Challenging Beijing's
Mandate of Heaven

Ming-sho Ho

Challenging Beijing's Mandate of Heaven

Taiwan's Sunflower Movement and Hong Kong's Umbrella Movement

TEMPLE UNIVERSITY PRESS
Philadelphia • Rome • Tokyo

TEMPLE UNIVERSITY PRESS
Philadelphia, Pennsylvania 19122
tupress.temple.edu

Copyright © 2019 by Temple University—Of The Commonwealth System
    of Higher Education
All rights reserved
Published 2019

Library of Congress Cataloging-in-Publication Data available from
    the Library of Congress

ISBN 978-1-4399-1706-0 cloth
ISBN 978-1-4399-1707-7 paper
ISBN 978-1-4399-1708-4 e-book

∞ The paper used in this publication meets the requirements of the American National
Standard for Information Sciences—Permanence of Paper for Printed Library Materials,
ANSI Z39.48-1992

Printed in the United States of America

9 8 7 6 5 4 3

Contents

List of Tables and Figures		*vii*
A Note on Romanization		*ix*
Acknowledgments		*xi*
List of Abbreviations		*xv*
	Introduction	*1*
1	A Tale of Two Societies	*21*
2	China's Impacts	*40*
3	Movement Networks	*71*
4	Opportunities, Threat, and Standoff in Taiwan	*95*
5	Opportunities, Threat, and Standoff in Hong Kong	*117*
6	Improvisation	*150*
7	The Morning After	*176*
	Conclusion	*209*
	Appendix 1. In-depth Interviews	*223*
	Appendix 2. Methodology of Protest Event Analysis	*229*
	Notes	*231*
	References	*237*
	Index	*261*

List of Tables and Figures

Tables

Table 2.1. Large-scale annual protests, 2006–2013	65
Table 4.1. Approval and disapproval ratings for the Sunflower Movement	114
Table 5.1. Approval and disapproval ratings for the Umbrella Movement	137
Table A.1. Taiwanese interviewees	224
Table A.2. Hongkonger and Macanese interviewees	226

Figures

Figure 2.1. Changing identities in Taiwan, 1994–2016	61
Figure 2.2. Changing identities in Hong Kong, 1997–2016	61
Figure 2.3. Protest events in Taiwan and Hong Kong, 2006–2013	63
Figure 2.4. Longer and larger protest events, 2006–2013	64
Figure 2.5. Confrontational protest events, 2006–2013	66
Figure 2.6. Pro-China protests and protests involving Chinese, 2006–2013	69
Figure 4.1. Taiwan's Legislative Yuan	102
Figure 5.1. Government buildings in Admiralty, Hong Kong	123

A Note on Romanization

In this book I adopt the pinyin system, as it is more commonly used internationally, with the understanding that Taiwanese and Hongkongers tend to employ other systems. I use conventional spellings for proper nouns—for example, "Taipei" (rather than "Taibei") and "Leung Chun-yin" (rather than "Lang Zhenying"). I use the romanization rule adopted by the Taiwan Ministry of Education in spelling some terms pronounced in the Taiwanese language (https://goo.gl/ABYSTW) and the Cantonese system proposed by the Research Institute for the Humanities, Chinese University of Hong Kong (https://goo.gl/onv5fs).

Acknowledgments

Before publishing my last book, *Working Class Formation in Taiwan: Fractured Solidarity in State-Owned Enterprises* (2014), I never would have thought that I would write a book on Hong Kong and how the former British colony's past and future is intimately related to my home country, Taiwan. As an observer of Taiwan's social movements, I am accustomed to following activists in their protests and discussions, and I found that their references to Hong Kong intensified as more and more exchanges and cross-pollination took place before the eruption of Taiwan's Sunflower Movement in March 2014. With the advent of Hong Kong's Umbrella Movement at the end of same year, I experienced an irresistible intellectual urge to make sense of the origin, the process, and the consequences of these two historical movements and to table other research plans to focus on this fascinating topic.

Born in 1973, I regretted not having visited Hong Kong before July 1, 1997, when the Union Jack still flew. Because of Taiwan's conscription obligation, a legacy of prolonged authoritarian rule, it was difficult for my male age cohort to travel abroad. But I must confess that my one-month visit to Hong Kong as a doctoral student in 1998 did not change my preconceived notion of that city as mercantile, pragmatic, and apolitical. While my fellow Taiwanese were engrossed in political and partisan debates about their future, I considered Hongkongers' seeming nonchalance rather perplexing. At that time, Taiwan's lawmakers were internationally notorious for their physical conflicts, a stark contrast to the gentlemanly demeanor of their Hong Kong counterparts. Yet I considered such feistiness better than a rubber-stamp legislature because at least the elected representatives were engaged in something serious. Who would appreciate the Soviet-style harmony of China's National People's Congress? Later I realized that my initial incomprehension was largely a product of historical tragicomedy for both Taiwanese and Hongkongers. In 1984, when I was still a junior high school student, I asked my teacher why Margaret Thatcher visited Beijing to conclude the Sino-British negotiation on Hong Kong's future when my government claimed to be the sole legitimate representative of all Chinese people. If my school textbook was right, the Iron Lady should have journeyed to my home city, Taipei. My contemporary Hongkongers were no less misguided in their wishful thinking. Chinese patriotism was an idealistic inspiration for the resistance against social injustices under colonial rule, but it swiftly degenerated into a convenient political tool for Beijing to maintain the status quo ante after Hong Kong's handover to Chinese sovereignty. In the twenty-first century, as younger Taiwanese and Hongkongers began to shed this historical baggage and consider their political destiny in their own terms, the two monumental protests that are the focus of this book emerged.

Taiwan's Ministry of Science and Technology generously sponsored this project (105-2420-H-002-051-MY3). Yun-chung Chen, Edmund Cheng, Yi Kang, Lau Ka-yee, Chi-hua Lin, Hung-Yang Tsai, Benson Wong, Wanling Yen, Ray Yep, and Samson Yuen offered much-needed help when I was collecting the research data. In various stages, the following people offered constructive criticism: Nathan Batto, Chun-Yen Chang, Heng-hao Chang, Tiehchih Chang, Edmund Cheng, Tsu-bang Cheng, Larry Diamond, Yun Fan, Dafydd Fell, Simona Grano, Stephan Haggard, Brian Hioe, Lawrence Ho, Tung-hung Ho, Shu-mei Huang, Xiaoqing Huang, Ian Inkster, Malte Philipp Kaeding, Leon N. Kunz, Pei-chia Lan, Chun-yi Lee, Da-chi Liao, Thung-Hong Lin, Yu-sheng Lin, Ngok Ma, François Mengin, Shelley Rigger, Ian Rowen, Gunter Schubert, I-Lun Shih, Ming Sing, Son Yu Liam, Jonathan Sullivan, Kyoko Tominaga, Hung-jeng Tsai, Steve Tseng, Sing Yan Eric Tsui, Sebastian Veg, James W. Y. Wu, Jieh-min Wu, Rwei-ren Wu, Ray Yep, and Samson Yuen. The manuscript was finalized during my stay in Boston, which was made possible by a one-year visiting grant from Harvard-Yenching Institute.

Finding a publishing house is always a formidable challenge for me, and I appreciate the suggestions of Salvatore Babones, Jeffrey Broadbent, Weitseng Chen, Thomas B. Gold, Stephan Haggard, Ho-fung Hung, Bruce Jacobs, James M. Jasper, Ching Kwan Lee, Yoonkyung Lee, Ya-Wen Lei, Doug McAdam, Tak-Wing Ngo, and Yen-tu Su. This book would not have been possible without the assistance of You-chen Cai, Chun-hao Huang, Mei Lan Huang, Yun-Nung Lu, Lungta Wei, and Lisha Wu.

Finally, I am grateful for the support of my family. After my father's funeral on the morning of August 18, 2013, Shuling and I attended the evening protest rally that led to the "Occupy the Ministry of the Interior," arguably the dress rehearsal for the Sunflower Movement. Our daughter, Little Plum, was born three months before the signing of the controversial free-trade bill that led to the Sunflower Movement, and our son, Little Sun, was born when the Umbrella Movement was raging all over Hong Kong. I consider myself very fortunate to have experienced the tremendous simultaneous changes in my intellectual and my personal life—none of which would have been possible without Shuling's companionship and understanding.

List of Abbreviations

BIY	Black Island Nation Youth Front
CCP	Chinese Communist Party
CEPA	Closer Economic Partnership Arrangement
CHRF	Civil Human Rights Front
CSSTA	Cross-Strait Service Trade Agreement
CUHK	Chinese University of Hong Kong
CUSU	Chinese University Student Union
DAB	Democratic Alliance for the Betterment of Hong Kong
DF	Democratic Front against Cross-Strait Service Trade Agreement
DP	Hong Kong Democratic Party
DPP	Democratic Progressive Party
ECFA	Economic Cooperation Framework Agreement
FNPP	Fourth Nuclear Power Plant
GPT	Green Party Taiwan
HK$	Hong Kong dollars
HKFS	Hong Kong Federation of Students
HKU	University of Hong Kong
HKUPOP	University of Hong Kong, Public Opinion Programme
HKUSU	Hong Kong University Students' Union
KMT	Kuomintang
LSD	League of Social Democrats
NGO	non-governmental organization

NOYDA	Network of Young Democratic Asians
NT$	New Taiwan dollars
NTU	National Taiwan University
OCLP	Occupy Central with Love and Peace
POS	political opportunity structure
PRC	People's Republic of China
SAR	special administrative region
SDP	Social Democratic Party
SEALDs	Students Emergency Action for Liberal Democracy
SPDM	Hong Kong Alliance in Support of Patriotic Democratic Movements in China
TCTU	Taiwan Confederation of Trade Unions
TSU	Taiwan Solidarity Union
US$	U.S. dollars
WTO	World Trade Organization

Challenging Beijing's
Mandate of Heaven

Introduction

It was around 7:30 P.M., March 30, 2014. Amid thundering cheers from the crowd, twenty-six-year-old student leader Lin Fei-fan took to the podium just a few hundred meters from the Presidential Office in Taipei, ready to deliver a speech to wrap up a mass rally that had reportedly attracted a half-million demonstrators, as well as spawned solidarity gatherings scattered over forty-nine cities in seventeen countries. Lin began the seventeen-minute speech by expressing his gratitude for the popular support that had been given to the protesters' occupation of the national legislature (Legislative Yuan) over the previous two weeks. Such an event, Lin contended, had already made history because "we have told the government that Taiwan's future belongs to all 23 million Taiwanese. Taiwan's future is our decision." He rejected the title "commander-in-chief" (*zongzhihui*) that the media had bestowed on him, saying, "The people are the real commander-in-chief and now we are here to command an out-of-order government," instantly drawing ecstatic applause from the crowd.[1] In concluding what has since been characterized as the best political speech in recent Taiwanese history, Lin reiterated the movement's core demands—withdrawing the free-trade agreement with China and enacting more supervision over cross-strait negotiation—and urged the audience to continue participating.

Between March 18 and April 10, Taiwan underwent an unprecedented mass protest that saw the nation's legislature occupied for twenty-four days. The dispute was over the Cross-Strait Service Trade Agreement (CSSTA), a sweeping trade liberalization pact that was intended to remove barriers to bilateral investment and migration in order to deepen economic integration. Dubbed the Sunflower Movement by the media because of an incidental gift of sunflowers to the protesters from a florist, the unusual episode grabbed national and international attention. At the end of the standoff, the government remained committed to promoting economic liberalization with China; nevertheless, the movement secured the legislative speaker's promise to prioritize enacting a legal procedure to handle cross-strait negotiations, giving the protesters an avenue to withdraw from the legislature voluntarily. On the last day of the legislature occupation, a festive farewell rally commemorated the movement's achievements and the protesters vowed to continue their activism.

At 10:30 P.M. on September 26, the final evening of a five-day campaign launched by Hong Kong students to boycott classes in protest against a Beijing decision regarding the electoral rule for the territory's chief executive, Taiwan's student protest elicited an unexpected rejoinder from Hong Kong. As thousands of participants were about to leave the rally outside of the Central Government Complex in Admiralty, seventeen-year-old university freshman Joshua Wong unexpectedly mounted the podium and pleaded with the audience to stay for a while. Wong, who had become famous for his successful leadership in a campaign against patriotic education two years earlier, began to share his personal feelings. Suddenly he changed the tone of the event by urging everyone to storm into an empty space nestled between two government buildings. Hundreds of participants joined the surprise sit-in, the "taking back of Civic Square," and Wong managed to climb over a three-meter-high fence. Police officers reacted quickly by surrounding the intruders and preventing others from entering. Although Wong and other student leaders were arrested, their supporters stayed overnight. On the afternoon of September 28, demonstrators bolted out from the sidewalks to block traffic, triggering a fateful police decision to shoot tear gas at the crowd at 5:00 P.M. Indignant about the brutal force used against unarmed protesters, citizens immediately took to the streets and three occupation zones emerged to usher in the advent of the Umbrella Movement.

Like its predecessor in Taiwan, Hong Kong's great protest was named by the media, which documented the conspicuous presence of umbrellas used as makeshift shields against police pepper spray. The Umbrella Movement, which lasted for seventy-nine days, became the largest protest incident in the territory since its handover to Chinese sovereignty in 1997; a poll indicated around 1.2 million Hongkongers had visited the scene at least once—roughly one-fifth of the area's population. Since the trigger topic for the Umbrella Movement was the democratization of leadership elections, the movement received enthusiastic responses from around the world, with international leaders such as U.S. President Barack Obama, British Prime Minister David Cameron, and German Chancellor Angela Merkel personally expressing their support. However, despite the international sympathy, the Umbrella Movement collapsed due to leader indecisiveness, mass fatigue, and bitter infighting, without securing any positive responses from the government. On December 15, Hong Kong police cleared the last occupation holdout with a mass arrest.

Although there was a stark contrast between the final outcomes of the two great protests, Taiwan and Hong Kong both experienced significant political changes in their wake. Protest activism proliferated and spread into newer issues, and many young people decided to enter the political arena by organizing new political parties and joining elections. Within the span of two years, both places witnessed the transition of erstwhile protest leaders into elected lawmakers. Taiwan underwent its third peaceful transition of political power in May 2016, as the independence-leaning party gained control of the presidency and legislature in defiance of Beijing. Post-Umbrella Hong Kong saw a surge in pro-independence forces as well as the imprisonment of dissident activists.

The Sunflower Movement and the Umbrella Movement belonged to a rare subset of social movements characterized by unanticipated emergence, large-scale and intense participation, and deep and far-reaching consequences. In his seminal article "Historical Events as Transformations of Structures," William Sewell (1996) called attention to these unusual protests, such as the storming of the Bastille prison during the French Revolution, which fundamentally altered the existing conditions and opened new horizons for subsequent actions. After the symbolic fall of monarchial despotism, there appeared no way to turn back the clock of history. Following this insight, Donatella della Porta coined the term "eventful protests" (2014: 17) to describe this kind of intensive, transformative, and history-making movement.

This book aims to make sense of the origins, the processes, and the outcomes of these eventful protests in Taiwan and Hong Kong. How did two massive and disruptive protests take place in culturally conservative societies where the Confucian norm of obedience to authority appeared to hold sway? Why were Taiwanese and Hongkonger citizens willing to take part in a protest that directly challenged the objectives of rulers in Beijing when their own political leaders had become increasingly accommodating to them? What were the sources of the bursts of creativity and artistry during the protests? How was it possible to orchestrate such large-scale collective action when the figurehead leaders of the movements did not possess extensive resources or real-time information? Finally, what were the regional and global consequences of these atypical protests? The following chapters tackle these questions, but first let me identify the shared features of these two eventful protests and set them in a global context.

Two Eventful Protests at a Quick Glance

Taiwan is a self-governing country, although its international statehood is overshadowed by an increasingly powerful and prosperous China that insists on holding sovereignty over this island. Hong Kong, a historical creation of British overseas expansion, transitioned to Chinese sovereignty in 1997, with a guarantee of a high degree of autonomy and the promise of full democratization. Both are successful economies in their own right. Taiwan maintains a vibrant democracy following a prolonged one-party authoritarian regime that lasted until 1987, whereas postcolonial Hong Kong is trapped in unfinished democratization.

Both societies remain fundamentally conservative in the sense that disruptive protests are not usually viewed as a legitimate means of expressing dissidence. Older Taiwanese grew up with an instinctive fear of politics because of protracted repression, whereas elder Hongkongers embraced a don't-rock-the-boat refugee mentality. Particularly in Hong Kong, colonialism has bequeathed a rule-of-law tradition that discouraged illegal protest actions (see Michael Ng 2017). In both places, political opposition arose in the mid-1980s and consistently adopted moderate strategies to further democracy. To illustrate the low tolerance for civil disobedience, consider the 2010–2014 World Values Survey. It showed the percentage of citizens in OECD countries with a principled disinclination to join a petition or peaceful demonstration to be 25.9 percent and 40.9 percent, respectively, whereas for Hong Kong the figures were 32.8 percent and 42.2 percent, and for Taiwan they were 56.7 percent and 71.4 percent.[2] The poll demonstrates the abiding power of political conformism in these two societies. Against this backdrop, Taiwan's Sunflower Movement brought the normal functioning of the legislature to a halt for more than three weeks, and Hong Kong's Umbrella Movement shut down key traffic arteries for more than two months. Clearly, both Taiwanese and Hongkongers somehow managed to overcome the unfavorable political culture in making these eventful protests possible.

Both movements challenged the political objectives of leaders in Beijing who had expressly indicated their intent to incorporate Taiwan and Hong Kong firmly into China proper. In spite of their different political status, both appeared permanently locked into economic dependence on China. In 2014, Taiwan's exports to China and Hong Kong amounted to 39.7 percent of total exports,[3] whereas Hong Kong's exports to mainland China were nearly half (47 percent).[4] In terms of cross-border travel, visitors from China made up 40.2 percent of visitors to Taiwan[5] and 77.7 percent to Hong Kong[6] in the same year. Given these close economic and social linkages, it is even more intriguing why Taiwanese and Hongkongers were willing to engage in protests that defied the agenda of Chinese leadership.

University students made up the core leadership, and young people were the main constituents of these two movements. Two on-site surveys (Cheng and Chan 2017; Chen and Huang 2015) provide a profile of the participants: In Taiwan, 74.8 percent of the sampled participants were under the age of thirty, while 25.6 percent were students, and 84.3 percent held a university diploma or above, whereas the respective figures for Hong Kong were 53.5 percent, 56.5 percent, and 54.1 percent. Young and highly educated people were the mainstay of these unusual political incidents. While these two protests essentially evolved around the future status of the two territories—centering on the likely economic and political absorption of Taiwan into China, and China's reinforced grip over Hong Kong—the young demonstrators clearly perceived that their own personal future was also at stake.

While the two eventful protests challenged the pro-China domestic political leaders, movement leaders took care to present their action as nonpartisan. For different reasons, Beijing has been persistently skeptical of the political opposition in both Taiwan and Hong Kong, the former because of its pro-independence tendencies and the latter for its insistence on democratization and the political rehabilitation of the 1989 Tiananmen Massacre. Yet throughout the episodes, opposition politicians played only a limited role, and they were not able to steer the movement direction. In both places, government officials attempted to portray the incidents as a political plot engineered by the opposition or foreign forces, in order to discredit the demonstrators, indicating that the nonpartisan image constituted a vital component of the broad appeal in these two eventful protests.

Both protests involved an unprecedented and risky confrontation with the authorities, and proceeded under a shroud of uncertainty and fear, yet without engendering social or economic crisis. Demonstrators maintained orderly, clean, and civilized encampment over the weeks, and except for the inconvenience in terms of traffic, civilian life went on as usual outside the occupation zone. There was no accompanying economic disturbance; the stock markets in Taiwan and Hong Kong fell over the first few days, but then went back to normal. As a matter of fact, both the Sunflower Movement and the Umbrella Movement sites became famed tourist attractions precisely because of their peacefulness.

Last, the eventful protests in Taiwan and Hong Kong were not unrelated. In the preceding years, there had been mutual exchanges and cross-fertilization among civil-society organizations and student activists as they became increasingly aware of the common threat posed by Beijing and the need for transborder solidarity. The occupation of the legislature in Taiwan provided an accessible reference case for Hongkongers.

Global Eventful Protests

What happened in Taiwan and Hong Kong cannot be isolated from the global wave of eventful protests that became more intensive in the preceding years. From a social movement perspective, the twenty-first century was ushered in by the "Battle of Seattle" on November 30, 1999, in which a coalition of environmentalists, unionists, and anarchists disrupted a World Trade Organization (WTO) conference (Flesher Fominaya 2014b: 84–89). Thanks to advances in communications technology, movement activists in different countries became more capable of coordinating their action and forging transnational networks (della Porta and Mosca 2005; Juris 2005; Smith 2002). Subsequently, a global justice movement, or alter-globalization and globalization-from-below movement, came into being in many places (Maeckelbergh 2013; Mason 2012; Notes from Nowhere 2003). There emerged a distinctive repertoire for "summit protests," in which protesters of different ideological tendencies and nationalities gathered to protest at meetings of the World Bank, the International Monetary Fund, the G8, and so on, protesting each summit with a prolonged encampment (MacDonald 2002; Tominaga 2017).

A parallel wave surged in the former republics and satellite states of the Soviet Union under the Color Revolutions, massive demonstrations in support of democratization in locations including Serbia (in 2000), Georgia (2003), Ukraine (2004), and Kyrgyzstan (2005). The existence of a transnational network of human rights activists helped to spread the tactic of nonviolent protests in these postcommunist countries (Bunce and Wolchik 2011). While the global justice movement mainly targeted neoliberalism, geopolitical factors played a visible role in the Color Revolutions, as these postcommunist countries were caught in the rivalry between the West and Russia (Way 2008). In his study on the Ukrainian Orange Revolution, Mark Beissinger (2011, 2013) discovered that participants were motivated by a number of diverse factors, and the aspiration for democracy was not the most predominant one. Ethnic and nationalistic politics were clearly involved in the Color Revolutions.

The global wave of eventful protests reached a climax in 2011, with the rise of the Arab Spring (heralded by the Tunisian and Egyptian Revolutions), the "European Summer" (stimulated by Spain's Indignados Movement), and the Occupy Wall Street Movement and its global diffusion through the autumn (Castells 2012; Flesher Fominaya 2014b: 148–193; Gerbaudo 2012). The Arab Spring was composed of popular protests against corrupt dictators in a number of countries in the Middle East and North Africa. Young people who chafed under political intolerance and economic stagnation made up the main contingent force, and their digital connectedness helped to overcome the fear instilled in them by the police and their informants (Bellin 2012; Ghonim 2012; Gunning and Baron 2014; Noueihed and Warren 2012;

Rand 2013). The European wave of protests initiated by the Spanish had a more visible economic origin as countries such as France, Italy, Greece, and Portugal were affected by the debt crisis and the austerity measures that had blighted a generation's future (Flesher Fominaya 2014a; Tejerina et al. 2013). Finally, the Occupy Wall Street Movement and its ensuing waves of global imitations identified as the "occupy protests" arose and became a truly global lingua franca in protest making (Gitlin 2012; Graeber 2013).

How can we position the Sunflower Movement and the Umbrella Movement in these successive tides of international eventful protests? East Asia was a region that seemed relatively immune to the global contagion. With the noticeable exceptions of the 2005 anti-WTO protest in Hong Kong and the 2008 anti-G8 meeting in Hokkaido, Japan (Tominaga 2014), this region witnessed fewer activities associated with the global justice movement. Furthermore, the Color Revolutions and the upheavals of 2011 stimulated weak responses in the region. Was the emergence of the Sunflower Movement and the Umbrella Movement a sign of convergence with the global eventful protest phenomenon?

As mentioned above, participation by predominantly youthful demonstrators and their political independence from political parties were similar to other international cases. Occupying a public space and using it as an ongoing bargaining chip with the authorities was also a familiar feature. In fact, the importance of spatial factors led many commentators to speak of "occupy movements" (Pickerill and Krinsky 2012), "square politics" (Krastev 2014), and "movements of squares" (Fernández-Savater and Flesher Fominaya 2017). Mobile and digital communication enabled youthful participants to launch a series of flash-mob-style protests that led to unusual confrontation with the authorities. Taiwanese and Hongkonger protesters also practiced a politics of inclusiveness by celebrating their cultural and ethnic diversities, and their occupation zones gave rise to a flurry of creative and artistic expressions.

Apart from these similarities, the Sunflower Movement and the Umbrella Movement diverged from the international eventful protests in many remarkable ways. First, they were emphatically not so-called leaderless movements, and the grassroots participants readily recognized some youthful faces as their figurehead leaders. In varying degrees, the decisions made by a small and closed circle of student activists shaped the movement outcomes. Second, although there had been a prevalent sense of economic deprivation among Taiwanese and Hongkonger youth, neoliberalism did not become a prominent issue in their protests. Even in the Sunflower Movement, which was triggered by trade liberalization with China, principled opposition to free trade remained a marginal voice. This reduced emphasis on economic demands was accompanied by a more salient role for geopolitical factors, as both the Sunflower Movement and the Umbrella Movement were inextricably opposed to an increasingly hegemonic China. Here, these two movements were more akin to the Color Revolutions, and more removed from the global justice movement. Last, unlike the European autonomous leftists and the American anarchists who shared an ideological aversion to institutional politics, Sunflower and Umbrella activists eagerly embraced party and electoral politics after the conclusion of their intensive mobilization. There was a rather smooth transition from street occupation to electioneering.

In short, the East Asian pair of eventful protests demonstrated a fascinating combination of convergence and divergence with what happened elsewhere around the globe. A closer look helps enrich our understanding of these unusual social movements as they have become increasingly important in reshaping our contemporary world.

The Six Puzzles to Be Examined

Social science is an intellectual craft that strives to provide a convincing account of those unlikely and unanticipated happenings that are incongruent with our received understanding. In this sense, the emergences of eventful protests, as well as their subsequent evolution await an explanation. Concerning Taiwan's Sunflower Movement and Hong Kong's Umbrella Movement, I raise six intellectual puzzles here:

Puzzle 1: Radicalism in Conservative Societies

In spite of substantial modernization on many fronts, both Taiwan and Hong Kong remain essentially conservative societies that frown on illegal protest behaviors. Yet, the two movements in question exceeded their global predecessors in terms of disruptiveness. The Sunflower Movement did not just occupy a public square; it occupied the national legislature, the citadel of contemporary democracy, and yet the movement enjoyed strong popular support. The Umbrella Movement managed to sustain a continuous road occupation in the city center for 79 days, surpassing the length of the Egyptian Revolution (18 days), the Spanish Indignados Movement (28 days with the protester decision to evacuate the Puerta del Sol square), and the Occupy Wall Street Movement (59 days with the police eviction of Zuccotti Park protesters). Why did Taiwanese and Hongkonger citizens decide to shelve their deep-seated suspicion over protest behaviors by supporting these ostensibly illegal acts of occupation?

Puzzle 2: "Hopeless" Protests?

Since protest making remains essentially a labor-intensive and risky activity, participants are more likely to join when they clearly perceive a chance of winning. However, such an optimistic outlook was conspicuously absent when the Sunflower and Umbrella Movements surged. Taiwan's ruling party was determined to ratify the trade bill with China with its parliamentary majority, and the major opposition party appeared to take a noncommittal stance in order to dodge confrontation over the sensitive issue. Opposition activists exhausted nearly every procedural possibility to delay the bill's passage and they also failed to draw public attention to the pernicious effects of free trade with China. In Hong Kong, despite an energetic campaign for a genuinely democratic chief executive election that lasted for more than one year, Beijing was determined to play hardball by announcing a package that was more restrictive than anticipated. To make matters worse, Hong Kong's opposition parties appeared utterly unprepared for such a hardline response and they were also too disjointed to present a common front. Many Hongkonger participants acknowledged that the chances of obtaining concessions from Beijing were slim in the early days of the Umbrella Movement (Cai 2017: 2). Apparently, Taiwanese and Hongkonger citizens took to the streets not because they saw that extracting concessions from incumbents was likely, but rather because something emphatically more vital was at stake.

Puzzle 3: Student Leadership

Both Taiwan and Hong Kong maintained a vibrant civil society, populated by a number of movement-oriented non-governmental organizations (NGOs) and political parties. Experienced movement activists and established politicians appeared the more likely candidates to lead these two massive antiregime protests. But in reality, movement veterans and politicians were practically sidelined in the decision-making process as students emerged as the indisputable movement figureheads. As such, both the Sunflower Movement and the Umbrella Movement were directed primarily by a group of university students who were in their twenties. Legally speaking, Joshua Wong was a minor without the right to cast a vote when he led the Umbrella Movement. How can we make sense of this atypical leadership?

Puzzle 4: The Curse of Movement Resources

At the onset of the two movements, there was a great contrast in terms of preparedness. Hong Kong's campaigners had been preparing for an eventual showdown, and they enjoyed the advantages of respected and recognized leaders, independent financing, volunteers trained in the tactics of nonviolence resistance, and a collection of logistical resources; yet the Umbrella Movement turned out to be ineffectively led and suffered from widening internal discord. In Taiwan, before student protesters stormed the legislature, the opposition movement was understaffed, under-funded, and not widely known. Nevertheless, the Sunflower Movement engendered a strong and coherent leadership core capable of executing its strategic decisions relatively smoothly. How did the possession of more abundant movement resources become a liability in the eventful protest?

Puzzle 5: The Sources of Unsolicited Contribution

Both the Sunflower Movement and the Umbrella Movement were made possible due to on-the-spot and decentralized decisions made by anonymous participants. Provisioning and maintaining order in the protest encampment areas were delegated to participants themselves, as leaders were too preoccupied with strategic responses. How was it possible for Taiwanese and Hongkonger citizens to sustain such orderly and prolonged protests? In a sense, the distinction between leaders and followers was blurred, because participants self-organized their own movements without receiving orders or authorization from anyone. The widespread ability to generate such spontaneous responses among the participants needs to be explained.

Puzzle 6: Solidarity and Schism

In terms of political outcomes, there was a noticeable difference between these two movements. The Umbrella Movement ended up further dividing Hong Kong's opposition, whereas the Sunflower Movement helped Taiwan's opposition party to secure a turnover of power. Hong Kong's post-Umbrella political landscape was further fractured with the entry of new political forces that emerged as contenders against the preexisting opposition parties, whereas Taiwan's post-Sunflower force became a partner to the main opposition party in its quest for national power.

This book aims to explain these six puzzles by answering from a social movement study perspective how, why, and when the Sunflower Movement and the Umbrella Movement occurred. What makes for a social movement? And what are its essential components? What may we learn from the existing research literature?

A Synthetic Perspective of Social Movements

I follow Sidney Tarrow's suggestion to identify social movements as the collective and sustained challenges mounted by a group of people with a common purpose and mutual solidarity (1994: 3–4). This brief definition stops short of specifying the content of the purpose, because social movements can be progressive or conservative in their agendas. Regardless of their ideological orientations, social movements are not reducible to protests, although these two terms are often employed interchangeably. A protest is an act of expressing one's objection, which can be highly individualized without involving a collaborative effort. Although a protest always takes place by violating an expected norm, it is not necessary that a protest evolve into sustained effort to challenge authorities. NIMBY (Not in My Backyard) is a particularly relevant category of protests that are not social movements.

One of the trademark characteristics of a social movement is its reliance on extra-institutional methods (Marx and McAdam 1994: 73). Apparently, there remain inherent difficulties in drawing a precise demarcation between what are the institutional ways to express one's dissidence and what are not. An extra-institutional act does not always go against the law, because there always remains an indeterminate gray zone. Whether peaceful or violent, an extra-institutional act is always something that departs from routine behavior and involves the collective presentation of the participants' worthiness, unity, numbers, and commitment (Tilly 2004: 2–3). Resorting to extra-institutional means has to do with the marginalized status of the people involved (Jenkins and Perrow 1977). In other words, if a group of people has routine and low-cost access to decision-making power, they tend not to launch social-movement activities in order to pursue their common purpose.

Ever since the theoretical revolution initiated by resource mobilization theory in the 1970s, researchers began to adopt an analytical perspective that was closer to the actions of movement activists, by focusing on the questions of how to organize collective action. The subsequent cultural turn, stimulated by new social movement theory and other theoretical orientations, helped to address the neglect of symbolic dimensions. Before the turn of the century, there emerged a well-established consensus on the image of social movements, as well as the conceptual tools to analyze them. Doug McAdam, Sidney Tarrow, and Charles Tilly (2001: 14–18) identified a "classical research agenda" that contains the following components: (1) political opportunities and constraints, or how the political environment shapes the development of social movements, (2) forms of organization, or the interpersonal relationship that encourages protest participation, (3) framing, or a symbolic construction that identifies social injustice, and (4) repertoire, or the way the dissent is performed and dramatized in public. The consensual understanding of social movements entails a number of assumptions. Social movements are a rational pursuit of shared interests or identities, rather than the result of abnormal psychological status as portrayed in the earlier approaches of collective behavior. While social movements entail a political bargaining process with opponents or the authorities, one cannot ignore their cultural aspects because movements also construct a shared understanding among participants, present a new interpretation of the dispute in question, and contest the existing norms and values. Social movements involve coordination and leadership, so they are distinct from spontaneous and unorganized responses at the individual level. As a corollary, social movements are a normal phenomenon in modern societies, which are expected to incorporate them as a permanent and conventional feature with growing democratic tolerance.

This consensus has helped to institutionalize social movement study by providing a shared vocabulary to the extent that a "standard model" of social movements is said to dominate the field (Amenta et al. 2010). To move beyond what they identified as a "classical research agenda," McAdam, Tarrow, and Tilly led the intellectual movement to reposition the research focus on "mechanisms," understood as universal causal sequences. Their collaborative attempt was to integrate the study of social movements with other related phenomena, such as nationalism, democratization, ethnic conflicts, and so on, into a single paradigm of "contentious politics" (2001; McAdam and Tarrow 2010; Tilly and Tarrow 2007).

From the classical research agenda to the study of contentious politics, there has been a clear rejection of universal laws. Yet for their opponents, the mainstream approach has not sufficiently recognized the role of human agency and its ability to construct a social movement by making creative use of preexisting symbols and meanings. This constructionist camp maintained the need to deepen the theoretical meanings of strategy from an enlarged perspective that involves biographical, cultural, or even aesthetic meanings of agency (Jasper 2004; Polletta 2002). One of their main criticisms was that the mainstream approach erred in reifying the state, as the concept "political opportunity structure" (POS) essentially entailed an excessively deterministic understanding of social movements (Goodwin 2012; Goodwin and Jasper 1999, 2004). As an effort to correct the structuralist assumption, constructionists emphasized the role of emotions in the genesis of social movements precisely because the affective dimension did not directly derive from the preexisting conditions, but more as a result of participants' shared understanding and interpretation (Goodwin, Jasper, and Polletta 2001; Jasper 2011, 2014). In a sense, the debate evolved around a perennial question in social science—that is, the classical structure-and-agency debate. Simply put, the question was about whether one should see the emergence of a social movement as a result of the conduciveness of objective conditions or as an achievement of participants' own efforts. In the literature on contemporary eventful protests, there appeared a clear divide of two theoretical orientations. Jeroen Gunning and Ilan Zvi Baron (2014) rigorously apply the mainstream approach by looking at the organizational mobilization in the Egyptian Revolution, whereas Jeffrey Alexander (2011) offers a cultural interpretation of how Egyptians manifested their political power via symbolic and moral performance.

While the existence of theoretical debates indicates the continuing vitality of a research field, there is a feeling that the divergences between these two camps are overemphasized so that their overlapping consensus is in danger of being overlooked (see Kurzman 2004a). Take the POS, for example, which has arguably sustained the fiercest gunfire from the constructionist camp; its practitioners have moved away from the original determinist formulation and concurred on the need for more conceptual specification (Meyer and Minkoff 2004; Ramos 2008). And there emerges the recognition that the impact of political opportunities is far from uniform (Almeida 2003; Meyer 2004). On the other hand, neither is it true that the mainstream approach has completely ignored the cultural processes of social movements. The mainstream approach researchers continue to pay attention to emotion (Aminzade and McAdam 2002), language (Tarrow 2013), and how these cultural elements structure the dynamics of movement contention.

The point is that social movements are inevitably a multidimensional process that involves how people organize themselves in order to mount a challenge to the political authorities and their protests would not be effective if they fail to appropriate the preexisting symbols and meanings and elaborate them into a passionate pursuit of the shared goals. In spite of theoretical crossfire, it is clear that the existing literature has already bequeathed an abundant set of conceptual vocabularies, which can be readily applied in different contexts. The task ahead is not about the differences in philosophical assumptions, but rather how we can use these theoretical tools to make sense of the ongoing evolution of contemporary social movements.

This book adopts a synthetic approach by making a selective use of the analytical vocabularies developed by the two camps. From the mainstream approach, I borrow network and generation (see Chapter 3) and opportunities and threat (see Chapters 4 and 5) to understand the origin of eventful protests in Taiwan and Hong Kong. Inspired by the constructionist camp, I analyze how biography affects movement leadership (see Chapter 5), the creative playfulness in protest (see Chapter 6), and the emotional aspect of movement activism (see Chapter 7). In place of paradigm warfare, I am hoping a theoretical syncretism offers the best intellectual guide to make sense of the contemporary social protests.

Having said that, I find that the existing theories are mostly geared toward understanding "routine" social movements that take place and end in an expectable fashion. Yet, the surge of eventful protests calls for newer conceptual tools precisely because they deviate from the received script of the interaction between protesters and the authorities. In order to fully explain such sudden, intensive, and transformative social movements, I theorize "standoff" as the exceptional moments of movement-government confrontation and "improvisation" as on-the-spot and decentralized decisions from the grassroots participants in order to sustain these two eventful protests in Taiwan and Hong Kong.

Research Data

The research data come from many sources. Based in Taiwan, I have more ready access to the Sunflower Movement, and in fact I entered the legislature two hours after the protesters stormed it on March 18, 2014. Given my prior familiarity with some of the student activists, I had the privilege of witnessing some of their inside meetings. I also conducted many rounds of field observation, both inside and outside the legislature. However, I do not consider myself an involved participant. During the twenty-four days, my engagement was largely limited to writing supportive newspaper op-ed pieces and delivering street-forum lectures. By comparison, my access to Hong Kong's Umbrella Movement was more limited. Nevertheless, I conducted a two-day field observation when the protest was still ongoing in the streets.

Furthermore, I carried out in-depth interviews with relevant persons in Taiwan and Hong Kong, in order to collect firsthand information from different subgroups and factions (see Appendix 1). In total, I interviewed 72 Hongkonger and Macanese, and 66 Taiwanese. My sample includes student participants and leaders, NGO activists, politicians and their aides, party workers, journalists, and university professors in both places. Since the Sunflower and Umbrella Movements were unusually large social movements in terms of scale, there has subsequently been a wealth of documentary films, published work, discussion forums, and speeches by both participants and observers, which also provide vital information.

Protests with and without Chinese Characteristics

Chinese political culture bequeathed a wealth of protest-making scripts for the would-be challengers. In particular, Confucianism bestowed an elevated status to literati because they exemplified the nation's conscience. It was scholar-officials' moral duty to remonstrate against the emperors' wrongdoings and the incidents of patriotic martyrdom were often lauded in the history textbook. Such preexisting cultural understandings created a shared expectation that protest movements led by intellectual elites should be treated with greater leniency, thereby constraining the regime's maneuvering space. Outright repression, such as the Tiananmen Square Massacre in 1989, remained a possibility, but it often came about when the besieged rulers ran out of other means for their own self-preservation.

In the twentieth century, the role of literati was inherited by university students whose sacred task was no longer the safeguarding of intellectual and moral orthodoxy but mounting a national salvation campaign with modern leanings. The famed May Fourth Movement of 1919 was a latter-day rendition of this Chinese intellectualism, and so were the subsequent students' nationalistic agitations in the 1920s and 1930s (Israel 1966). Craig Calhoun noted that in the 1989 Beijing pro-democracy movement the particular combination of elitism, heroism, and unselfishness was an enduring legacy of traditional culture (1997: 262–264). The students' attempt to couch their protest in the studied deference to the authorities and dramatized moralism clearly originated from the classical political theater (Esherick and Wasserstrom 1994).

The Sunflower Movement and the Umbrella Movement emerged partly because they made successful use of this cultural heritage by foregrounding the student role, even though students were not the sole participants. If those who stormed Taiwan's legislature were not students, but a group of plighted workers, it would be unlikely to elicit immediate and massive response to their cause. The same reasoning applies to Hong Kong's student protesters who were surrounded and badly treated by police after occupying Civic Square. It took students' victimization to arouse widespread citizens' sympathy and participation.

While both movements drew their strength from the moral force of student activism, there were clear deviations from the traditional script. In both the 1989 Tiananmen Movement (D. Zhao 2001: 284–285) and the 1990 Wild Lily Movement in Taipei (Wright 2001: 126), student participants maintained a cordon line to keep other citizens from entering their sit-in area, partly because of their fear of agent provocateurs sent by the government, which, however, symbolized the status distinction between student and nonstudent participants. Such spatial segregation was patently absent in the Sunflower Movement and the Umbrella Movement, as nonstudent participants played an important role in strategy making. In fact, Taiwanese activists made a formal decision in rejecting the characterization of a "student movement (*xuesheng yundong*)" in order to highlight the contribution of nonstudent participants (Yen et al. 2015: 142).

In place of the ultraserious tone of Chinese intellectualism, both movements were expressed in language that incorporated many elements from the youth popular culture. In many incidents, the government's response and the hostile media's detraction were treated with creative playfulness, such as in the Japanese *kuso* style. Personal life details of two Sunflower male student leaders, Lin Fei-fan and Chen Wei-ting, became insanely attractive to the public. Lin's Harry Potter–style glasses and green overcoat became an instant fashion, while a picture of Chen asleep with a teddy bear on the floor of the national legislature attracted the donation of more than eighty teddy bears overnight (hence the expression "Weiting-the-Pooh"). Hong Kong's participants also invented some playful and humorous forms of protest, including singing "Happy Birthday" to pro-government opponents to neutralize explosive situations (Gan 2017). As with Taiwan's Lin-Chen duo, Hong Kong student leaders Alex Chow and Lester Shum, often shortened as "Alexter," were portrayed in *fujoshi* (rotten women)–style cartoons that depicted the two males in a same-sex erotic fantasy (the "boys' love romance").

The waning of the relevance of classical political theater for Taiwanese and Hongkonger did not come from a deliberate choice, since both movement leaders were too engrossed in the strategic interaction with the government incumbents to pay attention to issues of style. More likely, the aesthetic shift reflected the change of university students' role in both places. The expansion of higher education in the 1990s had eroded their privileged status. Since a college degree no longer promised a decent professional job, it would become anachronistically incomprehensible if student activists decided to play the elitist role of classical intellectuals. Moreover, the prevalence of mobile digital communication and social media had leveled the distinction between student and non-student populations. What came in place was a shared youth culture in cyberspace that appeared more equalitarian, more creative, and funnier (M. Ho 2014c).

On the other hand, the cultural meanings of the Sunflower Movement and the Umbrella Movement can be discussed in light of the literature on protests in post-Mao China. The economic reforms and the gradual withdrawal of party-state control have generated many new social grievances that led up to growing numbers of petitions and protests. Yet, with the absence of a civil society and political liberties, Chinese protesters had to devise novel ways of making their collective claims, identified as "rightful resistance" (O'Brien 1996), "protest with rule consciousness" (Perry 2010), or "disorganized popular contention" (Chen and Kang 2016). Rather than mounting a bottom-up challenge, protesters were careful to make exhaustive use of the existing institutions (X. Chen 2008). Oftentimes, protesters professed their allegiance to the central leadership and used the preexisting socialist slogans to pressure the local cadres (F. Chen 2008). Despite its exponential growth, there was evidence that the Chinese government had found ways to manage and contain its political fallout.

Obviously what happened in Taiwan and Hong Kong did not share this Chinese characteristic because both episodes involved large-scale civil disobedience that confronted the government incumbents. Were a similar incident to take place in contemporary mainland China, it could have been a second Tiananmen Movement, ending either in the regime's collapse or crackdown. Nevertheless, "Chinese characteristics" are not a timeless and immutable essence, but subject to constant revision with the change of circumstances. During the Umbrella Movement, many Chinese visitors came to the occupation zones and personally witnessed how a protest could proceed in an orderly and civilized manner—a great contrast with the negative associations of protest behaviors with rowdiness in the mainland. It remains to be seen how these newer understandings take root and ferment over the years in redefining "Chinese characteristics."

The Mandate of Heaven and Its Peripheral Challengers

The two major incidents of resistance took place at the periphery of the People's Republic of China (PRC), and in different ways challenged its legitimacy claim. Hong Kong is currently a territory of China that enjoys administrative autonomy, whereas Taiwan remains independent, yet its de jure statehood is challenged and it now experiences more visible intrusion from China's visible hand. Despite their distance from China's power center, both Hong Kong and Taiwan bear strategic implications for the global rise of China.

For thousands of years, Chinese history has been animated by stirrings from distant places. Although the traditional perspective tends to consider Chinese civilization as evolving from its governing center, revolts in its periphery have actually punctuated many historical transitions. Nomadic invasions from the north by Turks, Mongolians, and Manchurians have decided the fate of ruling dynasties. The republican revolution of the twentieth century would not have been possible if a coterie of Cantonese-speaking revolutionaries led by Sun Yat-sen had not established an insurgent network in Hong Kong and among overseas Chinese societies. Similarly, the Chinese Communist Party (CCP) would not have come to power if it had not built guerilla bases in faraway locations and received aid from Russia. Over the course of Chinese history, things fell apart and the center did not hold, because of constant and robust challenges from the periphery.

Classical Chinese philosophy has long understood the vicissitude of ruling powers and developed a theory of "mandate of heaven" (*tianming*), which bestowed legitimacy on successful rebel leaders (Perry 1992: ix–x). A general, a feudal lord, a "barbarian" chief, or a peasant leader could rise to the throne of the Celestial Empire as long as he possessed such a blessing. More than a century after the fall of the last imperial dynasty in 1911, the Chinese ruler was again experiencing challenges from the periphery to the mandate to govern. The Beijing incumbents have implicitly renounced their allegiance to revolutionary socialism and have now embraced a militant nationalism to buttress their undemocratic rule. No longer denounced as a feudal vice, classical Chinese statecraft and its guiding philosophy of managing the periphery have now come back into fashion. For its enthusiasts, the traditional China-centered civilizational order (*tianxia*) was bound to dislodge the Westphalian system that saw individual national states as formally equal participants in international politics with the phenomenal rise of the PRC's economic and military might (for an engaged criticism, see Babones 2017). For Chinese President Xi Jinping, cultural assimilation (of Hong Kong and Macao), irredentism (of Taiwan as well as other "lost territories"), and other expansionist attempts overseas (such as in the South China Sea) have become a priority in the "Great Revival of the Chinese Race" (*zhonghua minzu weida fuxing*) political project. The more China seeks to reenact its historical imperial image, the more it encounters opposition from its periphery and neighboring countries.

I do not imply that the Sunflower and Umbrella Movements will result in a drastic change in China's political center. However, the multifaceted and contradictory center-periphery interactions should be taken into consideration when analyzing China's rapid ascendency to world power. Taiwan's future, indeed, is going to be largely shaped by the ongoing contention between "China's ambitions and America's interests" (Friedman 2013), whereas Hong Kong's prospects appear more complicated with the addition of the Taiwan factor. Nonetheless, these contemporary peripheral resistances to the inheritor of the Chinese empire do not strive for a mandate to the throne, as both Taiwanese and Hongkongers prefer to preserve their own distinctive political cultures, identities, and ways of life. The Sunflower and Umbrella Movements are the dramatic explosions of such powerful aspirations and they are sure to leave enduring legacies to future Taiwan-China and Hong Kong–China relations in the years to come.

Understanding the rise and fall of world powers and the implications for the global order has long been an area reserved for specialists in international relations and security studies. By contrast, social movement researchers have established a consensus to focus on short-term episodes of contentious mobilization, which appears to be detached from the sweeping changes brought about by the rise of a new world power. As expected, the advances of a more assertive China are often examined from the perspectives of military power and economic might, and less attention has been paid to the agitations from civil society. Here the insights of social movement study can help to fill the void, precisely because its analysis of mesolevel (interorganizational) and microlevel (interpersonal) processes enables us to understand how ordinary citizens are directly affected by macrolevel (supranational or national) changes, and why they are willing to engage in unusual protest behaviors. True, the evolution of geopolitics is largely shaped by top-down forces, such as military rivalry and economic strength; however, there also exists an oft-overlooked bottom-up dynamic of civil society, which is sometimes able to exert cross-border influence.

Plan of the Book

This book offers an account of the origins, the processes, and the consequences of Taiwan's Sunflower Movement and Hong Kong's Umbrella Movement. I tackle the genesis of the movements in Chapters 1 and 2, movement mobilization in the four middle chapters (Chapters 3 through 6), and domestic and international outcomes in Chapter 7 and the Conclusion. Here is a brief summary of the chapters.

Chapter 1 introduces the historical background of Taiwan and Hong Kong from their common origins as edges of contending empires. Both experienced prolonged colonialism and the resumption of Chinese rule. Social protests and pro-democracy movements in the two places first appeared in the 1970s, yet their subsequent trajectories diverged. Taiwan's political opposition was driven by a strong indigenous identity and the democratic transition finished before Beijing became capable of interfering with Taiwan's domestic politics, whereas Hong Kong's pro-democracy movement proceeded with an anticolonial Chinese nationalism and its progress stalled after the resumption of Chinese sovereignty in 1997.

Chapter 2 examines development in the twenty-first century, as Taiwan and Hong Kong began to experience more coercion from China. Although Beijing's strategic concession of economic benefits has cultivated a group of privileged local collaborators, grievances have emerged with its political intervention. Hongkongers rose to resist political and cultural assimilation, the "mainlandization," while Taiwanese reacted to the looming specter of Hongkongization. Both places witnessed a surge in self-defensive protests related to China impacts, accompanied by visible growth in indigenous identity over Chinese identity.

Both the Sunflower Movement and the Umbrella Movement were preceded by an increase in youthful protests. Chapter 3 looks at the similar economic circumstances that generated such waves of youth revolts. As young Taiwanese and Hongkongers engaged in protests more frequently, their movement networks expanded and thickened, which laid the interpersonal foundation for the two eventful protests. I also analyze the rise of the transborder network between Taiwanese and Hongkonger movement activists.

Chapters 4 and 5 form a pair in the examination of the eruption and the dynamics of the Sunflower Movement and the Umbrella Movement, respectively, through the theoretical lens of political opportunities, threat, and standoff. At the moment of their flare-up, political opportunities were not open to the protesters, whose demands appeared to have failed to elicit a positive response from the authorities. Yet both Taiwanese and Hongkonger government incumbents made fatal mistakes in dealing with the protest movements by creating an instant sense of urgency that heightened the cost of inaction. The attempt by Taiwan's ruling party to railroad the controversial trade bill through the legislature and the use of tear gas by Hong Kong's police unexpectedly stimulated protest participation beyond the anticipation of the activists. Therefore, both movements took place not because of favorable political opportunities, but rather because of the sudden rise of a threat.

Both the Sunflower Movement and the Umbrella Movement sustained a protracted confrontation with the government. In a standoff, movement leadership was post hoc constructed, making preexisting organizations and prior planning useless, or worse, a liability. Standoffs offered only a short window of opportunity for social movements; the longer they persisted, the more perilous they became. Standoffs were sui generis situations, in which contingency played a particularly important role in shaping the outcome, which explained why Taiwan's previously weakly organized movement turned out to command more effective leadership and to engineer a more graceful exit.

Chapter 6 surveys the widespread voluntary contributions and on-the-spot decision making among grassroots participants in light of the notion of "improvisation," defined as "strategic response without prior planning." These unsolicited efforts came in a rich variety and satisfied a number of needs to sustain protest encampment. In contrast to some literature that excessively glorified the so-called leaderless movements, improvisation could be just as hierarchical (as more experienced activists were able to play a more important role), conflict-prone, and even contradictory because it was essentially difficult to reconcile different ideological tendencies.

The consequences of the two eventful protests are investigated in Chapter 7. In Taiwan and Hong Kong newer protest activism emerged as a younger cohort of activists formed political parties and joined electoral politics. Post-Sunflower Taiwan experienced a turnover of power, while the post–Umbrella Movement witnessed the surge of political forces that advocated for independence or self-determination. I also look at both how Beijing responded to these unprecedented challenges and the regional reverberations. The Conclusion wraps up the preceding observation and analysis. I conclude the book by elaborating on the theoretical implications for the field of social movement study. Moreover, these two peripheral revolts provide a unique perspective by which we may broaden our understanding of the contemporary meaning of China's global ascendancy.

1

A Tale of Two Societies

Taiwan and Hong Kong were rarely considered suitable for comparison until Beijing came up with the "one country, two systems" design in the early 1980s. Deng Xiaoping originally invented this political formula specifically for Taiwan, and yet this model for national unification was first applied to Hong Kong as the colony's future became a topic of negotiation between London and Beijing. The result was the Joint Declaration in 1984, which promised to award special administrative region (SAR) status to postcolonial Hong Kong (Tsang 2004: 216). Since the handover of its sovereignty in 1997, Hong Kong has officially become a reference model for Taiwan (Bush 2016: 223–225).

This chapter examines the historical parallels and interactions of the two societies leading up to the era just prior to protest escalation around 2003. Both Taiwan and Hong Kong have been on the frontier of Chinese civilization, maintaining chronically contentious relations with the ruling dynasties, and were transformed into colonies as the decaying Qing Empire (1644–1911) succumbed to foreign powers piece by piece (H. Hung 2016). Colonialism brought about progress on many fronts; British rule (1841–1997) literally built Hong Kong from an obscure fishing village into a cosmopolitan global city, while the Japanese reign (1895–1945) laid down the political and economic foundations for modern Taiwan. With the postwar retroversion to Chinese sovereignty and the defeat of the Kuomintang (KMT) in the civil war in 1949, Taiwan became an "Island China" imposed with an anticommunist mission. While the outbreak of the Korean War in 1950 froze large-scale military hostilities in the Taiwan Strait, Hong Kong was among the few places where Nationalist and Communist supporters engaged in open struggles. The KMT encouraged Hongkongers (as well as Macanese) to come to Taiwan for higher education, and the procedures for their naturalization were deliberately easier—a legacy that persisted after Hong Kong's handover to Chinese rule. The early 1980s came with the international recognition that Taiwan and Hong Kong were among the few successful "tiger economies" that lifted their people out of poverty. It was during this same period that cash-strapped China eagerly sought to attract capital investment from Hong Kong and Taiwan, as evidenced by the establishment of four special economic zones in Guangdong Province and Fujian Province in 1980. Up to 2005, Hong Kong and Taiwan were the top two sources for foreign direct investment for China, if one includes the latter's detour funding via third places (Fuller 2008: 245).

Edge of Empires

Situated at the maritime periphery of the Eurasian continent, Taiwan and Hong Kong have been at the frontline of cold-war confrontation. Before they became "edges of empires"[1]—a zone of engagement among contending powers—they had historically been the frontiers of an expanding Chinese civilization, where the ruling dynasties encountered native peoples with varying degrees of sinicization and shifting allegiance. The Cantonese-speaking Guangfu people in the Pearl River Delta were not fully sinicized until the seventeenth century. In order to legitimize their newly civilized status, the Guangfu fabricated a lineage narrative in which they claimed to be the descendants of migrants from the northern Chinese heartland (S. Tsui 2015: 58–63). The boat-living Tanka people, a pariah group who were traditionally forbidden to purchase land or join the civil examination, excelled in seafaring and made a living out of trading and piracy in flagrant violation of the landbound Confucian values. Tanka seafarers were among those who provisioned the British expedition fleet that dealt a devastating blow to China in the Opium War (1839–1842). Seen as "traitors" by the Chinese government, these Tanka collaborators were rewarded with land grants after the British occupied Hong Kong, thereby experiencing a miraculous career advance from social outcasts to community leaders in the new colony (Carroll 2005: 21–32).

Across the 180-kilometer-wide strait, Taiwan was first ruled by a Chinese dynasty in 1683, before that having been controlled in part by the Dutch, the Spanish, and Zheng Chenggong (known as Koxinga) and his descendants. Chinese migrants arrived as land tillers under the auspices of the Dutch East India Company with the collaboration of Chinese seafaring traders, including Koxinga's father (Zheng Zhilong), or as soldiers when Koxinga took possession of Taiwan in 1662 by defeating the Dutch. Koxinga, eulogized as "a national hero" in postwar KMT historiography, was actually born to a Japanese mother in Nagasaki. Similar to Tanka seafarers, the Zheng family participated in a curious mixture of piracy and trading, thriving on the cosmopolitan coastal frontiers and maintaining situational loyalty to the Chinese state. Thus, while Koxinga's father defected to the rising Qing Empire, he chose to support the doomed Ming Dynasty.

For nearly two centuries, the Qing government practiced a largely passive policy by imposing restrictions on emigration and land reclamation—a piece of well-calculated statecraft that minimized the fiscal burden of governing this restless island frontier (Shepherd 1993). The conventional view has held that inexorable waves of migrants from Fujian and Guangdong eventually circumvented the official restriction and contributed to population growth; however, more recent study has stressed the gradual assimilation of plains aborigines who adopted Chinese surnames, ancestral worship, and rice cultivation (Brown 2004).

The opening of treaty ports in 1860 integrated Taiwan into burgeoning world trade, as its exports of tea, sugar, and camphor soared. The last two decades of Qing reign witnessed a turn toward a more pro-developmental policy, as foreign powers began to pose a security concern. Taiwan was promoted to provincial status in 1885, with railroad, telegraph, coal mining, and other modernization projects underway. The Chinese government remained unable to establish effective control over mountain aborigines and the eastern coast of Taiwan—a task eventually completed by the more advanced colonial state.

Collaboration and Resistance

It is a typical anachronistic error to characterize the "Chinese" in Hong Kong and Taiwan as having suffered colonization by foreign powers in 1841 and 1895, respectively, because the very notion of "the Chinese race" (*zhonghua minzu*) emerged as a nationalistic invention in reaction to the humiliating military defeats of the Qing Empire, particularly after the Sino-Japanese War of 1894–1895. As Arif Dirlik succinctly puts it, "Taiwan became a Japanese colony before the Qing became Zhongguo/China" (2018: 9). In other words, at the time of regime transition, people in Hong Kong and Taiwan maintained a situational loyalty to the imperial government, while willingly accepting belonging to a civilizational order. What was manifestly absent in their minds was the understanding of themselves as members of an indivisible nation. As such, the British were able to gain their foothold in Hong Kong with the voluntary collaboration of natives, only to meet armed resistance when they acquired the New Territories in 1899 (Hase 2008). The Japanese encountered years of armed resistance in Taiwan. As soon as the Shimonoseki Treaty of 1895 was signed, a short-lived Republic of Formosa led by mandarin officials and local gentry, arguably the first republic in Asia, was hastily formed (Lamley 1970). The Republic of Formosa soon collapsed amid internal discord, and other local resistance succumbed to the Japanese military. Sporadic armed rebellion continued until 1902, and the colonial regime encountered large-scale resistance in the 1915 Ta-pa-ni Incident and the 1930 Wu-she Incident.

Colonialism came in different tints and shades. The British originally aimed at securing a trade outpost. Envisioned as "the Great Emporium of the East" in the same fashion as Malacca and Singapore, Hong Kong's economic value would have derived from the entrepôt trade rather than extraction from the land and its people. The laissez-faire liberalism explained why the colonial regime was satisfied with indirect rule through a small number of English-speaking native elites as well as the fact that many Chinese businesspeople rose to eminence by playing the role of comprador servicing the foreign trade firms (Hui 1999; J. Tsai 1993: 147–153). Tolerance also attracted dissidents in the declining Qing Empire, from moderate reformer Kang Youwei to revolutionary Sun Yat-sen, who received medical training and developed his political ideas in Hong Kong (Carroll 2005: 76–81).

By comparison, Japan's imperialism set a more ambitious goal of territorial expansion and population acquisition, and the colonial state did not shy away from economic dirigisme and cultural assimilation of the conquered population—two legacies curiously inherited by the postwar KMT regime. Following the Meiji pattern of state-led industrialization, the early Japanese officials practiced "bureaucratic entrepreneurship" in modernizing land ownership, building harbors and railroads, and improving public health to make this new colony profitable (Chang and Myers 1963). Japanese conglomerates were encouraged to invest in the sugar industry, whose rapid growth elevated Taiwan to the world's number three producer. The rise of militarism in the mid-1930s gave rise to war-related industries, such as petroleum, cement, and metallurgy. As observed by Karl Marx (1974: 324–325) in the mid-nineteenth century, the British policy of free trade devastated the traditional handicraft industry in India; in contrast, Japanese colonialism was exceptional in that it "located modern heavy industry in its colonies" (Cumings 1987: 55). On the cultural front, early colonial rule adopted the gradualist policy of respecting "old customs" with the assumption that "backward" Taiwanese culture would naturally evolve to the Japanese level. The mid-1930s militaristic turn ushered in a coercive policy of assimilation as Taiwanese were deprived of the freedom of traditional worship and of publication in the Chinese language. Speaking the "national language," practicing Shinto rituals, and adopting Japanese names were eagerly promoted, as Taiwanese were becoming Japanized (Ching 2001).

Stimulated by the global trend of national self-determination and the emergence of anticolonial movements in Korea, India, and Ireland, a bourgeois-led home-rule movement rose in 1920 to demand the establishment of a Taiwan Parliament. The political awakening soon stirred the rise of peasant and worker movements, which led to a short-lived Taiwanese Communist Party (1928–1931) that championed political independence of a Taiwanese nation. The radicalization of the anticolonial movement incurred harsh repression, and by the early 1930s, these political movements appeared a spent force. Consequently, the colonial ruler merely implemented a highly restricted local election by popular vote in 1935—a token response to the Taiwanese pursuit of autonomy (Chou 1989).

The British colonial regime faced an entirely different situation, as Hong Kong's proximity to the mainland meant that it could not be immune from the revolutionary fervor in China. The Great Canton–Hong Kong Strike and Boycott of 1925–1926 was the largest prewar anticolonial struggle that brought commerce to a halt for over one year, because workers deserted their posts en mass to return to their native places in the mainland. The Strike and Boycott certainly had its local roots in rampant exploitation and racism, but it was triggered by the escalation of anti-imperialist confrontations in Shanghai and Canton, and the contention was supported by the KMT in alliance with the nascent CCP. In the end, the besieged British had to rely on Chinese business elites to negotiate with the Canton government, and these native collaborators played an assertive role in combating the local agitators (Carroll 2005: 131–158). By contrast, the Japan colonial government did not have a native collaborator class to neutralize the Taiwanese anticolonial movement; consequently, more often than not it had to resort to direct repression. Thus, in different ways, the two colonial regimes survived the tumultuous 1920s.

The Postwar Restoration

With the end of World War II in August 1945, both Taiwan and Hong Kong were lifted from Japanese rule. Hongkongers experienced their three years and eight months of Japanese occupation as a hellish period of mass murder, humiliation, evacuation, and shortage. In his autobiography, Szeto Wah (1931–2011), a veteran pro-democracy leader, portrayed how his family was forced to leave the city by taking refuge in their mainland hometown. This childhood witnessing of Japanese atrocities cultivated in him a life-long patriotic nationalism in the hope that a stronger China could defend itself (W. Szeto 2011: 17–23).

The Taiwanese farewell to fifty-one years of Japanese rule was complicated and ambivalent. The early years of military suppression and economic predation had become a faded memory, and the Taiwanese intellectuals who had embraced a cultural Chinese identity through classical learning were a dwindling group being replaced by a more cosmopolitan younger generation. Taiwanese born in the latter period of colonialism received universal education and experienced progress and development. The latter made up what was called "the war generation" (Chou 2003) because they grew up in an environment of fervent patriotic mobilization to the extent that more than twenty thousand Taiwanese volunteered to join the Japanese expedition forces, either as combatant soldiers or as military auxiliary personnel. Lee Teng-hui (born in 1923) had an older brother who died in Manila as a Japanese marine and was inducted into Tokyo's Yasukuni Shrine. Thus one of Lee's idolized heroes was Hatta Yoichi, the dedicated Japanese engineer who built a large-scale dam and irrigation system in southern Taiwan, the biggest in Southeast Asia at the time; apparently, he experienced the Japanese colonizer more as a modernizer than an oppressor (T. Lee 2015: 27–31).

The postwar future of Hongkongers and Taiwanese was decided by international power politics in which they did not have a say. The Allied Powers decided that Japan should be stripped of "all the territories stolen from the Chinese," which included Taiwan, but could be equally applied to Hong Kong. Immediately after Japan's surrender, there began "a race to Hong Kong" between the Nationalist Chinese and the British. Chiang Kai-shek's troops stopped at the border to allow the takeover by the former colonizer because Chiang did not want to provoke the British at that moment (Tsang 2004: 134–138). Later on, Communists also refrained from demanding the colony's return, since Hong Kong's diplomatic and economic value outweighed the political gain from an immediate "liberation." Guided by the policy of "long-term planning and extensive use" (*changqi dasuan chongfen liyong*), the nascent PRC allowed Hong Kong to be restored to the status quo ante in order to fully exploit its strategic advantage of being the sole trade outlet to the West during the cold-war-era embargo.

Ironically, the game of international politics ensured certain uncanny continuities with the prewar situation in both places. Hong Kong did not follow the postwar decolonization trend seen in India, Burma, and Malaya, and remained an anachronic Crown Colony that lasted well into the end of the twentieth century. Together with Gibraltar and the Falkland Islands, Hong Kong belonged to a unique class as relics of the British Empire (Sing 2004: 35). Originally, the resumption of British rule came with a power-sharing scheme that opened up public offices for election and replaced expatriates with local people in the administration. However, the 1946 Young Plan, named after Governor Mark Young, was abandoned because his successor reasoned that Hong Kong was a highly atypical colony that "can never become independent" (Carroll 2005: 131–132). Except for the removal of some overtly racist codes on residential segregation, postwar Hong Kong did not undergo significant changes in its governance structure. London continued to appoint governors, who possessed both executive and legislative powers, and the administration was entrusted to a group of expatriate bureaucrats who were in no way answerable to the people they governed. Until the gradual opening of elections in the early 1980s, formal channels for political participation remained non-existent, and the colonial government coined the euphemistic term "consultative politics" to make up for its democratic deficit (Lui 2015a: 83–102).

While Hong Kong's old-style colonialism was restored, Taiwanese actually encountered an acute deterioration. Nominally Taiwan was "retroceded" to Chinese sovereignty because it had been "ceded" to Japan previously; however, Taiwanese saw the installment of a corrupt, inefficient, and predatory regime in the immediate postwar years. In addition to having their expectation for liberation humiliatingly shattered, the Taiwanese faced even more challenging economic hardship than they had during the preceding war years as a result of the KMT's greedy extraction of the island's resources. Contemporary discussions unambiguously identified the situation as a continuation of colonialism (Philips 2007: 290–291). The unexpected recolonialization prompted an island-wide uprising in March 1947. In the February 28 Incident, Taiwanese elites attempted to mediate between armed insurgents and the besieged government, and at the same time they raised demands for political autonomy and equal treatment (Lai, Myers, and Wei 1991). In response, the KMT government mobilized troops from China in a crackdown campaign with approximately twenty thousand causalities and Taiwanese leaders being systematically eliminated. The bloody repression inadvertently stimulated a movement of clandestine communist insurgency that continued to the early 1950s (M. Ho 2014d: 33–64). With the beginning of the cold war and the "white-terror" reign, these underground challengers were systematically wiped out, securing the foundation for postwar KMT control of Taiwan—practically a continuation of Japanese domination, if not worse. To be sure, toward the end of Japanese rule, wartime mobilization enabled an expansion of government power, particularly in local administration, and ironically such a colonial legacy ended up facilitating tighter control by the émigré regime (Ts'ai 2009: 235–236).

Let us consider Taiwan's tragic experiences of the transition from Japanese to KMT rule as a fictitious contemporary Hong Kong analogy: After retroversion to Chinese rule, Beijing denigrates Hongkongers as "enslaved by British imperialism" and being unfamiliar with Mandarin Chinese is used as an excuse to sack those who used to work in governmental positions. To fill vacancies left by outgoing expatriates, Beijing sends mainland officials who have minimal local knowledge and do not understand English or Cantonese. Only a few natives with mainland connections are given official positions. All the British economic assets are summarily confiscated as "enemy property," and the public use of English is outlawed. After a failed revolt, similar to the February 28 Incident, Hong Kong elites are systematically wiped out. Beijing leaders consider lingering colonial influences and weak identification with the fatherland as contributing to the rebellion. Consequently, discussion of the colonial past is discouraged, and school textbooks promote anti-British thought, paint British rule as a dark and exploitative period, and glorify the resumption of Chinese sovereignty as a bright new beginning. The above conjectured scenario might sound too dystopian to be true; nevertheless, it is but a literal rendition of Taiwanese experiences in Hong Kong terms. And there is evidence Hongkongers are contemplating an analogously ominous future, as shown in the popular political film *Ten Years* (2015), released in the wake of the Umbrella Movement.

The Taiwan Independence Movement came into being after the suppression of the 1947 uprising. In 1948, Liao Wen-yi (Dr. Thomas Liao) and other exiles in Hong Kong first established a revolutionary organization to advocate this idea. Although Liao surrendered in 1965, the pursuit of political independence was taken up by a younger cohort of overseas Taiwanese (Fleischauer 2016). Before the lifting of martial law in 1987, these international campaigns failed to generate visible domestic reverberations because of the government's control.

Beneath Political Indifference

Due to unforeseeable vicissitudes, Taiwanese and Hongkongers shared the fate of being reduced to powerlessness in their own lands. Apparently, Taiwanese encountered a more miserable fate because of the protracted political repression. For a long time, "Formosans were either apathetic or fearful of political involvement" (Mendel 1970: 110) because the February 28 Incident and subsequent reprisals were such traumatic lessons that aversion to politics grew into a survival instinct. In private, Taiwanese expressed their discontent with nostalgia for the good old days of Japanese rule (Mendel 1970: 25; Wachman 1994: 96). For them, Japanese officials were abrasive, but at least they were law-abiding, dedicated, and fair. In a similar fashion, a perceivable current of colonial nostalgia emerged in posthandover Hong Kong; in both instances, romanticization of the colonial past with selective memories functioned as critique of the present, implicitly or not (Law 2014: 90–98).

On the surface, the majority of Hongkongers of the 1950s and 1960s demonstrated analogous apathy toward political activities. The shelving of the Young Plan did not rouse much public attention, indicating that Hongkongers did not prioritize political participation. Politics, however, did exist in another dimension. The civil war in China ended with the Communists' victory and the Nationalists' retreat to Taiwan, but in Hong Kong the two camps, armed with their own newspapers, schools, labor unions, and other mass organizations were competing for supremacy. In 1956, a dispute over a Republic of China national flag in a settlement area led to a five-day riot in which a pro-KMT mob launched a violent assault on CCP supporters; the result was sixty deaths and more than three hundred injuries.

Another contentious episode took place in 1967, and this time it originated from leftists and threatened British rule. Like the General Strike and Boycott of 1925–1926, the rising revolutionary wave from China spilled over, causing seven months of anti-imperialistic struggles in Hong Kong (Carroll 2009: 79–80). After Beijing's Ministry of Foreign Affairs fell under the control of ultraleftists during the Cultural Revolution, Hong Kong's CCP operatives followed the political wind by launching challenges over a labor dispute. In the summer of 1967, the communists adopted the terrorist tactics of assassination and homemade bombs to spread mass fear. The situation deteriorated to the extent that the British even made a contingency plan for evacuation. However, with solid local support, the colonial regime survived this challenge by exercising its emergency powers, arresting 4,998, convicting 2,077, and extraditing 221 persons (Yep 2014). That such draconian measures were popularly supported indicated that the longing for a stable haven remained prevalent.

Early postwar Hong Kong began as a city of recent immigrants. In 1945, Hong Kong's population was less than 1 million, and by the time the border with China was closed in 1951, it had swelled to more than 2 million. For those who newly arrived, Hong Kong was no less than a lifeboat in China's political turmoil, and such a "refugee mentality" brought about detachment and a tendency to "stay away from political tensions" (Matthews, Ma, and Lui 2008: 28). It was not an exaggeration to characterize early postwar Hong Kong as a third-world slum swollen with refugees, full of squalor and poverty. Even though the United Kingdom had decidedly embraced the idea of a welfare state, colonial administrators were reluctant to extend the government's obligation to take care of citizens. Social relief, medicine, and schooling were entrusted to private charities, religious groups, or political organizations. The colonial governors intended to minimize the fiscal burden, and one of their frequent explanations was that excessively "generous" provisioning of welfare would have led to more immigrants. To make things worse, corruption ran rampant, and grassroots Hongkongers chafed at the petty tyranny of policemen, firemen, and other governmental clerks.

Most Hongkongers might not have been interested in the KMT-CCP rivalry, but they cared about bread-and-butter issues. If their livelihoods were threatened, they did not refrain from protesting against the government. Throughout the 1950s and 1960s, protests erupted over the issues of rent control, telephone rates, ferry rates, and labor disputes (W. Lam 2004). The lack of an electoral venue led to these grievances being expressed in the streets. The 1966 protest against Star Ferry price hikes attracted the widespread participation of young people in an antigovernment riot (the Kowloon Disturbances), which was later seen as a watershed for giving rise to an indigenous Hong Kong identity (Law 2014: 227–230).

While Hongkongers expressed their discontent through a series of protests and riots, the existence of elections and the KMT's martial-law regime prevented Taiwanese from resorting to street protests. Since 1946, the KMT had implemented a local self-rule scheme by holding regular elections for representatives. As long as elections were restricted to the local level, competition for public offices did not pose a challenge to KMT rule. In fact, it helped the émigré regime to recruit native collaborators on a hostile island, thereby expanding its social support (Wu and Chen 1996). In addition to providing a safety valve for all sorts of social discontent, the existence of electoral politics allowed a certain space for political dissenters, and some of them were vocally critical of the KMT. While the government was willing to tolerate some free-speaking politicians, it strictly forbade any organizing effort. In 1960, when a group of liberal mainlander intellectuals worked with native politicians to attempt to organize an opposition party, the KMT swiftly threw them in jail.

The Free China Incident, named for the magazine managed by these mainlander intellectuals, demonstrated the limitation of the electoral strategy. Peng Ming-min, then director of the political science department of National Taiwan University (NTU), drafted a Declaration of Formosan Self-Salvation in 1964. Peng articulated a vision of civic nationalism by arguing that all Taiwanese people, natives or mainlanders, should reject the KMT's hopeless project of retaking the mainland and manage their common future via a new democratic government. The declaration was no less than an open call for Taiwan independence. Before this statement could reach a wider readership, the KMT arrested Peng and his associates.

Beneath the surface of political conformism, Hongkongers and Taiwanese mounted a series of collective challenges. With more difficult living conditions and the lack of electoral channels, Hongkongers launched successive protests to protect their livelihoods. By contrast, Taiwanese grievances were more political in nature, and elections had helped to channel some of their discontent to institutional avenues.

The Intellectual Awakening

The 1970s saw the rise of young reform-minded intellectuals in the two societies. By the end of that fateful decade, a full-fledged pro-democracy movement had come into being in Taiwan, while Hong Kong's protests had evolved into a strong current of social movements.

The KMT government encountered a series of external and internal crises during this period. The loss of the United Nations seat in 1971 shattered its claim to represent the only legitimate government of China as a whole, and the ensuing diplomatic setback, including Richard Nixon's visit to China and Sino-Japanese normalization in 1972, further discredited the KMT's proclaimed mission to retake mainland China, which had been used to justify the martial-rule dictatorship. When Chiang Ching-kuo began to take over command, an overhaul of the old system was clearly long overdue. In the early 1970s, tax burdens on farmers were relaxed, periodically reelected supplementary seats were added to the national legislature, younger Taiwanese talents were recruited to the government (with future president Lee Teng-hui [1988–2000] being the most prominent among this cohort), and anticorruption measures were implemented.

Making use of the more liberalized political environment, Taiwan's young intellectuals began to voice demands for more reforms though the platform of magazines, including *The Intellectual* (*daxue* [1968–1973]), the *Political Review of Taiwan* (*taiwan zhenglun* [1975]), and finally *Formosa* (*meildao* [1979]). That all three of these magazines ended up being closed down by the government indicated the restriction characterizing Chiang Ching-kuo's reforms. Nevertheless, this intellectual fermentation reverberated in other arenas. Literary writers, folksong lyricists, painters, and choreographers began to explore a novel style of incorporating elements from Taiwan's history and culture. They rejected the sterile rigidity of officially championed arts, as well as the mechanical borrowing from Western modernism. A renewed interest in Taiwan's colonial history and literature emerged. An unmistakable trend of indigenization simultaneously arose in many fields of cultural production, although its political connotations remained implicit and ambiguous. For instance, in the debate over "homeland literature" (*xiangtu wenxue*) in 1977–1978, it remains a contested issue whether the realistic writings on the plight of workers, peasants, and fishermen represented the sprouting of a Taiwanese consciousness or a pursuit of authentic "Chineseness."

According to Hsiau (2008), a new postwar generation was the main proponent of these intellectual campaigns. While their parents had developed different worldviews according to their ethnic backgrounds—a profound sense of rootlessness among mainlanders and nostalgia for the colonial past among native Taiwanese—this generation grew up with heavy indoctrination to the KMT's version of Chinese nationalism, and over the years, they began to fashion out a collective outlook of "returning to reality." In other words, regardless of the political future of "Republic of China," promoting social and political reforms in Taiwan should take precedence.

With the growing detachment from the KMT's orthodox nationalism also came a visible trend in university student activism. In response to the U.S. decision to declare Diaoyutai (or Senkaku Islands in Japanese) as part of Japan's Okinawa, Taiwan's students launched a series of patriotic protests in 1970, and this nationalistic fervor quickly spread to Hong Kong and overseas students in America. The movement to defend Diaoyutai amounted to the first major campus agitation since the government had neutralized the clandestine communist movement in the early 1950s. The KMT took care to channel the student activism into manageable venues, and the Diaoyutai Movement in Taiwan quickly subsided with the conclusion of a U.S.-Japan agreement in 1971 (E. Chiu 2003: 73–76). There was a great contrast between the short-lived student activism in Taiwan and its continuing vitality in the United States and Hong Kong. Taiwan's Diaoyutai activists in the United States split into a protracted rivalry between pro-CCP and pro-KMT camps. With the PRC's international ascendancy, the former gained the upper hand, while the latter were recruited into the Taiwan government. Among them was Ma Ying-jeou, whose presidency (2008–2016) encountered the Sunflower Movement's challenge. Due to its strong nationalistic sentiments, Hong Kong's Diaoyutai campaigns continued well into the 1990s, and became an integral part of the pro-democracy movement.[2]

In hindsight, the abrupt end to Taiwan's Diaoyutai Movement was in part due to surveillance by the KMT government, which had sufficient reasons to fear a further escalation. For Taiwan's patriotic students, it was patently clear that their nationalistic aspirations were going nowhere under the geopolitical reality, since the KMT survival had to rely on U.S. support. As such, there emerged a new concern for social issues. Students volunteered in urban impoverished neighborhoods, rural villages, and aboriginal communities to better understand Taiwan's social problems (M. Huang 1976: 44–45). This "social service" turn among students signified a bracketing of the ideological politics of nationalism, following the "returning-to-reality" trend (Hsiau 2008).

Riding on the wave of intellectual awakening, Taiwan's political opposition grew in its challenge to the KMT's authoritarian rule. In 1977, opposition politicians coordinated nation-wide electoral campaigns for the first time, and a *dangwai* (literally, "outside the party") movement came into being. Emboldened by their electoral success as well as the Chungli Incident, in which rioters torched a police station upon the revelation of election rigging, the opposition mounted a more vigorous campaign in the 1978 election, which the government canceled at the last minute, citing the emergency of the United States severing diplomatic relations with Taiwan. The opposition managed to form a de facto party under *Formosa* magazine to demand full democracy in 1979. On December 10, a mass rally turned into a violent clash with the police, and the Kaohsiung Incident resulted in a massive crackdown. Taiwan's nascent pro-democracy movement suffered a major setback because its leaders were jailed, and yet it made a quick rebound in the early 1980s.

The 1970s also witnessed the coming-of-age of a new generation in Hong Kong, commonly identified as the Baby Boomers. Unlike their refugee parents, who maintained emotional attachment to their mainland birthplaces, these Hongkongers were born or grew up locally, and regardless of their family origins, they were assimilated into a Cantonese-speaking everyday world and shaped by English-language education. According to Chan Koonchung (born in 1952 in Shanghai), a leading public intellectual of this generation, their appearance marked the emergence of "Hongkongers" as well as a distinctive "Hong Kong culture" (K. Chan 2008: 37). Perhaps, the launch of *City Magazine* (*haowai*) in 1976, co-founded by Chan Koonchung, represented the beginning of Hong Kong's cultural indigenization. The newspaper celebrated a cosmopolitan outlook, introducing the Western critical discourses and at the same time remaining fully aware of the local hybridity (Chun 2017: 109–123). In other words, there emerged a simultaneous disenchantment of orthodox Chinese culture in the 1970s: while young Hongkongers chose to embrace the Western modernities and their local elaborations, their Taiwanese counterparts began to examine the grassroots experiences in search of a distinctive cultural expression.

The growing Hong Kong consciousness was also made possible because of a series of social reforms initiated by the colonial government. The riots of the mid-1960s had revealed the fragility and explosiveness of an underprovisioned society amid rapid transformation. During the governor tenure of Murray McLehose (1971–1982), the government launched a massive public housing scheme, improved education and medical care, offered cash assistance to the needy, and cleaned up official corruption. These belated social and welfare modernizations came in a particular context. The colonial administrators needed to shore up their local support before Beijing began to raise the issue of Hong Kong's future. Critics and the Labour government in London also called for reforms in the colony (Lui 2012: 141–186). While Taiwan witnessed similar regime-initiated changes to buttress its challenged legitimacy, Hong Kong's colonial government reforms stopped short of changing political institutions, which entered the official agenda after the beginning of Sino-British negotiations in the early 1980s.

Hong Kong's collective actions evolved from sporadic riots and ad hoc protests to a more organized pattern in the 1970s. The Christian Industrial Committee, founded in 1968 and a precursor to the Hong Kong Confederation of Trade Unions, emerged as the most active labor organization of this decade by breaking the existing duopoly of labor unions by leftists and rightists. Under Szeto Wah's leadership, a professional teacher's union was established in 1973, later growing into a mainstay for the pro-democracy movement. The increasing intervention of the colonial government in urban planning and public housing provision encouraged organizing among tenants, and with the help of professional social workers, a community movement centered on housing issues took root (D. Ho 2000: 186–189). All these nascent forces made up what was called "pressure groups." By the end of the 1970s, there were signs showing the formation of a "social movement industry" (Lui and Chiu 2000: 8).

Hong Kong's student activism surged during this period, and similarly, there it was animated by an ardent Chinese nationalism. In the campaign to upgrade Chinese to become an official language (1970), as well as in the Diaoyutai Movement (1971), students became the vanguard of social activism, ushering in a "red and hot period" (*honghuo niandai*) (B. Leung 2000: 213–216). The nationalistic ideology, however, played a different role in stimulating student involvement. In Taiwan, the KMT version of Chinese nationalism was the official ideology, and student activism emerged initially under its aegis, but later evolved into growing disenchantment with it. In the context of Hong Kong, Chinese nationalism remained a subversive idealism that defied British rule, and hence was a taken-for-granted ideational component of the emerging student activism. Since Taiwan's KMT was losing the battle for the allegiance of overseas Chinese, Hong Kong activist students naturally identified with socialist China.

The nationalistic preoccupation explained the early predominance of the nationalist faction (*guocuipai*) over the social action faction (*shehuipai*) in the student movement. The nationalist faction was Maoist in orientation and was secretly supported by Beijing's operatives; since China remained committed to maximizing the utility of the colony, these student activists focused on promoting Chinese identity and avoided criticism of British rule. On the other hand, the social action faction, no less nationalistic in mindset, appeared more ready to rock the boat by targeting the existing social injustices in the colony. After the conclusion of China's Cultural Revolution and the fall of ultraleftists, the nationalist faction lost its influence. The social action faction's concentration on current problems gained ascendancy, evidenced in the campaigns to bring Peter Godber (a notoriously corrupt police superintendent) to justice (1973–1974), the scandal over mismanagement of Golden Jubilee School (1977–1978), and the dispute over resettling the boat people in Yaumatei (1978–1979) (B. Leung 2011: 353–354).

Albert Ho, the ex-chairperson of the pro-democracy beacon Hong Kong Democratic Party (DP) (2006–2012), was a social action faction leader during his student years in the early 1970s. His autobiography documented the struggles to combat the dominant nationalist faction. Despite his antagonism against the nationalist faction, he remained a dyed-in-the-wool Chinese nationalist who took personal pride in being a veteran participant in the Diaoyutai Movement and other anti-Japan campaigns (A. Ho 2010: 12–27, 139–159).

Albert Ho's career demonstrates the parallels as well as the divergence of younger activists in the two societies. Both the ascendancy of Hong Kong's social action faction and Taiwan's "return-to-reality" generation represented a pragmatic turn away from the high politics of nationalism. Yet, Chinese nationalism persisted as a leitmotif in the subsequent pro-democracy movement in Hong Kong, as evidenced by Albert Ho's vocal opposition to Taiwan independence, whereas its salience in Taiwan went into decline with the sprouting of an indigenous identity, which became a driving force in Taiwan's democratization.

Taiwan's Successful Democratization

In the 1970s, Taiwan developed a pro-democracy movement without social protests, while Hong Kong's social protests thrived without a pro-democracy movement. Over the following two decades, both societies began to experience political transition; Taiwan became a consolidated democracy, while Hong Kong traversed to a hybrid regime of semidemocracy.

Taiwan's pro-democracy movement bounced back from the Kaohsiung Incident, and grew in electoral seats in the early 1980s. At that time, social movements concerning consumer rights, aborigines, labor, women, and environmental issues made their entrance. An awakened civil society with the help of the resilient opposition made possible the significant breakthroughs in political transition (M. Ho 2010; M. Hsiao 1990). Defying the political restrictions, opposition politicians organized the Democratic Progressive Party (DPP) in 1986, and the government decided to lift martial law in 1987.

Taiwan made strides toward democracy in tandem with the decline of its preoccupation with China. There are several reasons why Taiwan's democratization necessarily accompanied such a "de-sinicization." First, the KMT justified its authoritarian rule by banning strikes, protests, and opposition parties in the name of wartime mobilization to suppress the communist insurgency. As long as the civil war remained officially "unfinished," civil liberties and political rights were suspended. Second, a genuine reelection of the presidency and national legislature was indefinitely postponed because the KMT contended that Taiwan made up only one province of the nation. Representatives elected in the 1948 election in China continued to exercise their capacity, and the KMT responded only by gradually increasing the share of supplementary seats periodically reelected in Taiwan. In short, the increasingly ridiculous claim of representing all of China stood in the way of democratization. Last, in despite of Chiang Ching-kuo's promotion in the early 1970s, native Taiwanese remained a minority in the mainlander-controlled government. The pursuit of democracy came with the aspiration for equality and dignity for Taiwanese, particularly during the late 1980s, when the more relaxed environment made it possible for opposition politicians to mention the tragedy of the February 28 Incident and to adopt the strategy of ethnic mobilization. The DPP adopted a Taiwan independence clause in its party charter in 1991. In short, there could not be democratization without indigenization or "Taiwanization" of politics (Jacobs 2005).

Taiwan's relatively peaceful transition to democracy was made possible in part by the leadership of Lee Teng-hui, who inherited the presidency upon the death of Chiang in 1988. Being the first Taiwanese president and surrounded by the mainlander old guards, Lee proceeded with extreme caution. The eruption of the pro-democracy Wild Lily student movement in March 1990 enabled Lee to expedite political reforms (Wright 2012: 115–116). Subsequently, electoral channels were gradually opened up, with full election of the national legislature in 1992, election of autonomous city majors and the provincial governor in 1994, and finally the presidential election in 1996. Lee, while personally an opponent of the Taiwan independence cause, attempted to craft a new national identity. He promoted the idea of "a community of life" (*shengming gongtong ti*) that included all the people in Taiwan, which shared many parallels to the Peng Ming-min's civic nationalism in 1964 (Hughes 1997: 97–98). Later, Lee's characterization of mainlanders as "new Taiwanese" helped to raise the notion of "Taiwanese" from an ethnic category to a more inclusive national identity.

Initially, China appeared willing to cooperate with Lee in normalizing cross-strait relations, as long as the latter demonstrated pro-unification commitment. However, Taiwan's democratization came with the quest for statehood, which began to unsettle Beijing leaders. China launched two missile exercises as an intimidation tactic as Taiwan was about to hold its first presidential election in 1996. Immediately before the 2000 presidential election, Chinese leaders issued a dark warning against the Taiwan independence movement. In retrospect, the two rounds of Chinese intervention not only alienated Taiwan's voters; they also failed to arrest the trends of democratization and indigenization. Lee won his reelection with 54 percent of voter support in 1996, and he proceeded to declare cross-strait relations as "a special state-to-state relation." The independence-leaning DPP's victory in 2000 amounted to a defiant rebuttal to China's threats.

Taiwan's democratization proceeded by successfully handling the "China factors," both from within and without. Internally, the boundary of a political community had to been redefined for the popular election of the top leadership, which was possible only after Taiwan gave up the pretentious claims that China's civil war was ongoing and the Republic of China continued to represent China. Externally, Taiwan had to withstand Beijing's successive attempts to disrupt domestic reforms. Luckily, Taiwan's democracy was consolidated with the 2000 turnover of power. Expectedly, Taiwan's political transition would have encountered a stronger external veto, if it had taken place a decade later when China had clearly emerged as a new world power.

Hong Kong's Stalled Democratization

Until the British introduced limited election to district boards in 1982, voting did not exist in Hong Kong. Expatriate administrators, who lived in a self-contained world with minimal contact with common Hongkongers, embraced a siege mentality that was instinctively suspicious of popular participation (Goodstadt 2005: 19–48). The 1970s witnessed the sprouting of student activism and pressure groups, which, however, never raised constitutional matters because "the question of democratization was simply seen as remote" (Lui and Chiu 2000: 11). During the Sino-British negotiation of 1982 to 1984, it became clear that the colonial status quo could not last. The British began to implement some measures of representative government in order to facilitate a graceful exit. Some seats in the legislative council were opened to popular vote for the first time in 1991, and the same year saw the passage of the Bill of Human Rights. Supported by the favorable political environment, Hong Kong's pro-democracy movement came into being. In 1986, a pro-democracy umbrella organization composed of pressure groups emerged, later succeeded by United Democrats of Hong Kong (1990), which later reorganized into the DP (1994).

The nascent pro-democracy movement proceeded with moderation and optimism, as reform-era China was experimenting with liberalization on many fronts. The Tiananmen Massacre in June 1989 not only crushed China's pro-democracy movement but also destroyed Hongkongers' confidence in their political future. In response, the last governor, Chris Pattern (1992–1997), expedited political reforms over Beijing's objection. The 1995 election for legislative council marked the first time all sixty seats were elected directly or indirectly. However, posthandover Hong Kong experienced a reversal in democratization when stricter regulations concerning voluntary associations and demonstrations were adopted and appointed seats in district councils reappeared (until 2011). The proportion of popularly elected seats in Hong Kong's legislative council grew at a snail's pace: 18 of 60 (in 1991), 20 of 60 (1995), 24 of 60 (1998), 30 of 60 (2004), and 40 of 70 (2012). The promise of the 1990 Basic Law for "the selection of the chief executive by universal suffrage" was repeatedly postponed. Hong Kong's top executive was decided by an unrepresentative election committee/selection committee whose numbers grew from 400 (in 1996), to 800 (2002) to 1,200 (2012); despite the piecemeal enlargement of the electorate, the ultimate decision was made by Beijing.

More alarmingly, pro-Beijing forces were improving their electoral capacity. The Democratic Alliance for the Betterment of Hong Kong (DAB), founded in 1992, showed steady growth, and by 2004, the DAB had surpassed the DP, the flagship of Hong Kong's pro-democracy movement, in legislative council seats to become the largest party (Ma 2012: 163–164). In local elections for district council, the DAB also began to outperform the DP from 2007 (J. Lam 2012: 117). Hong Kong's pro-democracy movement appeared to have lost steam, and its progress was bogged down in unproductive negotiations with Beijing over frustrating and mind-boggling details of constitutional reform. The government-proposed reform package of 2005 was vetoed by the pro-democracy opposition, and a newer version (proposed in 2010), no more progressive than the previous one, went into effect with the DP's support. Hong Kong's transition appeared trapped in the middle of nowhere, with it being characterized as "semidemocratic" or "competitive authoritarian" (Fong 2013).

In hindsight, there were many obstacles to a fuller democracy. The CCP's aversion to Western-style liberalism, undoubtedly, amounted to the most important factor. Before and after 1997, Beijing continued to embrace a conspiracy theory that perceived Hong Kong's pro-democracy movement as an international anti-China plot (Loh 2010: 175). Second, the local bourgeois persistently opposed democratization measures for fear of losing their economic privileges (Sing 2004: 88). In the 1980s, it originated from the fear of a populist increase in welfare expenses, and later on, with their growing investment in China, they had been recruited as Beijing's collaborators (see Chapter 3). Third, in spite of the growth of an indigenous identity in the 1970s, Hong Kong's political culture continued to encourage the "exit" option over the "voice" option, as evidenced by the mass exodus of educated professionals since the conclusion of Sino-British negotiation. "Emigration was never an issue of public debate. There was no moral condemnation of those who chose to 'exit'" (Mathews, Ma, and Lui 2008: 45). The weakness of Hong Kong's pro-democracy movement was due in part to the availability as well as the popularity of emigration, which certainly cast doubt on democracy as a desirable goal worth striving for.

While Taiwan's democratization grew in tandem with indigenization, Hong Kong's political movement evolved with an assumption that the city could not be democratized without a similar process in the mainland. Hongkongers' pursuit of freedom was framed under a larger project of democratizing China. In the early 1980s, idealistic student leaders first articulated the vision of "retrocession to the nation and democratic governance in Hong Kong" (*minzu huigui minzhu zhigang*), later often shortened as "democratic retrocession" (*minzhu huigui*), when the majority of Hongkongers preferred the extension of the colonial status quo. After the retroversion to Chinese rule had become inevitable, the "democratic retrocession" theory became the guiding philosophy by default. Although the Tiananmen Massacre shattered the wishful thinking regarding Chinese leaders, the annual commemorative rituals of the June Fourth candlelight vigil since 1990 popularized a particular "liberal patriotism" that combined pan-Chinese nationalism and Western liberalism (Veg 2017). In other words, unlike Taiwan, Hong Kong's pro-democracy movement had not been propelled by the urge for indigenization until the years before the Umbrella Movement.

Taiwan's democratization was propelled by a Taiwanese identity, whereas Hong Kong's pro-democracy movement continued to embrace a Chinese identity. It was largely due to the divergent pattern of national identities that

Taiwan's successful experience failed to become a positive reference for Hong Kong. Theoretically, an unprecedented peaceful transfer of power in a Chinese society should have generated a demonstration effect abroad, but it turned out to be quite the opposite. After the historical election that brought the DPP to power in 2000, Hong Kong's legislative council passed a unanimous motion to oppose Taiwan independence, with only one vote in abstention.[3] Albert Ho elaborated a legal theory explaining why Taiwanese belonged to a Chinese nation (Ho 2010: 237–239). When Emily Lau, the DP's chairwoman (2012–2014), indicated her respect for self-determination in a 2003 trip to Taiwan, for which she was savagely criticized by the pro-Beijing media, none of her pro-democracy colleagues came forward in her defense (interview #HK20-1). In other words, when it involved issues of Chinese nationalism, Hong Kong's pro-democracy politicians were actually willing to set aside the democratic ideals they professed to strive for. Belonging to a nation took precedence over the right of self-determination, and such an understanding remained entrenched in Hong Kong's opposition politicians until it encountered a strong challenge by the insurgent "localists" immediately before the Umbrella Movement (see Chapter 3).

Conclusion

Following postwar economic success, Hong Kong and Taiwan in the 1970s witnessed the nascent civil-society stirrings, manifesting in intellectual debates, student movements, and political activism. Both of the pro-democracy movements made major breakthroughs around the mid-1980s; however, the subsequent paths diverged. Taiwan was fortunate enough to complete its democratic transition before China grew strong enough to gain sufficient leverage over the island, whereas Hong Kong evolved into a semidemocracy after the handover to Chinese sovereignty. Hong Kong's pro-democracy movement proceeded with an unambiguous Chinese identity, while Taiwan's was powered by a current of Taiwanese consciousness. The diverging constellation of nationalistic politics explained why Taiwan's successful democratization failed to provide a positive lesson for Hong Kong, and such mutual ignorance lasted until around 2000, when the two societies began to experience a new round of impacts from China.

2

China's Impacts

By the turn of the century, Taiwan and Hong Kong appeared to be heading in opposite directions. Taiwan's democratization brought the independence-leaning DPP to power in 2000, while post-1997 Hong Kong returned to China's embrace with the new status of special administrative region that came with a guarantee of a high degree of autonomy. The two societies began to sustain a new round of China impacts, which generated waves of resistance and identity indigenization that planted the seeds for the two eventful protests of 2014.

In the first few years of Hong Kong's reversion to Chinese sovereignty, Beijing largely honored its pledge regarding local autonomy. The ill-fated attempt to legislate a national security bill (Article 23 of the Basic Law) in 2003, which outlawed vaguely described activities as "subversion against the Central People's Government, or theft of state secrets" and "establishing ties with foreign political organizations or bodies," provoked a large-scale mass demonstration. The setback led to a more assertive approach on the part of Beijing, as the Liaison Office, the central government's official representative in Hong Kong, began to play a more salient role in managing local affairs. Beijing delayed the promised political reforms, assisted loyalist politicians during elections, silenced criticism in the media, and promoted patriotic identification, which generated growing discontent. A Closer Economic Partnership Arrangement (CEPA) was implemented in 2003 to tighten the relationship between Hong Kong and the mainland, and yet the influx of Chinese tourists and parallel traders created acute grievances. Consequently, more and more protests emerged as a reaction against this perceived "mainlandization" (Lo 2008b: 42–44).

In Taiwan, the advent of the DPP government irritated the Chinese leaders, who had to look for other ways to curb what they perceived as secessionist tendencies. Reflecting on its failed saber-rattling interventions in 1996 and 2000 presidential elections, Beijing adopted a less coercive strategy of "encircling politics with business" (*yishang weizheng*), "promoting unification via economics" (*yijing cutong*), and "pressing officials through the people" (*yimin biguan*). With the KMT's comeback in 2008, Beijing saw this approach come to fruition. Ma Ying-jeou's government (2008–2016) prioritized rapprochement with Beijing; consequently, as many as twenty-three cross-strait agreements were signed, including the Economic Cooperation Framework Agreement (ECFA) (2010), which was modeled after Hong Kong's CEPA, as well as the CSSTA (2013), which led to the Sunflower Movement. Before the occupation of the legislature, the rapid cross-strait economic and political integration had generated more and more discontent, as civil-society organizations began to challenge the "Hongkongization" of Taiwan (Kaeding 2014; Lo 2008b).

In the literature on cross-strait relations, there has been a lively debate on how to define the "China factor" (S. Lin 2016; Schubert 2016; J. Wu 2016; Wu, Tsai, and Cheng 2017). The development of cross-strait relations is not a natural and spontaneous process, as if free market would have automatically led to closer economic exchange; in fact, it is planned, encouraged, and sponsored with a clear political agenda. In Hong Kong, there seems to be less use of the term "China factor" in academic and public discourses, but it is not because the influences are not felt. Quite the contrary, exactly because of its ubiquity and as well as the fact that Hong Kong is politically part of China, the term appears in a way to be superfluous. It is possible to find a middle-ground working definition that is applicable to both cases. When using the terms "China factor" or "China impacts," I am referring to the associated consequences that are clearly intended and promoted by the Chinese government to serve its agenda of politically incorporating Taiwan and consolidating its control over Hong Kong. In order to produce the desired results, Beijing needs to manufacture a group of local collaborators who might be ideologically or economically motivated. The China factor is not something entirely coming from the outside, but also appears as a "genuine demand" from within. Since Beijing is prevented from resorting to outright repression (as of Tibetans and Uighurs) and the use of surveillance and indoctrination (as of PRC citizens) toward Taiwanese and Hongkongers, a more delicate and less coercive strategy has to be crafted.

Some caveats are needed for this restrictive definition of "China factor." Unintended developments, such as Hong Kong's subway crowding and housing speculation due to the influx of people and money from China, might have elicited stronger popular resentment. There exists also a vast gray zone between intended and unintended outcomes. As of 2017, mainland immigrants arriving after the handover already made up 12.1 percent of Hong Kong's population.[1] Was it a political strategy of "demographic blood exchange transfusion" (*renkou huanxue*) according to its detractors? Beijing certainly made political use of these new immigrants' social and economic vulnerabilities after their arrival, but they did not migrate at the behest of Beijing. Last, even a carefully crafted strategy could backfire by bringing about unwanted effects. The attempt to foster a pro-Beijing media in Taiwan (see below) failed to generate favorable public opinion, and instead stimulated a new wave of resistance against Beijing's influence. Understanding the complexities in Taiwan-China and Hong Kong–China interactions, a narrower focus on clearly intended and formally stated policies by Beijing leaders, which I identify as "economic united front," is therefore helpful in identifying the agency and reactions in the process.

The Economic United Front Strategy

In 1939, Mao Zedong mentioned the united front as one of three fundamental problems confronting the Chinese revolution (the other two being armed struggle and party-building). Over the years, the CCP honed this political skill to perfection as they sustained themselves under the onslaught of the Japanese and won the civil war over the Nationalists (van Slyke 1967: 4–5). The united front strategy, in essence, meant the creation of internal divides within the enemy camp to isolate and defeat the main rival by making friends with the rest. While armed struggle represented a head-on approach to achieve the desired goal, united front was often employed when such a confrontational strategy appeared inadvisable or impractical. Prior to the 1980s, the united front strategy relied on ideological and political incentives in gaining the support of lesser enemies. Reform-era China saw the end of Maoist autarky, hence making possible the use of economic incentives, and such a modernized united front strategy was first deployed in Hong Kong, and then applied to Taiwan. In hindsight, this strategy foreshadowed what recently has been identified as "sharp power" for its mixture of coercion and incentives in achieving the geopolitical goals.

The conclusion of the Cultural Revolution brought about a fundamental revamping of China's policy toward Taiwan, as the professed goal of "military liberation" had long become outdated. In 1982, Beijing articulated the political formula "one country, two systems" in order to sweeten the deal with promises of a high degree of autonomy and an independent military force. To ward off these peace offensives, Taiwan's KMT government responded with a policy of no contact, no negotiation, and no compromise. Until the lifting of martial law that removed the trade ban with China in

1987, Taiwan was able to effectively neutralize the economic united front strategy (Kastner 2009: 47).

While China's initial peace offensive toward Taiwan did not make much progress, the Sino-British negotiation beginning in 1982 made Hong Kong a testing site for economic united front work. When Deng Xiaoping decided to dispatch Xu Jiatun, a veteran pro-reform cadre, to supervise Hong Kong affairs in 1983, the latter was instructed to broaden local support in preparation for the resumption of Chinese rule. Xu later fled to the United States to escape a purge, and afterward he published an unusually candid memoir that depicted how the united front strategy evolved from conventional channels to economic incentives during his tenure (1983–1989).

When Xu took office, there were around six thousand Communist Party members in Hong Kong, but only half of them were locals, who were mainly concentrated in the traditional bastions of the working class and leftist schools. Since the failure of the 1967 riot, communists virtually became social outcasts, as these underground members lived in a self-contained world isolated from mainstream society. Xu was told to make friends with the "rightists" by not shunning the relationship with the "pro-British, pro-U.S., and pro-Taiwan forces." He also encouraged contacts with youth, women, and neighborhood associations with the goal of broadening support for Beijing (J. Xu 1993: 76, 102, 116). All these attempts to establish relationships beyond the working-class core fell into the conventional tactics of united front work. Xu soon discovered the logic of Hong Kong's capitalism in that businesspeople's political orientations were intimately related to their transactions. This insight led to the following policy recommendation:

> We should use our "resources" to cultivate a group of pro-China capitalists. Our business units in Hong Kong should contribute to this goal without the fear of being criticized. We should learn to use the "resources" in the mainland, which are actually much larger, to gain popular support and contribute to continuing Hong Kong's prosperity. (J. Xu 1993: 130–131)

Xu maintained that such profit-based united front work worked both economically and politically for China: "With the growing attraction of mainland to Hong Kong, these Chinese capitalists are bound to change their mainland perception and their confidence will grow." He envisioned this scenario as a win-win situation because "merchants can make money and they contribute to the economic reforms of the mainland, increasing its export and attracting investment" (J. Xu 1993: 235).

The innovative application was made possible because China's economic reforms released market opportunities, which could be utilized as incentives for the business community. Xu took pride in securing a number of mainland business deals exclusively for Hong Kong capitalists. Tung Chee-hwa, the first Hong Kong SAR chief executive (1997–2005), demonstrated the effectiveness of this strategy. Tung's father was a Shanghai-born shipping magnate, who narrowly escaped a business collapse with an emergency Chinese loan, which resulted in the change of Tung family allegiance from pro-Taipei to pro-Beijing (He 2016: 134).

By making patriotism rewarding, Beijing aimed to create a class of loyalist businesspeople whose economic stakes in the mainland could be leveraged for political purposes. In the early 1980s, Hong Kong's businesspeople favored the continuation of the colonial status quo, but gradually they gravitated to an accommodating stance toward the resumption of Chinese sovereignty. An "unholy alliance" between Chinese communists and Hongkonger capitalists emerged with a shared antidemocracy agenda (So 1999: 119–122). A similar tactic was later deployed toward Taiwanese investors. In 1988, China established a national-level Taiwan Affairs Office with branches in many provinces and cities. The PRC officials made no secret of the fact that the preferential treatment they offered was geared toward the political goal (Kastner 2009: 94).

China's Economic Rise

China's economic ascendancy, eclipsing that of Japan and other newly industrialized Asian economies (including Hong Kong and Taiwan), was rapid and spectacular. By making use of its abundant low-cost labor and the international liberal trade regime, the rise of China has profoundly restructured international politics (H. Hung 2015).

In terms of China–Hong Kong and China-Taiwan relations, the speed of the enormous growth of China's economy clearly tilted the balance in its favor. When the economic united front strategy was first formulated in the mid-1980s, cash-strapped China was in urgent need of foreign investment. A milestone was crossed somewhere between the 2001 ascension of China to the WTO, which indicated its confidence to embrace the international market, and the overtaking of Japan as the world's second-largest economy in 2010. Since then China became more self-conscious of its growing economic might and became more ready to employ it for geopolitical purposes.

In 1990, the size of Taiwan's and Hong Kong's economies (measured in US$ GDP) were, respectively, roughly half (46.4 percent) and one-fifth (21.4 percent) of the economy of China, and by 2014 these figures had shrunk to one-twentieth (5.1 percent) and one-twenty-fifth (2.8 percent), respectively.[2] It was not that Taiwan and Hong Kong stagnated in this period. These two economies increased by more than three times, but their growth was effectively overshadowed by China's nearly thirty-fold expansion. Their relatively diminished economic significance encouraged Beijing leaders to adopt a more assertive strategy. The emergence of a "Greater China Economy" led to increasing dependence of Taiwan and Hong Kong on mainland China. Over the years 1998 to 2014, China received 63.2 percent and 39.8 percent of Taiwan's and Hong Kong's accumulated foreign direct investment, respectively.[3] In terms of trade volume, China swiftly emerged as the number one partner for both. China (including Hong Kong) accounted for 8.5 percent of Taiwan's trade in 1990, and it rose to 29.7 percent in 2014.[4] In Hong Kong, the share of trade with China was 32.7 percent in 1990 and 47 percent in 2014.[5] Both Taiwan and Hong Kong underwent a rapid de-industrializing process as China's low labor cost attracted the relocation of labor-intensive firms. By the mid-1990s, Hong Kong's manufacturing sectors virtually disappeared after their exodus to China (Lui 2015b: 35), while Taiwan continued to derive roughly one-third of its GDP from manufacturing despite the waves of factory closures (T. Lin 2009).

In the 1980s, small and medium enterprises from Hong Kong and Taiwan pioneered investment in China, followed by larger business groups. Over the years, the economic integration with China resulted in a massive wave of offshore business migration. As of 2012, "approximately 30 percent of the sum total revenues of 'Taiwan's top 300' enterprise groups came from China" (J. Wu 2016: 432). Hong Kong's top seven conglomerates also substantially increased their percentage of assets in China; by 2009 there were four major Hong Kong conglomerates whose assets in China accounted for more than one-quarter of their total assets (Fong 2014: 206).

Economic integration was, of course, a two-sided process; while Taiwanese and Hongkonger businesses grew more reliant on their offshore operations, China also needed access to the capital, technology, and financial skills controlled by Taiwanese and Hongkongers. Taiwan's exports to China were driven by demand for components from its relocated high-tech firms, which emerged as vital to the global production that integrated China as the world's factory. Hence, it was argued that Beijing was reluctant to impose economic sanctions on Taiwan for fear of negative impact on its own economy (Tung 2003). And Taiwan was said to have successfully taken advantage of the low-cost labor force in China to facilitate its own transition to a knowledge-based economy (Fuller 2008). Similarly, Hong Kong's status as international financial center played a vital intermediary role because China was still reluctant to lift capital controls in order to make its currency fully convertible. Hong Kong provided the access for China-based enterprises to attract international portfolio investment. As of 2014, Chinese companies listed on Hong Kong's stock exchange accounted for 60 percent of its market capitalization (Yick 2015: 185). China's financial pipelines, in a sense, were in the hands of Hongkongers.

Being the top two foreign direct investors, Hong Kong and Taiwan eagerly participated in China's economic modernization. It was estimated that

Hongkonger-owned factories employed over 10 million workers in Guangdong province in 2008 (Goodstadt 2014: 41). Taiwanese firms were said to maintain a labor force of nearly 16 million in 2014.[6] Their contributions gave rise to an economically stronger China, which gained the leverage to change the geopolitical status quo. Hongkongers lived with the expectation that someday Shanghai would replace their hometown city as the financial gateway to China. The political price for Taiwan was undoubtedly bigger; as John J. Mearsheimer observed, "By trading with China and helping it grow into an economic powerhouse, Taiwan has helped create a burgeoning Goliath with revisionist goals that include ending Taiwan's independence" (2014: 39).

Beijing's Collaborators

In China's transitional economy, political directives and personal connections took precedence over the rule of law. Businesspeople had to obtain a certain level of cooperation from communist cadres to ensure the smooth operation of their firms (Guthrie 2002). Willingly or not, Taiwanese and Hongkonger entrepreneurs had to accommodate Beijing's strategy of economic united front.

In Beijing's strategic roadmap, Hong Kong was ahead of Taiwan in many ways, foreshadowing the latter's future evolution. As noted above, Hongkonger capitalists had been prime targets of Beijing's friendship offensive. Well before the handover, the "bulk of the beneficiaries of colonial patronage switched allegiance and became openly critical of the British" (Goodstadt 2005: 112). To forestall the rising pro-democracy movement, Hong Kong's business elites formed the Liberal Party in 1994, which fought on the same front with local communists by opposing government-led political reforms (Chung 2001: 144–155). The commercial elites' dominance in the legislative council's functional constituencies and election/selection commissions for chief executive contained demands for democratization. Beijing was willing to reward these business collaborators by nominating them as deputies of the National People's Congress, members of the Chinese People's Political Consultative Conference, and other governmental positions (Fong 2014: 199–201). Although these official titles were mainly honorific, they provided privileged access to mainland cadres—a convenient tool for taking care of their investments.

Unlike their Hongkonger counterparts, Taiwanese businesspeople did not oppose democratic reforms during the country's political transition. Since the 1990s, Taiwan's capitalists have been consistently urging the government to liberalize cross-strait economic relations. As Taiwan became increasingly drawn into China's economic orbit, an estimated more than one million Taiwanese chose to reside in China, mostly for investment and job opportunities (Chiu, Fell, and Lin 2014: 1). These Taiwanese entrepreneurs, or "Taishang," clearly emerged as visible actors on the political scene. There were varying assessments of their roles and political influence; some argued that they skillfully dodged Beijing's attempt to utilize them as "agents for unification" (Keng and Schubert 2010), while some studies indicated their "subjection to the one-China principle" (Mengin 2015: 219–228) and participation in a "historic bloc" that successfully promoted closer cross-strait economic ties (Green 2015). Nevertheless, it was clear that Taishang constituted a "voting bloc" with a pronounced preference for the KMT, and their campaign donations and trips back to Taiwan to cast ballots were actively encouraged by communist cadres (Schubert 2016: 93).

In both places, the economic united front strategy gave birth to a group of local collaborators whose cross-border business interests became an auxiliary to Beijing's political agendas, ensuring a pro-unification party in power in Taiwan and forestalling democratization in Hong Kong.

"Conceding Benefits"

The DPP's success in the presidential election of 2004 prompted Beijing to reexamine its existing strategy. The result was an upgraded application of negative and positive incentives toward Taiwan.

In March 2005, China promulgated the Anti-Secession Law, which asserted the right to use military force in the event of Taiwan's declaration of independence or if the possibility of peaceful national unification was completely gone. Soon Chinese officials darkly warned that businesspeople who supported Taiwan independence were not welcome. Shi Wen-long, the founder of Chimei Group (a leading petrochemical and liquid crystal display producer), suddenly resigned and issued a public letter expressing his "regrets" for having supported Chen Shui-bian in the past. This "forced confession" came at the moment when Chimei's subsidiaries were unusually audited by local officials and denied access to bank loans. The Chimei incident had a chilling effect on the Taiwanese business community.

In addition to making an example of pro-independence Taiwanese entrepreneurs, Beijing provided exclusive rewards to some targeted groups. Chairman of the KMT Lien Chan, who was consecutively defeated in the 2000 and 2004 presidential elections and had previously served as vice president (1996–2000), made a visit to Beijing and met Chinese President Hu Jintao in 2005. Lien and Hu released a joint declaration to encourage more economic cooperation and to end hostilities on the premise of mutual acknowledgment of the "1992 consensus," which ostensibly meant that both Taiwan and the mainland belonged to one China. With the CCP's tacit understanding, the KMT leaders maintained that each side had different interpretations of the meaning of "one China," a proviso that avoided the impression that Taiwan had agreed to become a part of the PRC. The 2005 accord also marked the beginning of

China's more self-conscious use of "conceding benefits" (*rangli*) to achieve political goals. Having secured the KMT's endorsement of a pro-unification agenda, Beijing made strategic use of a more self-confident Chinese capitalism for the goal of political integration.

Following Lien's visit, Beijing abolished import duties on fifteen kinds of Taiwanese fruit in 2005. Since Taiwan's agricultural producers were primarily located in the pro-DPP southern region, Beijing aimed to create a group of dependent economic constituencies whose interests hinged on their privileged access to the Chinese market. Fruit growers were an ideal choice because their produce had a short shelf life and thus was more vulnerable to politically motivated economic sanctions. China's local governments launched several rounds of emergency "policy purchases" to stabilize the price when overproduction occurred in Taiwan. The result was that Taiwan's agricultural exports to China nearly tripled in the years from 2005 to 2015, and Taiwan replaced Japan as the number one importer.[7]

From 2006, there was an annual KMT-CCP Forum that promoted cross-strait exchanges by effectively sidelining the then-DPP government. Thus, after Ma Ying-jeou won the presidential election in 2008, the KMT was able to quickly put into practice what had been previously negotiated through party-to-party channels. A series of bold liberalization measures were swiftly implemented, including routine direct air flights from 2008, group tourist visits to Taiwan from 2008, individual visits from 2011, and the admission of mainland students to Taiwanese universities from 2011. The centerpiece of Ma Ying-jeou's effort to promote closer cross-strait ties was the 2010 ECFA, a bilateral agreement that minimized the barriers to economic exchange and envisioned a scheduled roadmap for further negotiations on investment protection, merchandise trade, and service trade. The ECFA contained an "early harvest list" on a number of trade items whose import duties were to be immediately lowered, which was "heavily skewed in Taiwan's favor" (Fuller 2014: 97).

In short, "conceding benefits" represented a more advanced application of economic united front work. Previously only Taiwanese entrepreneurs were targeted; now Beijing began to set its sights on Taiwan-based economic actors, particularly those who tended to support the DPP. There was evidence that Beijing was able to reap political advantages from Taiwan's growing economic dependence (Yuen 2014). After the turn of the century, Taishang gradually made known their pro-KMT inclinations, yet this partisan choice was carefully couched in terms of pure economic considerations. Nevertheless, such caution gave place to more forthright expressions. Shortly before the 2012 presidential election, many Taiwanese business leaders openly expressed their support for the "1992 consensus," which was eagerly championed by the KMT and rejected by the DPP. The eleventh-hour endorsement campaign by business magnates was remarkable not only for its scope, including nearly all leading firms in petrochemicals, microelectronics, transportation, and other industries, but also for marking the first time members of the business community expressly indicated their pro-unification preferences. One could legitimately surmise that Beijing was behind this campaign to interfere in Taiwan's election. Indeed, it turned out to be a successful tactic to mobilize "economic voters" (Y. Tang 2013), contributing to Ma Ying-jeou's triumph in his reelection bid.

Beijing's economic united front work toward Hong Kong did involve concession of benefits, but it paled in comparison with that toward Taiwan. In the wake of the 2003 outbreak of severe acute respiratory syndrome (SARS), Beijing put forward an individual visit scheme to allow mainland tourists to visit Hong Kong to revitalize the ailing economy. In that year, mainland tourists began to surpass international tourists, and their share climbed rapidly. By 2014, more than three-quarters (77.7 percent) of cross-border visitors to Hong Kong came from China.[8] The summer of 2003 also saw an increase in the speed of CEPA's implementation, which was framed as "mainland economic gifts" to Hongkongers who had manifested visible discontent with the SAR leadership.

Aside from these initiatives in 2003, Beijing did not adopt more preferential policies toward Hongkongers. Clearly the differential treatment had to do with the fact that Taiwan represented a more difficult target for Beijing for the following reasons. First, Beijing was able to maintain a strong presence in Hong Kong, but never in Taiwan. The CCP established its official representative in Hong Kong as early as 1938, evolving into the Xinhua News Agency, the precursor to the Liaison Office after the handover. Over the years, the CCP established a number of "parallel organizations" among professions, students, and labor to the extent that one could characterize Hong Kong's civil society as internally divided (Ma 2007: 186–189). That the pro-Beijing camp steadily enhanced its share of votes after handover also demonstrated Beijing's growing influence. By contrast, with a ban on the official presence of representatives of the PRC or CCP, there could not be an active Hong Kong–style Liaison Office in Taiwan. Evidently, Beijing attempted to establish some front organizations, but so far they remained largely obscure and marginal. For example, more than eighty new political parties were registered with explicitly pro-unification goals from 2008 to 2014; yet only a few of them actually fielded election candidates.[9]

Second, while posthandover Hong Kong willingly accepted economic incorporation into China, Taiwan's cross-strait policies oscillated several times. Hong Kong's first chief executive, Tung Chee-hwa, proposed the developmental strategy of "leaning on the fatherland and facing the world" (*beikao zuguo, mianxiang shijie*). Yet, when an economic crisis actually happened, Tung chose to prioritize the link to the "fatherland" rather than the "world." Under the tenure of Donald Tsang (2005–2012), further integration with China appeared to be the only way out of economic sluggishness, as there emerged a popularized perception that Hong Kong needed to eagerly embrace the "China opportunity." As such, ill-planned massive infrastructure projects to deepen the link to the mainland were hastily promoted, such as the Pearl River Bridge (2009) and the Guangzhou–Shenzhen–Hong Kong Express Rail (2010). Clearly Hong Kong had to pay the cost of establishing closer integration with the mainland. The rail, for instance, was the world's most expensive project in terms of construction cost per mile. As pointed out, this "mainland-oriented strategy" paid insufficient attention to the local conditions and put Hong Kong at the mercy of Guangdong Province and other agencies in the central government (Goodstadt 2014: 41–44).

By contrast, Taiwan experienced several rounds of policy reversals regarding cross-strait economic relations. Following the missile crisis of 1996, Lee Teng-hui unfurled a policy of "no haste, be patient" (*jieji yongren*), imposing constraints on certain investments in the name of national security. After winning the presidential election, Chen Shui-bian promoted the policy of "active opening and effective management" (*jiji kaifang youxiao guanli*) by removing a number of existing constraints in 2001. In 2006, in view of China's Anti-Secession Law and its policy of conceding benefits, Chen swerved to a more restrictive stance by announcing the policy of "active management and effective opening" (*jiji guanli youxiao kaifang*). With Ma Ying-jeou's presidency from 2008, Taiwan's cross-strait policy was again liberalized until the eruption of the Sunflower Movement in 2014. As has been pointed out, Taiwan's government alternated policy responses in view of cross-strait tensions, relaxing when Beijing appeared more conciliatory and restricting when the latter became hostile (S. Lin 2016: 44). Such strategic concerns were patently absent among Hong Kong's decision makers.

Hongkongers' Grievances

Observers agreed that the mass demonstration on July 1, 2003, which attracted half a million participants to oppose the legislation of a national security bill, served as a watershed (J. Cheng 2005). The eruption of this large-scale protest came from the accumulated discontent over a number of instances of government mismanagement since the 1997 handover, such as poor governance of the avian flu and SARS outbreaks, as well as plummeting property prices shortly after the Asian financial crisis also in 1997. While the protest eventually succeeded in forcing Tung's administration to withdraw the controversial security bill, it also invited more interventions from Beijing, which turned out to generate more grievances.

In April 2004, Beijing ruled out the possibility of holding direct elections for chief executive in 2007 and the legislative council in 2008. This move was seen as a hardline measure to ward off the rising pro-democracy movement as well as contagion from Taiwan, which had seen the DPP's successful re-election in the previous month (Lo 2008b: 13). Press freedom was another area where Beijing ratcheted up its control. Before Taiwan was democratized, colonial Hong Kong was the only Chinese society that enjoyed substantial press freedom. However, this legacy clearly eroded after the resumption of Chinese rule. Beijing officials frowned on reports on what they perceived as sensitive or disruptive issues, such as Taiwan's independence or the chief executive's low support rate, so a substantial number of journalistic professionals reportedly exercised self-censorship to avoid trouble. Beijing co-opted media owners with official titles to ensure friendly news coverage, and at the same time, more and more media were transferred to pro-Beijing or mainland owners (Chan and Lee 2012: 223–246). Outspoken radio hosts and columnists were silenced. As such, Reporters without Borders registered the rapid deterioration of Hong Kong's press freedom, from the 18th position out of 139 countries in 2002 to the 61st out of 180 in 2014.[10]

Beijing also launched a reengineering of its identity to deal with what was perceived as the problem of "lack of attachment to the fatherland" (*renxin wei huigui*). Mandarin-language teaching in primary school and lessons on Chinese history and culture in secondary school were introduced with a view to enhancing students' identification with China (T. Lau 2013: 746–749). The government's efforts to promote patriotic education culminated in an attempt to upgrade national and moral education to required courses in high school in 2012, a move that encountered a large-scale protest (see below).

Allowing mainland tourists to visit Hong Kong individually was one of the first steps toward economic integration, as well as a politically expedient move to buttress Tung's challenged administration. Mainland visitors grew spectacularly from 8.4 million in 2003 to 47.2 million in 2014, creating more and more visible negative externalities. Rising rents drove out mom-and-pop stores from the street corners, and they were replaced by shops that catered exclusively to mainland shoppers. Hong Kong's law granted the right of abode to the newborn babies of PRC citizens. With the individual visit scheme, pregnant mainland women literally walked into Hong Kong hospitals and delivered their babies there. True, the swarming of mainland tourists provided a timely economic stimulus; nevertheless, it came with intrusive inconveniences, as Hongkongers found it more difficult to make their way onto rush-hour metro trains, purchase daily necessities such as formula milk powder, be assigned a hospital bed, and obtain district school acceptances for the kids. A poll indicated the increasing dissatisfaction: Fewer Hongkongers agreed that mainland tourists "stimulated local consumption"; at the same time, a majority of respondents held that mainland tourists "worsened criminal problems" (63.8 percent), "increased rent" (71.4 percent), and "raised commodity prices" (69.5 percent) (Zheng and Wan 2013: 33–35).

In spite of the mounting discontent, there was evidence that Beijing gravitated toward a more unapologetically hard-line approach in dealing with Hong Kong affairs. In 2008, a Liaison Office staff member circulated the recommendation of "a second governing team" (*dier guanzhi tuandui*), which would be composed of mainland cadres in order to make up for a "deficiency" of SAR government. Such a suggestion amounted to a revisionist attempt to make room for Beijing's direct intervention. In the same year, Qiang Shigong, a Beijing-appointed legal scholar, published a tract that contended Beijing was obliged to assimilate Hongkongers into patriots as the first step toward the revitalization of Chinese civilization. Such hawkish discourse, diagnosed by Chan Koonchung as a doctrine of China's Celestial Dynasty (*zhongguo tianchao zhuyi*), or a new form of Chinese imperialism, was a peculiar mixture of Maoism, chauvinism, and Carl Schmitt's legal theory by envisioning the complete mainlandization of Hong Kong as necessary and inevitable (K. Chan 2012: 87–128). As such a hard-line outlook had emerged as the dominant thinking in the Liaison Office, the cavalier neglect of Hongkongers' opinions was bound to incur more vigorous resistance.

Resisting Mainlandization

Post-2003 Hong Kong witnessed reinvigorated resistance to the mainlandization. Many commentators have characterized the surge in protests as "civil society against the state" (Ku 2009: 43–45), "civil society in self-defense" (Ma 2007: 199–219), or "China's offshore civil society" (Hung and Ip 2012); all these portrayals emphasized that Hong Kong remained a contentious society in defiance of Beijing's coercive measures.

The resistance took place on many fronts and in many ways. Commemorating the June Fourth Tiananmen Massacre with a mass candlelight vigil each year has evolved into an inseparable part of Hong Kong's pro-democracy movement, as an overlapping personal network has developed between the Hong Kong Alliance in Support of Patriotic Democratic Movements in China (SPDM; founded in 1989) and the DP-led opposition camp. While PRC citizens were prohibited from mentioning this political taboo, and Taiwanese practically found it no longer relevant, Hong Kong remained the only city that continued to stage such political events to mark the incident. In a sense, the Tiananmen Massacre has grown to be an integral part of Hongkongers' collective memory (Chan and Lee 2010). One might argue that Hongkongers' obsession with the Tiananmen Massacre revealed a particular anxiety about their status within the Chinese nationhood because they appeared to be as vulnerable as those student protesters had been in 1989. For many younger Hongkongers, attending the June Fourth commemorative event was their first lesson in political enlightenment, thereby helping the pro-democracy movement to recruit a new generation of supporters.

In June 2004, shortly after Beijing postponed the direct election for chief executive, a group of professionals signed a declaration on Hong Kong's core values, which included liberty, democracy, human rights, rule of law, fairness, social justice, peace and compassion, integrity and transparency, plurality, respect for individuals, and professionalism.[11] It remained an open question whether pre-1997 Hong Kong had ever lived up to these ideals; nevertheless, the articulation of these goals represented a clear rejection of assimilation into mainland political culture. According to Margaret Ng, a signee of the declaration and a co-founder of the Civic Party (founded in 2006), "safeguarding the way of life of Hong Kong inhabitants" required democracy to shield them from the pernicious influences from Beijing (Margaret Ng 2008: 73).

At the same time when these professionals championed Western liberalism, there emerged preservation campaigns in opposition to government-initiated construction projects, including the redevelopment of Lee Tung Street (2005) (K. Ng 2013), the demolition of Star Ferry Terminal (2006) and Queen's Pier (2007) (Chen and Szeto 2015; Ku 2012), and the construction of the Express Rail (2008–2010) (H. Li 2013). These preservation movements began to attract a growing number of youthful participants who were willing to adopt more militant tactics, such as site occupation. Observers characterized this wave of antidevelopment protests as "postmodernism" (So 2008). Changing social values certainly underpinned these protests; nevertheless, these activists also identified themselves as taking part in "local action" (*bentu xingdong*), in that they were self-consciously defending the common experiences and collective memories of Hongkongers. Lee Tung Street used to be called the "wedding card street," famous for the concentration of print shops. While Star Ferry Terminal was the historical site that gave birth to the 1966 riot, Queen's Pier was the designated area of disembarkment for British governors and royalty. The Anti–Express Rail protest was primarily motivated by the attempt to protect Choi Yuen village, a New Territories settlement built by postwar migrants. This stream of participants in local action, or "local actionists" to distinguish them from the subsequent "localists," emphasized the everyday experiences of grassroots Hongkongers, but they did not problematize the Hong Kong–Beijing issues by concentrating their criticism on the collusion of local officials and business (M. Szeto 2011).

Starting in 2011, antimainlandization protests took an ethnic turn, as campaigns emerged to oppose mainland women giving birth in Hong Kong, as well as mainland parents sending their children to local schools. The antimainlander protest evolved into a campaign against the cross-border parallel traders whose activities had caused inconveniences. Mainland tourists and migrants were likened to "locusts" that would eventually exhaust local resources. These protesters identified themselves as "localists" (*bentupai*), who maintained that natives' interests should be prioritized and a proper separation of Hong Kong and China should be maintained. The appearance of these militant protesters effectively changed the meaning of localism, as the term no longer meant a defense of grassroots experiences against government-initiated projects, but a revolt of Hongkongers against Chinese. While previous local activists refrained from naming the China factor, newer localists blamed practically everything on China. Originally these new localist sentiments were circulated on the Internet; then a political organization, Civic Passion, was established in February 2012. Civic Passion remained the most salient anti-China force in Hong Kong before the Umbrella Movement, which gave rise to other more radical, organizations.

The Indigenization of Resistance

Commemorating June Fourth affirmed Hongkongers' Chinese identity and at the same time expressed their opposition to the communist dictatorship. Since Beijing frowned on such activities, the annual candlelight vigil became a symbolically defiant act. The SPDM and the DP leadership embraced the assumption that Hong Kong's democratization would not be possible without the same political transition in the mainland (P. Wong 2000: 73). As a result, the June Fourth commemorative events reinforced Hongkongers' patriotic identification with a Chinese nation.

With the 2004 Declaration of Core Values, the focus was shifted from China to Hong Kong, which was portrayed as an exemplary case of Western liberalism. In particular, the declaration began with the opening sentence "Hongkongers expressing their strong sense of a community of shared destiny" (*xianggangren biaoda le qianglie de mingyun gongtong ti yishi*), which echoed Lee Teng-hui's effort in forging an inclusive Taiwanese identity a decade earlier (see Chapter 1), indicating the sprouting of an indigenous consciousness by framing Hong Kong's problems in its own terms (H. Hung 2011: 115).[12] Implicit in this declaration was the assumption that Hong Kong's future would proceed in a way that was distinct from China's because of its own historical legacy. This amounted to an unstated refutation of the patriotic preoccupation that Hongkongers were morally obliged to pursue democratization in China.

After 2006, the rise of heritage preservation movements ushered in a bottom-up perspective with the emphasis on common Hongkongers' experiences. Led by local actionists, these campaigns envisioned a grassroots-based challenge to the SAR government. A protest rife with symbolism best illustrated such an outlook: On January 21, 2007, activists staged the landing of a ship, *The Local* (*bentuhao*). It was carrying new immigrants, residents from demolished neighborhoods, and foreign workers and arrived at Queen's Pier, which was slated for demolition for land reclamation. This ritualized protest reversed the meanings of the colonial heritage, with the privileges of

British dignitaries usurped by the less privileged Hongkongers (Ku 2012: 17). While these preservation activists aimed to empower those who would be victimized by the projects promoting closer Hong Kong–China ties, they refrained from criticizing Beijing. In the same fashion, participants in the Anti–Express Rail campaign made an effort to emphasize that they supported tighter integration with the mainland by carefully framing their protest as an opposition to the technical issue of site selection (interview #HK7). In leading the Anti–National Education protest, Joshua Wong declared his personal identification as Chinese in public (cited in Torne 2014).

While preservation activists articulated a multicultural and progressive vision for Hong Kong, subsequent protests erupted along the fault line of increasing tension between Hongkongers and Chinese migrants, tourists, and parallel traders. The newer version of localism came with a plethora of political demands, such as return to British colonialism, Hong Kong self-determination, or political independence, which all shared at their roots a profound distrust of Beijing. The localist tendency evolved from an attempt to preserve an endangered "community" to a nationalistic project to resist coercive mainlandization. Bitter recriminations emerged between local actionists and localists. Preservation activists were criticized for blind devotion to the universal values of human rights such that they ignored Beijing's declared intention to assimilate Hong Kong. A very colorful pejorative, "leftards," *zoogau* in Cantonese, meaning "retarded leftists," which carried sexual connotations, came into use and later expanded to include the SPDM and opposition party activists (C. Cheng 2013). On the other hand, the localist tendency was criticized as an inchoate rightwing antiforeign sentiment, which demonized mainlanders as invaders or agents of Beijing (Y. Chen 2014). In a number of subsequent issues, such as National Education (2011–2012), the Northeast New Territories Development Plan (2012–2014), and the denial of Hong Kong Television's operation license (2013),[13] this intramural rivalry became increasingly intense.

In short, within a decade after the 2003 July First demonstration, the resistance against mainlandization had been progressively radicalized. Patriotism and Chinese nationalism were eclipsed by an increasingly unambiguous Hong Kong identity. The successive frames of core values, collective memory, and finally natives' interests reflected the intensification of conflicts between Hongkongers and mainlanders. At least, right before the outbreak of the Umbrella Movement in September 2014, a Hongkonger proto-nationalism was in the process of fermentation (R. Wu 2016).

Taiwanese Discontent

Although Beijing's policy of conceding economic benefits increased cross-strait trade, Taiwan-based producers gained little from these emerging market venues because access to the Chinese market was monopolized by Taiwanese brokers, who enjoyed political connections on both sides of the strait. The consequence was that these intermediaries were able to secure the biggest portion of profit for themselves without benefiting the targeted farmers. Chinese officials knew that their patronage policy was abused, but they could not simply circumvent these political brokers to access local farmers directly (Jiao 2015: 165–181). Beijing's preferential treatment of Taiwanese firms was neutralized by local governments' protectionism such that profitability was increasingly squeezed (Yu, Yu, and Lin 2016). In other words, politics on both sides of Taiwan Strait constrained the actual results of Beijing's unilateral concession of economic benefits.

Taiwanese perceptions of cross-strait economics were also affected by the behavior of returnee businesses from China. The Taiwanese government has offered incentives in homebound investment for China-based enterprises. Returnee capital was welcomed because it was expected to bring new jobs and fill idle industrial zones. However, what these returnees have actually done in Taiwan is raise popular suspicion over these China-related businesses.

The Ting Hsin International Group, the number one producer of instant noodles and soft drinks in China, originated from a small firm in Taiwan. With its overseas business success, Ting Hsin came back to purchase Taiwanese food companies and expand to retailing and the telecommunication industries. Starting in 2013, a series of scandals among Ting Hsin's subsidiaries broke out, as they were found to have sold adulterated food to consumers, which gave rise to a boycott campaign amid public outcry. While Ting Hsin was perceived to have brought back its shoddy business practices from China, Want Want, another returnee food producer in China, had practically emerged as Beijing's mouthpiece in Taiwan. Want Want, originally a medium-sized food manufacturer from Taiwan that grew into a huge corporation due to its success in China, made its homecoming in 2008. Want Want immediately built its media empire by purchasing the *China Times* and two TV stations (one broadcast station and one cable), and its chairperson Tsai Eng-Meng made public his pro-unification preferences and did not refrain from using his media outlets to attack his opponents. There was suspicion that Tsai's venture into the media was not motivated by profit, but rather was at the behest of Beijing, whose support was vital to his business interests in China. Want Want's attempt to purchase a cable system company in 2011 gave rise to an Anti–Media Monopoly Movement, which was initiated by intellectuals and then evolved into a wider student movement in 2012 (Rawnsley and Feng 2014).

Ma Ying-jeou cited Want Want as a successful case of attracting returnee investment during a debate over the ECFA with Tsai Ing-wen.[14] During Ma's reelection campaign in 2012, Ting Hsin played a leading role in rallying business supporters.¹⁵ Consequently, the controversies of these two leading returnee business groups raised public concerns over the negative impacts of closer economic ties.

Resisting Hongkongization

Taiwan's acts of resistance reappeared with the advent of Ma Ying-jeou's government in 2008 as it made bold gestures to forge closer cross-strait ties. In November, student activism, which had lay dormant for many years, made a comeback to protest excessive policing during the visit of Chen Yunlin, the chair of China's Association for Relations across the Taiwan Straits, which marked the first visit by an official envoy to Taiwan. Just six months after Ma had stepped into office, Chen's visit signified a milestone for his rapprochement with Beijing. The Wild Strawberry Movement emerged as a sit-in protest that lasted for two months and ended without achieving its goals of obtaining a government apology over the brutal policing and revisions of the regulations on demonstrations. Nevertheless, the protest fostered a new generation of student activists, who played an instrumental role in subsequent activism leading up to the Sunflower Movement (see Chapter 3).

The Rebiya Kadeer incident of 2009 showcased how Beijing's growing influence began to draw the attention of Taiwan's civil-society organizations. Kadeer was an exiled Uighur activist, whose award-winning biographical documentary was to be screened at the Kaohsiung Film Festival. Beijing officials warned against the screening of the film, and later Chinese tourists were diverted away from the southern metropolis. Pressured by the local hotel business and KMT politicians, the DPP-controlled Kaohsiung city government hesitated for a moment, but later decided to stick to the original festival schedule due to protests by human rights organizations.

Commemorating the June Fourth Tiananmen Massacre had virtually disappeared in Taiwan. On the twentieth anniversary in 2009, a small-scale commemorative event was held in Taipei. In 2010, a group of college students from Hong Kong and Macao, in collaboration with exiled Chinese dissidents, organized a candlelight vigil on the NTU campus, marking the beginning of the involvement of a new generation. From 2011, it evolved into an annual mass rally staged by students and human rights activists.¹⁶ The reappearance of the June Fourth commemorative events in Taiwan was particularly noteworthy for the absence of Chinese patriotism, which continued to play a salient role in Hong Kong. The timing of its resuscitation also revealed an important clue. Just as cross-strait relations were making rapid strides, the effort to bring back Tiananmen's memory was no less than a warning that Taiwan's democracy could easily be sacrificed.

Previously, Taiwan's social movement organizations tended to be inward-looking, with occasional attention paid to transborder issues. The swift progress of the Ma Ying-jeou government's cross-strait policy brought about visible changes. Following the passage of ECFA in 2010, several labor, environmental, and human rights NGOs coalesced into the Alliance for Supervision over Cross-Strait Agreements (Hsu 2017: 140). The alliance marked the first time cross-strait affairs emerged on the agenda of Taiwan's NGOs, and later it evolved into the first organization to oppose the CSSTA, paving the way for the Sunflower Movement.

The emergence of the Anti–Media Monopoly Movement in 2011–2013 can be seen as civil-society defense of the freedom of expression. It started as a signature campaign by scholars, including Huang Kuo-chang, who later played a pivotal role in the Sunflower Movement. The turning point was when Chen Wei-ting, a student movement leader, shared a Facebook post that asserted that the openly pro-Beijing Want Want group had fabricated a news story to attack Huang Kuo-chang in July 2012. Want Want filed a libel lawsuit against Chen, which immediately sent a shock wave through the student population. Since the use of social media was immensely popular, many young users felt directly intimidated by the vindictive move of the pro-China conglomerate. On September 1, an Anti–Media Monopoly demonstration took place, attracting thousands of participants. In the end, the widespread student participation helped to stymie Want Want's ambition to build a larger media empire (Wong and Wright 2018).

Naming the "China Factor"

Protest activism in Taiwan underwent a process of indigenization similar to that in Hong Kong, as Taiwanese identity increasingly became the prominent feature in these protest campaigns.

During the troubled second tenure of Chen Shui-bian (2004–2008), a series of financial irregularities emerged, severely damaging the DPP's credibility. To shore up his challenged legitimacy, Chen opted for a strategy of firing up the base by adopting rhetoric and gestures of Taiwanese nationalism, which failed to reverse erosion of DPP support. With the KMT's victory in 2008, the demand for Taiwanese independence also suffered a setback, discredited as amounting to desperate and adventurist tactics. DPP lawmakers appeared to be rudderless amid their electoral debacle, winning only 27 out of 113 seats in the legislature. They were practically at a loss as to how to respond to the KMT's initiatives in liberalizing regulations regarding Chinese tourists, students, and investment because they were pressured by a clearly felt popular expectation for Ma's new cross-strait initiatives (interview #TW31-2).

It was in this context that the initial protesters took deliberate efforts to keep a distance from cross-strait politics. During the Wild Strawberry Movement of 2008, students avoided mentioning China even though police violence occurred during the visit by a Chinese envoy. Instead, student protesters framed the brutal policing as an issue of human rights violations, and demanded reform of the Assembly and Demonstration Law. Even independence-leaning students tacitly felt the constraint not to mention these "divisive issues" for the sake of movement solidarity (Y. Wei 2016: 64). As Chen Wei-ting, then a high school student participant, noted:

> The Wild Strawberry Movement did not touch the core issue by not confronting the China factor. At that time, the DPP had just stepped out of power, and Taiwan independence had become a dirty word always associated with Chen Shui-bian. That is the reason why the Wild Strawberry Movement's three main demands did not mention China.[17]

With greater perception of Beijing's presence in Taiwan, such strategic reticence gave way to a more forthright attitude. In 2012, when students mobilized to oppose the media monopoly, it became the first time that they put an emphasis on the "China factor," since the Want Want group did not disguise its pro-Beijing stance. At that time protest students were sufficiently emboldened to accuse China of interventions and call them out for the pernicious impacts on Taiwan's press freedom (Kaeding 2015: 210). In fact, the Anti–Media Monopoly Movement later listed "say no to the China factor" (*xiang zhongguo yinsu shuobu*) as one of the principal demands (J. Wang 2015: 222).

Student activists were not the only group who became more outspoken in naming the "China factor." In April 2013, a Declaration of Free Persons (*ziyouren xuanyan*) was issued by a group of liberal academics, which proposed to (1) develop cross-strait friendship on the basis of constitutionalism, (2) build mutual trust via human rights protection, and (3) sign a cross-strait human rights charter. Idealistic as it might seem, the declaration supported the universal values of democracy and human rights that had allegedly been slighted by Ma's rapprochement policy.[18] In fact, by agreeing to prioritize economic exchanges and deal with political issues at a later stage (*xianjing houzheng*), the KMT government had acquiesced to Beijing's professed economic united front strategy by surrendering Taiwan's political advantages in democracy, although the KMT might defend its position as a pragmatic approach to deescalate the cross-strait tension without conceding to the unification demand on the PRC's terms.

The rising attention paid to cross-strait politics by student activists and NGOs carved out a new space. Prior to that, the debate was more likely to be viewed through partisan lenses. The KMT traditionally maintained that Taiwan's economic vitality hinged on deepening cross-strait economic exchanges and investments so that a certain form of political rapprochement was necessary, whereas DPP politicians were more skeptical of closer ties with China, fearing negative impacts on national security. Now with growing civil-society interventions and the more upfront identification of the "China factor," the trajectory of these protests clearly evolved out of the old unification-versus-independence politics. The declining partisan connotation of resisting the influences from China was also made possible, with the DPP's subsequent turn to embrace a more centrist approach in cross-strait policy (see Chapter 4).

Identity Shifts

Under the shadow of an increasingly powerful China, both Taiwan and Hong Kong witnessed parallel resistances against political and cultural assimilation from approximately 2000, even though economic integration had become an accomplished fact. An unambiguous indigenous identity gradually surfaced and became the main thrust behind these protest campaigns. Longitudinal surveys also registered a clear ascendancy of indigenous identity over the Chinese identity. Figures 2.1 and 2.2 show the change in identities in Taiwan and Hong Kong.

By 2014 the exclusive indigenous identities had surpassed the exclusive Chinese identity, and in both places, the differentials between the identities were progressively widening. Taiwanese identity began to overtake Chinese identity from 1995, and by 2014 the former had evolved into a solid majority (60.6 percent), while the latter had shrunk to a mere 3.5 percent. Hongkongers' indigenization took a detour and evolved much later. The initial few years after the handover saw a continuing lead of Hongkonger identity over Chinese identity, followed by an interim reversal from 2002 to 2008, and finally the indigenous identity began to gain the upper hand again. Moreover, the mixed identity remained a popular choice in the two societies. It was the most favored choice for Taiwanese until it was surpassed by Taiwanese identity in 2008, whereas in Hong Kong it stayed neck and neck with the indigenous identity after 2011.

Starting from the early 1990s, the growth of indigenous identity appeared to be an uninterrupted process. However, a closer look at Figure 2.1 reveals that the two periods of KMT government (1994–1999) and (2008–2014) witnessed accelerated indigenization, with Taiwanese identity growing by 19.4 percent and 12.2 percent, respectively. Under the DPP's first government (2000–2007), it was merely a 6.8 percent expansion. In particular, Ma Ying-jeou's initiatives to portray Taiwan as a part of Chinese culture and history, a deliberate effort to reverse what he perceived as "de-sinicization" under his predecessor, achieved little "to change the long-term trend of public opinion moving away from identification with China" (Hughes 2014: 131). Contrary to the prediction that the ruling party's ideological inclinations would have an impact on popular attitudes, indigenization of Taiwan's identity was em-

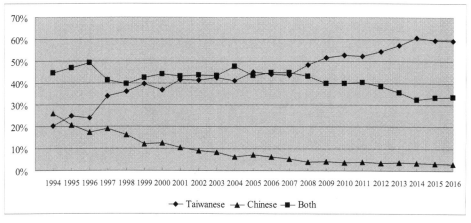

Figure 2.1. Changing identities in Taiwan, 1994–2016. (Election Study Center, National Chengchi University, https://goo.gl/cCVRax, accessed February 17, 2017.)

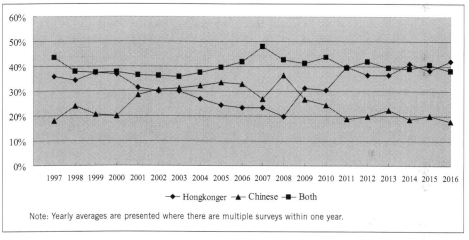

Note: Yearly averages are presented where there are multiple surveys within one year.

Figure 2.2. Changing identities in Hong Kong, 1997–2016. (Public Opinion Programme, University of Hong Kong [HKUPOP], https://goo.gl/DRpOjZ, accessed February 17, 2017.)

phatically not the intended result of politicians, but was rather a spontaneous evolution made possible by a freer political environment that encouraged self-exploration by individual citizens.

For Hong Kong, the year 2008 turned out to be a critical watershed. Hongkongers eagerly contributed to disaster relief following the Sichuan Earthquake in May and cheered for the Chinese team in the Beijing Olympics in August of that year, thus marking the zenith of exclusive Chinese identity (36.5 percent). Immediately afterward, the scandal over poisonous milk powder made in China and growing friction with mainlanders dampened fatherland attachment (S. Chiu 2016). Similar to Taiwan, Hongkongers' identity transition did not follow the incumbent's preferences, but came more as a response to changing relations with China (Kaeding 2011).

There is evidence showing that younger generations in both places were more likely to embrace an indigenous identity. From 2008, polls in Taiwan show that people in their twenties consistently surpassed those in their thirties and forties in preferring Taiwanese identity.[19] Taiwanese born after 1982 tended to identify themselves as Taiwanese and preferred independence more than their predecessor generations (Rigger 2016: 84–88). Since the University of Hong Kong's Public Opinion Programme (HKUPOP) began surveys with identity questions in 1997, a remarkably consistent affinity between younger people and the indigenous identity has emerged. Among the Hong Kong identifiers, people under thirty always exceeded those over thirty, while the reverse was true for Chinese identifiers.[20] Another study also showed that young Hongkongers were more ready to choose the indigenous identity and the trend was particularly noticeable after 2011 (Wan and Zheng 2016: 134). The conscious rejection of belonging to a Chinese nationhood among young Taiwanese and Hongkongers encouraged their intense participation in the occupy movements. Arif Dirlik (2016: 674) noted that the choice of a Taiwanese and Hongkonger identity was not only a rejection of "political homogenization" but also a challenge against the "de-historicized and de-socialized notions of 'Chinese.'"

Therefore, a reciprocal relationship exists between the rising resistance against mainlandization/Hongkongization and the identity shift. Taiwanese and Hongkongers were willing to take part in these protests because they began to cherish their distinctive ways of life, and these protest campaigns also helped to consolidate a growing indigenous identity.

The Dynamics of Social Protests

In the years before the outbreak of the Sunflower Movement and the Umbrella Movement, both Taiwan and Hong Kong witnessed rising trends in social protests, which became more frequent, more intense, and larger. The following is an analysis of protest events in Taiwan and Hong Kong from 2006 to 2013, as collected in journalistic reports. Here I choose the electronic databases of Taiwan's *United Daily News* and Hong Kong's *Mingpao* for my sources, and the selection and coding procedures are explained in Appendix 2. A protest is operationally defined as a public and confrontational act mounted by an intentional group of people whose claim involves a conflict of interest with their opponents. With this criterion, I find 4,644 and 698 protest incidents in Taiwan and Hong Kong, respectively, over these eight years. Figure 2.3 presents the development of protests in the two societies.

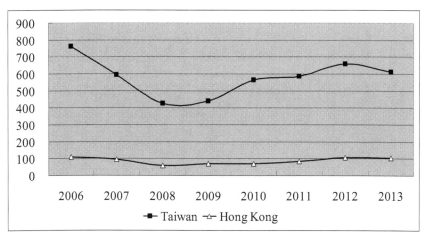

Figure 2.3. Protest events in Taiwan and Hong Kong, 2006–2013.

After the peak of protest activities in 2006, both societies witnessed a subsequent decline, with 2008 as the nadir. In Taiwan, 2006 was a highly anomalous year because the outbreak of the financial scandal involving Chen Shui-bian triggered a wave of anti-Chen protests culminating in the Red-Shirt Army Movement as well as pro-Chen mobilizations. Political protests, defined as those events launched by political organizations, political parties, and politicians, soared up to 190 events that year (or 24.9 percent of the total), whereas the following seven years had an annual average of 72. After the low point in 2008, a trend of gradual warming-up was visible in Taiwan and Hong Kong. The Sunflower Movement and the Umbrella Movement took place at the historical juncture when both of these civil societies became more contentious, a fact that encouraged mass participation in these two eventful protests.

Duration and Size

As the research method of protest event analysis inevitably conflates larger and smaller incidents, another way to examine the dynamic is to focus on the more significant ones of unusual duration and size. Figure 2.4 shows the distribution of protests that lasted longer and involved more participants.

Protest events that lasted more than one day were those involving sustained participation in the form of continuous sit-ins, occupation, or strike, which aimed to demonstrate the protesters' determination. Both in Taiwan and Hong Kong, such enduring protests reached a crescendo immediately before 2014. The amount of participation is another clue to measure the importance of protest events. In both places, larger incidents of collective action shot up in the years 2012 to 2013, after their previous climax in 2006 to 2007.

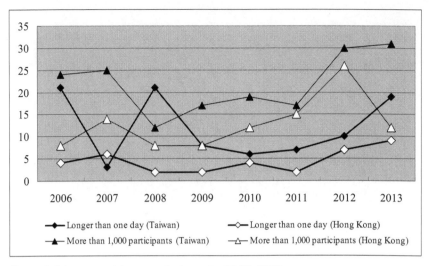

Figure 2.4. Longer and larger protest events, 2006–2013.

Clearly protesters in Taiwan and Hong Kong were becoming more used to a more confrontational style of protests.

Moreover, participation in annual protest events offers another perspective to gauge the extent of civil-society mobilization. In Hong Kong, the annual June Fourth candlelight vigil organized by the SPDM that had been held since 1990 and the July First demonstrations organized by the Civil Human Rights Front (CHRF) held from 2003 evolved into a signature political tradition as well as a yearly barometer of citizens' political discontent. Taiwan did not develop such a sustained tradition of annual demonstrations. Presidential inauguration day (May 20), which used to be an occasion for political protests in the late 1980s and the early 1990s, vanished as the DPP solidified its position in Taiwan's political landscape by giving up street activism. Throughout the 1990s, the antinuclear movement launched an annual demonstration, and the labor movement had its May Day rally, but they came to an abrupt end with the DPP's coming to power in 2000, symptomatic of the decline of street protests in this period. Although environmentalists and organized labor represented only specific sectors of Taiwan's civil society, their annual protest events remained an approximate estimate of protest mobilization. (See Table 2.1.)

In Hong Kong's two annual political demonstrations, there existed a considerable gap between the figures provided by police and organizers, as the former tended to underestimate the participation and the later exaggerated it apparently for different political purposes. Nevertheless, both estimations were consistent in that the June Fourth candlelight vigil saw a revival on the twentieth anniversary of the Tiananmen Massacre in 2009, and the

TABLE 2.1. LARGE-SCALE ANNUAL PROTESTS, 2006–2013 (IN THOUSANDS)

Year	2006	2007	2008	2009	2010	2011	2012	2013
Hong Kong's June Fourth candlelight vigil								
SPDM estimate	44	55	48	150	150	150	180	150
Police estimate	19	27	16	63	113	77	85	54
Hong Kong's July First demonstration								
CHRF estimate	58	68	47	76	52	218	400	430
Police estimate	28	20	16	28	20	54	63	66
Taiwan's May Day demonstration								
Media estimate	—	4	—	10	7	6	3	30
Taiwan's antinuclear demonstration								
GCAA estimate	—	—	—	—	—	10	5	100

Notes: (1) Beginning in 2013, there emerged a parallel June Fourth commemoration event organized by those who were dissatisfied with the Hong Kong Alliance in Support of Patriotic Democratic Movements of China's (SPDM) emphasis on Chinese patriotism. This table includes only the candlelight vigils held by the SPDM. (2) With the exception of 2009 and 2010, Taiwan's labor movement organizations and labor unions tended to hold separate May Day demonstrations. This table records only the largest event. (3) With respect to Taiwan's antinuclear demonstrations, this table shows only the events held by the Green Citizen Action Alliance, which were larger in scale. The figures presented here represent the organizers' estimate of the rally in Taipei only; they do not include rallies held in other cities. (4) All figures except for that of Taiwan's antinuclear demonstration in 2011 are based on the reports in *Mingpao* and *United Daily News* (Public Television News, https://goo.gl/XzaZM, accessed December 28, 2016).

July First demonstration gained new impetus in 2011. As such, the *Lonely Planet* recommended Hong Kong in its 2012 list of top-ten cities to visit because of the dynamism of protest actions (Chi-hua Lin 2013: 175).

During the first DPP government (2000–2008), the Taiwan Confederation of Trade Unions (TCTU) launched May Day demonstrations only twice in 2001 and 2005 (Y. Chiu 2011: 89). With the KMT's comeback to power in 2008, the TCTU began to play a more assertive role by mobilizing union members each year with the exception of 2012, indicating a resuscitation of participation among Taiwan's labor unions from then. The annual demonstrations began to attract new blood beyond the traditional constituents of blue-collar workers, as service workers in social work and nursing, and students joined the event. Taiwan's antinuclear movement experienced a drastic revival due to the Fukushima Accident of 2011, ending a decade of quietude and inaction. A mass demonstration was held less than two weeks after the nuclear disaster in Japan and continued to attract more participants in the following years (M. Ho 2014b; S. Wei 2016).

Intensity

If people take to the streets more frequently, and their actions last longer and attract more participation, it is a reasonable expectation that their protests are more likely to involve disruptive action and clashes with the police. Figure 2.5 shows protests that gave rise to (1) brawls or physical conflicts and (2) conflicts with the police.

Both societies witnessed a growing trend toward more aggressive protest behaviors; yet the surge in Taiwan was particularly noticeable as protests involving brawls or physical conflicts (106, with the exception of the atypical year 2006) and conflicts with the police (64) reached a new climax in 2013.

Immediately before the Sunflower Movement, discussions about civil disobedience (*gongmin bufucong*) became more prevalent among protesters who felt that they had nearly exhausted other peaceful means. Two episodes suffice here to show the escalated militancy. The Taiwan Rural Front, a movement organization founded in 2008 that opposed government-sponsored development projects, achieved an occupation of the Ministry of the Interior over August 18–19, 2013, which turned out to be a dress rehearsal for the occupation of the legislature seven months later. The dispute was in relation to a 2010 land expropriation case in Tapu of Miaoli County that had resulted in the suicides of two residents affected by government-ordered demolition. The Tapu tragedy was largely seen as an egregious example of

Figure 2.5. Confrontational protest events, 2006–2013.

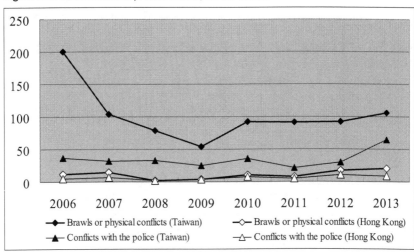

trampling on the lives of ordinary people for the sake of "economic development" (K. Chen 2017: 101–107).

The second episode was related to a group of laid-off workers who faced a government lawsuit over unpaid "loans" from the late 1990s.[21] The workers insisted that these "loans" originated as de facto compensation for wages and severance that their employers had been unable to pay, so the officials were expected to eventually request that the delinquent employers pay them.[22] In February 2013, laid-off workers and their supporters blocked the tracks at the Taipei railroad station, causing delays for thousands of commuters. Later on, to make timely use of Ma Ying-jeou's plummeting support ratings during an interparty power struggle in September, the laid-off workers threatened to mount a shoe-throwing protest at the KMT party congress originally scheduled for September 29. To avoid a potentially contentious situation, the KMT decided to relocate the meeting to a less easily accessible place in central Taiwan.

The unruly protests by people who were concerned about the land expropriation in Tapu and the laid-off workers incurred harsh official condemnation and negative journalistic coverage. Jiang Yi-huah, the premier from 2013 to 2014 and a former professor of political science with a Yale doctoral degree, denounced these protests vehemently. According to Jiang, these law-breaking actions did not qualify as "civil disobedience" because they were not "civilized."[23] However, later the two protest movements won belated vindication in court. In January 2014, the Administrative Court found that the government had violated proper procedures in expropriating private land in Tapu. Two weeks before students occupied the legislature, the Administrative Court decided in March 2014 that the laid-off workers did not have the obligation to pay back the government's "loans." Needless to say, such a drastic denouement discredited the authorities' insistence on law and order, and at the same time emboldened protesters to embark on more daring and disruptive protest strategies.

Data from Hong Kong reveal a similar trend of growing protest militancy, as brawls and physical conflicts, conflicts with the police, and public space occupation peaked from 2012 to 2013. According to Edmund W. Cheng (2016, 2018), the police statistics of legal processions demonstrated a continuous rise from 2004 to 2014. Larger-scale protests emerged at an accelerated tempo, indicating growing militancy on the part of Hong Kong's civil society. There was a clear upward shift in scale. Two preservation protests in 2006 to 2007 attracted 450 people, but when the protest against the Express Rail took place, more than 8,500 participants joined the demonstration. Finally, at its height, more than 90,000 protesters were present at the Anti–National Education rally in September 2012. In addition, there was a clear deviation from the conventional protest repertoire best exemplified by the annual June Fourth candlelight vigils and the July First demonstrations, which had been perceived as ineffectual and excessively ritualistic. Newer movements pioneered more disruptive actions; the preservation protesters launched site occupations to prevent the government's attempts at demolition, while the movements against the Express Rail and National Education launched massive sieges of government buildings.

Beginning in early 2013, the campaign Occupy Central with Love and Peace (OCLP) was underway, which avowed to paralyze Hong Kong's financial center with a mass sit-in in order to secure genuine universal suffrage for the chief executive. Due to its advocacy, a study has found increasing public understanding of civil disobedience (*gongmin kangming*), which explained why the Umbrella Movement could attract such large-scale participation (F. Lee 2015).

In sum, civil society in both Taiwan and Hong Kong became more active, more assertive, and more capable of launching larger-scale challenges to the government from 2008. The Sunflower Movement and the Umbrella Movement, in retrospect, represented an accumulated outcome of these state-and-society tensions (see J. Cheng 2014, Hsiao and Ho 2010, M. Ho 2014c).

Protests and China's Impact

Hong Kong and Taiwan experienced a heightened presence of the China factor from the turn of the century. Here I adopt a broader criterion for definition. A protest is about China if participants explicitly frame their issues as related to the behaviors of the PRC regime (both national and local governmental agencies), PRC citizens, or migrants. With this selection rule, I identify 130 China-related protests in Taiwan and 237 in Hong Kong from 2006 to 2013, or 2.8 percent and 34 percent of all protest events, respectively. The contrasting proportions demonstrate that the distinction between domestic and external affairs in Hong Kong was rapidly blurring under the "one country, two systems" framework, since nearly one-third of the protests were related to China or Chinese. By contrast, Taiwan's great majority of protests had an exclusively local origin. In the same period, Taiwan witnessed 19 protests about human rights issues in China, whereas Hongkongers took part in 46 protests on the same issue.

There were 10 pro-China events in Taiwan (such as anti-Taiwan independence protests) and 21 in Hong Kong (including the pro–National Education rallies and anti-OCLP protests), again an indication of the differing degrees of Beijing's penetration. More alarming is the escalating trend of pro-China mobilizations in the years immediately preceding the Umbrella Movement, 3 events in 2012 and 9 in 2013. Evidently Beijing and the SAR government were planning for an eventual showdown with the pro-democracy movement, while such developments were less visible in Taiwan (see Figure 2.6).

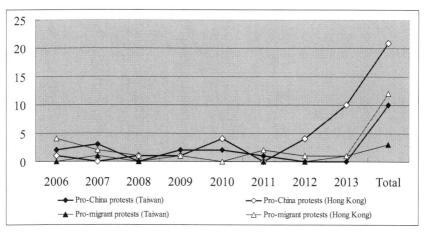

Figure 2.6. Pro-China protests and protests involving Chinese, 2006–2013.

There have been some China-related protests directly involving migrants or visitors from China. Chinese migrants and their family members in Hong Kong and Taiwan mobilized to further their interests, for the right of abode in the former and for shortening the waiting period for citizenship in the latter. Interestingly, new migrant campaigns in Hong Kong appeared more mainstream and supported by opposition politicians and NGO activists (such as the CHRF), whereas Taiwan's mainland spouse movement emerged as an exclusively self-help campaign, largely isolated from other social movements, and marked by a pronounced pro-KMT outlook (Momesso and Cheng 2017). In spite of these differences, only in Hong Kong did protests against Chinese migrants and parallel traders emerge. Angry Hongkongers took to the streets because they felt these uninvited intruders had worsened their quality of life, and the rapid growth of these protests eclipsed those protests mobilized by Chinese migrants from 2012, while such protest was absent in Taiwan. Hong Kong's deeper integration with China created tensions on the interpersonal level, fueling the localist sentiments that attempted to prioritize Hongkonger interests.

Conclusion

Shelley Rigger characterized Taiwan's challenging situation as "a canary in the coal mine for China's rise" that revealed how the new superpower would behave toward other neighboring countries (2011: 193). While most Taiwanese understood that growing economic ties with China were inevitable and perhaps beneficial, they also experienced actual deteriorations in civil liberties and press freedom. Although Taiwanese were lucky to have finished the political transition to democracy before the rise of China, their hard-won liberties were in danger of being eroded by Beijing's economic united front strategy and the concession of benefits for political purposes. This explained the seeming paradox of closer cross-strait economic integration and growing political disenchantment toward Beijing.

Taiwanese were not the only sentinel species to detect China's rising hegemony, because Hongkongers found themselves at a more advanced stage of Beijing's sharp power. Transforming the former British colony into a regular mainland city economically, culturally, and politically provoked waves of protest movements and an indigenization of identity as Hongkongers rose to resist the coercive assimilation. In Hong Kong and Taiwan, there emerged parallel processes of activation of civil-society actors to challenge the growing China factor within their territories, and later a transborder movement network connecting activists in the two places surfaced. Ultimately, "a locally perceived, PRC-originating threat to democratic and constitutional governance was a common feature" (deLisle 2017: 208) that paved the way for the occupy movements of 2014.

The above analysis lends a new perspective to the recent discussion of China's "sharp power," commonly seen as intervention to undermine democratic institutions with infiltration, bribery, and false information in the West. The term gains currency because China's "soft power" approach visibly fails to win hearts and minds among overseas targets and thus shifts to a more aggressive way to promote its influences. The stories of Taiwan and Hong Kong show that there is no clear distinction between soft power and sharp power, as China's economic united front strategy is simultaneously persuasive and coercive precisely because it aims to create political dependence through economic incentives. In a sense, China perfected the skill in exerting authoritarian influences first in Hong Kong and Taiwan before applying it to other countries. It remains to be seen whether similar negative syndromes and reaction will take place elsewhere in the world.

3

Movement Networks

"The interconnectedness of the thousands of demonstrators has created a reform movement that is organic, seemingly without well-defined leadership, and behaving like a single organism." Such was the observation of Hong Kong's Umbrella Movement by the acclaimed photojournalist James Nachtwey. Mesmerized by the participants' civic-mindedness and idealism, he went on to declare that "any nation which possesses people of such quality, capability and talent, would do well to embrace them and empower them, not crush them."[1] Similarly, a BBC report described Taiwan's Sunflower Movement and its preceding protests as mainly propelled by "rising young democrats" who were disillusioned by major political parties. These "participants tend to be ordinary people who want their voices heard, and want to protect Taiwan's future."[2]

Such an image of spontaneity on the part of ordinary citizens is actually quite prevalent in contemporary depictions of global eventful protests. Lin Noueihed and Alex Warren noted that Arab Spring protesters did not have "a clear program, a hierarchical organization with figureheads and followers" (2012: 6). Asef Bayat (2017) characterized the Middle Eastern upheaval as a "revolution without revolutionaries" because of the absence of revolutionary ideas. Surveying the global anticapitalist protests, Paul Mason contended that "there is no ideology driving this movement and no coherent vision of an alternative society" (2012: 45). David Graeber provided a firsthand account of how unorganized activists made possible the Occupy Wall Street campaign (2013: 41–54). All these characterizations seem to imply that these disruptive protests emerged out of nowhere because preexisting social movement organizations and parties played only a marginal role.

The progress of digital communication has often been identified as the most important contributing factor in the sudden explosion of these protests by unaffiliated citizens. As the Internet became more broadly available, faster, interactive, and mobile, protesters became more and more able to circumvent the authorities' censorship and the mainstream media's neglect. The Internet brought about "the power of organizing without organizations" because the transaction cost for launching a collective action has been greatly flattened (Shirky 2008). Social media made possible a distinctive logic of "connective action" (Bennett and Segerberg 2013). Manuel Castells maintained that the advent of information society ushered in a revolutionary era of "mass self-communication" that gave a powerful boost to the proliferation of "instant insurgent communities" (2012: 6–7). The sanguine expectation for cyberspace had led to a pre–Arab Spring prediction that "Islamic democracies will be born digital" (Howard 2010: 12). It was also observed that before the Egyptian protest was set in motion, the Western media had already created "an image of Facebook Revolution" (Holmes 2012: 402). The legendary story of how Wael Ghonim, a Dubai-based Google engineer, masterminded the protests in Cairo by managing a Facebook fan page seemed to confirm the power of online mobilization. Wael Ghonim later formulated a model of "revolution 2.0," which was "a spontaneous movement led by nothing other than the wisdom of the crowd" (2012: 293).

Nevertheless, there is increasing evidence indicating that the focus on the Internet is easily overdone and misleading if it is seen as the only determinative factor. The Egyptian Revolution had an offline origin because "protests had been meticulously planned by a small number of activists" whose collaboration evolved over more than a decade (Gunning and Baron 2014: 165–166). The revolt turned out to be successful largely thanks to the activation of preexisting networks of political opposition, labor movement, and Islamic organizations (Clarke 2014). Contrary to the banal image of a "Facebook Revolution," "a complex and laborious groundwork" was necessary to mobilize the opponents (Gerbaudo 2012: 61). In the case of the Spanish Indignados Movement of 2011, the preceding autonomous movements had laid the foundation of that campaign in spite of its ostensible claim of newness and spontaneity (Flesher Fominaya 2014a). Similarly, Todd Gitlin (2013a) warned against an overly romantic view of the Occupy Wall Street Movement because more numerous supporters and rally participants were members of labor unions or other progressive organizations. In short, the uncritical view of these mass protests as spontaneous occurrences runs the risk of overlooking the building of movement networks prior to the eruption of clashes with the authorities.

In social movement study, that protests emerge as "complex and highly heterogeneous network structures" has long been the received wisdom (Diani 2003: 1). Earlier dominant explanations embraced an excessively "undersocialized" perspective that reduced movement participation either to an emotional expression of unbalanced psychological conditions (the collective behavior theory) or to an individualized cost-and-benefit calculation (the rational choice theory). Both neglected the social ties that linked individual participants to their collective action. As such, how the preexisting network stimulated potential grievances into actual protests became a focal question among social movement students (Granovetter 1973; McCarthy 1987; Tilly 1978: 63; Useem 1980). Doug McAdam provided the classical formulation for why the existence of preexisting networks was conducive to movement participation (1982: 45–50). People with closer ties tended to view their participation as psychologically rewarding per se, and the presence of such a solidarity incentive made it easier to overcome the debilitating dilemma of free-riders. Furthermore, social ties facilitated internal communication so that people were more likely to accept novel messages from the persons they trusted. Therefore, while isolated individuals were self-regarding and uninformed, the mediating social ties helped to surmount these dual hurdles.

A great diversity of movement networks existed. Professionalized (led by full-time staff) and formalized (operating with codified rules) organizations were the classic models of movement networks that could sustain long-term participation (Staggenborg 1988). However, not all social movements were able to pool enough resources to maintain such institutionalized patterns. The great majority of existing movement organizations shared the characteristics of being segmentary, polycentric, and reticulate (Gerlach 1999: 85–90). In other words, they proceeded in a loosely coordinated fashion. On the least institutionalized pole in the spectrum, there were some social movements whose networks were embedded in existing organizations or interpersonal relations so that their campaigns tended to operate in an ad hoc manner. Researchers used a number of descriptions—"movement network" (Melucci 1985: 798), "social movement communities" (Staggenborg 1998), or "social movement families" (della Porta and Rucht 1995: 230)—to describe this loosely organized movement activism. Regardless of their different degrees of crystallization, movement networks were the building blocks that made possible the sustained challenge to the authorities.

This chapter examines the formation of networks in Hong Kong and Taiwan prior to the two occupy movements in 2014. Both societies experienced an escalated wave of protests that had brought about a new cohort of movement activists with interrelated networks spanning across universities, NGOs, and political parties. In particular, Hongkongers and Taiwanese who were born in the 1980s (whose ages were from 24 to 34 in 2014) made up the main contingent force of movement activism. I describe how economic grievances in the twenty-first century paved the way for youth revolts. Last, this chapter analyzes the formation of transborder movement networks that facilitated mutual learning as activists came to be aware of their common threat.

"Post-80" and "Seventh Graders": Profiling Youth in Revolt

As Taiwan and Hong Kong witnessed an ascending wave of protests, a new cohort of young activists had come of political age. They were acutely aware of generational differences with their seniors, and were more willing to explore novel and confrontational ways of making protests. In Hong Kong, people in their twenties and thirties spearheaded the preservation movements of 2006–2007. On the evening before the government evicted the sit-in protesters at the Queen's Pier in August 2007, Leung Man-tao, a renowned social critic, penned a prophetic essay that proclaimed, "Time is on our side." Leung perceptively pointed to the emergence of a young generation of activists with newer values and a more globalized vision, who consciously rejected the old-style politics of established politicians (M. Leung 2010). Although two historical piers were eventually bulldozed to make way for reclamation, these vanguards inspired more protest actions from Hong Kong's youth. The name "Post-80" (*bashihou,* those who were born in the decade of the 1980s) first surfaced in an intervention into the annual commemoration of the Tiananmen Massacre with the "P-at-Riot: June Fourth Festival for Post-80s Generation" (*bashihou liusi wenhuaji*) in 2009, clearly intended as a younger generation's playful rejoinder to the SPDM's patriotic obsession. In the Anti–Express Rail Movement, "Post-80" activists launched several rounds of a territory-wide Bitter March (*kuxing*) to demonstrate their opposition. Thereafter "post-80" emerged as a common identity in a number of subsequent movement campaigns, such as "anti-privilege post-80 youth" (*bashihou fan tequan qingnian*), "anti-hegemony-of-landed-property post-80 youth" (*bashihou fandiba qingnian*), and so on (Post-80 Self-Studying Youth 2012). In Hong Kong's popular discourse, the term became closely associated with a newer wave of protest activism organized by young people.

By contrast, there was no comparable generational identity that was intimately linked to protest activism in Taiwan. However, newer protests after 2008 were clearly led by university students or people in their twenties, locally called "Seventh Graders" (*qinianjisheng*)—a term that followed the Republic of China calendar to refer to those who were born between 1981 and 1990. The Wild Strawberry Movement of 2008, which marked the beginning of a rising trend in social protests in Taiwan, was visibly motivated by a generation consciousness. The student participants deliberately chose this self-mocking name in an attempt to challenge the seniors' stereotypical image of the 1980s generation as "a tribe of strawberries" (*caomei zu*) with the connotations of being good-looking on the outside, but fragile and soft on the inside. Afterward, the term "youth" (*qingnian*) was commonly used in protest movements. For example, in the Anti–Kuokuang Petrochemical Park Movement (2005–2011), the emergence of the student-led National Youth Alliance against Kuokuang Petrochemical Project (*quanguo qingnian fanguoguang shihua lianmeng*) had been a noticeable phenomenon. The Anti–Media Monopoly Movement was practically inseparable from the Youth Alliance against Media Monster (*fanmeiti jushou qingnian lianmeng*), a student-led organization founded in 2012. Finally, the student opposition to the CSSTA began with the formation of the Black Island Nation Youth Front (*heise daoguo qingnian zhenxian*) in 2013.

In Hong Kong and Taiwan, the terms "Post-80," "Seventh Graders," and "Youth" actually refer to the same age cohort, those born in the 1980s. They are essentially the "millennials" because they became conscious of their world around the turn of the century. This cohort turned out to be more protest-prone and keenly aware of generational differences between their seniors and them—a fact that has a common demographic and life-course root, as both societies underwent profound economic restructuring in the twenty-first century. In the American New Left movements of the 1960s, Baby Boomers who experienced the unprecedented prosperity of postwar capitalism were more likely to develop an idealistic and optimistic belief in progressive changes (Goldstone and McAdam 2001). However, in the Hong Kong and Taiwan contexts, it was not the experience of material bounty that stimulated their protest actions, but rather a realization that they would no longer enjoy their parent generation's economic success.

Economic Grievances

The eventful protests in North Africa, the Middle East, southern Europe, and North America in 2011 had been spearheaded by "a rapidly growing class of educated yet unemployed youth" who had fallen into an expanding army of "precariat" (precarious proletariat) (Tejerina et al. 2013: 380). In particular, appellations such as the Portuguese *Geração à Rasca* (the Desperate Generation [Baumgarten 2013]) and the Israeli "B Generation" (Grinberg 2013) vividly portrayed the economic plight and discontent among the young people. In the East Asian context, "the bleak economic future" is found to bring about the presence of youth in major demonstrations (Chua 2017: 3). Hong Kong and Taiwan also witnessed the youths' economic discontent, which fueled their protest actions.

Taiwan and Hong Kong were largely free of acute and dire economic hardship, as neither experienced the chronic stagnation as in North Africa and the Middle East, or sudden recession induced by debt crisis and austerity measures as in southern Europe. The pain of the 1997 Asian financial crisis, the 2003 SARS crisis, and the 2008 global financial tsunami was clearly felt, but both economies quickly recovered from the impacts. Still, there existed perceivable economic grievances. Both Taiwan and Hong Kong had bid farewell to the era of high-speed growth with full employment and entered a period of relatively slower development in the new millennium. Taiwan's annual growth rate in GDP was 7.6 percent from 1980 to 1999 and 3.8 percent from 2000 to 2014, whereas the respective figures for Hong Kong were 5.5 percent and 4 percent for those periods.[3] One of the common consequences was a rise in youth unemployment (those under twenty-five). Taiwan's average youth unemployment rate was 5.7 percent from 1990 to 1999, and it climbed to 11.6 percent from 2001 to 2014, whereas the situation for Hong Kong similarly worsened as it grew from 7.6 percent to 13.1 percent, respectively. While both Taiwanese and Hongkonger younger generations came to face a more challenging job market, they also had different grievances. Under the laissez-faire doctrine, colonial Hong Kong has been highly unequal in income, and the handover apparently aggravated the situation, as the Gini Index rose from 0.518 in 1996 to 0.537 in 2011. In Taiwan, the prolonged wage stagnation became a chronic problem. From 2000 to 2014, Taiwan's median monthly income actually declined by 0.14 percent.[4] Clearly, the two Asian tiger economies that became world-famous for their vitality and dynamism in the 1980s had lost their luster. In the new millennium, both saw the rising tide of unemployment as their manufacturing jobs were outsourced to China. With slower economic expansion, stagnant or slow growth in wages, and rising unemployment, young people were victimized by these adverse trends as the 1980s generation entered the job market in the twenty-first century.

The Post-80 Hongkongers were more likely to receive higher education, and yet a college diploma no longer automatically guaranteed a middle-class position. As the attainment of a middle-class position, defined by holding a professional job and owning a private apartment, had been a central component of the "Hong Kong Dream," the increasing inability among the youth to make this promise a reality threatened to destroy this implicit social pact (T. Lui 2014). Hong Kong's economy took a severe hit during the 2003 SARS epidemic, and it quickly recovered after the influx of investment and tourist consumption from China, which, however, fueled the housing speculation. A poll of Hongkongers under thirty-five in 2014 found that they were less likely to identify themselves as "middle class" than seniors (Ip and Chiu 2016).

Similarly, there was a widespread perception that Taiwan's era of abundant upward mobility during the industrial take-off had been irretrievably lost. Younger Taiwanese were less likely to experience the status change from "factory operatives to bosses" (*heishou bian toujia*) in their lifetime (T. Lin 2009). Taiwanese who were born in the years from 1946 to 1977 grew up in a highly mobile society, but such opportunity was denied to those who were born after (K. Su 2008: 207–211). Interestingly, while Taiwan has persistently been more economically equal than Hong Kong, studies found that more Taiwanese perceived inequalities as a grave social problem than Hongkongers (Wong and Yeh 2013; Zheng and Wan 2016). It is very possible that the prolonged wage stagnation and the diminishing chances for entrepreneurial and upward mobility worsened the subjective evaluation.

Hong Kong and Taiwan were luckily spared economic failures and upheavals, but an angst and sense of malaise prevailed in the twenty-first century, with the young people particularly penalized by the slower growth and rising inequality. The 1980s generation consisted of those who were born and grew up in the heyday of the boom years, yet encountered the harsh economic realities when they finished school and entered the job market. True, economic grievances per se did not stimulate protest behaviors, as the latter were triggered by other social and political factors, but the experiences of deprivation shaped a generation's mindset and these understandings had a prolonged effect on how they framed their discontents.

Public Perception and Activism

The peak of youth unemployment arrived earlier in Hong Kong (18.2 percent in 2003) than in Taiwan (14.5 percent in 2009), which partly explained its earlier manifestation of discussions on generational inequality in public discourse. Immediately after the handover and the Asian financial crisis in 1997, there was a growing perception that Hong Kong had passed its economic prime. In his widely read book on four-generation Hongkongers published in 2007, sociologist Tai-lok Lui contended that the fourth generation (born between 1976 and 1990) were "born to be losers" because they grew up in an environment with diminishing opportunities and were destined to fail the expectations of their seniors (Lui 2007: 13). Such a pessimistic diagnosis engendered an engaged and intense debate on Hong Kong's youth problems.

In Taiwan, *The Collapsing Generation* (*bengshidai*), a joint publication by academics and labor movement activists, was published in 2011. The book depicted a gloomy future for Taiwan's younger generation (defined as those who were between 20 and 40 years old at the time) because they were about to encounter the dismal prospects of pauperization, corporate domination, and bankrupt social insurance due to the declining fertility rate (Lin et al. 2011). Although *The Collapsing Generation* was not as widely circulated as Lui's small book, in 2012 it won the official Golden Tripod Award, the highest award in Taiwan's publishing industry, and was reprinted several times, an atypical achievement for serious publications in Taiwan.

The prevalent sense of relative deprivation among the youth per se did not automatically generate protest activism, which emerged as a combined result of political, organizational, and psychological factors. Nevertheless, the shared experience of economic grievances shaped the cultural understanding when young Hongkongers and Taiwanese launched their protests, highlighting the problems of social injustice. As such, in a number of protests that attracted young people, "justice" became a widely used frame. For example, in Taiwan's protest movements against the government-sponsored land expropriation and developmental projects, the slogan "land justice" (*tudi zhengyi*) was adopted by Taiwan's Rural Front and Hong Kong's Land Justice League (founded in 2011). Youthful Taiwanese participants protested forcible urban renewal projects and skyrocketing housing prices, raising the principle of "residence justice" (*juzhu zhengyi*), whereas their counterparts in Hong Kong attempted to challenge what they called "the hegemony of landed property" (*dichan baquan*), which was derived from a popular book that exposed the predatory behaviors of land developers (Poon 2010).

While young people suffered from a lack of opportunities, a seemingly opposite trend emerged that challenged the mainstream values that prioritized economic development over other social goals. In Hong Kong, the rise of the opposition movement to the government's developmental projects of urban renewal, land reclamation, and the Express Rail signified a rise in postmaterialist orientation that looked beyond monetary satisfaction (Ma 2011b). Other surveys, in 2010 and 2014, found the identification with postmaterialist values (freedom of speech and a more humane society) among Hongkonger youth was almost on a par with materialistic values (public order and price stability) (Wong and Chiu 2016). Taiwan witnessed an analogous rise of postmaterialist movements in this period. For example, science park projects that brought about large-scale investment of high-tech industries used to be eagerly solicited by local governments and residents, but more recently they have encountered resistance. The expansion of science parks was opposed by environmentalists, local farmers, and student participants (H. Chiu 2011). In the past, rural countryside was viewed as a social and economic backwater that ambitious young people should leave; now a reverse migration took place, as village life began to attract educated youth who were willing to experiment with environmentally friendly farming and community-supported agriculture schemes (Y. Tsai 2014). In other words, precisely because Hong Kong and Taiwan were lucky enough to be spared precipitous economic crises, their youth did not experience acute and debilitating hardships so that some of them decided to explore novel forms of political intervention that challenged the hegemony of economic development.

Rather than being passive victims of negative economic turns, the 1980s generation in Hong Kong and Taiwan attempted to express their experiences actively. In 2010, an "Our Post-80 Declaration" (*women de bashihou xuanyan*) was issued, which upheld the principles of truthfulness, historical sensitivity, action for social justice, inclusiveness, and so on.[5] In comparison with the 2004 declaration of Hong Kong's core values (see Chapter 2), which represented the moderate reformism of established middle-class professionals who upheld Western liberalism to counter mainlandization, this statement was clearly not anchored in any major ideologies, but came more as youth's rejection of the hypocrisy, materialism, and dogmatism of mainstream politicians. Interestingly, such sentiments were shared by Taiwan's 1980s generation. *Wild Strawberry's Song* (*yemei zhi ge*), created for the 2008 student movement, had the following lyrics: "I am not a flower in the greenhouse / You don't have to pretend to be considerate / I will never learn your hypocrisy / And will remain truthful to myself."[6] Clearly there existed the similar emphasis on the authenticity of personal feelings and their expressions through direct confrontation with social injustices.

Later on, these youth activists worked to fashion a more coherent worldview appropriate to their generation and time. A group called "Post-80 Self-Studying Youth" (*bashihou ziwoyanjiu qingnian*) published a book of their own writings annually from 2011 to 2013. Participants in the Anti–Express Rail Movement also documented the history of the villagers of Choi Yuen before its eventual demolition (Choi Yuen Village Support Team 2013). In Hong Kong, writing about and publishing Post-80 ideals had evolved into a thriving cottage industry. In Taiwan, there emerged 1980s generation writers, the "Seventh Grade Writers" (*qinianji zuojia*), who gained literary fame before turning thirty. In a collection of essays in which they were invited to describe their generational outlook, quite a number of pieces mentioned protest participation as a part of their formative experiences (Wen-cheng Yu 2016). In addition, there was an effort to articulate their social and cultural perspectives in an edited volume, *Island Nation's Keywords* (*daoguo guanjianzi*), that contained their analysis of nine fashionable topics, including "22K" (a synonym for the low monthly wage commonly offered to university graduates), "426" (a pejorative term for Chinese), "Emperor's Treasures" (shorthand for luxury mansions), and so on (Ting 2014).

Forging Movement Networks

The advent of a younger generation with similar critical outlooks was a sufficient but not necessary condition for the two eventful protests in 2014. Interpersonal links built during the preceding campaigns engendered networked communities for collective action. In both places, an expanding network connecting students, NGOs, and opposition parties came about, providing the backbone for activists and leaders. In Taiwan, there was a clearly identifiable lineage from the Wild Strawberry Movement of 2008 to the Sunflower Movement of 2014, as a core group of student activists developed their school bases, which brought about more participation both on and off campus. Hong Kong's equivalent to the Wild Strawberry Movement was the surge of student participation in the Anti–Express Rail Movement in 2010, which later stimulated student participation in electoral politics and deepened their links with the opposition parties and the NGOs.

The Lessons of the Wild Strawberry Movement

Taiwan's Wild Strawberry Movement took place in November 2008 to protest the excessive policing that ensued as the newly installed KMT government was rolling out the red carpet to welcome China's envoy. Protesters demanded an official apology, the resignation of responsible officials, and the revision of regulations on demonstrations, which failed to elicit positive responses from the authorities. The student sit-in protest at Taipei's Liberty Square dragged on for two months and finally collapsed from exhaustion. Despite its ostensible failure, the Wild Strawberry Movement was significant in many ways. First, it marked a new beginning of student intervention in national-level politics that had gradually subsided after the 1990 Wild Lily Movement (J. Ho 2001: 74). Afterward, student activism had contracted to some niche issues, such as the preservation movement for Lo-Sheng Sanatorium from 2004, and participants developed into a close-knit community that shunned involvement in partisan politics (S. Chang 2015). Due to the prolonged decline of student activism, the Wild Strawberry Movement had a unique origin in the Internet only because of the absence of prior student organizations (Y. Hsiao 2017: 48). Second, although the movement raised the issues of human rights and a possible authoritarian comeback, it was also the first time that students voiced their demands concerning cross-strait politics, reflecting the growing impacts of Beijing on Taiwan. Finally, students had taken a serious lesson from their failure and decided to go back to their campuses in order to build new organizational bases for the purpose of continuing and broadening their activism. Since the students' sit-in protests were not limited to only Taipei but also took place in Hsinchu, Taichung, Chiayi, Tainan, and Kaohsiung, a nationwide wave of campus organizing was immediately under way.

In many universities a proliferation of movement-oriented clubs emerged. In the schools where there was weak or no previous student activism, new clubs were organized, for example the Protest Club (*lingershe*) at National Cheng Kung University (Tainan), the Radical Notes (*jijin biji*) at National Tsing Hua University (Hsinchu), the Letting-Dogs-Out Club (*fanggoushe*) at National Sun Yat-sen University (Kaohsiung), and the Movement Club (*mufumen*) at National Chung Cheng University (Chiayi). In other places, dissident students revived movement clubs that had long been dormant, such as the Black Forest (*heisenlin*) at National Chung Hsing University and the

Humanity Workshop (*renjian gongzuofang*) at Tunghai University, both in Taichung. Student initiatives were facilitated by ex–movement activist professors who had taken part in the 1990 Wild Lily Movement and expectedly held sympathetic attitudes toward this new wave of campus activism. A study found that of sixty-nine active movement clubs scattered across the nation's forty-eight universities and with an average of ten members, the great majority of them emerged after the Wild Strawberry Movement (Jhuang 2015: 53, 59).

In the attempt to raise the consciousness of their fellow students, these Wild Strawberry activists experimented with a wide variety of mobilizing strategies. Some sought to bring outside political issues to campus. The Protest Club, for example, gained notoriety by staging graffiti protests on Chiang Kai-shek statues each year on February 28, while the Radical Notes activists devoted their attention to environmental protests. Others focused on daily grievances around campus in the hope that more students would be willing to become involved with public issues. For instance, the Letting-Dogs-Out Club started with the issue of motorcycle parking, and the Movement Club led a protest over the regulations on course requirements. The National Taiwan University (NTU) Student Association leaders provide another example of this student rights strategy. In 2009 they launched a series of protests against the university leadership's pursuit of academic excellence at the expense of student rights, which successfully raised the concern of students. To oppose a cut to teaching assistants' wages, these student activists organized a labor union of graduate students in 2011, the first in Taiwan's higher education (interview #TW54).

In short, on the eve of the Sunflower Movement Taiwan's universities were brimming with protest activism. One Sunflower activist, whose undergraduate and graduate student years spanned from 2007 to 2015, gave his personal observation:

> There was a discussion forum in 2007 about the issue of whether the DPP government should rename the Chiang Kei-shek Memorial, which attracted around eighty participants. It was so exciting then, but later I found everyone was staging a forum. There were not so many activities to attend in Taipei back then, and the participants were few. But later on, such events became so frequent that they sometimes took place at the same time. For example, at school, the Student Association held one event, and our club staged another, not counting those that happened outside the campus. In the past, we used to coordinate our events to avoid time conflicts for fear that participants might be diverted; afterward, such worry was no longer necessary. (Interview #TW59)

Intercampus Networks

These activist students were also conscious of the need to rebuild intercampus connections. As an activist noted, "The Wild Strawberry movement linked us like a bunch of rice dumplings" (*rouzong*) so that student leaders in different localities all came to know each other (interview #47). With this foundation, the intercampus or inter-regional network emerged in many ways. Sometimes networks expanded because activists changed schools. Two biographical stories of the 1980s generation, Lin Fei-fan (born in 1988) and Chen Wei-ting (born in 1990), the twin figureheads of the Sunflower Movement, suffice here. From 2008 to 2011, Lin was studying as an undergraduate in Tainan's National Cheng Kung University, where he co-founded the Protest Club. After 2011, he became a master's degree student in Taipei's NTU and served as the president of its Graduate Student Association from 2012 to 2013. With his move, Lin emerged as one of the nodal points linking students in Taipei and in southern Taiwan. Chen Wei-ting was still a high school student during the Wild Strawberry Movement. Because of his intensive participation, he became well known by Taipei-based activist students. Chen began to study in National Tsing Hua University in 2009, playing an important role in the Radical Notes club and thereby expanding his personal networks in Hsinchu.

These activist students also formed a nationwide network by launching joint campaigns. In 2010, a University Student Rights Investigation and Evaluation Team (*daxue xuesheng quanli diaocha pingjian xiaozu*) came about to protest an incident in which students' freedom of speech was violated. This organization evolved into a watchdog organization, with its annual reports, until 2013.[7] Student activists in southern Taiwan were particularly aware of their marginal status, and thus more willing to collaborate across schools. In 2011, they founded a quarterly magazine, *Praxis in the South* (*xingnan*),[8] and held rock concerts and evening forums, which lasted until the outbreak of the Sunflower Movement. As a matter of fact, the Anti-Media Monopoly Movement came into being largely thanks to the reactivation of student activist networks that were built after 2008 (Wang 2015: 133).

There were also occasions for mutual exchanges among activist students. The first event took place in 2011 as more than thirty students joined a three-day workshop held in Taichung (Y. Wei 2016: 89). In the beginning such exchanges were informal, small-scale, and limited to invited activists only; however, as news of such events traveled through social media, more students indicated their eagerness to join. As such, these events became more frequent and involved more participants (interview #TW59). In January 2014, two months before the Sunflower Movement, a five-day youth empowerment camp called Amateurs' Riot (*shuren zhiluan*) was held, with the participation of over two hundred students. As one organizer revealed, the networks formed in that camp played an important role in the subsequent occupation of the legislature (interview #TW46). Increasing participation and networking also brought sophistication: Before the legislature occupation, a group of activists had finished the manuscript of a manual to share the basic know-how of organizing a protest, which was put into print afterward (S. Chang, Huang, and Yu 2014).

Networking with NGOs and the DPP

The reemergence of student movements attracted the attention of NGOs and opposition politicians, who intended to build a close relationship with these new student activists. Despite their differing purposes and motivations, the result was that student activist networks extended beyond their own category. The Taiwan Rural Front was among the first to encourage and recruit student participants. From 2009, the Taiwan Rural Front held an annual summer camp that attracted hundreds of students (Y. Wei 2016: 116–123). While the NGOs intended to draw new blood from the emerging student activists, students also found it easier to access resources from the former. A group of students associated with the NTU Chuoshui River Club (*zhushuishishe*) began to undertake an oral history project on Su Beng (a Taiwan independence movement veteran) in 2009, and held an annual music festival on February 28 each year beginning in 2013 (Chuoshui River Club Editorial Team 2016: 54). These efforts emerged due to sponsorship from a number of pro-independence NGOs. Similarly, the Kaohsiung-based Praxis in the South forums and events were also made possible with monetary support from local NGOs (interview #TW50).

The opposition party attempted to harness the new student activism. Tsai Ing-wen, who led the DPP for six of its eight years in opposition (2008–2016), was originally a trade negotiation expert hired by Lee Teng-hui's government. With her technocratic background, she was perceived as less of a typical DPP politician and thus more acceptable to younger generation activists. Under Tsai's leadership, the DPP declared 2009 as "the year of social movements" and reestablished the Department of Social Movements in its party headquarters—a symbolic gesture to woo movement activists. After her failed presidential campaign in 2012, Tsai established the Thinking Taiwan Foundation, which recruited some young activists and operated an online forum for their writings.

Other DPP politicians also set their sights on these younger generation activists. People Rule Movement (*renmin zuozhu yundong*), a campaign launched by Lin Yi-hsiung in 2009, hired some ex–Wild Strawberry participants. As a result, when students mobilized to oppose media monopoly, they often had meetings in its office (interview #TW60). The Youth Synergy Taiwan Foundation founded in 2010 by Cheng Li-chiun, who became minister of culture under Tsai's administration, functioned as an important channel in this regard. In 2011, it sponsored ten NGOs all over Taiwan by subsidizing the salaries of their staff. All these efforts deepened the links between young activists and the DPP.

Hong Kong's Student Activism Reenergized

While Taiwan's students spearheaded the rising wave of social protests from 2008, Hong Kong student involvement came about later than other civil-society actors. In the two pier preservation movements of 2006 to 2007, there was only limited and intermittent student participation (interview #HK4-3). It was only after the high tide of the Anti–Express Rail Movement in December 2009 that student presence became more regular. The historical legacy of Taiwanese and Hongkonger student activism shaped the different trajectories of their revival. Hong Kong's student organizations, including the Hong Kong Federation of Students (HKFS) and campus-based student unions and student papers, were more institutionalized and better endowed with financial resources compared to Taiwanese counterparts. Consequently, Taiwanese students proceeded with a number of ad hoc coalitions and issue campaigns, whereas student movements in Hong Kong were revived by reactivating preexisting organizational networks.

Despite their flourishing in the 1990 Wild Lily Movement, Taiwanese student activists were unable to maintain a nationwide body to permanently represent their voice. There was no Taiwanese equivalent to the HKFS, founded in 1958, which formally incorporated the student union leadership of different universities. The HKFS enjoyed a solid financial basis by receiving membership fees from affiliated student unions and owning rent-generating properties.[9] Beijing fostered a parallel student organization to challenge the leading role of the HKFS, but without success (Ortmann 2012: 90–91). Hong Kong's campus-based student unions appeared more organizationally independent than Taiwan's counterparts. The Hong Kong University Students' Union (HKUSU) was a registered corporate with independent assets, while the Chinese University Student Union (CUSU) managed a HK$ 2 million (US$258,000) fund for the democratic movement in China, which sponsored the SPDM's activities (interview #HK16-2). Even Hong Kong's student papers were able to maintain a more autonomous and continuous operation. *Undergrad*, the student publication of the University of Hong Kong (HKU), first emerged in 1952 and enjoyed editorial autonomy. As of 2015, *Undergrad* operated with an annual budget of HK$200,000 (US$ 26,000), without the interference of school leadership or the student union (interview #HK21).

In spite of its more established status, Hong Kong's student movement underwent a prolonged period of decline following its involvement with the

Tiananmen protest in 1989. There had been several years that the HKFS was unable to select a secretary-general (Choy et al. 1998: 227, 230). Thanks to the rising student activism, the HKFS was able to continuously maintain a leadership structure after 2007. A participant of the HKFS from 2006 to 2007 characterized her tenure as "stillness without wind, quietness without wave" (*fengping langjing*), since the HKFS took part in only the annual rallies on June Fourth and July First. On these occasions, the participants who stood under the HKFS banner were few and limited to its core members (interview #HK67). Historically, the Chinese University of Hong Kong (CUHK) had maintained a stronger tradition of student activism than HKU. A CUSU president (2008–2009) described her tenure as the "low tide" (*lengdan*) of student activism because they were not able to attract attention from broader society while media reports concerning students were mostly about some campus scandals. In March 2008, the CUSU issued a proclamation to condemn Beijing's suppression of the Tibetan uprising, which drew severe criticism from mainland students (interview #HK57). At HKU, pro-Beijing students started to campaign for the leadership position in 2001, and a worrisome trend took place when the *Undergrad* began to adopt a more apolitical editorial policy by emphasizing lifestyle and consumption issues. An HKUSU president, who was suspected of maintaining clandestine linkages with Beijing, openly questioned the existence of any massacre during the Tiananmen protest on the eve of its twentieth anniversary in 2009, which turned out to be a critical turning point. This inadvertent whitewashing remark stimulated many protests among students, and the president was successfully deposed in a recall campaign, the first time in the history of HKU (M. Li 2015: 349).

The Impact of the Anti–Express Rail Movement

Although Choi Yuen villagers launched their opposition to forceful eviction in 2008, it was only in December 2009, when the Anti–Express Rail Movement launched its territory-wide Bitter March, that students began to become involved. As a CUSU president (2012–2013) put it, "I was a freshman when my seniors told me that Choi Yuen village needed help because they were facing the immediate threat of being evicted.... After I had been there, I found social movements were a good thing ... because there were experiences of mutual solidarity and a vision of alternative lifestyle" (interview #HK55). Another CUSU president (2010–2011) had a similar experience: "Students were willing to take part in this movement partly because they were touched by Choi Yuen villagers. They also experienced something meaningful in this campaign. Previous social movements were mostly about democratization and universal suffrage, which were not of interest to students. But the Anti–Express Rail Movement mentioned the issues of land justice, local attachment, rural culture, and development, which were novel and attractive to those who studied social work and cultural studies" (interview #HK65).

The legislative council decision to approve the rail budget in January 2010 signified a definite failure for the opponents. Yet Hong Kong's student interest in public issues beyond campus was reawakened. Since the budget was approved as a result of a questionable maneuver by functional-constituency representatives whose business interests were intimately related to the project, students became acutely aware of the problems of an undemocratic regime. Student leaders decided to form a coalition to take part in the Five District Referendum in May 2012, an attempt by opposition parties to expedite the process of democratization (see Chapter 5). To field all five candidacies, leaders from three university student unions joined the electoral campaign. As one participant explained her motivation for participation:

> When we were resisting the Express Rail, some students began to discuss the electoral rules for the legislative council. The existence of functional constituencies was simply unfair because it allowed monopoly by special interests. We began to be concerned about the issues related to political reform. The rules of the game for the legislative council were really in horrible shape. And it was worse when some [DP lawmakers] were eager to promote political changes through negotiation with Beijing. (Interview #HK62)

The era of political apathy was visibly gone. After 2010, students emerged as a regular contingent force in a number of social and political protests. There was clearly a spillover effect from the mounting campus activism. Scholarism, a movement organization of high school students led by the charismatic Joshua Wong, emerged in 2011 and played a leading role in the Anti–National Education Movement. There were social movements that gained support from the new wave of student involvement. In post-1997 Hong Kong, there had been two major strikes, by construction workers in 2007 and by dockworkers in 2013. The former incident was a traditional industrial conflict involving labor unions and pro-labor politicians, whereas the latter emerged as a civil-society-wide mobilization with the HKFS, Scholarism, and other students who joined the campaign to support the workers. Banners showing solidarity with striking workers were seen on many campuses (interview #HK37).

Linkages with NGOs and Political Parties

Similar to Taiwan, rising student protests brought about expanding networks that connected more and more activists. Scholarism rose to instant fame in early September 2012 with a hunger strike that forced the government to withdraw the plan to implement National Education. At its zenith, Scholarism included nearly five hundred members, mostly high school students or freshman university students (interview #HK46). Nevertheless, Scholarism's spectacular rise had to do with its reliance on links to "the existing social movement activists' network," which provided the necessary resources (Wang 2017). Left 21 was another new social movement organization formed in 2011. It was led by a former CUSU president (2007–2008), and had around seventy members including university students, activists in NGOs and opposition parties, and professors who shared a similar ideological outlook. Left 21 emerged during the Anti-Express Rail Movement, as some participants thought a class-analysis perspective was needed to counterbalance the predominant localist discourse (interview #HK66). In response to Occupy Wall Street, the Left 21 activists initiated an occupy movement at HSBC's headquarters in October 2011 (interview #HK53).

Movement network expansion led to more connections between student and nonstudent participants. The CHRF, serving as a coordination platform for staging the annual July First demonstrations, elected a CUSU student (then twenty-three years old) as its convener in 2011. He was the first student to lead this important movement organization and his predecessors had been established movement activists or opposition politicians. Clearly the NGOs attempted to tap into the newly emergent resources of student activism.

Both the CUHK and the HKU were prestigious higher education institutions, but the former was characterized by a radical tradition of student participation. The CUSU was in particular a hotbed of student activism, fostering generations of Hong Kong's intellectual and political leaders. Hence a closer look at the career trajectories of ex-CUSU presidents can be instructive. Among the fifteen ex-presidents from 2000 to 2015, only one took a pro-Beijing stance, whereas the others either continued to be active in opposition and social movements or stayed away from public engagement altogether. Among the five ex-presidents who took office during the period 2006 to 2010, four later joined opposition parties and embraced activist careers. The resuscitation of student activism clearly encouraged Hong Kong's opposition parties to recruit these younger generation leaders, similar to what Taiwan's DPP politicians had done over the same period. As a former CUSU president explained, "Opposition lawmakers more or less were more willing to trust those who had been involved with student unions" (interview #HK57). Consequently, Hongkonger young movement activists gained bridging networks to political parties and NGOs.

The Role of Social Media

The expansion of Taiwanese and Hongkonger movement networks took place in a period when social media rapidly evolved, resulting a radical reconfiguration of interpersonal relationships. Facebook launched its traditional Chinese platform in June 2008, and soon emerged as the most popular social networking service in both societies. With the addition of the global advent of iPhones in 2007, which marked the beginning of mobile online connection, protest making in the digital era has assumed a new contour.

As Joshua Wong revealed, when Scholarism initiated its campaign against National Education, the first thing he and his youthful associates did was to set up a Facebook fan page (cited from Torne 2014). In fact, Scholarism quickly evolved into a rising star on Hong Kong's protest scene precisely because of its digital technologies savvy. For instance, those who wanted to join the organization could simply sign up by filling in a Google document sheet (Wang 2015: 123). As a result, prior to the Umbrella Movement, a noticeable pattern of "online-based citizen self-mobilization" appeared in Hong Kong (F. Lee 2017: 3). The same observation can equally apply to Taiwan. As noted above, student involvement in the Anti–Media Monopoly Movement started when one of Chen Wei-ting's Facebook posts was threatened with a libel lawsuit by a pro-Beijing media tycoon. Hence it was no surprise that the following student protests relied heavily on social media. Like their Hongkonger counterpart, Youth Alliance against Media Monster campaigners made creative use of Facebook by sending out powerful memes to broader netizens (S. Wong 2016: 173). An episode suffices here to illustrate the progress of digitally enabled activism in pre-Sunflower Taiwan. On August 18, 2013, a rally took place in front of the Presidential Office to protest the Tapu land expropriation, which later evolved into an overnight "Occupy the Ministry of the Interior," arguably a dress rehearsal of the Sunflower Movement seven months later. There I encountered Shih-Jung Hsu, an activist scholar who led the Taiwan Rural Front, the event's main organizer. According to his on-the-spot estimate, the event attracted around ten thousand attendants and 80 percent of them came without being mobilized by the sponsor organization.

As the Internet became more widespread, interactive, and mobile, it was not a surprise that the development of Taiwan's and Hong Kong's activist networks was greatly facilitated by digital technology. Nevertheless, the significance of social media is easily overstated as the most important, if not the deterministic, factor contributing to the surge of protests, which is not supported by a realistic look at what happened in Taiwan and Hong Kong. In both cases, the rise of student activism was accompanied by the proliferation or resuscitation of campus-based organizations as well as the intensification of their face-to-face exchange and collaboration. Due to its advantages in low cost and speed, digital connectivity expedited the growth and thickening of activist networks without replacing offline efforts in organizing.

The use of social media is not a panacea for the problems inherent in collective action, and this understanding was widely shared among Taiwanese and Hongkongers. In preparing to launch their surprise sit-in protests in the Legislative Yuan and Civic Square, Taiwanese and Hongkonger activists deliberately refrained from using mobile phones to recruit participants, because they suspected the online communication was closely monitored by the police. As a matter of fact, OCLP made it a rule that participants in its internal meetings deposit their mobile phones in another room. The precautionary measure incidentally left OCLP leaders unaware of the students' storming of Civic Square on the fateful evening of September 26, 2014, creating initial confusion as the confrontation was about to unfold (interview #HK55). In addition, the progress in cyberspace does not one-sidedly benefit the challengers, since both the government incumbents and their allies can make political use of these digital tools. In Hong Kong, movement leaders' e-mails had been hacked and leaked to the press, and the websites of movement organizations and sympathetic newspapers were also paralyzed by spates of distributed denial of service (DDoS) attacks (L. Tsui 2017). These observations indicate the need for a critical, rather than a celebratory, assessment of social media's role.

Solidarity and Schism

A noticeable contrasting pattern of solidarity and schism existed. While Taiwan's network appeared more concentrated, Hong Kong's was rifted by the insurgency of localists (see Chapter 2), which was triggered by the abrupt outbreak of antimigrant protests in 2011. Amid this explosion, Chin Wan, a professor of Chinese folklore, published a best-selling book, *Hong Kong as a City-State* (*xianggang chengbang lun*), which called for Hongkonger ethnic mobilization to counter Beijing's colonial project, thereby breaking an existing psychological taboo among Hong Kong's opposition politicians and movement and student activists (Chin 2011: 17, 30, 150). According to Chin, Hong Kong was historically a city-state with a distinctive cultural heritage and political tradition so that its separation from China should be maintained. He mounted relentless criticism of opposition politicians for their futile obsession with democratization in China and of movement activists for their adherence to the nonviolence principle. Chin Wan's outspoken iconoclasm made him an extremely polarizing figure, a bête noire for his detractors, but revered as a "nation's mentor" (*guoshi*) by localists.

Representing an insurgent force, localists were not embedded in existing organizations, such as SPDM, CRHF, or HKFS, which have more or less consolidated their status as the spokespersons for Hong Kong's civil society, but rather made their way via the Internet. Since these established organizations were reluctant to address migrant issues, antimigrant mobilization was first initiated on Facebook or the Golden Forum, a popular online chatroom, before the advent of street protests (Chen and Szeto 2015: 438). Anti-tourist campaigns circulated the photos of ill-behaved visitors to visualize the threat of "locusts" from China (Ip 2015: 414). Chin Wan's groundbreaking book originated from a collaborative project by a number of Facebook supporters (Chin 2011: 17). The localist Civic Passion operated many new media outlets to mobilize its supporters. In other words, Hong Kong's movement networks were split with the emergence of online mobilization by localists, which represented a cautionary reminder that digital media did not always facilitate the connections among like-minded persons.

Evidently, the conflict between these two movement streams was worsening over the years. Chin Wan openly encouraged his followers to launch assaults on opposition parties and HKFS, because they were deemed as "traitors" who stood in the way of a genuine Hongkonger resistance against Beijing (interview #HK30). Localists grew more distrustful of the existing political and movement leadership. In spite of the fact that the SAR government decided to put off the National Education plan, localists maintained that the campaign was a failure because the controversial curriculum could still be adopted by individual schools. In the Hong Kong Television incident of October 2013, Civic Passion followers exposed two movement participants as affiliated members of Left 21, and called the campaign failure a deliberate act of sabotage. A spate of ad hominem threats ensued. An HKU student's personal information was revealed on the Internet, which invited anonymous harassment and verbal abuse from localists. Traumatized, she was afraid to attend class for a week (interview #HK37). The eruption of such excessive vigilantism demonstrated the widening gap between the two movement networks in Hong Kong.

In hindsight, Hong Kong's existing politicians and movement leaders appeared reluctant to look at the China factor. For example, on the problem of parents experiencing difficulties in securing a place in public kindergartens or primary schools for their children due to the influx of children of Chinese parents, a typical response was to blame the government for its fiscal retrenchment that had reduced school capacity. Yet, this argument simply looked away from the main issue, as babies born to Chinese mothers soared to nearly half of the total (46.1 percent) in 2012 (Lui 2015a: 404). Such a sectarian inability to address the ethnic and border issues was best exemplified by the controversy surrounding a protest advertisement placed in Taiwan's independence-leaning *Liberty Times* in September 2013. The "Open Letter to the Taiwanese Government and Taiwanese" stated that Hong Kong was under the severe stress of migrants and tourists from China and urged the SAR government to play a more assertive gatekeeping role to avoid becoming "communistic" (*chihua*). However, some movement activists criticized the effort as discriminatory, a move that was strangely lauded by pro-Beijing newspapers.[10] True, the initial explosion of the localist tendency appeared quite similar to populist xenophobia; it was due to the dogmatic rigidity of existing movement leaders who failed to address the growing frictions of Hong Kong–China relations that left a discursive space for the demagogues wide open.

Taiwan's movement network was largely free from such intramural conflicts. Nevertheless, before the resurgence of student movements in 2008, a narrow and sectarian mentality was prevalent in the small circle of student activists. A participant in this period described their dominant outlook as viewing both the KMT and the DPP as hopelessly rightwing parties, with the latter probably worse because its pursuit of political independence was at its core a populist mobilization (interview #TW50). The relationship between Lo-Sheng student activists and the DPP, for instance, remained troubled from the beginning (Cole 2015: 32–38).

In Taiwan's expanding post-2008 movement network, this sectarian tendency was swiftly marginalized. During the Wild Strawberry Movement, some participants insisted that McDonald's food should not be allowed in the sit-in area as a gesture of anti–American imperialism. Such an outlandish suggestion was not able to win the support of student participants. In the Anti–Media Monopoly Movement four years later, the ideological insistence on opposing all corporate ownership of media regardless whether their owners were pro-Beijing or not was practically sidelined by the student leadership's decision to highlight the harms of Beijing's interference (interview #TW60). A Sunflower Movement leader later acknowledged the gap between those student activists who were concerned about social justice issues and those who were more committed to political independence; nevertheless, he characterized the divide as "minor" and "more about personal issues than the difference in principles" (interview #TW57).

While Hong Kong's movement network was fractured by an ever-widening ideological cleavage, Taiwan's was relatively free of sectarian infighting. The different network configurations generated a profound impact during the two eventful protests, partly explaining why the Sunflower Movement was able to proceed under a more unified and effective leadership, a difficult achievement that was denied to the Umbrella Movement (see Chapter 5).

Taiwan–Hong Kong Nexus

A transborder movement network linking Taiwanese and Hongkonger activists came into existence during the fermenting years. What has been identified as a "transnational social movement network" that facilitated mutual sharing of information, strategies, and identities in different areas was already present (Flesher Fominaya 2014b: 39). The makings of this transborder linkage emerged as a result of the synchronized surge in protest activities as well as the more intrusive presence of Beijing in the two societies.

In the past, civil-society connections between Taiwan and Hong Kong had been intermittent, episodic, and issue-specific in spite of the lack of linguistic barrier. There had been regular exchanges between the opposition parties in the 1990s, but this came to an abrupt end when Taiwan's DPP came to power in 2000, as Hong Kong's opposition politicians shied away from contact to avoid being labeled as unpatriotic. In the early 2000s, independent labor unionists on both sides maintained regular exchanges, as Taiwan's TCTU activists were in constant contact with Hong Kong's Confederation of Trade Unions counterparts (interview #HK66). The Hand-in-Hand rally to protect the Victoria Harbor in March 2004 appeared to have been inspired by a similar campaign rally for Chen Shui-bian's reelection on February 28 in the same year (H. Hung 2011: 116). During the 2005 anti-WTO protests in Hong Kong, some Taiwanese participants were inspired by Korean farmers' "bitter-march" tactics, so they imported this peculiar approach for the Lo-Sheng Sanatorium preservation campaign. There were some exchange activities involving Hong Kong's pier preservation activists and Taiwan's Lo-Sheng activists. In building a new settlement for the displaced Choi Yuen villagers, some Taiwanese professionals in participatory planning were invited to contribute their expertise (interview #HK4-3).

The problems with the absence of more substantial civil-society exchanges were acutely felt in September 2012, when both Taiwanese and Hongkonger students were simultaneously leading large-scale protests against Beijing's interference. Taiwan's Anti–Media Monopoly Movement was opposing the merger bid of an avowedly pro-Beijing media tycoon, whereas Hong Kong's anti–National Education campaign resisted ideological indoctrination in schools. Given the highly analogous nature of the two movements, the lack of mutual understanding, let alone support, became particularly conspicuous. A Scholarism activist recalled that they were aware of the existence of a similar protest in Taiwan without really discussing it seriously (interview #HK46). Joshua Wong acknowledged that he did not know any Taiwanese counterparts at the time (interview #HK24-2). Taiwanese student activists admired the way their Hongkonger counterparts were able to lead a rally with thousands of participants, without the ability to know them personally. Face-to-face encounters took place later, after the climax of the two movements, as a group of Hong Kong student activists came to visit Taiwan and had a fruitful exchange with their local partners (interview #TW61).

The organization-based network started with the official launch of the New School for Democracy (*huaren minzhu shuyuan*) in May 2011, a tripartite collaboration involving overseas Chinese dissidents, Hong Kong activists, and Taiwan intellectuals. The idea of an institutional exchange platform originated from the needs of Hong Kong's opposition parties and movement activists, as they were pressured by the insurgent localists (interview #TW33).

Although the educational activities of the New School for Democracy failed to penetrate China, it succeeded in establishing a nexus between Taiwanese and Hongkonger activists. In a two-day workshop in January 2014, around twenty Hong Kong activists, including three legislative council members, traveled to Taiwan to meet their counterparts. It was due to these bridging efforts that the gestures of mutual solidarity emerged. On the eve of the July First demonstration in 2013, a group of Taiwanese showed their support via the Internet.[11] When the Sunflower Movement broke out, many Hongkonger activists stayed awake all night to watch the online broadcast, and some took a trip to Taiwan to witness the ongoing occupy movement (interview #HK38). After the conclusion of the Sunflower Movement, many Taiwanese activists flew to Hong Kong to take part in the July First rally of 2014, although some of the well-known leaders were denied entry at the airport. Minutes before Hongkonger students launched the surprise sit-in at Civic Square on the evening of September 26, Joshua Wong was speaking after the screening of a prerecorded video speech by Lin Fei-fan, who had become a persona non grata in Hong Kong. Clearly, the appearance of a Taiwan–Hong Kong nexus facilitated cross-fertilization, giving impetus to the two eventful protests in 2014. Valerie Bunce (2016) identifies demonstration effects and networks as the two main drivers of international diffusion of protests. Here, the emergence of Taiwan–Hong Kong connections emboldened movement activists in both places to launch more disruptive actions.

Conclusion

In her study of the Polish opposition in the 1980s, Maryjane Osa contended that the Solidarity Movement came about as a result of movement network expansion in the preceding decade spanning across intellectuals, the church, workers, and nationalists (2003: 154–168). The same observation is applicable to Taiwan and Hong Kong, as waves of youth revolts brought about increasingly dense connections among students, NGOs, and opposition parties over the years. Taiwanese and Hongkongers who were born in the 1980s enjoyed better material conditions and enlarged access to higher education; however, upon their graduation, they began to experience the economic pain of lack of opportunities, skyrocketing housing prices, and stagnant wages. The quest for social justice and a generational rebellion against paternalism were the driving motives for young people to take part in protests. Their participation brought about bolder and more connected civil societies that were capable of launching large-scale antiregime protests.

Therefore, it is not entirely accurate to describe the Sunflower Movement and the Umbrella Movement as originating from the spontaneous reactions of previously uninvolved citizens, because a group of core activists had been schooled and nurtured in a widening movement community. The two eventful protests might appear to have been unexpected to inattentive observers, but for those who were deeply involved in movement circles, in hindsight such a large-scale confrontation seemed inevitable, as both civil societies were becoming more contentious even as they became more connected, both internally and externally.

4

Opportunities, Threat, and Standoff in Taiwan

For the sake of narrative fluidity, this chapter analyzes the genesis and development of Taiwan's Sunflower Movement and Chapter 5 covers the genesis and development of Hong Kong's Umbrella Movement. A comparison of these two eventful protests and theoretical reflections is also included in the following chapter. Before the story begins, I discuss here the concepts of political opportunities, threat, and standoff.

Political Opportunities and Threats

The Sunflower Movement opposed further economic integration with China, while the Umbrella Movement demanded bona fide suffrage for the election of top leadership; both represented a collective challenge to the incumbents' core agendas, thus the fate of two movements was intimately related to a plethora of political factors. Was each movement able to gain support from political allies? Did the government enjoy a solid standing that enabled it to withstand the rising waves of protest? Under what conditions were the incumbents more likely to concede to the demonstrators' demands?

Researchers have conventionally analyzed the relationships between social movements and the state with the POS concept, or "the features of

This chapter was adapted from Ming-sho Ho, "Occupy Congress in Taiwan: Political Opportunity, Threat, and the Sunflower Movement," *Journal of East Asian Studies* 15, no. 101 (2015): 69–97.

regimes and institutions that facilitate or inhibit a political actor's collective action to changes in those features" (Tilly and Tarrow 2007: 49). According to this perspective, the movement's trajectory is commonly seen as a function of a POS whose expansion encourages movement growth and contraction brings about its decline (McAdam 1982; Meyer 1990; Tarrow 1989). Related, but clearly distinct, is the concept of "threat." While the POS enables the emergence of protest activism because its cost is reduced or the likelihood of success is enhanced, threat operates as an independent variable; it stimulates movement participation because of a sudden rise in the cost of inaction. As defined by Jack Goldstone and Charles Tilly, threat is best seen as "the cost it [a social group] expects to suffer if it does not take action" (2001: 183). Studies have found that, particularly for high-risk activism, the perception of the immediate and lethal threat brought about strong motivation for participation (Einwohner 2003; Maher 2010). Protest activism can possibly emerge when there is an acute spike in the threat level while the POS remains largely the same.

More theoretical discussion on POS is needed here, as there has been an ongoing debate over the analytical validity of the concept. A number of criticisms have surfaced as the POS approach has become arguably the dominant framework in analyzing the interactions of social movements and the state. It is argued that the POS theory assumes a "structural bias" that leads to underestimation of the agents' subjective capacity to perceive and seize opportunities (Goodwin and Jasper 1999; Jasper 2012; Kurzman 1996). There are studies that disconfirm the pro-movement effect of POS expansion; instead, they contend there is radical indeterminacy between POS and movement dynamics (Goodwin 2001; Rucht 1996). Skeptics are gaining the upper hand in these discussions, in that more and more students of social movements are suggesting shelving the term POS for other alternatives, such as "relational field" (Goldstone 2004), "political context" (Amenta and Halfmann 2012), and the "political reform model" (Amenta, Caren, and Stobaugh 2012). All of these suggestions attempt to provide a less rigid and less deterministic framework that allows more space for agency.

Central to the POS theory is the recognition that changes in political institutions affect social protests by lowering or raising the cost of collective action and that these state-related variables lie beyond the control of movement activists. It is possible to retain this core insight without incurring the risks of excessive structuralism or determinism, as long as we adopt the following revisions in conceptualization. First, there is a clear need for analytical distinction between political opportunities as ex ante conditions and how these opportunities are subsequently changed. It is erroneous to treat POS purely as a prediction variable to the outcome of social protests, because doing so fails to take into consideration that the onset of movement mobilization brings about interaction or mediation with the preexisting political conditions (Amenta, Halfmann, and Young 1999; Kriesi 2004). As such, Chapters 4 and 5 limit discussion on political opportunities to the conditions immediately surrounding the explosion of two protests, paying attention to how these conditions are subsequently remade due to the interaction with protest activism. Second, movement strategy matters and needs to be brought back into the analysis. An uncritical application of the POS perspective easily results in a biased view of "opportunistic protesters," implying that social movements are passively waiting for favorable political winds, and that is, of course, not tenable (Goodwin 2012). Instead, we need to pay attention to how social movements actively make, rather than just take, political opportunities by deploying certain strategies (M. Ho 2016). Third, there is a patent lack of consensus on what makes up a POS; conceptualizing a consistent list of its components (McAdam 1996: 27; Tarrow 1996: 54–56; Tarrow 2011: 164–165; Tilly and Tarrow 2007: 57) is not possible. Therefore, it is better to customize the analysis on political opportunities according to the social movements in question rather than to start out with a preconceived list of POS components. And in view of the fact that there is variation in how different aspects of a POS form a consistent pattern, in my subsequent writing I use "political opportunities" rather than "POS." Last, the addition of the threat concept, defined as the cost of "inaction" not action, sensitizes us to the pro-movement effect brought about by a "transformative event" (McAdam and Sewell 2001: 101–102) that exerts independent causal power. Threat involves the "power of negative thinking" (Jasper 2014: 104); in other words, the expectation of a worst scenario might encourage protest participation.

"Movement-and-Government Standoffs"

A standoff represents an unusual episode of contentious politics when movement activists (1) are capable of extracting the focal attention of incumbents with their disruptive acts, (2) generate protracted bargaining with the latter, and finally, (3) create the possibility for a high-risk outcome that either endangers the security of the ruling elites or incurs the risk of severe sanctions for the initiators.

Standoffs involve sustained confrontations between the protesters, who occupy urban public spaces and disrupt the normal functioning of political institutions, and the embattled authorities, who are ready to deploy force to restore order. Rather akin to the revolutionary situation, which Vladimir Lenin famously defined as the moment when the ruling class cannot maintain the old way and the suppressed people no longer want it, movement-government standoffs represent the rare occasions when movement participants are sufficiently emboldened to openly disobey the law, yet not powerful enough to change the will of government leaders. A delicate and momentary balance of forces arises, a tense period of suspense before the situation slides toward the final showdown.

Standoffs are justifiably well-covered headline news stories because of the high stakes involved for the conflicting parties. Movement organizers face harsh reprisals if they fail (such as with the 1989 Tiananmen Movement in Beijing), and government incumbents risk losing power in the case of regime shift (such as with the 2011 Tahrir Revolution in Egypt). In 2014, antigovernment mobilization in Thailand plunged the nation into an acute crisis, paving the way for a coup d'état by the armed forces, while Ukraine's Euromaidan protest gave rise to social unrest, civil war, and foreign territorial annexation.

Social movement studies conventionally focus on two main research topics: the movement's genesis and its impact. Movement versus government standoffs offer unique opportunities to observe the link between mobilization and its immediate outcome. Most movement activists take years or decades to achieve some significant results that observers can confidently identify as "successes," while exceptional movements unexpectedly step into an acute confrontation with the authorities with only days or weeks passing before their finale. Telescoped into a shorter observation period, we can more easily identify the logic of an "iterative strategic dance" (Fligstein and McAdam 2012: 84) between movement activists and government officials. The cycle of tactical innovation from below and the ensuing neutralizing adaptation from above, as identified by Doug McAdam (1983), can be closely observed. Standoffs represent an archetypal contingency situation, constituting a fundamental aspect of our action (Wagner-Pacifici 2000). As Francesco Alberoni (1984) points out, social movements represent a precarious intermediate status between "the nascent state" and "the everyday-institutional state" because their emergence signifies a creative force for change, but their goal is to make the change permanent. Seen in this way, standoffs exemplify the transitional characteristics of social movements, a particular observation niche for researchers. This chapter and the chapter that follows indicate that standoffs constitute a situation sui generis for which prior planning and preparedness tend to be of little use.

Opposing Cross-Strait Economic Integration

Taiwan's Sunflower Movement originated from the resistance to growing cross-strait economic integration, which witnessed an evolution from political parties to NGOs, and finally to students, as well as a concomitant shift to more radical protests.[1]

The second term of Chen Shui-bian's presidency (2004–2008) saw a more restrictive policy turn on cross-strait economic exchange. In the presidential election of 2008, DPP candidate Frank Hsieh opposed the KMT's proposal of intensifying cross-strait economic integration. He maintained that Taiwanese would suffer under a "one-China market," resulting in a miserable situation in which "men cannot find a job, women cannot find a husband, and the children will have to go to Heilongjiang (China's northeastern province) (*tsa-poo tsau bo kang, tsa-boo tsau bo ang, gin-a ai khi holiongkang*) (in Taiwanese)." After its dismal electoral performance in the 2008 election, the DPP continued in its skepticism over the growing cross-strait economic relationship, as evidenced in its opposition to the ECFA signed in June 2010. The DPP demanded a referendum on this trade agreement and its chairperson, Tsai Ing-wen, engaged in a televised debate with Ma Ying-jeou (S. Lin 2016: 181–182). After the ECFA was approved by lawmakers and went into effect in 2011, the DPP appeared to have mollified its opposition. When Tsai ran for president in 2012, she promised to uphold all signed cross-strait agreements, including the ECFA.

The DPP's defeat in the presidential election in January 2012 resulted in a new round of policy reorientation, particularly because the KMT was able to obtain endorsements from business leaders for its adherence to the 1992 consensus at the eleventh hour of the campaign. In its official reflection report on the defeat, the DPP noticed that the China factor had emerged as an economic issue to create a sense of dependence among voters. As such, the DPP needed to promote a new approach to cross-strait politics to shed the stereotypical "anti-China" (*fanzhong*) and "isolationist" (*suoguo*) image.[2] Some DPP politicians apparently thought they needed to do more than change the perceived image; otherwise, they might never have the chance to come to power again. Frank Hsieh, who had previously opposed economic integration during his presidential campaign in 2008, led an effort to build rapprochement with China. Hsieh maintained that the one-China principle was still enshrined in Taiwan's existing Republic of China constitution and thus should be the guiding principle of the DPP's cross-strait policy. He was invited for a trip to China in October 2012, a historical ice-breaking visit that promised to open the door for reconciliation between the DPP and Beijing. Afterward, there were voices calling for abolishing the Taiwan independence clause enshrined in the party charter in 1991 as a goodwill gesture.

When the signing of the CSSTA was announced in June 2013, Hsieh was attending a meeting with Chinese officials in Hong Kong and the media reported that he fully supported this economic bonus, although he later claimed the journalists had misrepresented his views.[3] The DPP did not oppose the CSSTA initially and, in fact, some of its leaders in the legislature showed their willingness to negotiate with the ruling party, which indicated their conditional acceptance of the free-trade deal with China (interview #TW32). DPP chairperson Su Tseng-chang had originally obtained Ma's agreement for a debate on the CSSTA, scheduled for mid-September, but that event was canceled at the last minute. The DPP decided not to talk to Ma because his support rating had dropped to a historic low because of internal strife in the KMT (see below). There was suspicion that the debate proposal from the DPP had been no more than a pro-forma gesture to placate pro-independence supporters, just as had been done concerning the ECFA dispute. In the cross-strait policy report released in January 2014, the DPP's official stance on economic agreements with China was that they should conform to "the international norms of reciprocity and transparency" and "mitigate the disadvantages faced by Taiwan's enterprises" (Democratic Progressive Party 2014: 35), seemingly implying that the party was prepared to support the CSSTA as long as these conditions were met.

On March 13, five days before the occupation of the legislature, the DPP publicized an opinion poll that revealed that around 41 percent of respondents were dissatisfied with the party's anti-China stance.[4] Why did the DPP leadership decide to release such information right at the moment when the legislature was about to process the CSSTA? It was widely surmised to be a symbolic gesture indicating the DPP's readiness to revise its cross-strait policy. Hence, student activists were highly critical of the DPP's "equivocal" stance on this issue prior to the occupation of the legislature.[5]

From NGOs to Students

While the KMT government mobilized a vigorous promotional effort for the ECFA in 2010, it chose to operate with shrouded secrecy for the CSSTA, one of the ECFA's follow-up agreements to liberalize bilateral trade in service sectors. Taiwanese came to know about the imminent and extensive liberalization only a few days before the official signing was to take place on June 21, 2013. The details of the sixty-four service industry categories that would be opened to Chinese investment and manpower were announced only after the treaty was finalized. Hao Ming-i, a staunch supporter of Ma Ying-jeou and a leading publisher, initiated the opposition to the CSSTA. According to Hao, allowing Chinese investment in Taiwan's printing industry without simultaneously asking China to lift censorship on published books from Taiwan would wreak havoc on Taiwan's publishing trade. He gave up his position as presidential advisor to protest the neglect of national security and violation of democracy. Artists, medical professionals, social workers, and hairdressing and cosmetic workers began to voice their concerns over the CSSTA.

The summer of 2013 witnessed brewing opposition to cross-strait economic liberalization. A coalition of NGOs on labor, gender, environmental welfare, and human rights issues, the Democratic Front against Cross-Strait Service Trade Agreement (DF), came into being on July 28, 2013, and was coordinated by activist lawyer Lai Chung-chiang. Lai had been working hard to increase the attention of civil-society organizations regarding cross-strait issues since 2010. The DF argued for more oversight and transparency over cross-strait negotiations and the protection of the livelihoods of those at the grassroots level. Moreover, it insisted that the medical and welfare sectors should not be commercialized and that Chinese investment in some industries with national security concerns should be prohibited. It was due to Lai's successful framing that the public came to view the CSSTA as a "black box" (*heixiang*) process in which public oversight had been minimal—a damaging criticism that the KMT incumbents found hard to shake off.

While the DF represented the more established wing of Taiwan's civil society, student protesters joined the foray with an attempt to break into the legislature on July 31. Afterward, they set up the Black Island Nation Youth Front (BIY), a group that later launched several disruptive rallies at the Presidential Office, the legislature, and the airport (to protest the visit of Chen Deming, the president of China's Association for Relations across the Taiwan Straits). A division of labor arose in that the DF's academics and NGO leaders were responsible for formulating the anti-CSSTA discourses, while students took care of direct actions.

The opposition movement persuaded the national legislature to collect more information before initiating the review of the CSSTA. From July 2013 to March 2014, twenty public hearings were held. There was intensive use of legislative tactics by both camps. The KMT attempted to expedite the process by hastily holding three public hearing sessions within eight days, while the DPP cautiously navigated between the pressure from the anti-CSSTA camp and its revisionist intent to avoid anti-China charges by chairing a public hearing regularly every two weeks. The final public hearing ended on March 10, and the CSSTA was then ready to be processed by the internal administration committee of the legislature. A DPP lawmaker was scheduled to preside over the committee on March 12, but the KMT did not accept the idea that the opposition party could set the agenda on the CSSTA's second reading. So the bill was delayed for one week until KMT lawmaker Chang Ching-chung became the rotating chair of that committee. In anticipation of a showdown, the DF launched a campaign called "120 Hours of Action Defending Democracy" (*hanwei minzhu yibai ershi xiaoshi xindong*) with five days of mass rallies, press conferences, and mobilization of students from central and southern Taiwan. A DF leader estimated that the KMT lawmakers could have probably taken action on March 19 (Wednesday) (interview #TW31-1); however, they turned out to be more hawkish than expected.

On the afternoon of March 17 (Monday), Chang Ching-chung attempted to mount the podium but without success, blockaded by the DPP lawmakers. Instead, he used a private microphone to announce that the second reading of the CSSTA was finished and ready for plenary review. In thirty seconds,

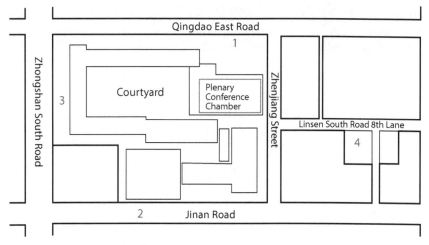

Figure 4.1. Taiwan's Legislative Yuan.

Chang formally concluded the session, leaving the DPP legislators and reporters bewildered. The KMT's parliamentary tactics amounted to a flagrant violation of the agreement to review and vote on the CSSTA on an article-by-article basis (hence the so-called 30-second Incident), thereby sowing the seeds for the student occupation.

On the evening of March 18, the DF and BIY staged a mass rally outside the Legislative Yuan as a planned event in their five-day campaign. At 9:00 P.M., protesters suddenly agitated in an attempt to storm the compound from three directions. Around fifty protesters were successful in climbing the premise's walls on Qingdao East Road (no. 1 in Figure 4.1) because policemen were caught off guard by diversionary tactics on Jinan Road and Zhongshan South Road (nos. 2 and 3 in Figure 4.1). The intruders gathered in the courtyard and shouted slogans for a while and then broke into the plenary conference chamber. The number of occupiers inside quickly swelled to around two hundred and they decided to hold their ground by erecting makeshift barricades and setting up a leadership core (interview #TW14). The news of occupying the legislature was immediately broadcast via the Internet, attracting supporters to the area. By midnight, around two thousand people had gathered on Qingdao East Road and Jinan Road to demonstrate their solidarity, effectively encircling the policemen who were attempting to pull the protesters out of the legislative building. Bottled water, food, first-aid, medicine, and other materials were quickly sent inside by supporters to sustain a potentially prolonged protest. By the early morning hours of March 19, as the protesters secured their occupation, the Sunflower Movement had emerged.

An Analysis of Political Opportunities

In the following section I look at three political opportunities (regime orientation, stability of elite alignment, and political allies) at the moment when the Sunflower Movement burst onto the scene, as well as their further evolution.

Regime Orientation

Ma Ying-jeou indicated his impatience with the slow progress of the legislative review of the CSSTA, which made up his core agenda in pursuing cross-strait rapprochement. In his New Year announcement of 2014, Ma sternly warned that the delay had "raised the concerns of our trade partners" so that they might become reluctant to sign free-trade agreements or increase investment in Taiwan.[6] Clearly, the KMT lawmakers had decided to railroad the CSSTA through the legislative review in response to demands from the top to speed things up.

Taiwanese activists were justifiably pessimistic about movement success. After all the public hearings on CSSTA were finished, the opponents felt that they had exhausted all the procedural possibilities for delaying its passage. In an emergency meeting after the KMT lawmakers forced its second reading on March 17, a participant revealed the pervasive sense of defeatism:

> The meeting proceeded in a delicate atmosphere because everyone felt pessimistic. After Chang Ching-chung's push through, it appeared that we were running out of means to stop the CSSTA. . . . Someone suggested we should launch a drastic protest, but such a proposal was opposed by some NGO representatives. (Interview #TW58)

Taiwanese activists were knowingly fighting an increasingly uphill battle as the KMT government had hardened its determination, and the chances for a concession were swiftly vanishing.

Stability of Elite Alignment

Disunity among the ruling elites has offered potential leverage to challengers because it has prevented the government from formulating and executing a consistent response. Such a political opportunity was more or less present in Taiwan.

After Ma Ying-jeou won his reelection bid in January 2012, his approval rating declined amid the emergence of intraparty competition for succession. With the growing waves of antinuclear protests, Taipei City Mayor Hau

Lung-pin and New Taipei City Mayor Chu Li-luan, two potential successors to Ma's presidency, had indicated their opposition to the disputed Fourth Nuclear Power Plant (FNPP), departing from the KMT's traditional pronuclear stance (M. Ho 2014a: 979). Aside from the rivalry over succession, the disunion was dramatized in Ma Ying-jeou's ill-fated attempt to sack Wang Jin-pyng, speaker of the Legislative Yuan, in September 2013. Ma cited a transcript of a wiretapped telephone conversation as evidence that Wang had meddled with the judiciary process involving a prominent DPP legislative leader. After firing the director of the High Prosecutors' Office and the minister of justice, Ma ordered the KMT to revoke Wang's party membership immediately, a move that would eventually lead to Wang being disqualified to serve as lawmaker and legislative speaker. Wang mounted an energetic fight in response by keeping his political position through legal action, gaining the support of other KMT heavyweights and popular sympathy. Nasty infighting within the ruling party fatally damaged Ma's support rating, which polls showed had plummeted to 9.2 percent.

The ruling party's disunion widened as the Sunflower Movement emerged. How Wang Jin-pyng decided to react to the student-led occupation in its first few hours was the key to the movement's survival because police action within the legislative building needed his consent, legally as well as politically. According to a DPP source, Wang initially ordered the police to evacuate the intruders, but later he adopted a neutral position by not allowing more police reinforcements at 4:00 A.M. on March 19 (interview #TW4). Why did Wang appear to be accommodating to the radical act of seizing the legislature given that there was no evidence of his opposition to the CSSTA? First, with Wang Jin-pyng's embittered relationship with Ma Ying-jeou, he certainly had no political reasons to thwart a movement protesting Ma's core agenda. Moreover, the result of the first trial over Wang's party membership was to be announced on the afternoon of March 19, less than twenty-four hours after the occupation took place. It happened that, if Wang lost the case, he would be immediately deprived of his party membership and the legislative leadership. There was no incentive for Wang to assume a hardliner position, since that would have risked his personal reputation and position, and helped his political enemy. In addition, in the first few days, both Hau Lung-pin[7] and Chu Li-luan[8] made conciliatory remarks about the Sunflower Movement and urged the central government to exercise more tolerance.

Political Allies

In the subsequent unfolding of the Sunflower Movement, opposition parties stood firmly behind the student leadership by providing their manpower and resources. But this situation had not been expected before the rise of the mass protest. In 2014, Taiwan's opposition parties, including the DPP (40 seats) and the pro-independence Taiwan Solidarity Union (TSU) (3 seats), were the minority in the Legislative Yuan (113 seats). The opposition bloc would certainly lose in a vote on CSSTA; yet the problem was not their numerical inferiority but that the opposition did not fully endorse the movement demand.

The DPP was in the process of adjusting its cross-strait policy by keeping its distance from the anti-CSSTA movement. Only the TSU vocally opposed the free-trade bill; however, its three seats could not make much difference if the bill were put to a vote. As pointed out above, the post-2012 DPP was exploring a more conciliatory approach toward Beijing and, as such, regarding the CSSTA its official stance was to call for an article-by-article review, implying that the DPP would not oppose the agreement as long as it was processed following due procedure. Before Hao Ming-i initiated his personal opposition, he had met the top party leaders but apparently failed to secure their endorsement (interview #TW3). Tuan Yi-kang, one DPP legislative leader, revealed the dilemma of his party:

> We knew the CSSTA was a double-edged sword. The DPP was in no position to oppose Taiwan's service industry's investment in China, but any trade opening would affect some industries in a small market like Taiwan. Therefore, the party leaders wanted to delay it and at the same time they also worried about the "anti-China" label. That was the reason why the DPP attempted to present a reasonable, well-balanced, and cautious attitude in dealing with economic relations with China. The DPP intended to focus on some problems of the CSSTA, but not outright reject it. As such, we only raised questions on technical details. (Interview #TW8)

Previously, Tuan estimated that the CSSTA could have easily finished legislative review before June 2014. Due to these considerations, the DPP maintained an ambivalent stance toward the anti-CSSTA movement until the "30-second Incident" on March 17. The KMT lawmakers' unexpected hawkish parliamentary tactic deprived the opposition parties room for negotiation. Three DPP legislators launched a hunger strike the following afternoon; however, their action was immediately eclipsed by the student-led break-in and sit-in several hours later. Without the 30-second Incident, it would have been unlikely that the anti-CSSTA activists would have had the determination to launch such a high-risk act as occupying the legislature, let alone enjoyed such subsequent popular support.

There was an absence of an unambiguously conducive political environment to encourage the eventful protest to take place in Taiwan. The only favorable political opportunity, the KMT's disunity, arguably existed only as a potential, and its activation needed the intervention of movement activism. Anti-CSSTA activists had originally planned to stage a sit-in in front of the Presidential Office in an emergency meeting on the evening of March 17. However, in the afternoon of the following day, they decided to change the plan by shifting the target to the Legislative Yuan (interview #TW39). Had the protesters proceeded with the earlier plan, the rivalry between Ma Ying-jeou and Wang Jin-pyng could not have offered political leverage for them, since there would have been little reason for Wang to intervene in this dispute.

Threat-Induced Mobilization

While existing political opportunities did not offer encouraging signals, threat suddenly surged as an effective force to encourage mass participation in unusual protest. As noted above, threat is better conceptualized as the cost of inaction, rather than action, as the latter should be understood as a negative political opportunity. It follows that protest mobilization is likely to emerge when participants become keenly aware of the urgency to take action before it becomes too late.

There were already a sizeable number of Taiwanese who held a negative view of closer economic ties with China, but few of them were actually involved in protest activities. According to the Taiwan Social Change Survey conducted in late 2013, skepticism over cross-strait economic integration was prevalent: 73.7 percent and 53.9 percent of respondents held negative attitudes toward "mainland Chinese working in Taiwan" and "Taiwanese going to mainland China for investment or work," respectively (Fu et al. 2014: 230–231). Taiwanese people appeared to be concerned about the political consequences of tightened economic relations, as the government's promotion of the CSSTA mostly stressed the economic benefits of the deal without reassuring the public about anxieties over losing political autonomy. Respondents were asked which conditions would contribute to a rise in popular support for peaceful unification. In declining order, there were 54.5 percent who chose "closer economic ties with mainland China," 44.2 percent "the rising international status and influence of the mainland Chinese government," 15.3 percent "mainland China's refusal to recognize the sovereignty of the Republic of China," and, finally, 7 percent "the communist one-party rule of mainland China" (Fu et al. 2014: 210–211). Clearly, there was a profound sense of uneasiness among Taiwanese people.

Thus the 30-second Incident served as a threat that facilitated movement participation. The KMT lawmakers' controversial maneuver actually substantiated the accusation that the CSSTA was an undemocratic black box. That Taiwan's democratic procedure suffered collateral damage in the effort to promote closer cross-strait economic integration lent credibility to the claims of anti-CSSTA activists. It made it possible to tap into a latent segment of the population who were worried about the economic and political consequences of the deal, but had remained detached from the controversy. Prior to that, opponents were struggling to raise more public awareness, as the DF was initiating a book-writing project and the BIY was planning a nationwide campus forum in order to highlight the perils of free trade with China. As such, one of the student leaders later jokingly acknowledged that they should write a thank-you note to Chang Ching-chung for bringing the national spotlight to the CSSTA issue.[9]

Once the protesters successfully broke into the legislature, a sense of urgency emerged to protect the occupiers, who appeared vulnerable to police action. It was clear that the more people there were gathering outside, the more difficult it would be for the police to evict the protesters. Therefore, students in central and southern Taiwan immediately mobilized the busing of volunteers on the hectic night of March 18. A student activist in Taichung City, around 150 kilometers from the epicenter of Taipei's legislature, noted:

> Our school's movement club was emotionally agitated. What Chang Ching-chung had done in thirty seconds was an irreversible CSSTA. It was akin to resistance to a forcible demolition, except the CSSTA affected everyone, not just a few residents. In my school, there were so many students who wanted to join the protest, but they could not find access. On my Facebook page, many unknown people wrote to me, asking how to join the movement. (Interview #TW23)

Clearly, the vulnerable fate of the occupiers in the plenary conference chamber of the legislature besieged by the police represented a symbol of resistance as well as a wake-up call for further mobilization.

Initiating the Standoff

As noted above, a standoff represents the rare moment when protesters have won mass sympathy and forced the government incumbents to tolerate their illegal behaviors. The campaign to oppose economic integration with China would not have grabbed national attention had protesters not occupied the legislature in the first place. Yet, a standoff emerged from a number of protesters' on-the-spot and swift responses.

The fateful decision by Taiwanese students to storm the legislature was finalized only a few hours before it took place. The contingent of protesters who spearheaded the break-in were recruited on the scene and the division of tasks, such as blocking policemen, carrying protest banners, and so on was arranged at the last minute (interview #TW51). When the students forced their way into the legislature, they had no intention of undertaking a sustained occupation; rather, they were seeking a highly dramatic sit-in that they expected to be terminated quickly by the police. As a student participant noted:

> I thought we would soon be pulled out, because we had tried to intrude on the legislature before. But this time was easier than expected. I was coming from the side of Qingdao East Road, and someone smashed the glass door to let everyone enter the building. We did not know why the plenary conference chamber was not locked. I was among the first wave of protesters to go inside. It was all darkness in the beginning. I immediately began to move chairs to barricade the main entrance, which was not planned, but out of a natural instinct in the hope that policemen would not be able to come in. Actually, the original plan was simply to unfurl our protest banners inside and wait for the police. (Interview #TW46)

The quick swelling of the crowd of protesters led to an instant change in the objective: preparation for a longer occupation. The sit-in participants' swift tactical decision was echoed by the equally fast responses from participants outside of the building. Some of them found other avenues to enter the building, while others were responding to the change in their own ways. According to an NGO worker:

> We only knew that students were planning for a break-in just one hour before. At that time, we were on Jinan Road, blocking police reinforcements. It was a chaotic situation.... [W]e [the NGO workers] immediately chipped in money and bought up all the bottled water, cookies, and medical stuff at the 7-Eleven convenience store on Qingdao East Road. (Interview #TW9)

Outside participants immediately knew that a sustained confrontation needed logistical support; many of them voluntarily contributed to purchasing and delivering materials for the protesters inside. For example, students from the NTU College of Medicine, located just two blocks away, instantly brought first-aid kits upon hearing that some protesters were injured (interview #TW17). As I entered the occupied plenary conference chamber around 11:00 P.M., two hours after the students had initiated the protest, piles of bottled water, food, and sleeping bags had already been sent in. Some protesters were munching on fresh, hot fried chicken fillets, the most popular nighttime snack among Taiwanese students. Based on the preexisting movement networks, a decision-making nucleus had been set up. I was present at its emergency meeting at around 1:00 A.M. on March 19. Lin Fei-fan brought an urgent message from a friendly professor to the effect that policemen would soon take back the occupied chamber by force, but they were willing to wait for a voluntary withdrawal. The students immediately rejected this ultimatum in unison. In the early morning hours, protesters successfully withstood several rounds of eviction attempts by the police with their makeshift barricades.

The opposition parties were also present on the scene. One DPP party executive had come to the scene in the afternoon and had seen that the students there were plotting some drastic action, based on their suspicious behavior. However, he thought it was impossible to enter the legislature by force and the students did not come to ask him for help. Upon learning that the students had successfully occupied the legislature, he immediately contacted DPP Chairperson Su Tseng-chang to come to support the students. Soon, Su, Tsai Ing-wen, Frank Hsieh, and other DPP heavyweights had decided to sit outside the plenary conference chamber to demonstrate their solidarity. TSU chairperson Huang Kun-huei later arrived and joined the ranks. That night, many DPP lawmakers personally helped to carry logistical materials to the besieged students because they enjoyed free access (interview #TW4). The involvement of opposition parties certainly raised the political stakes for the authorities if they insisted on expelling the intruding protesters by any means, thus facilitating the student occupation of the legislature.

The Post Hoc Construction of Leadership

Because of the rapid unfolding of the standoff, movement leaders had not anticipated that the larger-than-expected mass defiances might be tolerated by the government, so they were caught off guard by the development of events. Taiwan's movement evolved from a collection of loosely connected networks into a centralized one.

In the initial few hours after the students entered the legislative building, a decision-making core was formed, with the duo of Lin Fei-fan and Chen Wei-ting selected as the main spokespersons. Lin and Chen, in fact, had been only marginally involved with the CSSTA issue before, although the duo had established their reputations as student leaders in earlier activism. In the confused midnight hours of March 18–19, many students took turns holding the microphone to direct the protesters' defense against attempts at eviction. Nevertheless, the Lin-Chen duo soon emerged as the indisputable leaders, because no other student activists appeared as reliable as they (interview #TW1).

The swift selection of the Sunflower Movement leaders was in part due to the amorphous nature of the BIY, the only preexisting anti-CSSTA student organization. The BIY had only around twenty student members and many of them were simultaneously involved with other protest issues. In spite of this, the BIY was firmly embedded in a dense movement network of student activists (see Chapter 3), so it could always mobilize participants via interpersonal connections (interview #TW51). Therefore, a leadership structure could easily surface without regard to preexisting organizational boundaries.

In the chaotic situation with the occupied legislature cordoned off from the outside, relying on the informal old-timers' network proved particularly instrumental. Because many mutually unknown people were in the plenary conference chamber from the very beginning, sustaining an occupy protest required certain ground rules to be quickly established. In the first few days, students found suspicious and unclaimed objects such as cans of gasoline with lighters, electroshock guns, iron chains, and so on. Acts of sabotage, such as cutting the computer cables, occurred. Security team members (*jiuchazu*) identified many plainclothes officers attempting to blend in as protesters and journalists; they caught a record of eight undercover agents in one single day. The menace could also come from inside, as the security team members also had to deal with incidents of theft and sexual harassment (interview #TW43). As such, the core student participants tended to trust familiar faces initially, because they were afraid that strangers with ulterior motives might take over the movement (interview #TW47). It took a while for first-timers to be accepted into the decision-making circle. One student occupier described her initial frustrations at the lack of movement connections:

> If you had not taken part in the preceding movements, it was unlikely that you would be assigned any tasks. They mostly asked friends and acquaintances to be in charge of something, and the rest could only play the role of audience, which explained why many did not stay long in the plenary conference chamber. Later they decided to hold some events so that those who were free all the time would not feel bored. I was so anxious in the beginning about having nothing to do. Students who were assigned with tasks were always busy. And if you had a suggestion, they just told you it would be discussed in the meeting. (Interview #TW34)

While a decision-making core and the division of labor formed inside the legislature, sustaining the occupation on the outside was delegated to those DF-affiliated NGOs. In particular, staging events such as speeches, performances, opinion-sharing among participants, and forums on deliberative democracy at the entrances on Qingdao East Road and Jinan Road (see nos. 1 and 2 in Figure 4.1) was entrusted to NGO staff, who worked on a rotating schedule. These two strategically significant sites had to be continuously guarded by maintaining sizeable crowds in order to prevent police reinforcement. The legislature's main entrance on Zhongshan South Road (no. 3 in Figure 4.1) was managed by the Alliance of Referendum for Taiwan, a pro-independence organization that was not incorporated into the DF but fully supported the students' occupation. From day 2, there was a daily liaison meeting (*lianxi huiyi*) with the participation of student representatives and NGO representatives to coordinate protest actions both within and without. After the Executive Yuan Incident, the leadership structure was further centralized, with a 9-person group (5 students and 4 NGO staff or academics, including Huang Kuo-chang) responsible for emergency decisions, and a 30-person representative assembly (*daibiao dahui*) (20 students and 10 NGO staff) that met every evening. This decision-making structure functioned to the last day of the Sunflower Movement.

The Executive Yuan Incident

The standoff came as a result of the government's tolerance of mass defiance, which amounted to a tacit confession of their previous neglect of growing grievances. The authorities' inability to uphold law and order opened the floodgate for more disruptive protests and more aggressive demands.

Before Taiwanese students entered the legislature, they wanted the CSSTA bill to be sent back to the "article-by-article review and voting" stage. Having paralyzed the legislature, on March 20 (day 3), they issued new demands: (1) to withdraw the CSSTA and (2) to legislate a supervisory law for cross-strait negotiations. The government was given twenty-four hours to respond. Sunflower leaders also attempted to exert more pressure on the governments. On March 23 (day 6), Taiwanese students called for a nationwide class boycott and general strike.[10] None of these efforts to escalate the conflict beyond the initial scope of legislature occupation materialized. Due to pressure from education officials and school administrators, only a very few university professors suspended regular teaching. A Taiwan labor union of bank workers voted for a strike.[11] It was only on April 5 (day 19), five days before the conclusion of the Sunflower Movement, that Taiwan's labor unions issued a joint statement to oppose the CSSTA and support the students (Yen et al. 2015: 112–113). The weak, belated, and inconsequential rejoinder from Taiwan's organized labor was particularly noteworthy, since the trade bill in question threatened the livelihoods of Taiwan's service workers. Social workers, medical workers, book editors, and professionals in advertising and the ICT industry had launched protest actions in tandem with the students but none of them were unionized. Taiwan's labor unions, on the other hand, had experienced a secular decline for more than a decade, with its coverage shrinking to only large manufacturing firms and state-owned enterprises (M. Ho 2015a), which were little affected by the CSSTA.

The failure to ratchet up more pressure gave a respite to the challenged elites. The first response of Ma Ying-jeou was to denounce the occupation as an illegal act by refusing to negotiate with the protesters. In response, on the evening of March 21 (day 4), the Sunflower leaders invited supporters to stage sit-in protests at KMT party branch offices nationwide to create more pressure. Immediately, at least eighteen local KMT offices were besieged by protesters, and some protests lasted for several days. In major cities such as Taichung, Tainan and Kaohsiung, thousands attended spontaneous rallies. On March 22 (day 5), Premier Jiang Yi-huah came to meet the student leader Lin Fei-fan face-to-face, but he explicitly refused the demand of withdrawing the CSSTA. On March 23 (day 6), Ma Ying-jeou held a press conference to denounce the illegal behavior of the students. Ma continued to stress the economic advantages and necessity of the free-trade agreement with China, which further fanned the crowd's discontent. Right after the press conference, the students raised the idea of convening a citizens' constitutional conference (*gongmin xianzheng huiyi*) to solve the ongoing political crisis. For the previous few days, the Sunflower leadership had struggled to discourage the proposal to escalate the confrontation. After Ma's public announcement, the core leadership could no longer contain the radicals and tacitly agreed to their action.

On the third day of occupation, because of poor communication and lack of space in the legislative building, a group of student leaders decided to set up a logistics center (*houqin jidi*) in an auditorium of NTU's College of Social Sciences, which was conveniently located two blocks away. The College-of-Social-Sciences Faction (*shekeyuan pai*) hailed from the same student movement network, and yet their exposure to the outside crowd had encouraged a more sanguine assessment of the standoff. The College-of-Social-Sciences Faction thought the inside students were detached from and ignorant of the brewing crowd dissatisfaction, so they attempted to steer the movement into a more confrontational direction, which amounted to a growing split in the leadership of this nascent movement.

After several rounds of fruitless negotiations, the College-of-Social-Sciences Faction secretly decided to target the Executive Yuan (the executive branch of the national government), located one block away from the legislature. At 7:00 P.M. on March 23, they launched a sit-in there, and soon thousands of protesters swarmed its front square. Some participants broke into the government building, creating an excuse for an official crackdown. Starting at midnight on March 24, the police used batons, shields, and water cannons to disperse the crowd. More than five hundred protesters were wounded, some with severe head injuries. The police arrested and interrogated sixty-one people. The police spent several hours taking back the Executive Yuan, but the excessive use of force against a peaceful rally, which was vividly captured on mobile phone cameras and quickly spread across the Internet, shocked the public.[12]

The suppression at the Executive Yuan triggered a leadership crisis in the movement, as students were briefly plunged into a spate of mutual recrimination. Some inside leaders deliberately distanced themselves from the incident by asserting their ignorance about the "spontaneous" sit-in. Yet, such an attitude was criticized as selfishly "deserting" (*qiege*) their comrades (T. Yang 2014). Student activists spent several days afterward finding out the confusing antecedents of the Executive Yuan Incident. The College-of-Social-Sciences Faction collapsed soon after as the failure to paralyze another state organ discredited their radicalism, and some of its leaders went into hiding to escape a police manhunt. All of this consolidated the core leadership inside the legislature. The Executive Yuan Incident taught a bitter lesson on the futility of escalated militancy. From then on, it was tacitly understood that more disruptiveness was likely to be counterproductive, and such an understanding ironically helped the movement leadership manage a dignified exit when the situation became increasingly unfavorable.

The disproportionate use of force to drive away the protesters from the Executive Yuan backfired, as the government was criticized for "police brutality." A student activist who happened to be taking part in a television talk show experienced first-hand the instant reversal of public opinions:

> Many talking heads were criticizing me because they thought it made no sense to occupy the Executive Yuan after we had occupied the Legislative Yuan. I tried to keep cool in the beginning until I saw that someone had been arrested and many were beaten and bleeding. I started to cry and all of a sudden the opinions began to side with the students. Those talking heads said such bloody suppression was not necessary even though the students had made the mistake in the first place. The show was not able to continue, so they decided to turn it to an audience call-in session. And many callers criticized the talking heads for their previous remarks. (Interview #TW39)

The official attempt to whitewash the police violence flew in the face of video images showing people who were battered unconscious. As a result, the KMT incumbents made a minor concession to meet the mounting pressure of public opinion. On March 25 (day 8), the Presidential Office reversed its previous aloofness by showing willingness to meet student representatives unconditionally. Four days later (day 12), Ma held a second press conference in which he praised the Sunflower Movement as "the concrete practice of youth demonstrating their social concern and democratic participation" and then proceeded to respond to the demands item by item. Ma claimed to support the codification of cross-strait agreements and negotiation, but insisted its legislation could proceed simultaneously with the legal review of the CSSTA. As for the citizens' constitutional conference, he asserted that an alternative form of meeting ought to do the job. Nevertheless, he rejected the most important demand, which was to withdraw the CSSTA.[13] On April 1 (day 15), the Executive Yuan finished a draft on supervision of cross-strait agreements and negotiation;[14] however, this was no more than a restatement of the current practices with minimal oversight. Two days later (day 17), the government declared a national conference on economics and trade (*jingmao guoshi huiyi*) would be forthcoming. In short, following the Executive Yuan Incident, there were visible concessions on the part of the government, although they still fell short of the student demands.

The Perils of Sustained Standoffs

During the standoff, protesters enjoyed only a brief spell of tactical advantage as the continuing political stalemate incurred an increasing backlash that legitimized government crackdowns. In the beginning, the public tended to sympathize with the protesters as victims of excessive police force. As the standoff dragged on, the inconveniences brought about by street occupation became more intolerable. According to surveys in Taiwan, respondents indicated more support than disapproval for the Sunflower Movement until day 11; afterward there was a clear reverse trend (see Table 4.1).

Sustaining a standoff was immensely costly and labor-intensive, and easily gave rise to mass fatigue. Following a successful mass rally that organizers claimed had attracted a half-million participants the previous day, the Sunflower Movement experienced an unexpected drop in the number of street occupiers on March 31 (day 14). The authorities certainly kept tabs on the dwindling size of the occupation and waited for the time to be ripe to evict the protesters. Police officers were reinforced and equipped with antiriot gear on April 3 (day 17) and there was widely circulated speculation that the government was prepared for a forceful removal.

The Sunflower leadership understood that time was not on their side, and there was a pressing need to end their protests before they lost steam. The problem consisted precisely in that they had to secure certain achievements in order to persuade the participants to retreat; otherwise, a unilateral deci-

TABLE 4.1. APPROVAL AND DISAPPROVAL RATINGS FOR THE SUNFLOWER MOVEMENT (PERCENTAGE)								
	March 21 (day 3)	March 23 (day 5)	March 24 (day 6)	March 25 (day 7)	March 26 (day 8)	March 30 (day 10)	March 31 (day 11)	April 3 (day 14)
Support	48	65	51	70	63	55	48	26
Disapproval	40	27	38	20	20	36	38	33
Notes: (1) Twelve opinion polls were released during the twenty-four-day period, only three of which did not explicitly ask the respondents about their judgment of the students' occupation of the legislature. Because of its tendentiously leading question, I did not include the survey conducted by the official National Development Council on April 2. (2) Four listed surveys were conducted by the pro-KMT TVBS Poll Center (https://goo.gl/FxB0NP) and two by the pro-DPP Taiwan Brain Trust (http://goo.gl/MRcBUo) and Liberty Times Poll Center (http://goo.gl/XSblNz), while the other two were conducted by more neutral sources, Business Today (http://goo.gl/9X5E5A) and the Taiwan Indicators Survey Research (http://goo.gl/uZFb7V); all were accessed September 22, 2014.								

sion to end the occupation would have dealt a deadly blow to participant morale and wreaked irremediable damage on the leaders' credibility. The search for an exit strategy necessitated movement leaders to recalibrate their expectations, retreat from their previous maximalist stance, and obtain certain face-saving promises from the incumbents.

A Festive Finale

Seeing that Ma Ying-jeou would not concede to the core demand to rescind the free-trade bill, the movement gradually turned its focus to legislation for more oversight on negotiation with China and insisted on its passage prior to resuming the CSSTA review. On day 10, the students launched a campaign to collect pledges from lawmakers and announced their intention to end the occupation as long as more than half of the lawmakers promised to support the "legislation-before-review" demand.[15] For this purpose, the students needed the support of a sufficient number of ruling party lawmakers who formed the parliamentary majority. This campaign was designed to drive a wedge between the KMT lawmakers and Ma Ying-jeou. It was hoped that the former would act independently, thus thwarting Ma's intransigence and providing leverage to the movement. In tandem with this strategic reorientation, the Sunflower leaders toned down their criticism of KMT lawmakers.

Ma Ying-jeou held his second press conference on day 12 to announce his willingness to accept the legislation on negotiation but insisted on processing the legislation and the CSSTA review simultaneously, indicating that the political bargaining had been narrowed down to the timing of the new legislation. The rejection of Ma's new offer exposed the movement to the danger of an imminent crackdown in early April; however, it turned out that the students' insistence brought them a better deal. On the morning of April 6 (day 20), Wang Jin-pyng, the Legislative Yuan speaker, arrived at the occupied chamber and read a carefully worded announcement. He congratulated the idealistic devotion of student activism, and stressed that a working national legislature needed the ruling party's tolerance, the opposition party's wisdom, and the support of the citizens. To solve the present crisis, he pledged not to convene the interparty caucus discussion on the CSSTA before the law on supervising cross-strait negotiating was enacted. After reading his announcement, Wang made a brief visit to the occupied chamber, paying his respects to the inside protesters.

Before Wang's arrival, his intervention was previously known only to a very small circle of student leaders who had read his statement in advance (interview #TW57). Since Wang's offer was closer to the movement's aims than Ma's, it made it possible for the leaders to claim a success of sorts. Immediately after Wang's visit, the Sunflower leaders held a press conference to hint that a solution was looming. For the next twenty hours, student leaders and NGO activists were busy with internal meetings on how to foster an internal consensus for an exit. On the evening of April 7 (day 21), the Sunflower leaders declared that their occupation would end three days later. Although there was criticism about the decision to withdraw being made without proper consultation, and a lingering reluctance on the part of some die-hard activists, a cheerful and celebrative farewell rally was held on the evening of April 10.

Conclusion

This chapter has analyzed the rise and the unfolding of Taiwan's Sunflower Movement. In light of three political opportunities—the regime orientation, stability of elite alignment, and political allies—my survey indicated that the eventful protest came into being in the absence of a clearly favorable political situation. Prior to the onset of protest activism, the KMT government had firmly rejected the movement's demands. There was a significant degree of disunity among the ruling elites, which provided leverage to movement activists. The political opposition was in the process of a pragmatic turn and thus did not qualify as an unmitigated political ally. In other words, protesters did not launch action because they had become more confident of their power to bring about the intended result. In retrospect, the 30-second Incident violated a previous bipartisan agreement to process the CSSTA on an article-by-article basis and instantly drew national attention to this free-trade bill with China, thus paving the way for the student occupation of the Legislative Yuan the following day. Thus, the Sunflower Movement emerged more as a reaction to the suddenly imposed threat rather than to encouraging opportunities.

The ensuing twenty-four-day standoff eventually ended in favor of protesters. That student protesters were weakly organized turned out to facilitate the shift to reconstruction of a decision-making core. The costly defeat of the militant dissidents in the early phase unexpectedly consolidated the leadership, which was able to execute the retreat decision when the movement appeared to show its fatigue. The timely deepening of elite disunity enabled the leaders to voluntarily end the occupation with a claim of victory. Since standoff represented a radical break with the preceding situation, all these facilitating conditions only surfaced in the process. As the following chapter shows, the standoff in Hong Kong emerged without these advantages, which contributed to the collapse of the movement.

5

Opportunities, Threat, and Standoff in Hong Kong

While Taiwan's Sunflower Movement originated from an ever-widening controversy over economic integration with China, Hong Kong's Umbrella Movement emerged as an attempt to complete the unfinished project of democratization. This chapter first reviews Hongkongers' difficult pursuit of democracy and then analyzes the political opportunities and standoff of the Umbrella Movement. The conclusion to this chapter compares the unexpected trajectories of these two eventful protests and theorizes the meanings of contingency in standoffs.

As noted in Chapter 1, Hong Kong transitioned to a semidemocracy in which citizens were allowed to vote for only a certain proportion of their representatives. Hong Kong's political opposition appeared weaker than Taiwan's since its start in the mid-1980s. Before the 1997 handover, the DP, the flagship of Hong Kong's pro-democracy movement, stopped short of demanding direct and full election of representatives (Wing-yat Yu 2005: 263). Ever since the transfer of sovereignty, July First (officially a holiday for the Hong Kong SAR establishment) always invited protest rallies for various causes, including commemorating the June Fourth massacre, securing the right of abode for mainland immigrants, and other livelihood issues, without articulating a demand for constitutional reform.

The historical July First demonstration of 2003 raised the demand of "returning power to people" (*huan zheng yu min*), thus bringing the issues of direct elections and suffrage back to public attention. Democratization meant abolishing the appointed seats in district councils (which was realized in 2016); in the legislative council, it had to do with the seats selected by election committee (abolished in 2004) and the functional-constituency seats (which still accounted for half the seats in 2016). A full democracy would also require the top leader to be decided by popular ballot. The Basic Law had guaranteed the ultimate aim of having the chief executive and all members of the legislative council selected by universal suffrage, with the proviso that the process had to occur with "gradual and orderly progress," which provided ample room to maneuver for Beijing.

Facing the rising pro-democracy movement, Beijing made a decision in April 2004 to disallow universal suffrage for the chief executive in 2007 and for legislative council in 2008. In December 2007, the central government again denied the possibility of holding a popular election for chief executive in 2012, but specified its implementation for 2017, with the legislative council to follow in 2018. There was evidence that the politician-led pro-democracy movement was losing steam. As the pro-Beijing camp was strengthening its electoral competence by winning more and more seats, the pro-democracy camp underwent a fracturing process, as the successive formation of the Civic Party (2006), the League of Social Democrats (LSD) (2006), the Neo Democrats (2010), People Power (2011), and the Labour Party (2011) eclipsed the hegemonic role of the DP. The political opposition was split among the "pan-democrats," whose growing intramural bickering and electoral competition considerably weakened the pro-democracy movement.

The fracturing of political opposition was due in part to the introduction of the proportionate representative system in the legislative council election starting in 1998 (Ma 2007: 145–147). The new electoral rule favored smaller parties at the expense of the then-popular DP, clearly corresponding to Beijing's strategic considerations. The central government's reluctance to enact the promised suffrage exacerbated the pan-democrats' disagreements over the tactics. While the moderate faction led by the DP was in favor of negotiation, the radicals (exemplified by the LSD and People Power) opted for street protests and mass mobilization. Conflict soared when the LSD and the Civic Party launched the Five-District Referendum campaign in 2010, which was opposed by the DP and other moderates. The campaign aimed at creating political pressure on Beijing with the goal of realizing universal suffrage and abolishing the functional-constituency seats as soon as possible. Since Hong Kong did not have codified procedures for direct democracy, five lawmakers resigned and then signed up for the by-election in order to produce a de facto referendum in the hope that a strong show of citizen participation could pressure Beijing leaders. Boycotted by the conservative camp and condemned as a frivolous waste of taxpayers' money by the SAR government, the by-election of May 2010 generated a voter turnout rate of only 17.2 percent, far below the intended goal of 50 percent (Sing and Tang 2012: 150).

One week after the by-election, three senior DP leaders walked into the

Liaison Office for an ice-breaking negotiation. In what amounted to a historic compromise, moderate pan-democrats made conciliatory overtures with the intention of obtaining the promise for a roadmap to democratization. Nevertheless, they were able to secure only a rather modest reform package that included the popular election of five newly added functional-constituency seats (the "super district councilors") and the enlargement of the chief executive election committee from 800 to 1,200 (Sing and Tang 2012: 152). The DP leadership defended the result as a first step toward eventual democratization because it showed that Beijing was pragmatic enough to make concessions (Ma 2011a: 66). The detractors were legions. For them, the negotiation approach had failed to persuade Beijing to give up its insistence on "patriotism" as a precondition for chief executive candidates. The new system of super district councilors had helped to perpetuate the problematic system of functional constituency, rather than abolishing it. There emerged a walkout protest within the DP. In the 2011 district council election, People Power launched a "revenge campaign" (*piaozhai piaohuan*) by deliberately fielding candidates in districts where DP nominees took part. The radicals began to paint DP as a traitor, more despicable than the pro-Beijing camp. The 2012 legislative council election generated bitter and fierce infighting among pan-democrats such that they ended up receiving only 18 out of 35 directly elected seats, a significant setback from their previous 19 out of 30 seats.

Occupy Central Campaign

The disappointing results of the 2012 election demonstrated the dim prospects for a pro-democracy movement led by fractious and fragile opposition parties. Benny Tai, a HKU law professor, published a newspaper op-ed piece titled "Civil Disobedience as the Most Lethal Weapon" in January 2013 (Tai 2013: 32–34). Reflecting on the previous failures of mass rallies, referendum campaigns, and negotiation, Tai proposed a mass occupation by tens of thousands in Central, the financial and political hub in Hong Kong, to change Beijing leaders' mindset. He envisioned the campaign would proceed nonviolently and be led by respected opinion leaders and accomplished professionals who would willingly shoulder the legal consequences. He contended that the preparation of such a deadly weapon would in and of itself create political pressure and its actual deployment would have to be postponed until the possibility for authentic universal suffrage had completely disappeared (Tai 2013: 34). Tai's seminal article reverberated widely, leading him to later join hands with Chan Kin-man (a CUHK sociology professor) and Chu Yiu-ming (a Baptist minister) to launch the Occupy Central with Love and Peace (OCLP) campaign in March 2013. The trio pledged to paralyze the financial hub with a mass sit-in if the design of the 2017 universal suffrage failed to meet international standards. Citizens would first deliberate on the ideal suffrage package and indicate their preference by a popular vote. Should Beijing continue to ignore these democratic voices, they would execute the occupy plan in protest.

Initially, the OCLP campaign reunified the fractured landscape of Hong Kong's pan-democrats and movement activists by providing a common platform and redirecting attention to the suffrage issue. Scholarism, for instance, immediately decided to devote full attention to the pro-suffrage campaign after concluding their intensive mobilization against National Education (interview #HK46). An Alliance for True Democracy came into being to coordinate action among pan-democratic parties. OCLP raised funds, recruited volunteers, and trained security brigade members in preparation for the eventual showdown. Benny Tai published a book that eloquently spelled out the campaign's mission and methods. Making use of the transborder movement network (see Chapter 3), OCLP leaders made several visits to Taiwan to meet movement activists, and a Taiwanese veteran activist was invited to provide lessons on nonviolent resistance to the volunteers (interview #TW33).

Pro-Beijing media and conservatives portrayed OCLP as a recipe for disaster and lawlessness, and the government rejected its registration application, creating difficulties for fund-raising activities.[1] OCLP leaders' use of the transborder movement network was savagely denounced as "collusion with Taiwan's pro-independence forces." Countermovement organizations and mass rallies also came into being, ostensibly at the behest of Beijing. Aside from this expected repression and harassment from the pro-Beijing camp, OCLP leaders began to encounter criticism of being too cautious from within. Being a legal scholar, Tai once insisted that the core participants had to sign a pledge to uphold the principle of nonviolent civil disobedience and to take part in a public swearing-in ceremony presided over by retired judges (Tai 2013: 54). Chan Kin-man argued for the necessity to see the mass sit-in as a last-resort act because Hongkongers had never experienced repression like Taiwan's February 28 Incident so they were reluctant to take drastic actions for the sake of democracy.[2] Since OCLP leaders made it clear that the planned mass sit-in was a bargaining chip with Beijing, they initially appeared reluctant to accept proposals, including the "civil nomination" (signature endorsement by citizens) for chief executive candidates, which appeared to violate the requirement of approval by a nomination committee in the Basic Law. Moderate pro-democrats were anxious to preserve some negotiation space so they opposed the idea of civil nomination and the OCLP trio seemed to concur with them.

OCLP leaders believed that a pro-democracy movement worth its salt needed to be internally democratic. Extensive forums on deliberative democracy were to be held before there would be a citizen vote to pick the ideal package for chief executive election, which was scheduled for mid-2014. The insistence on procedural justice certainly added legitimacy to the planned mass civil disobedience; however, it did not silence conservative detractors, nor did it appeal to militant supporters who were growing more restless and impatient with the ostensible lack of progress. In a peculiar way, the OCLP campaign had to fight on both fronts, reproducing the dilemma faced by moderate pan-democrats, as it was simultaneously criticized for fomenting irresponsible disruption by pro-Beijing conservatives and for excessive precaution by the radicals. More discouraging was the fact that there was no sign that Beijing had softened its ingrained opposition to a chief executive election without prior screening. In early 2014, one OCLP leader privately acknowledged that the probability of a concession from the central government was low. "Perhaps a real change is possible only if we are sent to jail," he pessimistically said. Under this condition, he viewed it as a "difficult achievement," as the poll support rate for the OCLP hovered around 25 percent (interview #HK1-1).

Students Take Charge

As the OCLP campaign was mired in sluggishness, students took the initiative by radicalizing the demand for universal suffrage. In February 2014, Scholarism and HKFS jointly put forward a student proposal that included not only the system of civil nomination but also reform of the nomination committee. Taiwan's Sunflower Movement in March had further strengthened determination among Hong Kong's students to take bolder steps because they had seen the possibility of a successful occupy protest even without prolonged deliberation and planning. Immediately HKFS decided to "rehearse" occupying Central after the annual July First demonstration, overriding opposition from the OCLP leadership. As an HKFS veteran put it:

> The biggest disagreement the students had with the OCLP trio was concerning the degree of action. We felt it acceptable to mount a disruptive protest as long as we had sufficient reason. We thought OCLP was too slow. They talked too much without really organizing action, and that was the reason why we kept pushing them toward more decisive action in the internal meeting. (Interview #HK55)

By contrast, the OCLP leadership did not view the Sunflower Movement as a positive case to emulate. As Benny Tai explained, "We are not going to plunge into an immediate confrontation like Taiwanese students."[3] As the moderate and radical tendencies further diverged within the OCLP campaign, Beijing hardened its response with the publication of a State Council publication on June 10, which basically asserted the primacy of "one country" over "two systems" and the priority of national security concerns in designing the suffrage system. Such intransigence fanned Hongkongers' indignation such that the OCLP's citizen vote ended up with nearly 780,000 participants in late June, much better than originally expected. After the conclusion of the July First demonstration, thousands of people took part in an overnight "civil disobedience rehearsal" defying police eviction, with 511 arrestees the next morning.

While the students were pushing the OCLP campaign in a more aggressive direction, Beijing appeared poised for a showdown. On August 17, the pro-government camp launched a mass demonstration to oppose the OCLP campaign, which purportedly attracted 190,000 participants. Beijing showed its true colors with a National People's Congress Standing Committee decision on August 31, which turned out to be more conservative than anticipated. The "August 31 Framework" not only rejected civil nomination and other more liberal designs but also raised the required support threshold for a chief executive candidate to qualify from one-eighth of the nomination committee members to one-half. This new system threatened to bring about a "sham election without choice" to the extent that pan-democrats could no longer field their candidates as they did in 2005 and 2012.

The announcement signified that the OCLP's expressed preference for negotiation ended in total failure. For a moment, the movement leaders appeared hesitant about whether to launch the original mass sit-in plan. Privately, they thought only a few thousand would join despite their preparatory work of more than a year.[4] In a news interview, Tai admitted that their campaign had been "a failure up to this point," and yet this defeatist appraisal was denied by other leaders.[5] In mid-September, they decided to start the action on a public holiday (October 1), which indicated their intention to reduce disruption by holding the mass occupation of the financial center on a nonworking day.

While the senior movement leadership showed indecisiveness, students seized the initiative again by announcing a five-day class boycott starting on September 22. As the campaign proceeded, HKFS and Scholarism judged that more drastic action was needed. On September 25, the fourth day, students attempted a "siege" of the Government House to demand a dialogue with Chief Executive Leung without success. Throughout the campaign, student participation was below expectations. An HKFS leader described the discouraging conditions: "We thought the campaign was a failure because it attracted only a few hundred participants each day. At HKU, students were still attending class. Those who supported us came to Admiralty only in their free time, and then they went back to school for class" (interview #HK52).

Occupying Civic Square

With their class boycott campaign on the brink of a collapse, students opted to take more militant actions on the final day. The contingency plan to oc-

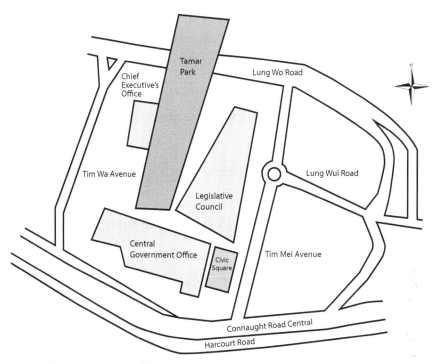

Figure 5.1. Government buildings in Admiralty, Hong Kong.

cupy Civic Square was made only two hours before its execution. The decision was made without informing OCLP leaders, and only one opposition lawmaker, Leung Kwok-hung (known as "Long Hair") of LSD, knew in advance. According to the original plan, if student intruders were arrested, those who remained outside would immediately stage a hunger strike (interview #HK16-1). At 10:30 P.M. on September 26, hundreds of students launched a surprise sit-in of Civic Square, an empty space nestled between the Central Government Offices and legislative council in Admiralty (see Figure 5.1). Policemen reacted much more harshly than expected, denying the encircled protesters water for hours, using pepper spray and batons, and arresting sixty-one participants. Female students were forced to urinate in plastic bottles (Umbrella People 2015: 22–23). Student leaders, Alex Chow and Lester Shum of HKFS and Joshua Wong of Scholarism, not only were detained for nearly forty-eight hours, the legal limit for police custody before pressing criminal charges, but also had their residences thoroughly searched.

Sympathy for the students immediately surged, and supporters began to gather outside the Central Government Complex overnight. The next day witnessed an escalation as more and more supporters gathered in Admiralty. The OCLP leaders, however, were slow to react. The trio had an emergency meeting in the morning, with the conclusion to stick to the original plan to start action on October 1. This decision encountered vehement criticism both from within and without. The trio was savagely bombarded throughout September 27, as students and citizens emotionally shouted, "Why are you so late to come here? Do you know that we have been attacked by many rounds of pepper spray?" (interview #HK34) The escalating pressures led to a last-minute revision, and at 1:00 A.M. on September 28, Benny Tai took to the podium on Tim Mei Avenue to announce the immediate beginning of the mass sit-in to demand Beijing retract the August 31 Framework. Although the late-night declaration was sudden and confusingly criticized as "taking the credit from students," the next day saw more citizens come forward to support the students. By that afternoon, supporters gathered on Tim Mei Avenue and Lung Wui Road had broken free of the police cordon line by occupying the eight-lane Harcourt Road (interview #HK36), a major traffic artery of Hong Kong Island (see Figure 5.1). At 5:00 P.M., the police fired tear gas to disperse the crowd, and the images of the brute force being used against citizens who had nothing to protect themselves with except umbrellas, goggles, and plastic wrap released a mighty shockwave. The Umbrella Movement emerged as Hong Kong's citizens braved the harsh attack from the police.

Afterward, the SAR government did not reveal the decision-making process on the use of tear gas, which, in hindsight, was clearly an error in overestimating the security threat. There were suggestions that Hong Kong's police made the swift resolution to use force because they felt obliged to act decisively in order to preclude the possible intervention of the People's Liberation Army. Moreover, learning the lesson of the Sunflower Movement, Hong Kong's police were determined to prevent protesters from entering government buildings, which had made restoring order more intractable.[6]

An Analysis of Political Opportunities

Before the fateful decision to release tear gas on protesters, Hong Kong's OCLP campaign was fighting an increasingly difficult battle, as favorable political opportunities in terms of regime orientation, elite alignment, and political allies were clearly absent.

Regime Orientation

During the consultative stage, the SAR government officials claimed that they welcomed all kinds of proposals for political reform and were willing to negotiate. Later they chose to ignore the OCLP campaign for genuine suffrage by encouraging Hongkongers to "pocket it first" (*doizyusin,* in Cantonese), implying that an imperfect suffrage package was better than nothing. Beijing's unveiling of the tough-talking white paper in June and the announcement of the August 31 Framework were an in-your-face rejection of the demand for a fair and uncensored election.

Previously Joshua Wong anticipated "a void period of political reform" (*zhenggai kongchuangqi*) of nine months after the citizen voting in June because protesters would have to passively wait for Beijing's response (J. Wong 2015: 47). There was evidence that their rivals shared the same appraisal, as a well-known pro-government academic categorically asserted, "Hong Kong is not Taiwan. We will not have a Sunflower Movement" (I. Chen 2015: 84). Beijing's opponents and supporters concurred that a concession from the central government was highly unlikely, which was confirmed by the subsequent development.

Stability of Elite Alignment

Chief Executive Leung Chun-ying assumed power after a bruising election, by defeating Henry Tang, the candidate favored by business elites, in March 2012. Even though it was a "small-circle" election of 1,200 voters who largely followed Beijing's dictate, Leung's campaign relied on intensive mudslinging by attacking his rival over extramarital affairs and violation of building codes. As such, Leung's government began without the blessing of conservative business leaders. Leung's vindictiveness earned him the sobriquet "Wolf Ying," which also indicated his alienation from the pro-government camp. While his predecessors used to appoint some moderate pan-democrats into government positions, Leung gave up the attempt at co-optation and his personnel decisions were heavily criticized as "excessively leftist and narrow-minded" (*yizuo erzhai*), the stereotypical error of sectarianism among the communist leadership before Beijing revamped its Hong Kong policy in the mid-1980s. Therefore, Leung began his term in office with a lower approval rating and his performance was persistently below the two preceding chief executives in monthly surveys.[7] It went without saying that Leung's unpopularity lent credence to the OCLP campaign's demand for authentic suffrage for chief executive. Nevertheless, Leung had to toe the line dictated by Beijing, which had the ultimate power to decide on the suffrage issue. Before the announcement of August 31 Framework, Beijing had succeeded in solidifying the pro-establishment bloc for the support, hence narrowing the degree of elite disunity.

After the appearance of the Umbrella Movement, elite disunion further worsened. On October 8 (day 11), an international report embroiled Leung in a financial scandal for not having declared overseas income, which appeared to be a reward for corruption. It has been widely speculated that the revelation of such damaging information came from the mainland, seemingly indicating that Beijing was not necessarily supporting Leung. On October 29 (day 32), James Tien, a Liberal Party legislative council member, publicly demanded that Leung step down because of his mishandling of the student protest, bringing the rift within the pro-government camp to the surface. The defection of the Liberal Party, a conservative ally to Beijing, was politically significant because the last time it had openly challenged the SAR leader in 2003 the result was the failure to enact the National Security Bill. Beijing clearly understood the magnitude of this elite split, and thus swiftly reacted, removing Tien's membership in the Chinese People's Political Consultative Conference in order to forestall further widening of the crack. Throughout the Umbrella Movement, there were a number of conservative politicians who made overtures to the students with the hint that they could secure certain understandings from Beijing, which indicated Leung's precarious relationship with local elites (interview #HK58).

Political Allies

Hong Kong's pan-democrats occupied 27 out of 70 seats in the legislative council. Despite their minority, the opposition lawmakers possessed veto power of varying degrees either by filibuster or other parliamentary tactics; yet the problem was that they did not fully support the movement demands.

As shown above, the OCLP campaign emerged precisely because its leaders understood that a fractured political opposition could no longer spearhead Hong Kong's pro-democracy movement. The proposal for large-scale civil disobedience aimed to build a common platform, uniting pan-democrats, NGOs, and the students. To achieve this goal, Benny Tai contended there needed to be reconciliation between pan-democratic moderates and radicals for a "unity of reason and passion" (Tai 2013: 157). Yet, when it came to the design of the election of the chief executive, the old sectarian conflicts surfaced again. The Alliance for True Democracy was at first successful in bringing together all twenty-seven of the opposition lawmakers. While the coalition was able to persuade moderates to accept the civil nomination plan, Wong Yuk-man, a radical firebrand, walked out in protest against the retention of the nomination committee. Later, People Power decided to initiate its own version to compete with the one endorsed by the Alliance for True Democracy.[8] When the OCLP launched citizen voting in late June 2014, three options were presented: the student proposal, the People Power proposal, and the Alliance for True Democracy proposal, all containing civil nomination. Moderate pan-democrats were highly critical of this arrangement because they thought such an aggressive gesture would leave no room to find middle ground with Beijing. Therefore after the conclusion of citizen voting, which showed the Alliance for True Democracy proposal to be the most favored one (42.1 percent), the DP and Ronny Tong of the Civil Party left the coalition.[9] In their view, the OCLP campaign had been hijacked by radical forces, as represented by the students, so that a deal with Beijing appeared less likely. In early August, a number of moderate pan-democrats crossed the aisle to join hands with some pro-government conservatives to sign a joint declaration that pleaded for a cool down in order to reach a consensus on political reform.[10]

Therefore, the OCLP campaign encountered the perennial problem of disunited pan-democrats. The situation appeared inauspicious for the pro-democracy movement because a reform package needed two-thirds approval in the legislative council, or 47 votes, and the SAR government needed to secure only 4 defection votes from the 27 pan-democratic lawmakers. The widening fissure among opposition parties lent itself to a divide-and-conquer strategy by the incumbents. Nevertheless, such a scenario did not materialize because Beijing's hardline approach left no choice for compromise by pushing the pan-democrats to adopt a confrontational stance. Immediately after the announcement of the August 31 Framework, the 4 moderate pan-democratic lawmakers targeted for cooptation expressed their opposition, and except for Wong Yuk-man and Ronny Tong, the other 25 opposition lawmakers signed a pledge to support the OCLP campaign.[11] In short, Hong Kong's fractious opposition parties did not play the role of a solid political ally to the pro-suffrage movement.

As the ex ante variables, the examination of political opportunities on the eve of Umbrella Movement indicated that Hong Kong's campaigners were facing the political headwind at that time.

The Tear-Gas Shock

The students' last-minute decision to occupy Civic Square triggered a chain of reactions, culminating in the police's use of eighty-seven tear-gas canisters on the afternoon of September 28. The use of chemical weapons was highly atypical in Hong Kong's context, as the last time it had occurred was during the 2005 WTO meeting, when the police tried to break up a protest by Korean farmers armed with Molotov cocktails (J. Ng 2016: 31–32). As such, the deployment of tear gas against unarmed citizens was seen as outrageous and unacceptable. A schoolteacher participant recounted her initial response:

> "What happened? It [the government] must be insane." I could not believe my eyes and ears from that moment. I saw people falling to the ground. My bodily instinct led me to cry out loudly, "Keep cool! Go immediately! Don't trample on other people!" . . . I was so emotional and angry. I kept shouting, "This government has gone nuts! What have we done to deserve this treatment? Why?" (Hong Kong Christian Institute 2015: 52)

An eyewitness journalist noted, "Once the tear gas was fired, people were immediately frightened. We saw soaring smoke and [heard] loud sounds, as everyone was fleeing from the scene. There were many rumors, and mobile phones were circulating some pictures of the People's Liberation Army in town and tanks entering the Cross-Harbor Tunnel" (interview #HK6).

The police failed to take back the occupied streets, as protesters kept coming back each time the tear gas diffused until the police decided to pull back.

> People were still gathering on Harcourt Road. Cardinal Joseph Zen [the cardinal and bishop of Hong Kong] was urging everyone to leave via a loudspeaker without success. At that moment, I do not think anyone could possibly have evacuated the crowd. This was the most moving part of the movement; so many people chose to stay in defiance of the lethal risk. I was so moved that people were chanting the slogans, such as "free Joshua Wong," "free Alex Chow," and "we want true suffrage," all night long. (Interview #HK6)

The aggressive use of tear gas backfired as the suddenly imposed threat stimulated more protest participation. Subsequent onsite surveys discovered that the participants who were already present before September 28 tended to have more experience in movement activism, whereas those who took part afterward were less experienced. This finding showed that many previously unconcerned Hongkongers were galvanized into action more because of the police repression than because of their support for genuine suffrage (G. Tang 2015; Yuen 2015).

Threats in Taiwan and Hong Kong

While the political opportunity perspective provided an inadequate explanation for the rise of two eventful protests in Hong Kong and Taiwan, the concept of threat turned out to be more useful in both places. Ultimately, what motivated the unprecedented number of people to take to the streets no longer amounted to the movement issues of suffrage design (Hong Kong) or a free-trade bill (Taiwan) per se, but an acute sense of crisis that they were about to forfeit something more valuable. Hongkongers were indignant at the sight of the police's brutal application of tear gas to unarmed and peaceful citizens, whereas Taiwanese were shocked at the forceful way that ruling-party lawmakers processed the free-trade bill in apparent violation of democratic procedure. While a favorable opportunity was readily identifiable through a rational appraisal, threat exerted its pro-mobilization power via strong emotional reactions. Citizens decided to take part in these two unconventional protests because they were rightfully angry with governmental leaders, sympathetic with the mistreated protesters, and fearful that something worse was to come.

On a closer look, threat came about as a combined result of the protesters' strategy and the incumbents' mistakes. Overriding the more cautious OCLP leadership, Hong Kong's students mounted waves of sit-in protests that invited an aggressive response from the police. Taiwan's anti-CSSTA protesters exercised sufficient pressure on opposition party lawmakers, who reluctantly felt obliged to process the review according to a strict procedure. In what could be described as movement brinkmanship, the activists in Hong Kong and Taiwan persisted in exploring every possible venue and adopting increasingly disruptive protests until the government incumbents lost their poise and made some damaging mistakes. In a sense, they struggled to "make opportunities" rather than passively waiting for the emergence of favorable chances. Compared to politicians, NGO leaders, and university professors, college students appeared more suitable to play the role of radical fringe. Not only were they less confined by routine schedules and rules, which facilitated swift and impromptu protest making; they also were seen as more or less the "nation's conscience," and their rule-breaking behaviors were better tolerated by the public. Equally important was the fact that government leaders erred by taking some counterproductive harsh measures. Counterfactually, if the Hong Kong police had shown more self-restraint on September 28, the street occupation might have naturally declined or at least become more easily handled because the next day was a Monday. In Taiwan, had the ruling party lawmakers evinced more patience by processing the CSSTA according to the original agreement of article-by-article review, its passage might have had to wait for a few more months, but the protesters might have found it difficult to mount a drastic act of legislature occupation.

An Occupation in Spite of Leadership

When the police deployed tear gas, many student leaders were still in custody, rendering HKFS and Scholarism rudderless at a critical moment. Since there were many Internet rumors about the deployment of more lethal weapons, OCLP leaders, who had just announced the initiation of their civil disobedience action less than twenty hours earlier, urged citizens to leave the scene for their own safety. HKFS, Scholarism, and opposition lawmakers also spread the same message to "preserve strength for another day" (*baoliu liliang zeri zaihui*).[12] At 11:00 P.M., HKFS organized an emergency rally on the campus of CUHK—around an hour's metro ride from Admiralty—which attracted thousands of students. They decided to continue the boycott campaign indefinitely (interview #HK10). Some Scholarism students decided to rush back to their offices to remove computers, for fear of a police search (interview #HK46).

Student and nonstudent leaders' calls for retreat failed to persuade the citizens, as they kept fighting back until the police decided to pull back. Spontaneous occupation took place in Mong Kok, Causeway Bay, and Admiralty, ushering in the Umbrella Movement. A smaller incident of occupation took place in the shopping district of Tsim Sha Tsui, lasting from September 30 to October 3. In a sense, the Umbrella Movement surged not because of, but in spite of, the movement leaders' decisions. Leung Kwok-hung later described the unexpected turn of affairs: "If pan-democratic leaders and the OCLP figureheads had not asked the crowd to retreat, would the Umbrella Movement have blossomed in many places to witness the heroism of the crowd in Causeway Bay and Mong Kok? It was due to righteous indignation that the crowd animated their spirit and evolved into a decisive force" (M. Lam 2015: 20).

When Hong Kong's students stormed Civic Square, OCLP leaders and staff were not present at the scene, which gave rise to a widespread perception that the senior leaders did not care about the students. The prevailing sense of mistrust erupted when Benny Tai announced the OCLP's launch at midnight, with nearly one-third of the crowd immediately leaving to show their disapproval. It was erroneously perceived that the OCLP leaders had attempted to take the credit from the students' sacrifice. As the movement momentum was at the brink of a premature collapse, Leung Kwok-hung made a highly dramatic move to kneel down before the crowd and plead for solidarity, helping to stabilize the situation. In fact, before Benny Tai mounted the podium, HKFS activists had warned of the danger because they knew the participants came out of sympathy for the students, rather than identification with the OCLP's agenda (interview #HK52). Apparently, the OCLP trio failed to notice that the students had emerged as the de facto leaders in the public mind. Later one OCLP leader acknowledged that the crowd's reaction amounted to "a clear signal that OCLP had forfeited leadership." In subsequent official statements, the OCLP leaders felt it necessary to downplay their role by always maintaining that decisions were jointly made by the "two student organizations and the trio" (*shuangxue sanzi*) (interview #HK1-2).

It was difficult for the students to instantly organize a decision-making core because their key leaders were taken into custody immediately after the storming of Civic Square. When they were released two days later, what they saw was a transfigured city on the verge of a popular uprising. Student leaders needed time to digest what had happened in their absence, and thus, they could not "clearly explain what to do next because they did not fully understand the situation" until September 30 (day 3) (interview #HK55).

Leadership Compared

The standoffs in Hong Kong and Taiwan came about after a number of tactical decisions were haphazardly made by movement activists in response to rapidly changing situations. These decisions were often ad hoc, on-the-spot, and involved abrupt changes or even reversals that invited unintended consequences. Student leadership in both instances demonstrated their capacity to launch large-scale protest actions in a flash, outpacing and outsmarting the authorities, to arouse citizen support. As experts in this flash-mob-style protest, they practiced an asymmetrical warfare with the government. Protesters could endure repeated failures without being demoralized because all they needed was a flare-up or an incumbent misstep to gain national attention. Nevertheless, there were different degrees of coordination and leadership capacity between Taiwan and Hong Kong.

In terms of biographical background, Taiwanese movement leaders appeared more experienced than their Hongkonger counterparts. Both Lin Fei-fan (26 years old then) and Chen Wei-ting (24) were graduate students and had been involved with movement activism since 2008, whereas HKFS's Alex Chow (24) and Lester Shum (22) were undergraduate students, and most Scholarism members, led by Joshua Wong (18) were high school students. Chow, Shum, and Wong had been involved in movements for no more than two years. The DF convener Lai Chung-chiang had been coordinating NGOs since 2010, whereas the OCLP's trio were respected professionals whose movement experience had not started until their 2013 campaign. Differences were also apparent in the opposition parties. A number of DPP lawmakers and party staff had begun their political careers with street protests, which facilitated their swift response to the student protest. In contrast, Leung Kwok-hung, the iconic Trotskyite street warrior, and Lee Cheuk-yan of the Labour Party were arguably the only two pan-democratic lawmakers who had movement experience. Thus, when Taiwanese students opted to storm the legislature, they had the advantage of better liaison with NGOs and opposition parties than Hongkonger students did.

Aside from these subjective differences, Hongkongers were facing a more formidable regime backed by Beijing, whose ruthless determination to squash popular uprisings at all costs was well known. While a Tiananmen-style solution weighed heavily on the minds of Hongkongers, Taiwanese were immune from this fearful obsession. Hong Kong's policing also appeared more aggressive in the use of weapons such as pepper spray and tear gas, with which Taiwan's policemen were not equipped. Thus, there seemed sufficient reason to be cautious, which explained why the Hongkonger leaders were unanimous in calling for a retreat during the confusing melee on the evening of September 28. As it turned out, this decision erred in its underestimation of the militancy of the protesters.

The Main Stage in Admiralty

On October 1 (day 4), a main stage (*datai*) was erected on Harcourt Road to replace the original one on Tim Mei Avenue, which had been used during the class boycott campaign, symbolizing the intention to centralize the movement leadership. There was a five-person "master of ceremonies" team, called the MC group, which took turns directing and holding events every evening, and all five of these MC members had backgrounds in movement activism (interview #HK59). Previously, Leung Kwok-hung had suggested that a more inclusive commanding team needed to be set up immediately after the launch of the occupy action; however, this proposal did not win the consent of the OCLP trio.[13] After the chaotic beginning, it was only in the early days of October that a "five-party platform" (*wufang pingtai*)—with the participation of HKFS, Scholarism, OCLP, pan-democratic parties, and NGOs—emerged as a new coordination mechanism. Nevertheless, the students remained the movement's public face. HKFS, in particular, played the dominant role and its actions did not always follow the conclusions reached by the five-party platform. As the occupation continued, pan-democratic lawmakers and OCLP leaders suggested a quick withdrawal, a move that was opposed by the more militant students. On October 18 (day 21), the trio announced their intention to surrender to police as a formal gesture of their detachment, thereby leaving the students at the movement's helm.

Hong Kong's standoff involved three simultaneously formed zones of mass occupation, but the student leadership was effective only in Admiralty, the epicenter of the Umbrella Movement. Although there had been earlier attempts to set up main stages in Mong Kok and Causeway Bay as well, they were aborted following the onset of violent assaults by pro-government mobs, the "Blue-ribbon supporters," on October 3 (day 6). HKFS and OCLP immediately asked participants to evacuate Mong Kok to reassemble in Admiralty. Yet, the protesters courageously resisted the onslaught of violence and defended the occupation, which again damaged the credibility of the student leadership. Until the Mong Kok occupation was cleared by police on November 26 (day 60), there existed only a podium at which everyone was allowed to speak for up to two minutes, a system that failed to serve as a command center. In the Causeway Bay occupation, which was the smallest in size and lasted until December 15, the last day (day 79), the students were able to maintain their presence only occasionally. Without an equivalent of the main stage in Mong Kok and Causeway Bay, student leaders could only make use of the podiums of Mobile Democracy Classroom (*liudong minzhu jiaoshi*), a series of street lecture activities that came into being on September 30 (day 3), in order to communicate to the protesters there (interview #HK4-1). This platform allowed the student leaders to reach only a limited number of participants.

Dialogue with Officials

Taiwan's protesters staked more aggressive claims after their successful occupation of the legislature. Likewise, when Hong Kong's students launched the class boycott campaign, their demands were (1) to rescind the August 31 Framework, (2) to include civic nomination for the chief executive election, and (3) to abolish functional-constituency seats in the legislative council. After Hong Kong's citizens had bravely resisted police repression, on September 29 (day 2) HKFS called for the resignation of Chief Executive Leung Chun-ying as well as Chief Secretary of Administration Carrie Lam and two other officials who were responsible for political reform, and they demanded a reply from the government before October 2 (day 5). A nascent standoff offered the movement leadership a bargaining advantage, and attempted to exert more pressure on the government.

HKFS launched a "noncooperation movement" (*buhezuo yundong*), including class boycott, general strike, and the "cessation of market transactions" (*bashi*). Immediately after the police launched tear gas, the Confederation of Trade Unions and the Professional Teachers' Union urged their members to strike in protest.[14] However, the noncooperation movement failed to gain traction, as most schools continued their teaching activities. And only one labor union of a soft drink company mounted a one-day work stoppage in solidarity.[15]

With the similar appearance of radicalizing drifts, two movements diverged in the initial period, with profound consequences for their subsequent trajectories. While Taiwan's students opted for militance that resulted in the bitter failure of the Executive Yuan Incident, Hong Kong leadership effectively suppressed the tendency in the first few days, resulting in a costlier and more destructive explosion later on.

In the late evening hours of October 2 (day 5), Chief Executive Leung responded by announcing that he would not step down and he deputized Carrie Lam, the number-two government official, to have a dialogue with the students. Leung's press conference immediately set off scattered protests; however, the student leadership opted for moderation by abandoning the announced plan to besiege the Office of the Chief Executive. In reciprocation, HKFS issued a carefully worded statement, emphasizing (1) "political reform is the only issue" (read: not insisting on the resignation of Leung), (2) "upholding the 'one country, two systems' framework" (read: upholding the Basic Law), and (3) "Hong Kong's problems should be solved locally" (read: not spreading the protest wave into mainland cities).[16] On October 11 (day 14), HKFS publicly rejected the name "Umbrella Revolution," which was circulated by the mass media, and emphasized their campaign was not a "color revolution" because they did not intend to "seize power" but sought only "high-degree autonomy"[17]—clearly a friendly gesture of self-limitation to gain Beijing's trust.

There were many reasons why the Hong Kong students decided to deescalate tension at this critical moment. As the specter of the Tiananmen Massacre haunted Hong Kong, pan-democratic moderates, in particular, warned that attempting to storm government buildings would force the police to pull the trigger. In the initial days, the students relied on the more informed OCLP leaders for political judgment. According to one of the OCLP trio, a number of "middlemen" from Beijing contacted them and brought the same message from the central government, "no bloodshed [*buliuxue*], no compromise [*butuoxie*], and a dialogue is the biggest concession [*duihua shi zuida de rangbu*]." These emissaries maintained that Beijing leaders could not afford the political consequences of rescinding the August 31 Framework with the hint that some modifications based on that decision could be negotiable (interview #HK1-2). Finally, learning a lesson from the Sunflower precedent in which the rivalry between Ma Ying-jeou and Wang Jin-pyng had played a crucial role, HKFS intended to exploit the split in the government to its advantage. Carrie Lam hailed from the colonial officialdom and was seen as an acceptable alternative to Leung, who was widely suspected to be an underground CCP member; therefore, giving her the credit for handling the stalemate could help to realize the movement's goal (interview #HK19). Thus, the students stopped denouncing Carrie Lam in order to prepare for dialogue, an attempt to make an opportunity by leveraging the elite disunity, which did not pan out in the end.

While Taiwan's Sunflower Movement leaders channeled the growing impatience of the crowds by encouraging protesters to stage sit-ins at local KMT branch offices, the Hong Kong leaders chose to contain such explosive undercurrents for the sake of negotiation. On October 1 (day 4), Scholarism launched a human chain outside Golden Bauhinia Square to prevent protesters from entering and disrupting the official ceremony for the PRC's National Day (*Passion Times* 2016: 231).

It took more than two weeks for the talk between students and officials to take place on October 21 (day 24). The hardliner camp headed by Chief Executive Leung Chun-ying apparently intended to undermine the forthcoming dialogue with a series of provocative gestures, and as a result the student leaders decided to suspend the preparation for negotiation after the pro-government violence (day 6) and the police attempt to clear the Mong Kok occupation zone (day 20). Carrie Lam also decided to put off the dialogue, citing the reason as being that the students agitated for a noncooperation movement (day 12). Leung Chun-yin asserted that the occupation movement was being aided by "external forces" (day 22)—a trite and baseless accusation in China's media and Hong Kong's pro-Beijing newspapers.[18]

Through the intermediation of an HKU professor, HKFS and Carrie Lam had shared a basic understanding that both sides should not set preconditions for their meeting and the negotiation would subsequently be continued. There was also agreement on the conclusions of the dialogue in that the government was willing to give some concessions in exchange for the students acknowledging the officials' good faith. During the televised talk, Lam and other officials promised more consultations to reflect the citizens' opinions, which fell short of the HKFS's insistence that a new government report must include the popular demand for genuine suffrage. After the dialogue, the student representatives mounted the main stage at Admiralty and vehemently denounced the government as "shameless" and "deceitful," rather than giving some credit to Lam's team of negotiators. In the eyes of the government, HKFS had reneged on the agreement and Lam was severely criticized by hardliners in the government (Umbrella People 2015: 238–249). However, from the student perspective, it was Lam and her officials who first broke the promise by (1) deliberately omitting that the government report on political reform would be specifically sent to Beijing's Hong Kong and Macao Affairs Office and it should contain the demand to revoke the August 31 Framework, and (2) scheduling the follow-up talks after the 2017 election rather than before it (interview #HK58). Regardless of which side should be held responsible for the failure, it became nearly impossible for the moderates in the government and student leadership to collaborate afterward.

The Surge of Militants

The HKFS's failure to obtain significant concessions from the government unleashed the formerly restrained grassroots militancy. Originally the movement had largely followed the principle of nonviolent civil disobedience; now the "militants" (*yongwu pai*) were gaining ascendancy with the belief that protesters should fight back against police violence and protect themselves from injury or arrest. A student participant reflected on his change in mindset:

> In the beginning, I supported the idea of winning citizens' sympathy by playing the role of pitiful victims. Later on, I thought we should at least protect ourselves, and finally, I even found it acceptable to attack the policemen. The radical forces were becoming more popular, spreading the idea that we should not be passively beaten because it was useless. (Interview #HK8-1)

More and more participants began to wear masks and carry homemade shields in the occupation zones, and some of them were even practicing and teaching martial arts. Incidents of militant initiatives occurred, including the attempt to block an elevated walkway in Admiralty to prevent government employees from going to work (day 42), the storming of the legislative council (day 53), and the "shoppers' revolution" (occupiers pretending to be shoppers) (days 61 and 68). As the idea of "using (mass) militancy to deter (police) violence" (*yiwu zhibao*) gained currency and thereby threatened to eclipse the nonviolence principle, some moderate NGO and pan-democratic activists denounced these militants as government-planted provocateurs and they were willing to report these troublemakers to the police, which fueled the sense of betrayal among the militants.

It was in this context of polarization that the two student organizations gravitated toward a more militant stance. On the evening of November 30 (day 64), the students launched an offensive to besiege the Central Government Offices, with the intention of disrupting functioning the next morning. As a tacit nod to the militants, HKFS and Scholarism encouraged every participant to bring "whatever was necessary." A bloody overnight fight ensued on Long Wo Road, with the police eventually succeeding in taking back the streets by force and arresting forty protesters. The two student organizations acknowledged the failure and apologized to those who were injured.

The evolution of the Sunflower Movement and the Umbrella Movement shows that the standoffs generated a strong current of bottom-up militancy. Even the more centralized and coherent leadership in Taiwan was unable to prevent its eruption in the first week. By contrast, the Hongkonger leaders appeared successful in restraining radicalization for the purpose of negotiating with the government; yet after the failed dialogue, the mounting pressure became so irresistible that HKFS eventually succumbed to and launched an ill-thought and doomed disruptive protest, which in hindsight amounted to a last-ditch gamble by a visibly exhausted movement.

A War of Attrition

Table 5.1 indicates that a reversal of public attitude toward the Umbrella Movement happened after the third week. From then on, the number of people who wanted the occupation to stop immediately was more than double that of those who preferred it to continue. An increasingly unpopular movement was exhausting its moral capital in its challenge against the authorities.

A comparison with Table 4.1 shows that the Sunflower Movement enjoyed greater and more persistently popular support than the Umbrella Movement. There were a number of reasons for the difference, such as Hong Kong's incomplete democratization and the concomitant lower tolerance for social protests, as well as the organizational strength of the pro-Beijing camp and their previous counter-mobilizations. Nevertheless, the spatial pattern also mattered. Hong Kong's protesters blocked Admiralty's Harcourt Road, Mong Kok's Nathan Road and Argyle Street, and Causeway Bay's Hennessey Road, all of which were traffic arteries whose disruption caused great inconvenience to motorists, cabdrivers, and commuters. By contrast, Taiwan's Sunflower Movement closed only a section of Qingdao East Road and Jinan Road, neither of which was designed to sustain substantial traffic. In addition, Mong Kok and Causeway Bay were vibrant shopping districts whose store owners' business were severely affected by the ongoing protests, whereas the area

TABLE 5.1. APPROVAL AND DISAPPROVAL RATINGS FOR THE UMBRELLA MOVEMENT (PERCENTAGE)

	October 15 (day 18)	November 5 (day 39)	November 10 (day 44)	November 18 (day 52)	November 19 (day 53)	December 9 (day 73)	December 12 (day 76)
Approval	38	25	27	28	28	31	34
Disapproval	34	70	73	58	55	49	42

Notes: (1) Nine opinion polls were released during the seventy-nine-day period, and because of their tendentious questions, I did not include two surveys conducted by a pro-government party and a pro-Beijing newspaper. (2) Four surveys were conducted by HKUPOP (https://goo.gl/BAAAD3), and three by the CUHK's Centre for Communication and Public Opinion Survey (https://goo.gl/77WQxV), all accessed August 27, 2015.

around Taiwan's legislature was filled mostly with government buildings and schools, which helped to minimize the disturbance to other citizens. As such, the Hong Kong students had attempted to reduce the disruption with an official HKFS apology to citizens (day 8),[19] a proposal to limit occupation to evening hours (day 12),[20] and the suggestion to evacuate Admiralty's Queensway in exchange for the government opening Civic Square (day 16);[21] the last two plans did not pan out due to objections from other protesters. In Mong Kok, there were initiatives to encourage protesters to patronize the mom-and-pop stores, as their business was severely affected.

As the movements continued, they became more vulnerable to counter-protests and violent assault by pro-government mobsters. Journalistic sources indicated five anti-Sunflower rallies in Taiwan and fifteen anti-Umbrella events in Hong Kong. Physical attacks or threats by gangsters against movement participants emerged much earlier than organized counterprotests (day 2 in Taiwan and day 3 in Hong Kong). While the political function of counter-protests was to change public perception by showing the voice of the "silent majority," violence appeared more often as a psychological weapon to intimidate participants. Such violence appeared to have worked particularly well in Mong Kok, as some female students reported avoiding the area because of safety concerns (interview #HK56). In Hong Kong, the government consciously made use of the popular respect for the rule-of-law tradition. Since October 20 (day 20), the court had issued a series of injunctions to evacuate the occupation, which discouraged participation from moderate supporters because they did not want to defy the judiciary. There were lawyers who avoided being charged with presence in the occupation zone for fear of "contempt of court," which might lead to the revocation of their licenses (interview #HK35).

A protracted standoff also meant the gradual erosion of enthusiasm and morale among movement participants, which made it possible for the government to practice an attrition strategy (Cheng and Yuen 2017). My Hongkonger student interviewees indicated that class attendance went back to normal in the first week of November. Hong Kong's police began to disperse

Mong Kok protesters by force on October 17 (day 20). Clearly the standoffs represented a temporary truce at best; once the movements began to show signs of fatigue, the government was poised to retake the lost territory.

A "Pilotless Plane" Crash

Umbrella leaders demonstrated tactical flexibility by tacitly giving up the demand for Leung's resignation and focusing on the issue of universal suffrage. They also made use of disunity among the elites to further the movement's goals—for example, by agreeing to negotiate with Carrie Lam and sidelining Leung. Nonetheless, the Hong Kong movement was inherently crippled by its loose structure and weak decision-making capacity.

The HKFS's decision not to reciprocate the offer from moderate officials during the dialogue proved consequential. Seeing the decline in movement participation, the government closed the door on further negotiations, despite pleas from HKFS on November 28 (day 62) and Scholarism on December 3 (day 67). Facing the government's hardened attitude, the Umbrella leadership had to scramble for alternative exit proposals, which did not pan out as a viable solution in the end. The suggestions were an electronic vote by participants (day 26), the resignation of five-district opposition lawmakers for a de facto "referendum" on political reform (day 34), and an "Umbrella Opinion Day" (opinion poll by participants) (days 48–50). More challenging was the fact that participants in the occupation zones had shrunk to only the hardcore members who rejected any form of compromise and yet whose endorsement provided the legitimate grounds for the student leaders to announce a retreat.

The Umbrella Movement came to a discouraging end with police eviction and mass arrest, as three occupation zones were forcibly cleared one by one. Chan Kin-man aptly described the Umbrella Movement as a "pilotless plane";[22] we might add that the lack of coherent and effective leadership made for an erratic journey in which the flight eventually ended in a crash when the fuel was exhausted.

Resources and Resourcefulness

The unexpected emergence of a standoff brought about a retooling of the preexisting leadership structure. Here Marshall Ganz's (2000) key finding that the possession of material resources is not synonymous with resourcefulness or the strategic capacity to formulate viable decisions was relevant. In his classic study on the American farm worker movement, he argued that the well-endowed labor unions failed to organize immigrant workers, since they were accustomed to a top-down bureaucratic approach, whereas Cesar Chavez succeeded because his intimacy with the grass roots made the appropriate decisions possible.

The Hong Kong's OCLP had been preparing for the showdown with Beijing for more than year and thus had accumulated donated funds and materials in advance. OCLP maintained a security brigade (*jiuchadui*) of more than two hundred, who had received training in nonviolence (interview #HK39). Anticipating mass arrests or even casualties, OCLP had organized professionals with expertise in medical care, legal aid, and psychological counseling (interview #HK49). There were other parallel preparations. Inmediahk, an activist online media, held a training workshop to recruit citizen journalists in order to report on the planned sit-in protest (Inmediahk 2016: 15). Intellectuals and professors initiated a public education project, the University of Democracy to Come (*weilai minzhu daxue*), two weeks before the onset of the Umbrella Movement, which later evolved into a vibrant street forum in the occupation zone (P. Ho 2015: 13).

In Taiwan's Sunflower Movement, soliciting donations, arranging the logistical supply of materials, and mobilizing professionals took place only after the standoff had begun. DF was merely an ad hoc and loose coalition of NGOs with only one part-time staff member, whose meager resources paled in comparison to those of OCLP. There was no parallel preparation by media and intellectuals in Taiwan. While there was no involvement of religious groups prior to the occupation of the national legislature in Taiwan, the OCLP leadership made a conscious decision to appropriate Christian themes, such as love and peace, to legitimatize their advocacy of disruptive actions (interview #HK1-3). There was a two-day theological seminar on the Christian meaning of civil disobedience (S. Chan 2015: 387), while such religious preparedness was absent in Taiwan.

In terms of student participants, Hong Kong also held a comparative advantage over Taiwan. HKFS, as an official federation of the student associations of eight universities, had long been recognized as the territory's representative of students for its long-term participation in social and political movements. Scholarism, which earned its fame in leading the Anti–National Education campaign, had up to five hundred members in its prime.[23] Since there was a gradual warming of student mobilization prior to the standoff, efforts to cultivate more awareness among university and high school students were already under way. Immediately before the class boycott campaign, CUHK's Student Press published a special issue with a detailed analysis of contemporary worldwide student protests, including the Sunflower Movement.[24] Here again, Taiwan's BIY appeared almost like a non-entity in comparison because of its rudimentary structure.

Since standoffs represented a drastic rupture with the status quo ante, it became difficult, if not problematic, for movement leaders to convert their resources into capacity, which was urgently needed in the swiftly evolving confrontation with the authorities. More specifically, there were two reasons for the discontinuity. First, be it attempting to railroad through a controversial free-trade bill with China or firing tear gas against unarmed citizens, the threat induced by the government's misconceived responses functioned much like what James Jasper (1999) called a "moral shock," exerting a significantly more electrifying effect than what movement leaders could have elicited on their own under normal circumstances. Although DF did not prepare material resources as OCLP did, the occupation of the legislature attracted the immediate pooling of manpower, money, and logistical supplies, in similar fashion to what happened in Hong Kong. In both cases, the post hoc resource gathering turned out to be more powerful than prior preparation because it was able to tap voluntary contributions from citizens who had previously been unconcerned.

Second, prior planning always lagged behind the rapid unfolding of standoffs. One of the reasons why the OCLP trio hesitated in response was that they had previously announced October 1 as the initiation day. Accordingly, many of OCLP's trained volunteers had applied for leave from work on that day and could not join the protest as the confrontation intensified from September 26 (interview #HK55). OCLP had formulated a detailed action plan for a massive sit-in in Central, but when the conflict flared up in Admiralty (a metro stop away), the leadership appeared slow to adjust. Originally, they anticipated that the arrest of famous sit-in participants, such as Cardinal Joseph Zen, would garner international attention; yet what happened was that the police officers' brutal treatment of students generated citizen sympathy (interview #HK39). Arguably, the OCLP leadership was entrapped by their own plan. The fact that movement leadership had to be constructed post hoc during the standoffs made preexisting organization and prior planning of little use, or worse, a liability for the ensuing movement.

Leadership Effectiveness Compared

Making decisions in the unusual moments of standoffs was inherently complicated for a number of reasons. Core activists suffered from sleep deprivation and hygiene and health problems because of prolonged encampment and emotional upheavals. The behavior of Taiwanese and Hongkonger students was criticized by other participants. A Taiwanese NGO leader complained that students were faction-ridden, inconsistent, and irresponsible to such an extent that meetings with them were often inefficient because much time had to be spent on moderating their emotional responses (interview #TW10). A Hong Kong pan-democratic lawmaker criticized students for being rude and taking everything for granted (interview #HK22). Students often came late for meetings as if they were reluctant to share decision-making power with their seniors (interview #HK36). The source of such complaints was not only nonstudents; students also found the quality of discussion and decision making to be unsatisfactory. As a Hongkonger student noted:

> They often had long debates without coming to a decision. HKFS was always criticized for its slowness in reaching a conclusion. In the meetings, students often came back with different ideas. Student leaders played multiple roles, dealing with different crowds, and contacting diverse groups, and that was the reason why students always reported inconsistently in the meetings. (Interview #HK37)

Taiwanese students also felt frustrated that their meetings were often disrupted by unrelated issues or emergency incidents, so that a focused exchange of ideas became nearly impossible (interview #TW46). More irritating was the fact that a smokers' chat during recesses sometimes overturned the conclusions previously reached in the meeting (interview #TW39). Particularly in larger meetings, students often dozed off, or played with their mobile phones without paying attention to the ongoing discussion.

Aside from these common problems, establishing a leadership structure did not necessarily guarantee the capacity to direct the movement during standoffs. Hong Kong's five-party platform meetings were intermittent and non-decisional, finally collapsing before the police eviction, whereas Taiwan's leadership remained operational till the very end, when it managed to execute an orderly retreat. The contrast in effectiveness, however, was due to a number of situational factors.

First, social movement researchers have argued that space matters as an independent force that serves to pattern protest mobilization (Sewell 2001; D. Zhao 1998). The Sunflower Movement clearly enjoyed advantages in spatial arrangements that were denied to the Umbrella Movement. There was only one occupation zone, which facilitated coordination, and the core protesters were ensconced inside the legislative building, separated from outside supporters by the police. With the DPP lawmakers taking shifts to guard the eight gates to the plenary conference chamber, it was possible for some activists with connections to exit and enter repeatedly. The police cordon kept outside participants on the street, inadvertently elevating the status of the student leadership. Huang Kuo-chang described such spatial segregation as "the isolated island effect" (*gudao xiaoying*), which made the inside occupiers appear vulnerable, thus encouraging supporters to extend their stay on the outside. Rejecting the proposal for a full occupation of the legislature, Sunflower leaders in the legislature argued that the presence of the police cordon actually protected the occupiers as long as the authorities did not attempt a forced eviction (interview #TW46).

In retrospect, "the isolated island effect" defended the student leadership from the challenges of radical dissenters. On the afternoon of March 23 (day 6), Lin Fei-fan and Chen Wei-ting went to the entrance on Qingdao East Road in an attempt to dissuade angry protesters from storming their way inside. With tears in his eyes, Lin pleaded to the crowd for more patience:

> I have four pending legal cases. I have not graduated yet. I have been inside for six days, and I did not leave for the first three days. If you have better ways and careful planning, you are free to occupy anywhere, as long as you are willing to take the responsibility. (Quoted in Taipei Documentary Filmmakers' Union 2014)

Ironically, Lin was speaking in front of police officers, and it was their presence rather than Lin's emotional pleading that eventually prevented the protesters from coming in. By contrast, the Umbrella Movement leadership did not enjoy such spatial protection, and were thus directly exposed to insurgency from radical participants. The Main Stage on Harcourt Road represented the command center of the whole movement, with the evening rally as its daily highlight. As the standoff dragged on, participants became impatient with the lack of decisive action from student leaders. With the accumulated frustration, some participants began to target HKFS and Scholarism, as the Main Stage instantly became a resented spatial symbol of ineffectual leadership. The slogan "No Main Stage, Only the Mass" (*meiyou datai zhiyou qunzhong*) circulated in the occupation zones. Consequently, some participants had to volunteer to form a "defense line" (*fangxian*) in order to protect the speakers on the podium (interview #HK17)—a task that oddly enough was relegated to the police in Taiwan.

In order to calm the growing discontent, the MC group that managed the daily event on the main stage conceded by inviting up participants who were willing to speak for two or three minutes at a time, starting on November 9 (day 43). Thus it happened that militant followers of Wong Yuk-man and Civic Passion members mounted the podium almost every evening and cursed the student leaders using foul language, which gave rise to nasty brawls (interview #HK59). The situation deteriorated to such an extent that a "demolish the Main Stage" (*chai datai*) protest took place on November 21 (day 55), as hundreds of participants threatened to end by their own hand what they called "the one-stage dictatorship" (*yitai zhuanzheng*) because they were fed up with the "monopoly" of HKFS and Scholarism.[25]

Second, both movements needed some collaboration from the opposition parties. Hong Kong's opposition lawmakers provided physical space in the legislative council building where the students camped out. The pan-democratic parties also mobilized their members for volunteer work in the occupation zones. Taiwan's DPP mobilized its supporters for two major rallies on March 21 and 30 (days 4 and 13), and its Department of Social Movements maintained a liaison person inside the occupied chamber twenty-four hours a day to report on logistical needs, to which the DPP contributed quite substantially (interview #TW4).

There was a difference between using the opposition parties' resources and incorporating them into the decision-making process. DPP limited its participation to a subsidiary role by refraining from taking part in the decision-making process, whereas their Hongkonger counterparts sat in on the five-party platform meeting. Hong Kong's opposition was disjointed, ranging from gentlemanly moderates to street-warrior radicals, and their ideological differences exerted a polarizing influence. In the initial few days of the standoff, the moderate pan-democrats had suggested that the students should end the occupation quickly because they were more sensitive to voter responses. On the opposite end of the ideological spectrum, People Power and Civic Passion were among those who preferred more militant actions, and the two parties' followers waged territorial warfare in the Mong Kok occupation zone to vie for supremacy (*Passion Times* 2016: 120–121, 213).

Last, preexisting organizations with clear boundaries, hierarchical structures, and loyal membership turned out to be a hindrance to coordinated strategizing. As an established, property-owning student organization with representation in affiliated universities, HKFS should have been a valuable resource; however, its reliance on consensus rule for major decisions to maintain its territory-wide legitimacy made it extremely inflexible when on-the-spot judgment was needed. An HKFS leader acknowledged that their representatives at the five-party platform meeting were not authorized to make any promises. On many issues, HKFS later overturned conclusions reached in the five-party platform meetings, which partly explained why the pan-democratic politicians regarded the students as being inconsistent and lacking discipline (interview #HK16-1). Moreover, student leaders came from two distinct organizations, thereby increasing the costs of coordination. In the past, cooperation between HKFS and Scholarism had been problematic because of a lack of trust, making collaboration difficult during the Umbrella Movement. For instance, when five Scholarism members launched a hunger strike on December 1 (day 65) to continue the momentum of an apparently depleted movement, HKFS leaders were caught unprepared because Scholarism had just promised to collaborate on managing a withdrawal (interview #HK58). This incident indicated the existence of a subtle rivalry between these two student organizations.

Taiwan's case demonstrated the strength of prior organizational weakness. The twenty student delegates to the decision-making body were selected for their functional roles (media liaison, materials distribution, security, and others) in the legislature occupation. Since the existing organizations were rudimentary, there was no need to consider the participant students' prior affiliations in designing the leadership structure. Thus, although BIY was the first anti-CSSTA student group, its organizational significance quickly dissipated with the onset of the standoff.

There was a clear difference in the influence of leadership over rank-and-file participants between the two movements. Starting in the second week, the Sunflower leadership appeared firmly in control of the movement's direction, as evidenced by the fact that it was able to make the consequential decision to withdraw on the evening of April 7 (day 21), overcoming the reluctance of some die-hard participants. Such a decisive move remained an elusive goal for the Umbrella leadership. who had perennial difficulties with hardcore participants who refused to withdraw without achieving the goal. In fact, as noted in Chapter 3, there had emerged two conflicting movement networks in Hong Kong prior to the Umbrella Movement. In the first few days of the standoff, localists mounted a smear campaign against the student leadership by distributing wanted posters and handouts throughout the occupation zones. A number of targeted activists were personally threatened or humiliated by these assaults (Chan et al. 2015: 2, 10). Such infighting was hardly imaginable under the stronger leadership of the Sunflower Movement, which was even capable of suppressing dissenting voices on some occasions. On March 19 (day 2), a banner hanging in the occupied chamber, which characterized the anti-CSSTA protest as "opposition to free trade" (*fan ziyou maoyi*), was ordered to be removed (Hsieh 2016: 14). On March 30 (day 13), when the students staged a mass rally, the security team members forcefully confiscated flyers from a dissenting group called "Wings of Radical Politics" (*jijin ceyi*) before they could be distributed to the crowd (Yen et al. 2015: 104–105).

Yongshu Cai (2017: 116) pointed out that the Umbrella Movement's weak leadership originated from lack of organization, so the leaders had no authority over those self-motivated participants who tended to make decisions on their own. Taiwan's Sunflower Movement also drew strength from such unsolicited participation, which, however, did not weaken leadership effectiveness. In fact, the Umbrella Movement actually enjoyed more organizational resources, at least in the initial stages, due to the existence of HKFS and OCLP. As argued above, ex-ante variables did not necessarily predict the ensuing standoff evolution. The Sunflower Movement was able to maintain a more functional decision-making core because it possessed many spatial advantages, which gave rise to a secured and elevated leadership.

Contingency in Standoffs

The above analysis reveals that movement-government standoffs are highly "contingent" events as defined by their threefold meanings of indeterminacy, conditionality, and uncertainty (Schedler 2007: 70–73). First, standoffs are indeterminate because they are not inevitable developments that flow inexorably from the previous evolution. The scenario could have been different if

Taiwan's ruling party had not been so impatient to push the disputed free-trade act, or if Hong Kong's police had not been as aggressive in using tear gas against unarmed citizens. Second, whether standoffs can be concluded in favor of the movement depends on the existence of centralized and capable leadership, which cannot be guaranteed in advance. That Hong Kong's occupation simultaneously emerged in three disconnected zones constrained leadership effectiveness; Taiwan's student occupiers in the legislature, in contrast, were safely secluded behind the police cordon, which not only elevated their symbolic status but also protected them from dissident radicals. Last, the trajectory of standoffs is not easily predicted. Hong Kong's movement had more preparation, international attention, and stronger perseverance for sustained mobilization, yet it ended without being able to claim a symbolic victory for the movement. The hindsight advantage of having witnessed the Sunflower Movement turned out to be of little use, if not counterproductive, for Hong Kong's student leaders, since they placed so much hope in the elite's disunity that they missed their chance when the regime was most vulnerable during the first few days.

How can we account for the unforeseeable effect of contingency here? Standoffs represent a radical rupture with the routine state of affairs by suspending normal expectations. Movement agendas and leadership have to be constructed anew, rather than being inherited from the status quo ante. In his study on the Iranian Revolution, Charles Kurzman (2004b: 49) contends that the system of mosques was not a preexisting network for Islamists, but "a potentially valuable resource that had to be commandeered before it could be mobilized." Clearly, the onset of extraordinary activism reconfigured the circumstances that had engendered the protest in the first place, as obstacles were transformed into resources, threats into encouragement, organizations into rigidities, and loose networks into leadership structure. That standoffs constitute a fundamental break with the normal state of affairs explains why Hongkongers' preparedness, well-known leadership, and strong organizations quickly became liabilities once occupation occurred.

Contingency and Its Theoretical Meanings

Here the attention on contingency can offer us a complementary insight to revisit the existing perspectives from (1) the strategy model and (2) the theory of emergent norm.

First, recent years have seen calls for a more strategy-focused approach in the study of social movements. James Jasper is the main proponent of this strategy approach in opposition to the rational choice perspective that has adopted a narrowly instrumental conception of movement strategy. Instead, making strategic choices should be viewed as a matter involving biographical, cultural, and aesthetic meanings of the agency (Jasper 2004, 2014).

The strategy model and my exploration on contingency above are dissatisfied with the structuralist approach (which tends to see protests as an outcome of objective conditions) and the rationalistic approach (which reduces social movements to the result of individual action); both fail to explore the creative and interactive dimensions of social movements. No matter how well calculated a particular tactical choice is, its consequence is always indeterminate and conditional because the result is also based on the incumbents' responses. Nevertheless, there are noticeable differences in emphasis. The strategy model appears more geared toward making sense of "artful creativity" among movement participants (Jasper 1997: 11), which constitutes the essence of human agency, whereas this chapter focuses more on the situational rather than the personal dimensions of strategy making. As an atypical scenario, standoffs allow creative responses from the movement participants because of the inherent uncertainties. Standoffs also generate the inevitable movement fatigue and pressure for escalated conflicts, which obviously constrain the range of strategic choices. In other words, the contingency perspective is more akin to the view that both "the structural limitations and opportunities" need to be examined in the study of movement leadership (Morris and Staggenborg 2004).

Second, the stress on the novel properties of standoffs appears to hearken back to the tradition of emergent norm theory. Ralph Turner and Lewis Killian (1957: 12) maintain a categorical distinction between routine action and collective action, because the latter has to develop new rules of interaction in order to give orientation to the participants. The dynamic of social movements follows the crystallization of new norms, which gradually become the dominant definition of the situation in order to offer clear guidance to the crowd. The findings of the theory of emergent norm are subsequently eclipsed by resource mobilization theory, which contends that social movements are regular phenomena in modern society and hence follow routine logic similar to other organizations. With the proliferation and institutionalization of protest behaviors in democracy, it seems increasingly questionable to view social movements as a departure from the everyday world. The newer perspective, however, has been criticized for the opposite error of "normalizing collective protests," because it has unjustifiably marginalized those cases in which protesters deployed disruptive tactics (Piven and Cloward 1992).

Clearly, the two theoretical perspectives are looking at different subsets of social movements. The emergent norm theory is interested in revolutionary movements that intend to bring about a systemic change, whereas the resource mobilization theory attempts to explain those run-of-the-mill movements aimed at piecemeal and partial changes. With the advent of "social movement society," in which protests have been institutionalized as a permanent feature of modern democratic polity (Meyer and Tarrow 1998), one can safely argue that routinized movements have become the norm, accounting for the majority of social protests. Still, the world-wide rise in eventful protests and the dramatic confrontations with the authorities remind us of the significance of these arguably exceptional protests, which refuse to follow the expected script.

This chapter concurs with the theory of emergent norm in the sense that we need to pay attention to the nonroutine aspects of social movements while taking into account that they represent only a few, yet meaningful and consequential, cases. Even in democratic countries that legalize and tolerate protest behaviors, very few movements are able to illegally occupy public space and demand an immediate response from the authorities. The emergent norm theory is premised on symbolic interactionism that prioritizes construction of meanings that provide orientation to human conduct. By contrast, my investigation does not support the view of shared norm as a necessary precondition for sustained challenges to the government. The participants might be motivated by different values, yet what really brings about an atypical scenario of standoffs involves a number of factors, including the rising protest wave and miscalculation by incumbents.

Conclusion

On the eve of the second anniversary of the Umbrella Movement in 2016, Alex Chow told the media that he regretted not having prepared enough in advance. "If I had been more capable and my mind had been more steady, I would have offered comfort to my comrades by helping them to stabilize," he candidly reflected.[26] In a subsequent interview, Chow further explained:

> During the Umbrella Movement, it was rumored that the government would evict the protesters by force and the army would be mobilized, for which we did not have any psychological preparation. The talk about Occupying Central had been around for nearly two years, and yet there was no discussion of this possibility or any preparation for communication and strategy. It was due to this deficiency that none of us were able to respond to the situation cool-mindedly, and neither was there any preconceived idea that could be implemented immediately. We just responded in a haphazard way. (Interview #HK58)

Indeed, the standoffs emerged as such unanticipated and unusual situations that even the most engaged movement leaders were surprised by the rapid unfolding of the confrontations with the authorities.

The same characterization was equally applicable to Taiwan's Sunflower Movement, which initiated from a hastily cobbled-up plan to stage a sit-in protest inside the legislature. The Umbrella Movement was far more prepared than the Sunflower Movement in terms of communication, trained volunteers, financial donations, and logistical supplies. As this chapter has demonstrated, standoffs represented such a radical departure from the ex ante situation that the subsequent construction of leadership, rather than preparedness, played a more important role in shaping the outcome. A number of situational factors, including underdeveloped organizations, the spatial segregation of core participants, and the collapse of radical factions helped to consolidate a strong leadership structure in the Sunflower Movement, which facilitated an orderly retreat once it became clear that the government would not concede to its principal demands. In a documentary interview, Chen Wei-ting made this frank revelation:

> Occupation ... is like running a government, with me being the vice-president and Lin Fei-fan as the president. It is so disgusting and horrible that what we have been doing is almost like a government. Fei-fan and I are in charge of responding to Ma Ying-jeou and Jiang Yi-huah, and the other minor issues are delegated to our spokespersons. ... Now I fully understand Ma Ying-jeou's situation. My feeling is that I am fearful of democracy. (Quoted in Taipei Documentary Filmmakers' Union 2014)

Chen's confession revealed the inherent difficulties in reconciling the contradictory demands between leadership effectiveness and participatory democracy. Toward the end of occupation, one Sunflower leader appeared to lose his composure by defending the retreat decision as "at least more democratic than Ma Ying-jeou."[27] The irony was that successfully leading a movement during the standoff required certain minimal degrees of centralization of command, which not only ran counter to the spirit of spontaneity that animated these eventful protests all over the world but also was unforeseeable, no matter how well one might have previously prepared.

To sum up, this chapter contends that (1) movement leadership is constructed post hoc, making preexisting organizations and prior planning useless or, worse, a liability; (2) the effectiveness of the emergent leadership is the most unpredictable variable, since it is largely determined by a plethora of circumstantial factors; (3) standoffs set off a relentless drift toward more disruptive protests that tend to result in destructive escalation of confrontation with the authorities; (4) standoffs offer only a short window of opportunity for social movements (the longer they persist, the more perilous they become for participants); (5) as a corollary, movement leaders are willing to settle for a less satisfactory outcome, but a viable exit strategy hinges on the existence of a robust leadership, which is not always available. The gist of my observation is that standoffs are sui generis situations, in which contingency plays a particularly important role in determining the outcome.

If there is a practical lesson to be drawn from the above observation, it is that movement leaders need to be flexible, adaptive, and ready to accept a suboptimal outcome. Standoffs are fleeting, precarious, and high-risk situations precisely because the initial tolerance of incumbents is always provisional at best. With the full panoply of repressive forces still intact, they are simply waiting for an opportunity to restore the status quo ante.

6

Improvisation

Common to the Sunflower Movement and the Umbrella Movement was the high number of citizens who volunteered their effort, donations, and money to the ongoing protest.[1] Arguably, it was largely due to such an unsolicited, anonymous, and fearless outpouring of enthusiastic support that the government incumbents were forced to tolerate the mass occupations in the initial stages. For many participants, it was one of their most memorable experiences to receive gestures of kindness from strangers who required nothing in return. Even less well-off citizens contributed their share to the movement; cabdrivers declined to take fares from riders heading toward occupation zones, street vendors gave out food free of charge, and occupiers volunteered to collect garbage and sort recyclables as meticulously as possible. Rain gear was distributed when it was wet, warm soup when it was cold, and water when it was hot. An upside-down world came into being where indifference gave way to caring, estrangement to common purpose, selfishness to altruism, and suspicion to trust. According to a Sunflower occupier who decided to quit her job to stay in the movement:

> Doctors inside the legislative building paid attention to our health conditions by sanitizing us and cleaning the environment. Doctors and lawyers often chatted with us and solved our puzzles. They were

This chapter was adapted from Ming-sho Ho, "From Mobilization to Improvisation: The Lessons from Taiwan's 2014 Sunflower Movement," *Social Movement Studies*, September 18, 2017, 1–14, www.tandfonline.com.

the people with great professional capacity, but they chose to stay with us and offer their professional help. I felt hope for Taiwan because everyone here trusted each other. My feeling was that we would not fail or lose! (One More Story Citizen Voice Team 2014: 45)

The feeling of being empowered by widespread solidarity and generosity was also found in Hong Kong. A group of Christians described a rather unusual situation as follows:

Most participants and supporters experienced a kind of utopia, more or less, as life in the occupation zones was a kingdom of love and solidarity, and everyone underwent a baptism of spirituality. To use the language of Christianity, it was closer to living in the Kingdom of Heaven.... The occupation zones were transformed into an alternative community with shared ideals, free exchange of opinions, artistic flavor, and clean orderliness. They were simultaneously givers and receivers, leading a different life style in the Hong Kong society that was used to competition and alienated human relationships. (Hong Kong Christian Institute 2015: 20)

Such personal testimonies of invincibility or religious rapture pointed to a powerful current released by the unprecedented number of citizen participants who made their own decisions to contribute to the movement. They were not simply followers who waited to take orders from the leadership; instead, they essentially made a movement of their own through individual effort. It was not an exact characterization that they were "mobilized" into a movement because they took a personal stake in it. Observing the contemporary movement activism in the West, W. Lance Bennett and Alexandra Segerberg (2013: 23) identify an emerging pattern of "personalization of contentious politics" that is both self-expressive and self-satisfying. The same description can equally apply to Taiwanese and Hongkonger protesters.

In a sense, the phenomenon of widespread participation and contribution was akin to the surge of volunteerism following a disaster, as many citizens instantly felt obliged to do something for the benefit of others. In Taiwan's Sunflower Movement, one popular slogan was "We Have to Save Our Own Nation Ourselves" (*ziji guojia ziji jiu*), which powerfully portrayed the image of a nation plunged into a sudden danger that called for immediate patriotic responses. The same slogan was later borrowed and adapted in the Umbrella Movement as "We Have to Save Our Hong Kong Ourselves" (*ziji xianggang ziji jiu*) (Veg 2016: 670). Clearly, many Taiwanese and Hongkonger citizens viewed their own participation as an emergency rescue operation that could not afford any hesitation.

Among global eventful protests such a decentralized pattern of participation was common. With the emergence of spontaneous and uncoordinated collaboration, some writers contended, organizations and leadership had become obsolete (Graeber 2009; Invisible Committee 2009). The contemporary antisystem movements were said to take place "without the need for a leader and without any individual having a privileged insight" (Karatzogianni and Robinson 2010: 131). Michael Hardt and Antonio Negri (2017: xiv, 15–24) observed that "leadership" had become a dirty word in an age when the "multitude" became capable of strategy making. The abolition of the leader/follower distinction seemed to vindicate the anarchist belief in mass spontaneity over organization and discipline. In particular, the notion of "prefigurative politics" envisioned an alternative to the mainstream instrumental view of participation as a means toward the movement goal. Instead, what people did at the protest scene presaged the new social configuration to come (Graeber 2002: 72).

The movements in Taiwan and Hong Kong were emphatically not leaderless. As the previous chapters indicate, both movements constructed decision-making cores in the early stages of the standoffs, albeit with contrasting degrees of effectiveness. Nevertheless, both movements drew their strength from the unsolicited involvement of anonymous citizens. How can we explain the source of this mass enthusiasm? Where does this sudden outburst come from? What role does it play in the sustained confrontation with the authorities? This chapter contends that the existing conceptual tools of social movement studies are not well prepared for these unusual protests, since most theories devote their attention to routine, institutionalized, and hence more predictable social movements that are led by preexisting organizations. Here I conceptualize "improvisation," defined as "strategic response without prior planning," as a vital mechanism that made possible the orchestration of these atypical protests in Taiwan and Hong Kong.

This chapter provides an overview of improvisation in these two movements, with a classification of their functions and degree of innovation. The Sunflower Movement and the Umbrella Movement would have been nipped in the bud if there had been no unsolicited and instant input from anonymous citizens. However, there is a difference between recognizing these voluntary efforts and glorifying the wisdom and capacity of the "multitude." Such naive populism errs in the excessive homogenizing of movement participants without paying attention to the role played by seasoned activists. I present a realistic appraisal of improvisation by identifying its inherent tensions and limitations. Spontaneous responses from the participants constituted the very source of the movement's power but their role should not be overestimated.

From Mobilization to Improvisation

Ever since the 1970s, students of social movements have focused on the episode of mobilization as the basic unit of analysis. The *Oxford English Dic-*

tionary indicates the dual origins of "mobilization" as "the action or process of bringing into circulation or realizing assets, capital, etc." and "the action or process of preparing or organizing an army, fleet, etc."[2] The founding theorists' deliberate choice of such a term with financial and military etymologies aimed to highlight the disciplined and purposeful aspect of movement participation, which was often obscured by the stereotypical image of "a madding crowd" in earlier collective behavior theory (McPhail 1991: 219).

Tilly and Tarrow (2007: 219) define mobilization as the process whereby a political actor gains control over resources that are vital for political contention. As has been pointed out, earlier theorists did not provide a precise definition of "resource," but used the term to loosely refer to anything that was useful for the movement (Kitschelt 1991: 331). As such, mobilization covers a number of related but distinct activities, such as cultivating awareness, recruiting participants, fund-raising, building organizations, and establishing personal relations. In spite of its broadness, mobilization always presupposes the existence of a prior group, whose various degrees of coherence and coverage are supposed to have a direct bearing on the scale of movement participation. Hence, Tilly (1978: 84) proposes the hypothetical formula "mobilization = f (organization)," with the implication that the more organized a social movement is, the more capable it is of bringing people to the streets.

It is not that the organization-based mobilization model fails as an accurate portrait of contemporary movement activism. Quite the contrary, with the gradual institutionalization of social movements in democratic polities, it is a reasonable expectation that the majority of protests would take place in a preplanned and organized manner. There is a need to develop an alternative conceptual scheme to understand those rare but consequential moments when social movements depart from business-as-usual. There are times when preexisting organizations play only a limited role in stimulating popular participation and the required resources are voluntarily contributed by previously uninvolved citizens. To fill in the theoretical lacuna, David Snow and Dana Moss (2014) conceptualize "spontaneity" as a subtype of protest actions that are not "planned, intended, prearranged, or organized in advance of their occurrence." They identify some situations conducive to these spontaneous responses, including nonhierarchical organizations, uncertain and ambiguous moments, the existence of prior emotional priming, and so on. Clearly these conditions were present in the standoffs in Taiwan and Hong Kong.

This chapter uses the term "improvisation," defined as "strategic responses without prior planning," to shed light on unsolicited, yet consequential movement participation. As a core component of human agency, improvisation is the ability to generate creative responses to new situations. People do not improvise when they fail to take proactive action or when they closely follow the given script. Analyzing face-to-face interactions, Erving Goffman (1967: 261) contends that self-command under fluid and ever-changing circumstances should not be taken for granted, but rather is a social skill to be mastered. In this sense, the actor "must give himself up to certain rapid resolution of an uncertain outcome. And he must give himself to fate in this way when he could avoid it at reasonable cost." Just as an impromptu instrument performance is a hallmark of accomplished musicians, the ability to improvise interaction, even in a less familiar milieu, is a necessary social competence for human agents.

Social movement scholars have noticed the importance of improvisation. Tilly uses the term "repertoire" for the range of possible forms of protest that are available under certain historical conditions. Making a protest often involves a process of selecting the most appropriate action to challenge the authorities. Tilly and his collaborators recognize the improvisatory character of repertoire performance, which relies on the flair and finesse of movement practitioners. Hence, repertoire evolves "as scripted interactions in the improvisory manner of jazz or street theater rather than the more repetitious routines of art songs or religious rituals" (McAdam, Tarrow, and Tilly 2001: 49). Focusing on the role of improvisation helps us overcome the limits of the conventional model that views movements as organized mobilization. The issue here is not that the mainstream hierarchical and centralized social movement organizations are not effective, but that they do not exhaust all the possible ways of protesting. Especially in the unusual and dramatic situation of a standoff, in which the government is forced to tolerate mass law-breaking and the protesters appear vulnerable to police crackdown at any minute, such creative and unanticipated responses are more likely to take place.

Varieties of Improvisation

Both the Sunflower Movement and the Umbrella Movement involved prolonged and large-scale confrontation. Movement leaders made the executive decisions in bargaining with the authorities, leaving protest site management to the discretion of activists from NGOs and political parties. Because of the unprecedented scale, preexisting organizations were not able to provide enough resources and manpower, so citizens' initiatives filled in the gaps. In hindsight, there were five major types of improvisation: maintaining the logistical supply, encouraging stay and participation, maintaining morale, presenting a formidable image, and relaunching movement offensives.

Maintaining the Logistical Supply

Provisioning for the needs of the thousands of participants was inherently difficult, if not impossible, for any of the movement organizations, no matter how well-endowed they were. Once a standoff began, numerous supporters immediately volunteered to purchase and deliver materials to the occupation zones. In fact, the names of the two movements unmistakably originated from the largesse of the citizens. "Sunflower" came from a young florist's gift that was placed on the podium of the occupied chamber and that was later reported in the media (C. Li 2014: 202), whereas "umbrellas" first made their appearance on the protest scene when on-lookers on an overpass threw their parasols to the besieged students in Civic Square in order to provide them with protection from the police pepper spray.[3]

In Taiwan, in the early morning hours of March 19, when the students were still resisting police eviction, supporters had already ordered boxes of bottled water to be delivered to the legislature. Only a few hours later, the cardboard boxes they received from PChome (a popular shopping website) could have lined the whole section of a street and some of them were large enough for a person to fit inside (One More Story Citizen Voice Team 2014: 123). The swift delivery of materials took place in Hong Kong as well. At the intersection of Nathan Road and Argyle Street, passers-by who were on their way to work brought food, water, and other daily necessities to the remaining protesters on the morning of September 29 (day 2). It took only half a day for the stockpile of materials to amass into a small mountain, thus giving birth to the first depot station in Mong Kok (M. Lam 2015: 76).

Taking inventory, managing, and distributing these materials required a substantial amount of time and effort. At its zenith, there were twenty-six supply units in Admiralty, seven in Mong Kok, and two in Causeway Bay. They functioned like convenience stores in the occupation zones so that protesters could "easily spend all day in the village without spending a dime" (J. Ng 2016: 209). "Hospitality for others" became a prominent feature in the occupation zones (Huang and Rowen 2015: 33–36). In Taiwan, the materials team that serviced occupiers in the legislature was composed of twelve volunteers, who worked in shifts around the clock (interview #TW21). More numerous activists were responsible for the materials stations outside the legislature.

In both cases, there had been efforts to coordinate voluntary contributions in order to balance supply and demand; however, these did not function well partly because anonymous donors made individual decisions based on their own personal judgment as well as their possessions. A Taiwanese student participant was surprised to find daily contact lenses of all prescriptions, dry bodywashes, guitars, and condoms among the supplies (interview #TW14). In one interesting episode, the day after a picture of Chen Wei-ting holding a teddy bear as he slept was circulated on the Internet, more than eighty stuffed toys were delivered to the legislature.[4] In Hong Kong's Admiralty, the female restrooms were kept meticulously clean and provided with all kinds of hygiene, skincare, and cosmetic products (interview #HK47).

Clearly, what constituted daily necessities varied widely among the supporters, and donations involved not only an objective assessment of what participants needed but also subjective satisfaction from the act of donating.

In addition to material resources, professional skills were required to meet the needs of the protesters. Around three hundred volunteers, including medical doctors, registered nurses, and medical students, took shifts to deal with emergencies in Admiralty (J. Ng 2016: 207). In Taiwan, more than two hundred medical doctors, emergency medical technicians (EMTs), and other paramedic personnel managed four outside first-aid centers nonstop (interview #TW41). Dozens of medical professionals took shifts on duty inside the legislature.[5] Skilled technicians might not enjoy the privileged status of medical professionals, and yet their contributions were no less significant. Hong Kong's carpenters assembled makeshift lighting equipment for the convenience of occupiers (S. Lau 2015: 95–97). Taiwan's occupiers inside the legislature suffered from a lack of air-conditioning in the first few days, but a makeshift ventilation tube built by a plumber enabled them to breathe fresh air again (H. Xu 2014: 167).

Encouraging Stay and Participation

Both movements involved prolonged confrontation and, as such, it became strategically important for them to constantly maintain large enough crowds in the occupation zones to keep up pressure on the authorities. To achieve this goal, those who were already onsite needed incentives to extend their stay, and those who were not onsite required encouragement to come. Both in Taiwan and Hong Kong, drinks, meals, and snacks were regularly distributed to all participants. Volunteers set up stations to recharge mobile phone batteries. A group of Hongkonger students with a background in electronic engineering fashioned emergency recharging devices out of automotive batteries (interview #HK15-1).

In order to extend the protesters' stay in the occupation zones, activities such as speeches, musical performances, film screenings, and opinion sharing were held on Admiralty's main stage as well as at the two side entrances to the legislature on Qingdao East Road and Jinan Road in Taipei. As mentioned in the previous chapter, these events were largely organized by NGO activists who were trusted by the student leaders. However, these events were insufficient to hold the attention of the numerous and diverse participants— a need that was met by improvisation. Both in Hong Kong and Taiwan, university professors took shifts giving street lectures on related topics. Hong Kong's Mobile Democracy Classroom operated continuously for fifty-three days by holding events in three occupation zones.[6] In Taiwan, a similar Street Democracy Classroom Action (*jietou minzhu jiaoshi xingdong*) began on March 20 (day 3) and continued until April 2 (day 16).[7] University students also volunteered free tutoring services for high school students who were facing greater pressure from examinations. The effort to promote deliberative democracy as a policy-making procedure in Taiwan had been under way since 2000 (Chen and Lin 2008), and during the Sunflower Movement, a "Dstreet" project emerged to experiment with its application in a protest situation. From March 26 (day 9), Dstreet held ten days of such activities by inviting protesters to share their ideas on cross-strait trade.[8]

As for those who had stayed away from the scene, both Taiwanese and Hongkonger activists improvised on how to bring more accessible information to the public, because both the CSSTA and political reform involved a number of esoteric technicalities that were difficult to explain to laypeople. Immediately after the 30-second Incident, Internet activists from Watchout (*wocao*), an online congress-monitoring organization, decided to produce infographics, called "lazy people's packages" (*lanren bao*), to highlight the CSSTA's potential harm. Their infographics were finished a few hours before the students rushed into the legislature and were viewed by more than 100,000 computer users on the first day (C. Hung 2015: 103–104). In Hong Kong, a group of students formed Speak for the Truth (*tuyan*), which also worked to produce easily readable infographics. Later, they received financial sponsorship to print the contents as handouts (M. Lam 2015: 224–225). A group of g0v.tw programmers established an online platform to facilitate the sharing of real-time information during the Sunflower Movement and, later on, the digital technology was exported to Hong Kong.

In Hong Kong, it was easy to take a metro or bus ride to the occupation zones, whereas the cost of transportation to travel to Taipei from outside the city might have prevented some supporters from attending in Taiwan. Starting from the midnight hours of March 19, there was emergency busing for students in central and southern Taiwan. Such initiatives proceeded under the auspices of university professors, NGOs, and pro-independence organizations. Afterward, a campaign emerged to finance transportation for students. Student participants who did volunteer jobs in the occupation zone could be reimbursed for their tickets (One More Story Citizen Voice Team 2014: 86).

Maintaining Morale

Taking part in an unexpectedly prolonged movement was fraught with anxiety and frustration; yet the leaders seemed to be too preoccupied with executive decisions to pay much attention to the psychological needs of participants. There appeared to be an excessive instrumentalism on the part of movement leadership. A Taiwanese activist revealed the unpleasant experience of always being told to do something without really knowing the meaning or purpose of such action (interview #TW 46). Another Hongkonger student complained about the utilitarianism among leadership:

Their way of making a movement was totally dehumanizing. . . . If someone felt sick or fails, it did not affect how they work. It was your own business that you were not able to keep up with them and they did not have the time to pay attention to why you failed. In the end, they did not bother to communicate. They just assigned a task to anyone who has free time. (Interview #HK44)

Such cavalier disregard for mass participants was certainly not conducive to maintaining morale, particularly when quite a number of protesters personally experienced police violence and developed traits akin to posttraumatic stress disorder. Taiwan's clinical psychologists intervened on March 23 (day 5) upon learning of strong emotional reactions among movement participants. Soon a support team of practitioners formed to take care of mental health inside the legislature (I. Su 2014). After the Executive Yuan Incident, a "March 18 psychological service team" (*sanyiba xinli fuwu tuandui*), composed of more than fifty medical doctors and social workers, set up a tent on Jinan Road to offer counseling to victimized participants.[9] Hong Kong's psychological professionals also launched initiatives. More than half of the local clinical psychologists and educational psychologists signed a statement of support for the students. In Admiralty, they managed a station providing professional help on the spot (interview #HK49).

There was an outburst of handicraft activities in the occupation zone as participants began to work on artistic projects such as paper folding, leatherwork, knitting, and carving to share with others; consequently, there emerged a large number of sunflower-themed and umbrella-themed memorabilia. A Taiwanese participant who worked in screen-printing said people without money could also find a way to contribute their support (H. Xu 2014: 129). A Hong Kong student who shared her handmade rubber stamps explained, "It is better to preserve some souvenirs before it is over someday" (interview #HK56). Supporters intended to make their participation personally meaningful, rather than being there passively as a member of the crowd. Making handicrafts and sharing them not only transformed the seemingly idle and purposeless waiting time into productive labor but also reinforced the sense of community with a common purpose.

There were innovative ways to maintain movement morale. A group of Hong Kong's artists created an art installation project called "Stand by You: Add Oil Machine" (where "add oil" in Chinese is an expression of encouragement and support). For the project, artists collected messages of support from social media from all over the world and projected them onto the wall every evening. It was meant to bring support from those could not make it to the scene to cheer up the occupiers. The Add Oil Machine, which made its debut in Admiralty on September 29 (day 2) and lasted until the occupiers there were evicted, received messages from more than ninety countries (interview #HK63).

While Hong Kong's Add Oil Machine was designed to boost the spirits of participants, Taiwan's "Intestine Flower Trash Talk Forum" (*dachanghua leshehua luntan*) (the name deriving from a word play on "Sunflower") was meant to release tension and frustration among participants. After the students announced the decision to withdraw on April 7, a music activist, Indie DaaDee, hosted a talk show event by inviting participants to come forward to express their discontent. The forum went viral for three consecutive nights starting on April 8, tallying more than 100,000 online viewers at its peak. Lin Fei-fan and Chen Wei-ting also showed up at the event and, following a prescribed script, declared personal support for Taiwan independence, drinking beer, and mouthing profanities—the exact opposite of the uptight and clean image of the Sunflower Movement. As Indie DaaDee later revealed, he decided to create a collective platform for catharsis because he saw so much unexpressed frustration among the participants.[10] In a way, one might say that the Sunflower Movement was able to execute an orderly retreat partly because those frustrated participants had their voices heard.

Presenting a Favorable Image

Traditionally, both Taiwanese and Hongkongers had low tolerance for disruptive protests; therefore, winning the citizens' hearts and minds became a vital task for the movements. Movement participants appeared conscious of the need to gain social acceptance for their law-breaking behavior. Cleaning up garbage, sorting, and recycling were certainly necessary to maintain hygienic conditions, but these acts also powerfully showed the demonstrators' civic-mindedness and willingness to take responsibility for the mess they brought about, without passing it on to the cleaners. Lecturing and tutoring helped to encourage students to stay longer in the occupation zones, but these events were also instrumental in neutralizing conservative criticism that the students had abandoned their studies for something more exciting. Hong Kong's student protest, starting on September 22, proceeded under the slogan "boycotting class, but not the study" (*bake bu baxue*), whereas Taiwan's professors staged their street lectures with the idealistic claim that "where the students are, there are classrooms" (*xuesheng zaina jiaoshi jiu zaina*). Both these framing strategies aimed to preempt criticism that students and teachers had forfeited their duties.

Arguably the most iconic spectacle of Hong Kong's movement was the "Umbrella study corner" (*zheda zixiu shi*), which evolved from a few tables and chairs to a well-lit and paved reading area with Wi-Fi connection and food that could accommodate hundreds of students who could access free and on-demand tutoring help. International correspondents appeared to marvel at this ostensible display of civility among demonstrators, even to the extent that the Umbrella Movement was described as "orderly," "the tidiest," and "the most polite" protest ever.[11]

Although cross-strait trade liberalization and universal suffrage were different issues, both movements challenged the authorities in the name of democracy. Protesters attempted to display their diverse backgrounds so that their movements could appear to represent voices across the spectrum. There were deliberate acts to celebrate multiculturalism and diverse identities in the occupation zones. In Hong Kong, people with disabilities and of South Asian origins were present on the scene (Hong Kong Christian Institute 2015: 39–46, 202–209), while expatriate professionals' contributions were also a notable phenomenon (J. Ng 2016: 211–213). Although most mainland students stayed away from the Umbrella Movement—and actually quite a number of them were vocally critical because of their ingrained nationalistic sentiments—some of my interviewees insisted that there were pro-Umbrella mainland students who contributed their share (interview #HK5-1).

Taiwan's indigenous people, roughly 2 percent of the population, had a high-profile presence in the Sunflower Movement. Some indigenous students were among the first protesters who broke into the legislature, and they immediately invited more compatriots to come. The Anti-CSSTA Black Box Indigenous Youth Forum (*yuanzhuminzu qingnian fan heixiang fumao luntan*) was set on March 22 (day 5) and held an event every evening in the occupation zone. It was due to their presence that deliberative democracy street events included topics on how free trade affects indigenous people (interview #TW11). Partly because of the encouraged inclusiveness, a study found that some of Taiwan's housewives who were previously absent from street protests were empowered to "make private public" by expressing their daily concerns during the Sunflower Movement (C. Yang 2017).

Enjoying international attention and the spotlight also helped to gain bargaining power for the movement. In this aspect, Hong Kong apparently possessed an advantage that was denied to Taiwan. As a former British colony, a gateway to China, and a global financial hub, Hong Kong's movement attracted more international attention than Taiwan's because more foreign correspondents were stationed there. Taiwan's participants were conscious of the need for better liaison with the international media. A working group, composed of more than eighty participants, came into being on March 24 (day 7), and functioned as the international face of the Sunflower Movement by immediately sending out news releases in thirteen languages (interview #TW19).

Relaunching Movement Offensives

As the standoffs in both Hong Kong and Taiwan dragged on, the mobilizing capacity of movement leaders declined. Not counting the disastrous attempt to blockade government buildings on November 30 (day 64), the last mass rally held by Hong Kong's students took place on October 10 (day 13). Similarly, after a successful gathering on March 30 (day 13), Taiwan's student leaders did not attempt to stage a comparable event. Clearly, time was not on the side of protesters. Practically speaking, all that was left for the movement leaders to do was prolong the precarious stalemate in the hope that elite disunity might bring about more acceptable concessions, which happened in Taiwan but not in Hong Kong.

The leaders' inability to launch more offensives gave the challenged governments a chance to recoup from the initial shock. As the movements were in danger of losing their momentum, acts of improvisation helped to open new zones of engagement to maintain pressure on the governments. On the evening of October 14 (day 17), Hong Kong's protesters launched a spontaneous sit-in to block Lung Wo Road, which was put down by the police, with forty-five people arrested and dozens seriously injured. Social-worker activist Tsang Kin-chiu was taken to a dark corner and savagely beaten by seven police officers for around ten minutes, an incident that was filmed by television cameramen. The "Dark Corner Incident" dealt a mighty blow to Hong Kong's policemen, who had been accused of conniving with violent progovernment mobsters. The Social Workers' General Union immediately launched a protest that evening at police headquarters, which attracted hundreds of participants. It was due to this pressure that the police decided to suspend the seven officers involved and place them under investigation.[12] A campaign to bring the "Seven Black Policemen" to justice ensued.

On October 23 (day 26), a group called "the Hong Kong Spidie" hung a giant banner with the slogan "I Want Real Universal Suffrage" (*woyao zhen puxuan*) from the highest point on Lion Rock, arguably the most symbolic place in the territory, signifying Hongkongers' hard-working spirit (Umbrella People 2015: 250–257). Although the Lion Rock banner was removed within hours, the improvised act developed into a protest repertoire of its own, representing the defiant spirit of resistance, as many activists were inspired to replicate it on other mountain peaks or high buildings, both before and after the end of the Umbrella Movement.

The Sunflower Movement witnessed the proliferation of diversified movement tactics as its confrontation with the authorities entered the third week. Newer campaigns were independently launched with little or no consultation with movement leaders. Democracy Kuroshio (*minzhu heichao*), a student organization primarily in southern Taiwan, started a series of street demonstrations at the local offices of KMT lawmakers starting on April 4 (day 18). These events turned out to be more successful than expected because hundreds of participants showed up to support the student initiatives.[13] Beez (*xiaomifeng*) was a decentralized organization formed on April 3 (day 17), with more than a hundred cells (which they called "beehives") all over Taiwan. Beez activists staged street speeches; led impromptu singing of *Island's Sunrise* (*daoyu tianguang*), a rock song created to support the Sunflower Movement; and distributed leaflets. Beez participants created a variety of flyers to highlight the negative impacts of a free trade treaty with China and placed them in relevant places; for example, flyers discussing the impact on medical care were placed in hospitals, and flyers on publishing were placed in bookstores. At its climax, more than seven thousand people were involved in this activism (interview #TW18).

These initiatives represented ingenious ways to open new zones of engagement when the movement leaders appeared to have exhausted their capacity to mobilize mass rallies. They helped to spread the movement's messages, encourage participation, and maintain pressure on the authorities.

Degrees of Originality

In addition to categorizing these numerous acts of decentralized collaboration by their function, it is also possible to view them in terms of the degree of deviation from routine activities. Broadly speaking, there existed three types of improvisation: improvisation by replication, improvisation by adaptation, and improvisation by innovation.

Improvisation by Replication

Applying previously used solutions to meet a new situation was the simplest form of improvisation, since past experience provided a more or less reliable guide when facing uncertainty. In Taiwan, hours after the successful occupation, many independent efforts emerged among those who were not involved at the start. Student activists outside Taipei immediately rallied their friends and chartered buses to join the protest in the early hours of the morning (interview #TW27). Internet activists also quickly responded by setting up an online broadcasting system to cover the incident before television camera crews arrived. These efforts were unplanned and uncoordinated, but not unprecedented. Soliciting financial support to transport students to Taipei had been put into practice during previous campaigns, for example in the 2012 Anti–Media Monopoly Movement. The same goes for the instant establishment of online broadcasting, since participants knew that mainstream media tended to adopt negative framing by magnifying the conflict scene and downplaying movement demands in their previous campaigns (C. Hung 2015: 64).

With the onset of standoff in Hong Kong, many university student associations immediately galvanized into action to support the movement, even without being requested to do so by the HKFS. The City University of Hong Kong Students' Union, for example, quickly recruited volunteers for a variety of tasks: collecting and transporting materials, liaising with school leadership, lobbying for professors' support, and encouraging students to join the protest (interview #HK40). Another instance of replication was that a veteran activist of the Anti–Express Rail campaign wrote an FAQ, particularly with Chinese mainland readers in mind. The article, which eloquently defended the students' action and clarified a number of rumors (such as the involvement of foreign forces and political instigation), was posted online immediately after the police's tear-gas assault and gained instant and widespread circulation in China's social media, with more than a million online users sharing the piece (interview #HK7).[14]

These supportive acts were executed by people with previous activism experience. True, they reenacted what they had been doing before, but the real contribution consisted in their timely and autonomous reaction when the movement leadership was in disarray.

Improvisation by Adaptation

Replicating a previously used tactic was effective when it aimed at satisfying an analogous need; for example, encouraging more participation or spreading the movement's message without it being distorted by the hostile media. There were times, however, when the same task required a different approach, since the change in circumstances had rendered the previous methods inadequate or inapplicable. A relevant case was how the Taiwanese activists reacted to the apparent failure of a nationwide class boycott campaign, which was announced on March 23 (day 6) by the movement leaders. In a number of universities, students had negotiated with the school administration for a temporary suspension of classes but to no avail.[15] Students then decided to stage a series of "democracy classrooms" on campus, in which the issues of civil disobedience and free trade were discussed. In other words, students adapted to campus conservatism with these onsite teach-ins in order to reach those students who had not visited the occupation site and create an impression of intercampus solidarity.

Another instance was the formation of the "Independent Company of Lane Eight" (*baxiang duli lian*). That military appellation referred to an ad hoc group of participants who took turns guarding an intersection on Linsen South Road, Lane Eight (see no. 4 in Figure 4.1), where police reinforcements could easily be deployed without encountering the crowd on Qingdao East Road and Jinan Road. The Sunflower leaders within the legislature had apparently overlooked this area because they were primarily concerned with drawing supporters to location numbers 1 and 2, which were closer to the occupied chamber. Outside activists discovered the strategic location and managed to stage events and activities on their own because they shared the same goal of preventing a police assault. The expression "independent company" meant that they did not receive orders from headquarters directly, yet they remained an integral part of the network of combatants.[16] That military metaphor summed up the gist of improvisation rather nicely.

Hong Kong's security brigade members also needed to adapt to unexpected and swift turns in the situation. The OCLP trio had originally envisioned an orderly sit-in with a division of nine areas, each assigned a number of security brigade members who were authorized to turn away those who refused to follow the nonviolence conduct code. However, as the Umbrella Movement came into being with the unexpected resistance of ordinary citizens, the security brigade members immediately found themselves unwelcome at the occupation, let alone able to enforce the OCLP rules. As such, they decided not to wear prepared uniforms or badges in order not to draw attention to their presence. Nevertheless, since they were equipped with walkie-talkies provided by the OCLP, they were able to handle certain emergency situations in Admiralty's occupation zone. An adapted and less intrusive method to maintain order continued to the very last day (interview #HK39).

Improvisation by Innovation

The most inventive improvisation moved a step further by actively finding new needs and then devising means to satisfy them. This represented a bolder departure because these new needs were discovered independently, often unknown or ignored by movement leaders, and they had to be met by unconventional or untried methods. A relevant case here is how a "team of 3,621" in Taiwan experimented with online crowd funding to place a full-page advertisement in the *New York Times* on March 29.

This independent project was initiated by a group of Internet activists who wanted to be helpful beyond just joining the crowd. At first, they were busy reworking the complex details of the CSSTA into easily readable infographics. Later they discovered a generational digital divide, since senior citizens were not used to receiving online information, so they decided to try online fundraising to place advertisements in major domestic newspapers. The crowd-funding campaign began at the stroke of midnight on March 24, which happened to coincide with the police suppression of the sit-in at the Executive Yuan. Within three hours, they had collected contributions of NT$ 6.3 million (US$200,000) from 3,621 donors, more than four times their goal. With this money, they were able to fund three waves of local newspaper advertisements plus an additional pamphlet, and with the help of overseas compatriots, they were able to reach an international audience by placing a full-page advertisement in the *New York Times*.

In Hong Kong, a similar crowd-funding project was initiated by a football fan, who was incensed by a pro-Beijing politician's use of the motto of

Liverpool Football Club "You'll Never Walk Alone" to support the police. Within twelve hours, more than five thousand supporters answered this call by contributing HK$70,000 (US$9,000). A full-page advertisement to support the Umbrella Movement in the name of football fans appeared in a local newspaper two days later (Umbrella People 2015: 188–195).

Improvisation as Decentralized Collaboration

The emergence of these anonymous acts of improvisation filled the vacuum in the confusing initial stages of the protests and, later on, even with the formation of a decision-making core, decentralized collaboration continued to provide indispensable resources and assistance as the standoffs dragged on. There were objective difficulties for the leadership to exercise comprehensive command once the movements exceeded a certain size. Movement leaders often possessed insufficient or incorrect real-time information so that a great majority of their decisions were not proactive but rather came as responses to the evolving situation. Moreover, their discussions tended to focus on a few select issues of strategic significance. Given their protracted and inefficient ways of conducting a meeting, it was practically impossible for the movement leaders to take care of every detail. For example, there had been an urgent suggestion that HKFS should provide first-aid services to injured participants in the first few days. Yet Hong Kong's student leaders failed to respond to this request because they were too preoccupied with other issues (interview #HK45). As such, there appeared to be no way to satisfy emergent needs in such a large-scale and sustained movement other than relying on decentralized collaboration.

Improvisation made possible the invention of some novel protest repertoires. For example, to neutralize provocation by pro-government protesters, Hong Kong's demonstrators devised a humorous way of collectively singing "Happy Birthday" to the troublemakers. Wishing someone a happy birthday soon was adopted as an effective tactic to defuse the tension deliberately created by counterprotesters (Protesters in Occupation Zones 2015: 170–171). After the police dispersed the occupation in Mong Kok, a "shoppers' revolution" sprang up, as protesters made their attempts to occupy by pretending to be shoppers (Gan 2017). In Taiwan, the police turned a blind eye to a counterprotest of mobsters led by a Beijing-related mafia boss on April 1 (day 15) and described his action as merely "passing by" (*luguo*) on the way to the legislature for a petition. After the conclusion of the Sunflower Movement, a number of these "passing-by" protests took place, such as the siege against the police precinct office on April 11 (see Chapter 7).

There is evidence that such decentralized patterns of decision making sometimes worked better than top-down coordination. The OCLP's detailed plan for an orderly mass sit-in became impracticable as soon as its leaders declared the launch. In Taiwan's Sunflower Movement, two episodes vividly demonstrated the limit of hierarchical decision making.

On the second day of the occupation, Sunflower leaders were worried that if they were not able to fill Qingdao East Road and Jinan Road with people, they could be dispersed at any time. They requested that the opposition party send in its supporters. Since the DPP had scheduled a public hearing on the CSSTA for the following day, March 21 (day 4) was the earliest possible time they could arrange. On that day, the DPP mobilized roughly 160 busloads of supporters from central and southern Taiwan. Including those who came from the greater Taipei metropolitan area, the DPP chairperson claimed to have brought more than ten thousand people to back up the student occupiers, which unexpectedly proved to be a publicity disaster. Since there had been thousands of protesters on the street by then and the police had long ceased pulling occupiers out, there were complaints that the DPP had attempted to "steal the thunder" from student activists. An inadvertent remark by the DPP chairperson was perceived as an attempt to gain electoral advantage; he later had to issue an apology for that (interview #TW4). Consequently, mass mobilization by the opposition party turned out to be of little help even though it was first proposed by the movement leaders. The traditional organizational mobilization failed precisely because its rigidity failed to keep up with the rapidly evolving situation.

The second case consisted of the call for people to take shifts in protecting the occupiers after the climax of the March 30 rally (day 13). At that time the Sunflower leaders were concerned that the third week might see a sharp decline in participation. Thus in the concluding speech of that evening, Lin Fei-fan urged the audience to form seven-person groups to rotate their attendance in a weekly pattern by familiarizing themselves with strangers and exchanging contact information. The attempt to maintain mass participation failed completely, as the morning of the next day saw only a few hundred protesters on the streets. Lin later embarrassingly acknowledged that supporters did not respond eagerly to his plea.[17]

This disappointing result deserves a closer look because Lin's speech was widely acclaimed as such a success that there were even suggestions that the twenty-six-year-old graduate student should run for president.[18] There was a glaring gap between the leader's charismatic performance and the participants' lukewarm response. The plan to rotate participation in a week's protest among mutual strangers was too inflexible to be improvised. This top-down request failed because it disregarded participants' own decision making by turning their presence into a mechanical duty to a randomly formed seven-person group with which they did not identify.

In short, improvisation played a critical role that made two eventful protests possible precisely because they emanated from individual participants' initiatives. These acts of unplanned collaboration were quick, flexible, and innovative only insofar as participants did not take orders from the movement leadership.

Limits of Improvisation

Recognition of the valuable contributions made possible by improvisation does not mean that movement leadership had become unnecessary or obsolete. Improvisation fulfilled many vital needs to sustain the movement, but it was not fit for all purposes or ready for deployment at all times. It took unusually shocking events such as the police tear-gas attack and the student occupation of the legislature to activate the groundswell of improvisation by anonymous citizens. It follows that most other social protests have been unable to tap into the vast pool of latent resources because they remained conventional and routine.

Moreover, granted that both Hongkonger and Taiwanese movement leaders were prone to making mistakes and at times appeared to lose their grip on the direction of the movement, decentralized decision making was also not immune from this flaw. In Taiwan, the failed attempt to occupy the Executive Yuan originated from an ill-planned, arguably irresponsible, act of improvisation, as some radical student activists were determined to escalate the confrontation despite the core leaders' initial reservations. The radical faction succeeded in seizing the right moment, as public indignation soared after Ma Ying-jeou's press conference on the morning of March 23 (day 6). They did not anticipate that participants would bear the full brunt of an all-out police crackdown. In Hong Kong, the first few days witnessed chaotic circulation of rumors of army deployment, which led to the call for retreat by the OCLP and student leaders. As such, many participants thought the provision of exact real-time information was a critical task. As many as one hundred students formed a clandestine reconnaissance network by fielding volunteers to some strategic locations on a rotating basis and reporting the situation around the clock via social media (interview #HK8-1). In hindsight, such efforts were of only limited use, as the government decided to pull back the police force after it failed to disperse the crowd. When pro-government mobsters launched their violence on October 3 (day 6), mainstream media carried instant messages about the development, which made the scouting team's work virtually redundant. In other words, improvisation did not always lead to an optimal decision or allocation of resources.

Improvisation derived from the willingness of individual participants to contribute their share, from which they derived the subjective satisfaction of being an integral part of the movement. Yet there were times that their psychological need for self-affirmation created coordination problems because they followed nothing but their personal convictions. Conflicts over spatial management in the occupation zones were ubiquitous. Many Hongkonger participants commandeered police fences and used them to build barricades to prevent the police from advancing. As they volunteered to guard these protection barriers, a proprietorial sense took root, as if they were entitled to the turf. They did not allow other people to make changes to their barriers because it had become a personal trophy after battling the police (Protesters in Occupation Zones 2015: 93). OCLP leaders once spent an entire morning conducting a deliberate democracy forum on whether to remove a section of barricades that had lost their protective function after the police retreat and had become an obstacle blocking the flow of protesters (interview #HK1-2).

In Taiwan, there was no preorganized security brigade, so all those who volunteered to maintain order were recruited on the spot, which made teamwork and cooperation more difficult. Activists who took over a shift frequently did not know the identity of their predecessors (interview #TW55). Misunderstandings and miscommunications were common. There was a period of time when as many as seven groups took charge of security on Qingdao East Road, and all of them insisted on acting independently (interview #TW2-1). These security members were untrained and inexperienced, and therefore they tended to abuse their authority. Especially during the first week, when Qingdao East Road and Jinan Road were filled with participants, the security members attempted to impose strict rules on the direction of flow and maintaining an emergency corridor (*yiliao tongdao*), which caused inconvenience and resentment. A student activist observed:

> Those amateurs often appeared bossy and arrogant once they got a bit of power. This was a trait of human fragility because everyone loved to be seen and to be affirmed. One night I was assigned leadership over the security team on Qingdao East Road. When patrolling my assigned area, I was surprised to meet another guy who claimed to be the leader. He even challenged my credentials by provokingly asking whether I had authorization from the top. (Interview #TW13)

Quite a number of volunteers falsely claimed that their authorization came from certain persons or organizations. The Citizen 1985 Action Coalition, a movement organization formed one year before the Sunflower Movement, mobilized around two hundred volunteers to maintain order on Qingdao East Road in the first few days. But later on, many unaffiliated people claimed to be members of that organization and their problematic behaviors caused a number of misunderstandings.[19] A Citizen 1985 Action Coalition leader even encountered an unknown volunteer who justified his authority to maintain order as a "member" who had "received permission from above" (interview #TW58).

Compared to Qingdao East Road, Jinan Road was wider and farther from the Executive Yuan, the epicenter of the violent clash on March 23–24; nevertheless, a number of conflicts over the spatial arrangements took place there as well. Pariah Liberation Area (*jianmin jiefang qu*), a coalition of counterculture activists and veterans from a number of movement issues, began to hold an evening forum on Jinan Road starting on March 20 (day 3). As the self-mocking name suggested, they were conscious of their marginalization from the movement leadership, of which they were highly critical. Pariah Liberation Area activists contested the necessity of maintaining an emergency corridor, which they viewed as an imposition of medical authority that caused inconvenience to their events. After a heated argument with medical volunteers, the corridor was reduced in width (interview #TW17). On the other front, Pariah Liberation Area came into conflict with activists from Parent Participating Education (*qinzi gongxue*), a home-schooling organization that maintained a tent to support the Sunflower Movement. Parent Participating Education activists encouraged parents and their children to come to the site to learn a real lesson in democracy, and yet their need for quiet nights for preschool kids was not respected by the Pariah Liberation Area, which held activities until 3:00 or 4:00 A.M. After a fruitless negotiation, Parent Participating Education activists raised a protest slogan in the tent, which read, "We Are Here to Support Big Brothers and Big Sisters in the Legislative Yuan. Big Brothers and Big Sisters of Pariah Liberation Area, Please Support Our Sleep" (interview #TW44).

Finally, improvisation provided no solution to the inherent dilemma faced by the occupy movements in the context of a conservative political culture. People joined the protest because they felt anger toward the government, and yet their protests were more likely to gain social acceptance if they behaved civilly. In Taiwan, the protesters inside the besieged legislature were always under the watchful eye of media cameras, and the demands to comply with social expectations were so great that the occupied conference became a highly regimented area. Under the omnipresent gaze of the camera twenty-four hours a day, the occupied legislature was likened to "a miniature of the fictional surveillance society" (M. Lee 2015: 33). A strict code of conduct was promulgated and vigorously enforced, and people who entered the room had to be searched (for security purposes) and their body temperature measured (as an anti-epidemic measure). When protesters first broke into the legislature, there were people who celebrated by drinking beer and having a smoke, which was repeatedly broadcast and savagely criticized in the pro-government media, so later on such "inappropriate" behaviors were strictly forbidden. Lesbian and gay participants who shared pictures of physical intimacy via social media in the first few days were later discouraged from doing so for fear that the hostile media might create a negative association between the movement and promiscuity (Yen et al. 2015: 267–272). As such, the plenary chamber on the ground floor was said to be populated with "clean and well-behaved kids" (*ganjing guaibaobao*)—in great contrast to the second floor of the legislative building, which evolved into a "wildlife area" (*yesheng dongwuqu*) where libidinal gratification and other unbecoming behaviors were tolerated (interview #TW34). In Hong Kong, Jason Ng (2016: 168–169) noted that condom sales went up in Admiralty during the occupation and the protesters' tents were a perfect shelter for intimate behaviors. A participant noted that he often saw boozing and smelled marijuana in the occupation zone in his nighttime patrol (interview #HK69). Had the pro-government media known this, it would have been perfect material to discredit the eventful protests as licentious lawlessness. Similarly, while Hong Kong's student leaders demonstrated their pro-LGBT stance by taking part in the annual pride parade, which took place during the Umbrella Movement, there surfaced some discussions on whether the issue of sexual minorities would have "distracted" from the focus on political reforms.

Speaking about Occupy Wall Street, Todd Gitlin (2013b: 31) maintained, "All movements have to work out a proper relationship between the expressive impulse and the strategic act." While demonstrators in New York deliberately prioritized the playful and participatory aspect of the movement by rejecting a clear leadership structure, Taiwan's and Hong Kong's protests were torn between the two contradictory demands. Acts of improvisation did not solve this deep-seated problem, but rather replicated and multiplied the tension between the expressive and the instrumental throughout the occupation zones. As pointed out by Jasper (2014: 2–3), all social movements encounter the "Janus dilemma": precious resources and time are devoted to either the internal participants or the players outside the movement. An improvised movement allows more latitude for individual creativity and personal sense of involvement, but at the cost of efficiency in decision making.

Pariahs and Passion

Improvisation came from the willingness of individual participants to contribute their effort, and consequently if they were able to share a consensus over the movement goals as well as an affinity in ideological outlook, their improvisation would be more likely to bring about a collaborative result. And if there were fundamental disagreements, improvisation could worsen the internal strife, weakening the solidarity among movement participants. In Hong Kong, as noted in Chapter 3, the rise of localists since 2011 had created a fissure among the anti-Beijing camp. There was a heated debate concerning movement tactics (nonviolence versus militancy), the attitude toward mainland immigrants (acceptance versus exclusion), and movement networks (NGOs versus Internet mobilization) even though they were fighting the same foes. During the Umbrella Movement, this tension flared into numerous incidents of internecine conflict. By contrast, such ideological divide and disagreement over tactics was patently absent in Taiwan.

In a sense, the Sunflower Movement was the mirror image of the Umbrella Movement. In the former, the core leadership came from the pro-independence tendency, while the leftwing activists, represented by the Pariah Liberation Area, played a marginal role, whereas in the latter HKFS made up the movement leadership, and the localist camp, best exemplified by Civic Passion, agitated from the periphery. Both Lin Fei-fan and Chen Wei-ting had publicly announced their personal support for Taiwan independence prior to the Sunflower Movement, which explained why pro-KMT media often alluded to the Lin-Chen duo as clandestine members of the DPP, which was manifestly incorrect.

Despite this inverted configuration of the two movements, what really influenced the result of improvisation was the degree of solidarity among movement participants. A comparison of Hong Kong's Civic Passion and Taiwan's Pariah Liberation Area offers insight into the difference. From the very beginning, Civic Passion had challenged the leadership of OCLP, HKFS, and Scholarism because they argued that it was the citizens who spontaneously occupied the streets who actually disregarded the call to retreat. Civic Passion followers mounted a series of vigilante assaults against some movement activists whom they called traitors, which amounted to an organized witch-hunt campaign. Particularly in Mong Kok, where localist sentiments were visibly higher, many party and movement activists who were identified as "leftards" had to avoid contact with each other in order to avoid trouble (interview #HK20-1). Later, Civic Passion followers attempted to seize the command center in Admiralty by launching a number of protests against the Main Stage. Afterward, Civic Passion published *A Chronicle of Umbrella Failure,* which documented their "crimes" in excruciating detail. According to its postmortem examination, the Umbrella Revolution (which they insisted was the correct name) failed not only because of the regime's repression but also because of "the smear campaign by the mainstream media as well as the full-scale sabotage by pan-democrats, leftards and the OCLP trio" (*Passion Times* 2016: 14).

Civic Passion followers gained such notoriety among the Umbrella Movement leaders that they were often derogatively referred to as "hotdogs" for their ignorance. Among my interviewees who were party and NGO activists, it had become the well-received view that Civic Passion acted at the behest of Beijing with the purpose of creating dissension within the opposition, although they took care not to voice such allegations in public. Toward the latter half of the movement, as the leadership was mired in indecision, Civic Passion's advocacy for more militant action appeared to gain wider acceptance among the participants. Thus, the ill-fated decision by the students to blockade government buildings on November 30 could be seen as a desperate attempt to hold onto their endangered leadership in the face of the escalating challenge of a rival faction.

In Taiwan, the Pariah Liberation Area leaders articulated a different movement philosophy from that of the Sunflower leadership. They insisted on framing the protest as anti-neoliberalism rather than as anti-China. They opposed the leadership-centered style that created stars such as the Lin-Chen duo, and instead they contended that grassroots participants should have their own voices. They appeared more vocally critical of the DPP's involvement. All these demands placed the Pariah Liberation Area solidly on the radical end of Taiwan's movement activism ideological spectrum. Similarly, there was criticism of the "pariahs" as a disguise for those movement veterans who had failed to make it into the decision-making core and their advocacy of a leaderless movement flew in the face of that leadership. Nevertheless, such suspicions paled in comparison to the accusation that Civic Passion constituted Beijing's agents in Hong Kong.

In spite of the disagreements the Pariah Liberation Area did not launch protests against the Sunflower leadership. Its activists acknowledged that they chose a "milder form" of expressing disagreement because they "did not want to disrupt the movement" and had certain expectations for the movement leaders (Hsieh 2016: 63). An episode suffices here: Lin Fei-fan once showed up unexpectedly at the Pariah Liberation Area's evening forum, sitting on the ground as other members of the audience did. The host immediately noticed his presence and asked him to take off his signature green overcoat to remove his symbolic distinction from the "pariahs," and proceeded to chastise his leadership style to his face. Lin appeared to accept the criticism in good humor by applauding.[20] Such an episode of "The God Fan Descending upon the Earth" (*fanshen xiafan*) (Hsieh 2016: 50) was hardly imaginable in the Hong Kong context. If a student leader had dared to set foot at an event organized by Civic Passion, mob violence would probably have ensued. With the comparison to Hong Kong in mind, a Taiwanese student activist explained:

> There were more shared experiences in previous movement activism in Taiwan, which provided the base for trust even though there existed differences in ideological stands. Young localists in Hong Kong had little movement experience, which only started in the Umbrella Movement. They did not trust the student leaders because they had not been working together before. (Interview #TW59)

In short, the higher degree of overlap in movement networks made possible a more collaborative pattern of improvisation in Taiwan, whereas the preexisting conflict engendered antagonism in Hong Kong's improvisation.

Differential Contribution

Improvisation relied on not only participants' enthusiasm but also their skills, which explained why it was wrong to see everyone as equally capable.

Large protests typically involved participation among those who had previously been unconcerned or unmotivated, but first-timers were seldom capable of making strategic decisions beyond a certain level. Surveying the contemporary occupy movements, Paolo Gerbaudo (2012: 141) maintains that these protests actually rely "heavily on the intervention of highly involved and experienced participants" in spite of the dominant rhetoric of being leaderless, spontaneous, and horizontal. Thus, when it came to improvisation, skilled activists could always rely on their past experience and familiarity with the activist network to devise novel solutions. In many subsequent published books of witness accounts and oral history, most Taiwanese and Hongkonger first-time participants tended to be involved with some voluntary work, such as sorting the waste, provisioning the food, and making handicrafts, but rarely higher-level improvisation that required executive decision making.

My interviews with experienced activists revealed that they were constantly adjusting their strategic responses independently as the situation unfolded. For example, student activists in central Taiwan suspended their bus mobilization on the fifth day because there was already enough of a crowd around the legislature, and hence they redirected attention to other activities to support the movement (interview #TW28). A Hongkonger professor with extensive movement experience knew that student leaders were under enormous pressure so he adapted his improvisation to offer auxiliary assistance to meet the changing situation. In the chaotic first few days, the rumors that police would employ rubber bullets had spread fear among the supporters. To back up the student leaders, he and some professors formed a "bullet shield group" (*dang zidan zu*). Afterward, he invited HKFS leaders to speak in the street classroom forums in Mong Kok and Causeway Bay in the hope that they could establish better liaison with the participants beyond Admiralty. Later on, as the students were pressed by pan-democratic politicians and OCLP leaders for an earlier retreat, he co-created an NGO coalition to stand behind the student leadership to counterbalance this pressure (interview #HK4-1).

Sometimes these anonymous leaders might have misleadingly claimed to be "amateurs" (*suren*) or "netizens" (*xiangmin*); however, they were actually more experienced than regular participants. In Taiwan, the key person who coordinated the efforts of the "team of 3,621" insisted he was a "novice" (*xinshou*) because his prior involvement in social movements had been less than six months. Nevertheless, he had been administrating a number of online forums for more than a decade, including some 800,000 Internet users (interview #TW15-1). Similarly, the incident of police violence in Hong Kong that gave rise to the campaign against the "Seven Black Policemen" certainly had to do with the video image, a sort of Hong Kong Rodney King moment, but the victim's background also played a certain role. Tsang Kin-chiu had been a student activist with the HKFS, and he was also an activist social worker with electoral participation in the Civic Party (interview #HK48). Tsang's movement network helped to stir up sympathy and support that crystallized into a spin-off campaign within the Umbrella Movement.

To sum up, depending on one's past experience, skill, and personal network, how one contributed to the movement varied greatly. It follows that improvisation should not be seen as synonymous with impromptu performance by laypeople. What appeared to be a spontaneous overflow of the crowd might actually have been a trained response and coordination by seasoned activists, who were experienced enough to provide necessary on-the-spot judgment, yet not so well-known as to be mentioned in the mainstream media.

Conclusion

For decades, theorizing social movements has been an ongoing effort to elucidate what movement activists actually have done to promote their agendas. As social movements became a predictable and routine phenomenon in advanced democracies, researchers grew used to the view of social movements as organization-led campaigns. As such, research questions tended to focus on the decision making of movement leaders to see how they utilized their mobilizing networks, grasped political opportunities, framed collective grievances, and deployed protest repertoires.

The recent eruption of eventful protests all over the world urges us to develop new conceptual tools to understand these unusual yet consequential forms of activism. Both in Taiwan and Hong Kong, massive civil disobedience would not be possible without the anonymous, innovative, and courageous contributions of rank-and-file participants. That a substantial number of citizens voluntarily adopted these altruistic behaviors not only constitutes the most moving vignettes in the whole episode of contention but also challenges the conventional leader/follower distinction, since these volunteers did not take orders from above but acted on their own judgment. Therefore, it is not entirely correct to say that these participants were mobilized, as if a preexisting organization were capable of bringing about participation and contribution on such a scale. Rather, these participants essentially made their own movement. A Taiwanese activist described this unusual experience:

> I have been taking part in social movements for ten years and I never saw such spontaneity and freedom. Anyone present on the scene was allowed to do anything she or he saw fit. She or he did not have to ask for permission or have to belong to an organization, and no one was authorized. . . . Anyone who stood up from the crowd could be a

director of the garbage station or the materials station. They were totally unrelated to the movement leadership or those speakers on the podium. No one knew who these volunteers were and where they were from. In fact, these questions did not matter at all. (Interview #TW49)

This chapter has developed the concept of "improvisation" to understand the proliferation of these strategic responses without prior planning in the Sunflower Movement and the Umbrella Movement. There was a great variety of functions and different degrees of innovation in improvisation, which filled in the gaps when movement leaders appeared incapable or unwilling to take care of these aspects that actually proved vital to sustaining participant morale. To be fair, provisioning such an army of occupiers exceeded the capacity of any movement organization, no matter how well-endowed it might have been in the first place. Therefore, a decentralized pattern of decision making emerged as the only viable solution because of its advantages of being swift, flexible, and innovative.

Improvisation was not a panacea to solve all the dilemmas of collective action. Most social protests fail to attract such an outpouring of spontaneous support because they do not flare up into a direct and acute confrontation with the authorities. Neither was decentralized decision making less prone to error than movement leadership. It sometimes happened that individual participants' subjective quest for meaningful involvement ran counter to the objective requisites of the movement. Improvisation varied according to the participants' skill and background so that it was not true that everyone could equally contribute to the movement. All these caveats warned against a naive populism often seen in contemporary anarchist-leaning writings that tend to glorify leaderless movements or the "multitude." Instead, my investigation suggests that improvisation and leadership are mutually complementary rather than contradictory.

Finally, the contrasting finales of Taiwan's Sunflower Movement and Hong Kong's Umbrella Movement highlighted the different impacts of improvisation. The Sunflower Movement was able to execute an orderly and peaceful retreat with a claim to success because improvisation took place in a less antagonist milieu, whereas the Umbrella Movement collapsed in leadership indecision, participant exhaustion, and internecine strife, results that were actually exacerbated by improvisation among those who were hostile to movement leaders. A more collaborative and productive pattern of improvisation could come about only with the existence of a prior consensus among movement activists.

7

The Morning After

Joshua Wong (2017) reflected that both Taiwanese and Hongkonger protests "exemplified a clear rejection of Beijing's increasing interference" and were propelled by the younger generations who had decidedly shifted away from the Chinese identity. Indeed, both incidents shared many similarities in terms of not only origin (growing contention in civil society against the pernicious impacts from China) but also process (post hoc construction of leadership during the standoffs and improvisation by participants); yet nothing could be less alike than their respective finales.

The occupation of Taiwan's legislature was peacefully concluded with a voluntary withdrawal, and a festive farewell rally on the evening of April 10 to celebrate the incident. In Hong Kong, defying the government's final warning, hundreds of protesters gathered on the street in Causeway Bay on the morning of December 15. The numerically superior police forces quickly removed the last holdout, thus terminating the Umbrella Movement with a mass arrest. In Taiwan, with a statement "Turning Defensive to Offensive by Leaving the Fortress to Plant the Seeds" (*zhuanshou weigong chuguan bozhong*), the Sunflower leaders framed their movement as having "fulfilled the preliminary tasks and obtained significant achievements." They called for continuing vigilance over the government and cross-strait negotiations, and encouraged youthful participants to continue their activism.[1] While the Sunflower Movement ended on a triumphant tone, the end of the Umbrella Movement was characterized by bitterness, frustration, and anger, as student leaders were too exhausted to produce an official statement.

The contrasting emotional expressions certainly had to do with the difference in government responses. The Sunflower Movement not only postponed the immediate ratification of the CSSTA but also won bipartisan agreement to legislate the procedure for cross-strait negotiations. In contrast, Beijing and the SAR government stood firm with the August 31 Framework that nad reduced universal suffrage to a meaningless choice. After the failure of the student-official dialogue, the SAR government did not honor its promise to submit another new report to Beijing or initiate a new round of public consultation. The subsequent vetoing of the political reform package by the legislative council in June 2015 was largely seen as a setback for the government, as it had previously counted on the defection of some moderate pan-democrat lawmakers to pass the bill. Hong Kong's democratization was still mired in impasse, as the 2017 chief executive election proceeded in a similar "small-circle" fashion based on the decision of a 1,200-member election committee, with the Beijing-handpicked Carrie Lam being selected as the successor to Leung Chun-ying.

The eruption of these two large-scale protests dealt a mighty blow to the credibility of the top political leaders domestically as well as in the eyes of the Beijing leadership, because they vividly showed these leaders' unpopularity and inability to resolve the political crises on their own. Yet their subsequent responses differed. Undeterred by the Sunflower Movement, until the end of 2015, Ma Ying-jeou's KMT government remained committed to deepening economic linkages with China by still calling for the lawmakers' early approval of the CSSTA, submitting an application to the China-initiated Asian Infrastructure Investment Bank in March 2015, and continuing negotiations over the Cross-Strait Trade in Goods Trade Agreement (another free-trade deal whose negotiation continued until December 2015, two months before the DPP clinched the presidential election). Nevertheless, Ma adopted conciliatory rhetoric to appear accommodating to the Sunflower Movement. In his 2015 New Year's Day Message, Ma Ying-jeou said:

> The student movement of last March certainly had an effect on Taiwan. Outspoken youth and their online networking reenergized our society. Some people welcomed it, while others had reservations. But I think it was a good thing when seen from a long-term perspective. If our country has young people who are concerned about society, and a civil society that respects democratic rule of law, seeks rational dialogue, and opposes violence and autocracy, Taiwan will be filled with vigor and continue to grow stronger.... We must recognize that young people have lofty ideals and a strong sense of justice. They are particularly incensed by unfairness and misconduct. If the government does not explain itself clearly, or acts inappropriately, misunderstandings and criticism are likely to result.[2]

These laudatory remarks on student idealism as well as the implicit self-criticism should be interpreted in the context that Ma's ruling party had just suffered a fresh defeat in the 2014 local election (see below), forcing Ma to give up his party chairmanship.

While there was a clear divergence between rhetoric and practice in Taiwan's political leadership, Hong Kong's Leung Chun-ying persisted in his hardline approach. In his annual Policy Address in January 2015, Leung chided the students for their "misunderstanding" of constitutional matters, which needed to be "corrected." He followed by severely criticizing the HKU student paper, *Undergrad,* for its advocacy of "self-reliance and self-determination."[3] It was highly unusual for Hong Kong's governmental leaders to pick a student publication as a target in an official statement and, with that move, Leung insinuated that the Umbrella Movement was instigated by independence-minded extremists. Later Leung encouraged the citizens to "vote out" the pro-movement politicians, practically a declaration of war on Hong Kong's opposition by a top leader who was required by the Basic Law to remain nonpartisan.[4] Pro-Beijing organizations mounted smear campaigns against the Umbrella Movement that portrayed the movement as constituting lawless disturbances.

Police and judicial responses also differed. While both Taiwanese and Hongkonger authorities turned a blind eye to violence by pro-government mobsters and the disproportionate use of force by police, there were clear distinctions in the way movement participants were prosecuted and judged. Immediately after the final clearance of the occupiers, the Hong Kong police commissioner vowed to put all leaders in jail within three months.[5] By contrast, on the evening of April 11, the first day after the Sunflower Movement ended, a protest emerged over an incident involving police mistreatment of the remaining demonstrators. As hundreds of participants laid siege to a police precinct office, its commanding officer tendered his resignation and made an official apology. Throughout the Sunflower Movement, the only time the police arrested movement participants on the spot was during the Executive Yuan Incident of March 23–24, which generated 61 arrests. In Hong Kong, police arrests happened on several occasions, amounting to 955 arrests, and as of June 2016, 123 people had already been prosecuted,[6] whereas Taiwan's prosecutors indicted 119 people for their involvement.[7] Hong Kong's court also generated quicker verdicts; in August 2016, twenty-one months after the Umbrella Movement's end, three student leaders were found guilty, although they were given unusually lenient punishment.[8] The decision was overturned in an appellate court in August 2017 that threw Joshua Wong, Alex Chow, and Nathan Law into jail (see below). In Taiwan, one of the DPP government's first decisions was to withdraw the lawsuit against the Executive Yuan Incident participants on the charge of trespassing and damaging government property, although participants had to face other prosecutor indictments (W. Chang 2017: 46). In April 2017, three years after the Sunflower Movement, a court decision found twenty-two people charged with occupying the legislature not guilty, and the verdict elaborated a theory of civil disobedience to exonerate the defendants.[9] Clearly the harsher treatment of Hong Kong's movement participants had to do with their more repressive political regime.

The two movements differed in terms of public reception. In a joint survey carried out at the end of 2014, 53.3 percent of respondents in Taiwan indicated their approval for the Sunflower Movement (with 46.7 percent disapproving), whereas 46.8 percent of Hongkonger respondents thought positively of the Umbrella Movement and 53.2 percent negatively (Hsiao and Wan 2016: 137). The divergent public evaluations were also evident when it came to electoral campaigns. In Taiwan, the Sunflower Movement's image was less contested and arguably evolved into a symbol of youthful idealism. During the local election of November 2014, not only DPP politicians but also some candidates from the TSU and the KMT attempted to appropriate its positive symbolism to attract votes, either by employing the visual image of sunflowers in their fliers or playing the tune of *Island's Sunrise* (interview #TW45). During Hong Kong's district council election of 2015, most of the candidates inspired by the Umbrella Movement actually chose to deemphasize their movement background in order to avoid its disputed implications. As a DP district councilor wryly observed, these activists did not "mention the Occupy Central or the Umbrella Movement . . . and those candidates who emphasized it were not serious about being elected" (interview #HK26).

In short, there seems to be sufficient reason to characterize the Sunflower Movement as a "success" and the Umbrella Movement as a "failure," given their noticeable differences in terms of the ending of mass occupation, policy concessions, incumbent responses, prosecutorial and judicial treatment, and public reception. Nevertheless, such a simplified view runs the risk of premature judgment. While it is less ambiguous to identify winners and losers in social revolutions because they often end with the collapse of one contending force, a definite balance sheet for social movements appears more difficult because it depends on the time horizon one uses to evaluate their impact. The episode of intensive contestations tends to be brief and exceptional. The ultimate outcome of social movements depends more on the subsequent mobilizing strategies on the part of movement participants (Andrews 2004: 198–200).

This chapter surveys the post-occupy flurry of activism in Taiwan and Hong Kong. I first examine emotional outcomes of the unusually intense participation in these two eventful protests and how their successful management was critical to follow-up activism. In both places, younger and newer activists emerged to carry out the unfinished projects and open up new fronts of social and political reforms. While occupying public space was an extra-institutional act of civil disobedience, these activists also set their sights on institutional avenues to promote change, as many of them joined elections, giving rise to a new cohort of representatives and lawmakers with a professed commitment to movement activism. Political changes came about as a result of these waves of political participation. Tsai Ing-wen led her DPP to a landslide victory in the general election in January 2016, initiating Taiwan's third peaceful turnover of power, whereas Hong Kong's Leung Chun-yin announced his decision not to seek a second term. This chapter concludes by examining the changes in Beijing's policies toward Taiwan and Hong Kong.

"Movement Injuries": Managing the Emotional Consequences

Social movement researchers have recognized the pivotal significance of emotional process in a belated effort to correct the rationalistic bias that has perceived feelings, affects, and moods as irrational or irrelevant. Thinking and feeling are intimately combined in social actions, individual or collective. Movement solidarity not only rested on the cognition of shared interests but also required an emotional confluence that empowered collaborative effort. The arousal of certain emotional states, such as indignation, pride, compassion, and hopefulness, acts as a more powerful stimulus to protest action than rational argument. As such, it has been argued that practically all of the key concepts in social movement research—including identity, opportunity, networks and repertoire—hold an accompanying emotional aspect (Aminzade and McAdam 2002; Goodwin, Jasper, and Polletta 2001; Jasper 2011). In the studies of global eventful protests, scholars also identified an underlying psychological process. Gunning and Baron (2014: 203–239) contended that the transmutation "from fear to defiance" encouraged the Egyptians to challenge Hosni Mubarak's police state. Gerbaudo (2012: 115) found that the Occupy Wall Street organizers failed to elicit mass enthusiasm in the social media because their online language was cast in "a cold informative tone," amounting to "an uninspired and uninspiring monologue." Chapters 4 and 5 document how the passionate reactions to the suddenly escalated threats—the railroading of the CSSTA through the legislature and the police deployment of tear gas—prompted massive acts of defiance in Taiwan and Hong Kong.

While most scholars focus on explaining pro-movement emotions before or during protest mobilization, less attention has been devoted to the emotional consequences, which actually have a prolonged impact on subsequent movement politics. Generally speaking, both the Sunflower Movement and the Umbrella Movement generated complex and ambiguous feelings when the sit-in protests came to an end. On the one hand, some participants felt confident and elated about having been present during these history-making moments, no less than once-in-a-lifetime personal experiences. The creative and spontaneous expressions of solidarity in the occupation zones helped to strengthen the shared convictions among participants. On the other hand, there was also a widespread sense of frustration, disappointment, and powerlessness because the achievement was less than expected. Among those who spent more time in the occupation zones and those involved in the decision-making process, such negative emotions were particularly strong. From my interviews, there were Sunflower activists who canceled a scheduled wedding or were immediately married afterward. In Hong Kong, there were abundant stories of inter-generational conflicts and family breakups.

In Taiwan, the term "movement injuries" (*yundong shanghai*), a homonymic pun on "sports injuries," began circulating to describe the pain and other negative feelings that came out of the concentrated and sustained participation, an expression equally applicable in Hong Kong's context. Among those who experienced or witnessed police force, some were clearly traumatized with an instinctual fear at the sight of the police. A Taiwanese surgeon who treated injured protesters at the makeshift first-aid booth was later unable to perform a routine medical suture because of involuntary shaking in the hands (interview #TW41). In spite of the ensuing litigation against the responsible officials and police officers during the Executive Yuan Incident, many participants still suffered physical and mental harm. On its second anniversary, an investigative report of the oral-history accounts by participants was published online, and a ritual of "environmental theatre" was held, in which participants were encouraged to reenact the incident symbolically and share their personal experiences for therapeutic purposes.[10]

Hong Kong's student leaders appeared to sustain more severe "movement injuries" because their protest lasted longer and encountered more hostile responses from the government. As revealed in the media, many of the student leaders underwent a profound process of soul-searching and self-healing. Alex Chow developed acute depression; for three months he avoided going out and decided not to wear his trademark eyeglasses in order not to be recognized on the metro. Later on Chow started to practice Buddhism, helping him to gain a clearer and calmer perspective.[11] Yvonne Leung, Chow's HKFS colleague, admitted having a visceral sense of guilt for some mistakes for which she was responsible and said she "would devote a life-long effort to pay back her obligations."[12] Taiwanese student leaders suffered from similarly negative feelings, but their symptoms appeared milder. In an interview,

Chen Wei-ting acknowledged a sense of relief when he later learned that victims of police force did not harbor grudges against the decision makers.[13]

In Hong Kong, there arose an idiosyncratic emotional response among grassroots participants that was absent in Taiwan. A pervasive sense of disappointment turned into anger over the student leadership who were perceived to have "misled" or even "betrayed" the movement. Less than two weeks after the conclusion of the Umbrella Movement, HKU students initiated a walk-out campaign to take their student union out of the HKFS, which immediately snowballed among other universities. Four universities opted to exit via student voting, which dealt a devastating blow to the student organization that had played a leading role in Hong Kong's social and political movements for more than half a century. After the setback, the HKFS represented the students at only the four remaining universities, practically forfeiting its claim as a territory-wide organization. Ironically, the HKFS's disintegration was not due to the pressure from the pro-Beijing camp, in spite of its decades-long defiant opposition, but rather was a result of a grassroots revolt by those who thought the federation was not militant enough.

The resentment against the student leadership took an ugly sexist turn against some female students. One Hong Kong student noted:

> Nice-looking girls often experienced personal assault. Some localists criticized them for making use of their good looks to gain something in the movement.... If the identity of the girlfriends of some student leaders was revealed, they lost creditability among their peers because they were automatically perceived as supporting their boyfriends. These attacks were never about the issue, but rather were personal. They called them things like "stinking vagina," "bitch," or "public toilet"! (Interview #HK37)

Therefore, a self-help group, "Young Girls' Heart" (*shaonu dexin*), was formed among these victimized women. It began with internal sharing and evolved into formalized academic events on patriarchy and social movements. Although such gender-based violence was less explicit in Taiwan, there were also some collective efforts to deal with the traumatic experiences. A psychoanalyst organized a peer group of the victims at the Executive Yuan for therapeutic purposes (Peng 2016).

Many ways of coping with "movement injuries" emerged. Overcoming the psychological stress and the debilitating emotions of guilt, shame, and humiliation provided the impetus for further involvement. There were individual leaders and participants who opted to withdraw from public involvement permanently, out of disillusionment or frustration. Most of the first-timers were less exposed to negative emotions and were therefore more likely to be inspired to take part in subsequent movement activism.

Taiwan's Post-Sunflower Activism

Many young Taiwanese participants received their first lesson in movement activism during the legislature occupation and subsequently became committed activists in a number of protest events. The movement's positive image focused the national spotlight on some of its leaders, such as Lin Fei-fan, Chen Wei-ting, and Huang Kuo-chang, who became the new faces of Taiwan's energized civil society. That the Sunflower Movement secured a peaceful exit with a victorious claim was particularly inspiring, showing that changes were possible with collective effort. Riding this new tide of enthusiasm, Taiwan's antinuclear movement and anticurriculum revisionism campaign achieved their own milestones.

Antinuclear Movement

The post-Fukushima resuscitation of Taiwan's antinuclear movement had been one of the streams contributing to the Sunflower Movement, as indicated in Chapter 3. Yet, in spite of the rising antinuclear sentiment, the KMT government remained committed to nuclear energy. Five days after the end of the occupation of the legislature, Lin Yi-hsiung, a respected senior leader of Taiwan's pro-democracy movement, announced his intention to stage a hunger strike, which would begin on April 22, and his determination to carry on to the very end unless the government stopped construction of the FNPP. Since Lin's steadfast determination and willingness to assume martyrdom for the antinuclear cause was well known, his protest not only exerted great moral pressure on the KMT government but also provided powerful stimulus to the antinuclear activists. In the end, Lin's hunger strike lasted seven days and he was hospitalized on April 28. During these seven days, Taiwan's antinuclear movement experienced an unprecedented high tide. On the evening of April 24, at least 4,000 people took part in a human-chain protest. On April 26, an antinuclear "road running" with 7,000 participants took place in the morning, and an evening rally attracted more than 10,000 people. The climax came with a demonstration on April 27. More than 50,000 joined the march that afternoon, and when they arrived at Taipei Railway Station on Zhongxiao West Road, a mass sit-in took place. The confrontation lasted until early the next morning, when police used water cannons to disperse the crowd.

These activities took place in Taipei, but during the hectic week, other cities also witnessed massive outpourings of sympathy for Lin Yi-hsiung, such as staging candlelight vigils and poetry readings, and tying yellow ribbons on trees lining the streets (signifying concern for Lin's deteriorating physical condition). Facing the unexpected surge of antinuclear activism, the KMT first tried to keep its pro-nuclear stance. On the first day of Lin's protest (April 22), Ma Ying-jeou insisted the FNPP would be operational once construction and safety inspections were finished. On the third day (April 24), KMT lawmakers and the Executive Yuan decided to hold a referendum before inserting the fuel rods. Finally, when it came to the sixth day (April 27), an emergency meeting of local KMT executives decided to mothball the FNPP's first reactor and to stop construction of the second one.

Taiwan's dispute over the ill-fated FNPP had persisted for three decades, accompanying the country's transition from martial-law authoritarianism to multiparty democracy. When the DPP first became the ruling party in 2000, Chen Shui-bian ordered a halt to the FNPP project, which generated a backlash from the KMT-dominated legislature. To the disappointment of antinuclear activists, Chen soon decided to resume construction in order to secure a political compromise with the opposition. By the time the KMT made its comeback in 2008, the FNPP appeared to be a settled issue and Taiwan's nuclear enthusiasts eagerly expected a major expansion. The Fukushima Accident breathed new life into a seemingly depleted movement; however, it was not strong enough to change the KMT's pro-nuclear stance. Lin Yi-hsiung's hunger strike inspired the frenzied week of antinuclear protests in late April 2014, but the huge momentum bequeathed by the Sunflower Movement made these actions effective. Traditionally Taiwan's antinuclear movement had proceeded with middle-class professional leadership and moderate tactics. The precedent of the legislature occupation clearly expanded the accepted boundaries of protest making, making possible the overnight mass sit-in of April 27–28, which turned out to be instrumental for the movement breakthrough. In a sense, the FNPP, presumably Taiwan's last major nuclear project, became collateral damage of the Sunflower Movement (M. Ho 2018). Afterward, Tsai Ing-wen's DPP government promised to phase out the existing nuclear reactors with the expiration of their forty-year operating permits, and an ambitious renewable energy program was underway to fill the gap. Taiwan is expected to become completely free of nuclear energy as of 2025, the first Asian country to embark on this decidedly pro-environment path.

Anti-curriculum Revisionism Campaign

Analogous to Hong Kong's Anti–National Education Movement (2011–2012), Taiwan's anticurriculum revisionism campaign of 2015 originated with high school students' resistance to an explicit attempt by the government to implement indoctrination. While Hongkongers opposed the glorification of contemporary China under the name of patriotism, Taiwanese fought against the resinicization of their identity.

In early 2014, Taiwan's Ministry of Education announced a revision to the curriculum guidelines for senior high school courses, which included some ideologically motivated changes to restore the outdated China-centric worldview. The decision attracted immediate criticism and protests from historians and high school teachers. The outbreak of the Sunflower Movement effectively drew attention away from the curriculum dispute until high school students initiated their protests in May 2015.

Overriding the criticism, education officials scheduled the new curriculum to be implemented in the fall semester of 2015. Starting in early summer, high school students voiced their opposition and organized their regional and national mobilization networks. The official intransigence added fuel to their escalated activism. On July 23, a group of high school students broke into the education minister's office to stage a surprise occupation. Twenty-four students, as well as three journalists and six nonstudent participants, were promptly arrested and threatened with legal action by the Ministry of Education, planting the seeds of a tragedy. One student participant committed suicide, which immediately sparked a sit-in protest. Hundreds of high school students occupied the front square of the Ministry of Education from July 31 to August 6, a move dubbed by the media as "the high school students' Sunflower Movement," and the confrontation came to an end when education officials agreed to respect each school's autonomous decision on whether to adopt the new textbooks.

The anticurriculum revisionism campaign was in many ways linked to the preceding Sunflower Movement. Both protests had to do with the China factor, as the new curriculum was designed to resinicize Taiwanese students, while the CSSTA would have resulted in deeper economic ties to China. Many high school students were also present during the legislature occupation, personally witnessing their seniors' actions on this rather unusual occasion. Some Sunflower veterans also offered logistical and other backend support (interview #TW55). The campaign was propelled by a familiar slogan, "We Have to Save Our Own Curriculum Guidelines by Ourselves" (*ziji kegang ziji jiu*), and the official process of revisioning was criticized as a "black box" for the lack of transparency and consultation (Chou 2017). Subsequently the DPP Ministry of Education abolished the controversial curriculum and broadened the participatory procedure for future revisions by allowing student representation.[14]

Political Activism in Taiwan

The successful movements against nuclear energy and the curriculum revisionism represented spillovers of the mass enthusiasm released by the Sunflower Movement. Other movement issues, concerning urban renewal, workers' grievances, environmental protection, and gender equality, resulted in an influx of new participants. There also emerged new organizations and campaigns that claimed to carry out the spirit of the Sunflower Movement.

Taiwan March (*daoguo qianjin*), a movement organization led by the Sunflower stars Huang Kuo-chang, Lin Fei-fan, and Chen Wei-ting, was established in May 2014. Taiwan March was incorporated as a foundation because it enjoyed secure financial support, including corporate donations. It launched a nation-wide campaign to initiate a referendum on the referendum law, and despite its failure to collect enough signatures, the organization transformed into the New Power Party (NPP), which emerged successfully as the third-largest party in the legislature after the 2016 general elections (see below). The establishment of Taiwan March truncated the development of Democracy Tautin (*minzhu douzhen*, "tautin" meaning "fighting together" in Taiwanese), which had been originally planned as a representative organization for the Sunflower Movement's core members. Democracy Tautin remained one of the few post-Sunflower organizations that continued activism for two years (interview #TW34). Student activists from southern Taiwan, who largely stayed out of the decision-making core during the occupation of the legislature, formed Democracy Kuroshio to continue the subsequent participation. Though smaller in scale, the Youth against Oppression in Taiwan (*taizuo weixin*) and the Formoshock (*fuermosha huishe*) were also new movement organizations initiated primarily by young people.

The Appendectomy Project (*gelanwei*, "removing the bad/blue lawmakers") came about as a recall campaign against some KMT lawmakers. The Appendectomy Project experimented with the novel method of online crowdfunding to mount its vigorous campaign. Surmounting daunting legal barriers, it achieved a recall vote in February 2015. Although the targeted KMT lawmaker survived the challenge with the help of a high legal requirement of 50 percent voter turnout (25 percent of the electorate showed up at the polling stations), it made possible the first recall vote against an elected legislator in two decades. Subsequently, the Appendectomy Project devoted its attention to three KMT lawmakers who ran for reelection in 2016. The "blacklisting" campaign turned out to be rather successful because all three of these KMT incumbents lost their seats to DPP challengers.

There also emerged campaigns for constitutional revision. The Civil Movement for Constitutional Reform (*gongmin xianzhen tuidong lianmeng*) was an umbrella organization of NGOs pressing the demand for a citizens' constitutional conference, first raised by the Sunflower Movement. Youth Occupy Politics (*qingnian zhanling zhengzhi*) launched the campaign to lower the voting age to 18 from 20. Finally, prior to the student occupation, the effort to strengthen public supervision of lawmakers had already gotten underway with a newly founded watchdog organization, Watchout, which aimed to utilize digital communication to improve public understanding of how the legislature actually worked. Since the Sunflower Movement emerged precisely because lawmakers could easily railroad through a controversial agreement with minimal regard for public opinion, Watchout received much more attention afterward.

Whether they focused on constitutional reform, referendum law, recalls, congressional oversight, or cross-strait politics, these new organizations or campaigns were avowedly more political, and they did not abstain from partisan politics. There existed a shared, albeit implicit, consensus to target the KMT because of its recalcitrance against reforms both before and after the Sunflower Movement, a contributing factor to its consecutive electoral debacles in 2014 and 2016.

Hong Kong's Post-Umbrella Activism

Although the Umbrella Movement collapsed in a cloud of mass fatigue and leadership indecision, it also engendered new waves of movement participation, as evidenced in the mushrooming of a number of "post-Umbrella organizations" (*sanhou zuzhi*), an expression that was curiously absent in Taiwan. The proliferation of movement discourses was another noticeable feature in post-Umbrella Hong Kong. Reflecting on the failure to obtain compromises from Beijing on the issue of electoral reform, movement activists began to explore other avenues of continuing the movement's momentum. The OCLP leaders envisioned a society-wide Citizen Charter Movement (*gongmin yuezhang yundong*) in which activists from different sectors were encouraged to formulate their core values to form a common front (interview #HK1-2). The idea gave rise to the Community Charter Movement (*shequ yuezhang yundong*), which involved grassroots-level organizing in order to realize democracy at the scale of communities. At the same time, another group of intellectuals jointly published a programmatic *Discourse on Reforming Hong Kong* (*xianggang gexinlun*), which maintained that Hongkongers should capitalize on their local advantages to maximize and perpetuate self-rule (Fong 2015). Hong Kong's subsequent protest activism appeared more self-defensive than pro-active in nature, and there were no comparable movement breakthroughs. With the exception of Beijing's new restrictions in April 2015 on mainlander individual visits and the announcement in December 2016 of allowing pan-democratic politicians to visit the mainland, the regime made no concessions to the increasingly agitated civil society, as evidenced by the following two episodes: the HKU personnel controversy of 2015 and the "Fishball Revolution" of 2016.

The HKU Personnel Controversy

After the Umbrella Movement, the SAR government was apparently attempting to implement more surveillance on campus. There were some dissident academics who were penalized with demotions or non-renewal of contracts. Chin Wan's dismissal in April 2016 for his divisive Facebook comments was the most noteworthy case. Chin denounced it as an act of political repression and claimed to be the "first victim in academia after the occupy movement."[15] Amid such heightened attention to academic freedom, two top-level personnel decisions concerning HKU generated protest activism.

Johannes Chan, the former HKU dean of the Faculty of Law and a vocal pro-democracy scholar, was selected in 2014 to fill the vice-chancellor position. Normally, such a personnel decision was approved pro forma by a governing body of the HKU Council; however, pro-Beijing newspapers initiated a smear campaign over his close relationship with Benny Tai, Chan's colleague and the co-founder of the OCLP movement. Apparently, due to the political pressure, the HKU Council deliberately delayed the confirmation procedure, stimulating protests from pan-democratic politicians, HKU alumni, lawyers, and students. On July 28, 2015, dozens of students stormed the conference room of the HKU Council and disrupted its meeting. A pro-government council member claimed to be injured in the protest, and education officials and HKU leaders jointly condemned the "student violence." The incident prompted the school leadership to enforce tightened policing of student representatives, who were always escorted by security guards when attending official meetings (interview #HK50). On September 29, the HKU Council finally came to an anonymous vote rejecting Chan's appointment. The unprecedented vetoing of a recommended candidate prompted HKUSU President Billy Fung to break the confidentiality protocol by revealing how pro-government council members raised ridiculous arguments to oppose Chan's nomination. In early October, a demonstration as well as a rally, both involving thousands of participants, took place on the HKU campus to protest the violation of academic autonomy.[16]

The SAR government appeared determined to staff higher education with loyalists. Arthur Li, a keen supporter of Chief Executive Leung Chun-ying, was widely viewed as having been heavily involved in the decision to veto Chan's appointment. The rumored prospect of appointing Li to lead the HKU Council gave rise to several protests. Yet the government simply ignored these complaints and installed Li as HKU president. The HKUSU launched a class boycott campaign demanding a revision to the HKU Council's composition;[17] however, this failed to elicit widespread student participation. In 2017, Billy Fung was sentenced to community service for disrupting the HKU Council meeting, which forced him to postpone graduate study at Taiwan's NTU.

"Fishball Revolution"

Immediately after the unsuccessful class boycott campaign at HKU, an unexpected incident of unrest took place in Mong Kok, a popular shopping district with an unmistakable working-class flavor, arguably the polar opposite of the elitist citadel of higher education. Nicknamed the "Fishball Revolution" in the media, the conflict originated from a clampdown on food hawkers during the Lunar New Year holiday, which generated mass resentment over the overzealousness of law enforcement. In the preceding years, the SAR government's policy of zero-tolerance of cooked-food peddling had sparked sporadic protests and a heated debate over the use of urban space. Outlawed by a regime bent on eradicating street food in the name of sanitation, hawkers became a symbol of Hong Kong's endangered popular culture that easily aroused sympathy. Moreover, since Mong Kok was an occupation site during the Umbrella Movement, which had displayed a grassroots and radical style of protest making a clear distinction from prudish and well-mannered Admiralty, the plight of the Mong Kok peddlers immediately attracted the attention of militant participants who had been dissatisfied with the nonviolence-oriented student leadership. As such, physically confronting the law-enforcing policemen emerged as unfinished business for those who opted for a head-on confrontation with the authorities.

On the evening of February 8, 2016, the clash between law enforcement officers and pro-hawker protesters started to brew. As the policemen attempted to disperse the crowd with batons and pepper spray, the latter fought back by throwing pavement tiles, erecting makeshift barricades, and burning garbage. A policeman fired warning shots and aimed his pistol at demonstrators, further fueling the anger. It was in the morning hours of the following day that the ten-hour confrontation finally ended with 124 injuries and 74 arrestees, the most violent disturbance since the handover (Kwong 2016: 436). As expected, the SAR government and its pro-Beijing allies condemned the incident as a lawless "riot" (*baoluan*), while the pan-democratic opposition was again caught in the embarrassing position of denouncing the protester violence and criticizing the government for its rude law enforcement at the same time. In hindsight, the event took place in an escalating disenchantment among young Hongkongers, as a survey indicated their declining trust over the SAR government and growing support for radical protests (W. Lam 2017).

The Fishball Revolution also had political implications. Hong Kong Indigenous, a radical localist organization founded shortly after the Umbrella Movement, mobilized its supporters to join the fray throughout the incident. Its leader, Edward Leung Tin-kei, a charismatic HKU student who was running for a legislative council seat in a by-election (New Territory East) on February 28, took part and was arrested, which gave him instant publicity territory-wide. Leung advocated a "theory of unlimited resistance" (*kangzheng wudixian lun*) to keep escalating the pressure on the government until the latter made a mistake by resorting to disproportionate force, and this defiant attitude particularly attracted young voters, who were increasingly disillusioned with the nonviolence philosophy embraced by the Umbrella Movement leadership. Leung's surge in popularity posed a threat to Alvin Yeung Ngok-kiu of the Civic Party, a rising political star who originally expected to obtain an easy win. In the end, Yeung obtained 37.2 percent of the vote share and narrowly defeated the pro-Beijing candidate by less than 3 percent, while Leung received a better-than-expected 15.4 percent. The pan-democrat's Pyrrhic victory foreshadowed the political coming-of-age of the localists, who had once seemed to be a bunch of unelectable outcasts, but who were now threatening to push Hong Kong's opposition in a more radical direction. After the election, Leung prophetically argued that the political landscape was now divided among pro-Beijing forces, pan-democrats, and localists.[18]

Profession-Specific Organizations

There emerged many post-Umbrella organizations that were based in particular trades or professions. The Progressive Lawyers Group, for instance, sprang from the legal volunteers during the Umbrella Movement. Formed in January 2015, the organization had around 80 solicitors and barristers whose activities spread across different arenas, such as writing weekly media columns, offering legal education in high schools, and writing legal studies on contemporary policy debates (interview #HK35). Financier Conscience was another organization with around thirty members who were employees of banks and securities and funds firms, and which also maintained a media column (interview #HK34). There emerged similar organizations among medical doctors, psychologists, insurance agents, radiologists, and so on. Oftentimes these post-Umbrella organizations had to devote their attention to issues specific to their own trade (such as the downgrade of Hong Kong's credit rating), but they attempted to develop alternative perspectives differing from the dominant ones offered by the government and their employers.

True, these activists represented only a self-conscious minority of white-collar workers whose professional interests were intimately tied with business opportunities in China or Chinese investment in Hong Kong. Many activist professionals also simultaneously took part in community-based organizations, so there was a substantial overlap among these newly formed movement networks. One participant estimated the total number of active participants was somewhere between 1,000 and 2,000 (interview #HK69). Nevertheless, these profession-based activist groups were a novel feature in Hong Kong, since most professionals were traditionally apolitical or conservative, with the notable exceptions of lawyers and schoolteachers. Moreover, since the thirty-seat profession-based functional constituencies in the legislative council continued to be a bastion of the pro-Beijing camp, these professional activists made efforts toward a change in electoral rule by launching an intensive lobbying campaign (interview #HK68).

A Comparison

Given the flourishing of subsequent protests in Taiwan and Hong Kong, it is clear that sources for continuing mobilization were not depleted after the intensive deployment of the occupation. Enthusiasm for deeper civic engagement appeared to be a renewable resource, provided that "movement injuries" were carefully tended. Arguably the effect was particularly strong among the young people who formed the main contingent forces in the two occupy movements. As McAdam (1989) demonstrated in his study of the American civil rights movement, concentrated participation in an unusual movement episode produced profound and everlasting biographical consequences, because it took place during the formative years of one's life trajectory. Thus it was not a surprise that many of these post-occupy organizations and activism were spearheaded by young people.

There were also obvious divergences between the two ensuing movement trajectories. Taiwan's post-Sunflower activism, which tended to target political institutions, successfully challenged the policy priorities of government incumbents, such as the nuclear energy program and the introduction of a Sino-centric curriculum. Although constitutional reforms did not materialize in the end, the emergence of such demands per se indicated that the horizon of possibilities had been broadened, as many participants genuinely believed in the feasibility of systemic changes. By contrast, there were practically no post-Umbrella organizations that focused on electoral reform, the very issue that generated the Umbrella Movement. Although discussions on self-determination, self-rule, or even independence from China thrived in post-Umbrella Hong Kong, it remained difficult to put these political proposals into practice. In the wake of the Umbrella Movement, a crescendo in mobilization for "peripheral nationalism" emerged (Fong 2017: 23–26), and "the debate over relations with China for the first time displaced universal suffrage as the dominant campaign issues" (Kaeding 2017: 158–159). The lack of interest in constitutional matters signified widespread disenchantment with the political formula of "one country, two systems," best exemplified by the dramatic act of burning a copy of the Basic Law by student representatives during the June Fourth candlelight vigil in 2015.[19] While senior pan-democratic politicians understood the mini-constitution as a guarantee for eventual democratization, the younger generation despised it as a broken lie.

While Taiwanese mobilized for progressive changes and their wide-ranging demands read like a wish list of political reforms, Hongkongers' activism appeared more self-defensive, aimed at preventing the volatile status quo from deteriorating. Inheriting institutions designed in the colonial era, the SAR government enjoyed a degree of leverage to direct university administration, and such political meddling had already occurred before the Umbrella Movement without provoking major resistance. Yet it was precisely because of post-Umbrella fears that campus control would be tightened that the HKU personnel controversies generated an intense wave of public scrutiny and protest actions. Clearly what was at stake was not merely endangered academic autonomy but also a regime-initiated project to eradicate campus-based opposition. The relatively limited ambition and scope of Hong Kong's post-Umbrella activism was related to the increasingly unfriendly political environment created by a vengeful chief executive and the powerful presence of pro-Beijing organizations.

While Hong Kong's new activists largely refrained from raising demands for political reform, they spent more energy exploring new areas for further activism. There arose a tacitly pessimistic understanding that bona fide democratization was not possible in the foreseeable future. By channeling their enthusiasm to communities and professions, Hong Kong's activists expanded and multiplied the zones of engagement with Beijing. Fixing HK (*weixiu xianggang*), in this regard, was an interesting example of broadening movement commitment in the wake of protest activities. This team of plumbers and electricians provided pro bono services to those who needed household maintenance in order to reconnect the grassroots neighborhood (S. Huang 2018). In contrast, although the CSSTA threatened to impact a number of service workers' livelihoods, profession-specific activism in Taiwan was sporadic and sparse (such as the Taiwan Publishing Freedom Front by book editors), or limited to students (such as medical school and social work students). There were more than 400 lawyers involved in providing free legal consultation for Sunflower participants, whereas there were slightly more than 100 pro-Umbrella lawyers in Hong Kong; yet there was no equivalent to the Progressive Lawyers Group in Taiwan. Apparently, the lower degree of devotion to professional interests in Taiwan had to do with the fact that the conclusion of the occupation of the legislature had indefinitely delayed CSSTA ratification so that the flurry of profession-based activism did not continue afterward.

Last, while the different types of post-Sunflower activism shared a more or less similar ideological outlook, the various types of post-Umbrella activism were riven by divergent tendencies. A Democracy Tautin convener acknowledged in an interview that there were not many ideological differences between the new movement organizations, since all of them presented a youthful image and supported Taiwan independence and social reforms (interview #TW55). As another interviewee cynically explained, post-Sunflower organizations mushroomed because "many activists wanted to compete for financial support" while they still enjoyed national fame (interview #TW43). In contrast, Hong Kong's preexisting mutual distrust only deepened after the Umbrella Movement, which provided the impetus for the above-mentioned wave of HKFS walk-outs. A heated debate emerged over movement strategy, as more and more Hong Kong activists became disenchanted with the nonviolence philosophy. As such, the Umbrella supporters appeared to be profoundly divided over the Fishball Revolution, eulogized as a heroic act of resistance by militant localists and deplored as misguided violence by existing movement leaders (interview #HK39).

From Protest to Electioneering

Occupying a state organ or public space in a sustained confrontation with government incumbents was undoubtedly an unlawful act, often the last resort when opponents had exhausted other available channels. However, such drastic and disruptive protests did not mean that the participants rejected engagement with legal procedures in principle. If they had perceived a realistic probability of effecting desired changes through these avenues, chances were they would have eagerly embraced this opportunity, rather than avoiding it. Nevertheless, both sympathetic and critical observers of contemporary occupy protests tended to overemphasize their inherent anti-institutional characteristics and thus often failed to analyze subsequent electoral participation. In his global survey of protest activism, Castells (2012: 227) concluded that these movements were rarely programmatic and their leaderless structure made it nearly impossible for them to "be co-opted by political parties." From the opposite perspective, Ivan Krastev (2014: 20, 59) faulted the occupy protests for their refusal to propose viable alternatives because they were largely propelled by "rejectionist ethics." Without a concrete program or a guiding ideology, street occupation became "a kind of performance art" for its own sake. Such a diagnosis tended to ignore that fact that major protests generated new political parties as well as enthusiasm for elections. The Spanish Podemos, the Greek Syriza, and Isreal's Yesh Atid were recent cases of protest-driven party formation (Talshir 2016: 274). In Chile, the leaders of the 2011 student movement became elected officials (Sznajder 2016: 243). Taiwanese and Hongkonger activists chose similar strategies of electioneering.

On the theoretical front, a contemporary effort emerged to bring interaction between social movements and political parties back into the research agenda, since both activities involve organized efforts to promote social change via the multiple channels of the modern state (Goldstone 2004). Political parties have emerged in the wake of movement mobilization, and it has not been uncommon for politicians to engage in protest activities. The insufficient attention to the movement-party interaction partly originated from discipline specialization, where institutionalized electoral studies are housed under political science, and social movement studies in sociology, which unfortunately gave rise to a polarized perspective that political parties are institutional and rational, while social movements are extra-institutional and irrational. Newer studies have emerged to address this neglect of the reciprocal relationship between elections and social movements (Halfmann 2011; Heaney and Rojas 2015; McAdam and Kloos 2014; McAdam and Tarrow 2010; Mudge and Chen 2014; Skocpol and Williamson 2012).

This section reviews the major elections after the Sunflower Movement and the Umbrella Movement. Taiwan's local election in November 2014 and legislative election in January 2016 and Hong Kong's local election in November 2015 and legislative election in September 2016 offered institutional channels to absorb the new political energy unleashed by the two eventful protests. In both places, significant political changes happened as erstwhile occupiers were voted into political office, resulting in a major transfiguration of the political landscape.

Taiwan's 2014 Local Election

The "nine-in-one" local election took place on November 29, 2014. It was the largest in scale, with more than 11,000 public offices up for grabs, including executive positions (autonomous cities, cities/counties, townships/indigenous districts, and wards/villages) and representative positions (councilors in autonomous cities and cities/counties and representatives for townships/indigenous districts). Many movement activists joined this election, either as candidates or campaign staff.

Councilor positions in autonomous cities and cities/counties (907 seats in total) provided the most advantaged entry point for aspirants, because these intermediate-level positions were mostly elected under the multiple-member district rule, increasing the first-timers' winning chances. From Central Election Commission sources, I was able to identify 37 candidates with movement background in the local councilors election, including 9 from the Green Party Taiwan (GPT), 8 from the Trees Party, 5 from the Wings of Radical Politics, 14 from the People's Democratic Front, and 1 independent. The number of candidates fielded by these movement-oriented parties surpassed all previous elections (Ho and Huang 2017). Two young GPT members (ages 26 and 34) were successfully elected. The surge of interest in politics among young people apparently reenergized the GPT, which was founded by environmentalists in 1996 and underwent a sustained period of inactivity following its one and only electoral success in that year.

Taiwan's 2016 National Election

The legislative and presidential election was held on January 16, 2016. Before the Sunflower Movement, the rising tide of social protests had stimulated an effort to form a new movement-oriented party in the summer of 2013, and the Taiwan Citizen Union (*gongmin zuhe*) was established shortly before protesters seized the legislature. The KMT's disastrous setback in the 2014 local election, in which it conceded three autonomous cities (Taipei, Taoyuan, and Taichung) and four other cities/counties to the DPP and its ally, became an inspiring lesson showing that real change was possible. The competition for the 113 legislative seats in the 2016 election gave rise to an unprecedented explosion of electoral participation among movement activists and the formation of new parties, which were dubbed the "third force" (*disan shili*) by the media. In early 2015, the Taiwan Citizen Union split into two new parties, the NPP and the Social Democratic Party (SDP), over whether to support Tsai Ing-wen for the presidency and coordinate with the DPP to field a single candidate in district elections. The NPP opted for a more collaborative approach with the DPP, while the SDP insisted more on its independence and entered an alliance with the GPT.

The NPP, the SDP, and the GPT all nominated some young Sunflower participants as their candidates. These three parties fielded 23 candidates in the election for 73 district-seat lawmakers, while other Sunflower activists chose to align with other pro-independence parties, including the TSU and a newly established Free Taiwan Party. As expected, there was intense competition between the third force candidates and the DPP. In the end, three NPP district nominees, including Huang Kuo-chang, successfully ousted KMT incumbents and the new party also gained 2 proportional seats by earning 6.1 percent in the party vote. With its 5 seats in the legislature, the NPP became the third-largest party, trailing the DPP and the KMT. The SDP and the GPT, on the other hand, failed to win any seats either by district or proportionally.

Although there was some resentment that the NPP took advantage of the Sunflower Movement by cornering its celebrities and receiving the most financial donations, its surge symbolized a rather smooth transition from civil disobedience to electoral campaigning, taking the movement commitment into the formalized political arena. NPP leader Huang Kuo-chang (age forty-three when elected in 2016) was a legal scholar who played a critical role in the nine-person decision-making core during the legislature occupation. Huang's transformation from an activist academic to a popularly elected lawmaker helped the Sunflower Movement to secure a solid footing in the new legislature.

Hong Kong's 2015 Local Election

There were eighteen district councils in Hong Kong, whose members were selected in 431 electoral areas in the first-past-the-pole manner. The size of these areas roughly corresponded to Taiwan's village and ward chief areas. District councils used to be a training ground for political parties to groom their next generation of politicians. Over the years, the pro-Beijing camp had established its supremacy at the grassroots level with stronger organization and abundant resources. With its capacities limited to consultation over community-level sanitation, welfare, and recreation, the district council was not an ideal place to translate movement passion into electoral politics. Nevertheless, post-Umbrella Hong Kong saw new entrants in the district council election held on November 22, 2015. These participants were called "umbrella soldiers" (*sanbing*) in the media, clearly indicating their origin in the Umbrella Movement. There were some young people who decided to join the election on their own upon learning that some pro-Beijing incumbents would be automatically reelected because of the lack of challengers (interview #HK20-1).

It proved more difficult to provide a precise estimate of movement-inspired electoral participation in Hong Kong for several reasons. With the absence of a legal regulation for political parties, candidates could fill in the political affiliation column with any organizational name they preferred or conceal their real membership. Since the Umbrella Movement appeared controversial in the public mind, many activist candidates deliberately avoided mentioning their movement involvement. Last, localists, such as six Civic Passion candidates who denounced the Umbrella Movement as an utter failure, rejected being categorized as pan-democrats or umbrella soldiers.

Consequently, the estimated number of umbrella soldiers varied in the media: 51 according to the *Stand News*[20] and 49 according to the *Apple Daily*,[21] with substantial discrepancies in the list of candidates. Seven umbrella soldiers were successfully elected, and some even unexpectedly defeated entrenched conservative veterans. Among them, Youngspiration, a post-Umbrella organization with a noted localist tendency, fielded 9 candidates and 2 were elected. The election represented a moderate win for Hong Kong's opposition (including pan-democrats, democracy-leaning independents, and umbrella soldiers) by gaining an additional 25 district councilor seats, whereas the pro-Beijing camp lost 11 seats. The result was certainly a disappointment for the conservatives, because they had anticipated a clear knock-out over pan-democrats for their involvement in the Umbrella Movement.

Hong Kong's 2016 Legislative Election

Presaged by the New Territory East by-election in February 2016, the legislative council election on November 4 that year witnessed the rise of localists and movement activists to the extent that pan-democrats felt threatened by these new players on the field. The SAR government introduced a legally questionable screening process (a required affidavit that upheld Hong Kong as an integral part of China as well as an examination of their previous public statements) that deprived six would-be localist candidates of the right to join the election. These contenders openly advocated for a change in Hong Kong's constitutional status, and they included Edward Leung Tin-kei of Hong Kong Indigenous and Chan Ho-tin of Hong Kong National Party, two pro-independence star leaders.

The electoral competition mostly revolved around the thirty-five seats of geographic constituency, which were decided by the democratic one-person-one-vote principle. Since the geographic constituency election proceeded under a proportionate representative system that generated multiple elected lawmakers (five to nine) in one district, the rule of the game encouraged intramural competition because a winning candidate had to garner only sufficient rather than a majority of the votes. As an insurgent force, localists even found it difficult to coordinate their electoral participation. Splintered into two alliances, localists were represented by a senior wing composed of Wong Yuk-man (a former pan-democratic incumbent), Chin Wan, and three Civic Passion candidates, as well as by a younger wing of four candidates related to Youngspiration. On the other hand, Umbrella Movement activists also joined the foray and raised the self-determination demand (insisting on Hongkongers' right to decide their future options, including independence) in order to carve out a middle ground between localists and pan-democrats. These activist candidates included Eddie Chu Hoi-dick, a veteran preservation activist who has been active since 2006; Lau Siu-lai, a college lecturer who became famous for operating a street forum in Mong Kok during the Umbrella Movement; and Nathan Law, the HKFS successor to Alex Chow and the only nominee of Demosisto, which was co-founded by Joshua Wong.

The election generated success for both localists and self-determination movement activists. Three localists won seats: Cheng Chung-tai (age 32) of the Civic Passion, Baggio Leung (age 30), and Yau Wai-ching (age 25) of Youngspiration. In addition, Eddie Chu Hoi-dick, Lau Siu-lai, and Nathan Law (age 23) succeeded in winning office. Although Hong Kong's opposition harvested a moderate gain in the 35 geographic constituency seats, from 18 seats in 2012 to 19 in 2016, the growth was secured at the expense of pan-democrats, as many incumbents failed in their reelection bids, including the seasoned labor activist Lee Cheuk-yan. Clearly the Umbrella-inspired contenders made their entrance into the political arena by edging out pan-democratic veterans, further fracturing Hong Kong's political opposition.

The Political Consequences

In Taiwan, the ruling KMT suffered consecutive defeats in the 2014 local election and the 2016 general election. Taiwan underwent its third peaceful transfer of power, as the DPP's Tsai Ing-wen won the presidency and secured the legislative majority for her party for the first time (with 68 out of 113 seats). In the wake of the Sunflower Movement, the slogan "Taiwan will be better only with the collapse of the KMT" (*guomindang bu dao taiwan buhui hao*) went viral among young people, clearly illustrating the unpopularity of the ruling party. Apparently, both the DPP and the KMT leaders understood the momentous consequences of the Sunflower Movement. In her acceptance speech on the winning night, Tsai Ing-wen cited the lyrics of *Island's Sunrise:* "At the dawn, a group of people gather here and they become more courageous in order to protect us." Tsai further added that her DPP was this group of people and they had also become more courageous after the election.[22] At her inauguration ceremony on May 20, she cited the same stanza again to conclude her speech and invited the rock band to perform the song in front of the Presidential Office. While the DPP was celebrating the legacy of the Sunflower Movement, the KMT acknowledged the incident as one of the reasons why it lost popular support in its reflection report.[23] The bipartisan consensus indicated the historic significance of the Sunflower Movement.

In a less dramatic fashion, Hong Kong also underwent significant changes. Localist sentiments surged in the wake of the Umbrella Movement. A poll of HKU students by the *Undergrad* in mid-2016 showed that 41 percent of the respondents favored independence, closely trailing those who supported maintaining a one-country-two-systems framework (43 percent).[24] Although the localist candidates failed in their attempts to secure seats in the 2015 district council election, they succeeded in the 2016 legislative council election. The pro-Beijing conservatives did not win the anticipated electoral victory in either case. Leung Chun-ying's sudden decision not to run for reelection in December 2016, apparently at the behest of leaders in Beijing, might be seen as a belated vindication for Hong Kong's Umbrella supporters.

On closer inspection, the electoral route for the young movement participants in both places was fraught with difficulties. The chance of a successful candidacy was disappointingly low: There were only 2 winners out of 37 movement candidates in Taiwan's 2014 local councilor election, 3 out of the 23 in the 2016 legislative election, and 7 out of 50 in Hong Kong's 2015 district election. The 2016 legislative election in Hong Kong might look like an exception, as 3 out of 9 localist contenders succeeded. The result was actually distorted in part due to the government's intervention to disqualify 6 pro-independence candidates, who would otherwise have split the votes. Clearly these first-time electoral contenders were facing an uphill challenge against the established politicians. In addition, there appeared to be inherent difficulties in coordinating the electoral efforts for the best return even among like-minded contenders, as demonstrated by the splits in Taiwan Citizen Union as well as the proliferation of localist and other new parties in Hong Kong. The rising activism brought about an overtly optimistic assessment of the electoral prospect, which easily brought about a suboptimal outcome.

Despite the low odds of success for a movement-oriented candidacy, its impact was not limited to the seats actually won. Movement-oriented parties "did not need to win election to exert influence on the policymaking decision of major party politicians" because the latter were more likely to concede to the movement's demands for fear of losing votes (McConnaughy 2013: 259). The challenges of Taiwan's third force had already made the mainstream parties more responsive to the voices of social movements. In the 2016 general election, the DPP's list for proportionate representation seats amounted to an impressive snapshot of contemporary social movements in Taiwan in that activists in environmentalism, human rights, feminism, rural preservation, disability, and social enterprises were nominated. Two ex-GPT members now served as DPP lawmakers. Even the KMT now had a pro-same-sex-marriage legislator. Similarly, in Hong Kong's 2017 legislative election, established pan-democratic and even conservative parties felt "compelled to respond to the localist agenda" (Kaeding 2017: 167).

By sending new faces like Huang Kuo-chang and Nathan Law into the legislature, the Sunflower Movement and the Umbrella Movement have secured a place in the political institutions. A new political generation has come of age in both places, replacing the preceding era of the 1980s generations in Hong Kong and Taiwan who pioneered the protest waves. Now younger figureheads like Joshua Wong (born in 1996) and Nathan Law (born in 1993, the youngest legislator in Hong Kong's history, but later deprived of legislative council membership in July 2017) came to represent the future opposition movement that was destined to face an eventual showdown with Beijing, as the expiration date of the one-country-two-systems design approaches in 2047. Similarly a group of young activists in their twenties or early thirties eagerly became political workers for the DPP, the NPP, the SDP, and the GPT, injecting fresh energy into Taiwan's politics.[25] How this cohort of new politicians, who were originally schooled in street protests and then toughened in electoral politics, will reshape future politics will unfold for years to come.

Cooperation or Conflict: Relations with the Opposition Parties

The relationship between the preexisting opposition parties and the new political forces also showed contrasting patterns. In first-past-the-post elections, such as those for Taiwan's district-seat legislators and Hong Kong's district councilors, if the opposition parties and the new forces could not agree on a single candidate, they would have given a windfall to the pro-government camp. If we exclude the NPP's "task nominees" whose participation was merely a means to meet the legal threshold in order to be able to contend for proportional seats, Taiwan's 2016 legislative election saw six cases of conflict between nominees from the DPP and the third force (the NPP, the SDP, and the GPT). In Hong Kong's 2015 local election, there were six such cases between pan-democrats and umbrella soldiers, not including another six conflicts with localists who actually chose the same district on purpose. On the surface, the number of district conflicts was the same, but their significance varied greatly. There were 73 district-seat legislators in Taiwan and 431 district councilors in Hong Kong, so it should have been easier for the latter to avoid such conflicts. Moreover, Hong Kong's pan-democratic parties and democracy-leaning independents fielded only 272 candidates, leaving around 40 percent of the districts without challengers from the opposition camp.

Given their fragmentation, Hong Kong's pan-democratic parties even had difficulties in coordinating nominations among themselves, let alone making a deal with the umbrella soldiers. In the 2015 local election, Youngspiration nominated nine candidates and three of them were in the same district as pan-democratic candidates. The group's spokesperson revealed that a prior negotiation with the DP leadership had failed to reach a consensus (interview #HK28). In contrast, Taiwan's DPP appeared more resourceful and capable of avoiding a mutually harmful rivalry with the third force. The DPP decided to temporarily suspend the nominations in 30 out of 73 districts, where its nominees did not perform well last time, in order to make room for coordination with allies. In fact, as Huang Kuo-chang made his decision to join the election rather late, the DPP deliberately vacated three possible districts for his choice in spite of internal criticism. The DPP's seemingly friendly gesture toward the third force did not originate from altruism, but rather political calculation. In the districts where it was not able to field a competitive member, the DPP endorsed 12 candidates, including 6 nonpartisans (5 of whom were former KMT members), 3 NPP, 1 SDP, 1 TSU, and 1 People First Party candidate. Evidently there was no favorable treatment toward the third force in spite of its rhetoric. The fact that the DPP encouraged its supporters to vote for ex-KMT or People First Party politicians who were competing against third force candidates clearly demonstrated its political realism.

While young political aspirants were busy organizing new political parties and organizations, there emerged a perceivable alienation from existing opposition parties in Hong Kong that was absent in Taiwan. As a Labour Party legislative council member lamented:

> Hong Kong's citizens felt that the opposition parties were useless because we have spent more than two decades without being able to overthrow the rule of the communist party. As a result, every time new faces came on the scene, they placed all their hope on them. (Interview #HK22)

Such sentiment was echoed by an interviewed LSD leader, "Do you think Joshua Wong and we have different ideas? No, but he does not collaborate with us." In comparison, the Sunflower-inspired activists generally had a more favorable attitude toward Taiwan's main opposition party. In the 2014 local election, the DPP launched a Democracy Grassroots (*minzhu xiaocao*) campaign by recruiting and training young people to join elections for village and ward chiefs. Among the thirty-seven participants, more than one-third of them mentioned their experiences in the Sunflower Movement and other protests in their resumes,[26] and the TSU launched a similar program, which was, however, less successful. There were Sunflower participants who later joined the DPP and became professional political workers. There were at least ten Sunflower activists who were directly involved with Tsai Ing-wen's campaign, and some of them began to work in the Presidential Office after the turnover of power. In the new legislature from February 2016, around one dozen Sunflower activists worked as aides to DPP lawmakers.

Such cordial relations between the main opposition party and young activists were entirely absent in Hong Kong, where the new political force emerged more as a competitor than a partner. The DPP was able to gain allegiance mostly because it was more resourceful than Hong Kong's underdeveloped pan-democratic parties, a clear advantage to young contenders for initiating their political careers. By being able to attract new blood, the DPP gained the opportunity to groom a new generation of leaders.

International Responses

The Sunflower Movement and the Umbrella Movement presented an unparalleled challenge to the Taiwan-China and Hong Kong–China relationships, which were embedded in an evolving geopolitical order shaped by the ascendancy of China and the American reactions in this region. As such, both occupy protests engendered reverberations beyond their borders.

The international media generally presented favorable accounts of the protesters, by highlighting their youthfulness, nonpartisanship, civility, and sophistication with digital communication, almost the identical image of the Arab Spring in the Western mainstream media. Hong Kong's government officials and conservative politicians, in fact, regarded these sympathetic reports as sufficient proof of the alleged "intervention of foreign forces." Because of the denser concentration of international journalists in Hong Kong, the Umbrella Movement drew more attention than the Sunflower Movement, as evidenced by cover stories in *Time* and *The Economist*.

Political leaders from the United States, the United Kingdom, Germany, Canada, Japan, and other major nations explicitly expressed their support for the Umbrella Movement. Hollywood paid its tribute too, as Oscar winners mentioned the incident during the 2015 Academy Awards ceremony. In Feburary 2018, U.S. senators launched the campaign to nominate Joshua Wong and his young associates for the Nobel Peace Prize. As expected, Chinese officials reiterated their insistence that Hong Kong remained a domestic issue and their intolerance of any interference by other countries.[27] Taiwan's Ma Ying-jeou surprisingly declared his endorsement of Hongkongers' pursuit of genuine universal suffrage and in his Double Tenth Day speech of 2014 urged Beijing to concede to the demands of demonstrators, which incurred insulting criticism from a hawkish China mouthpiece.[28] Ironically, the apparent global support failed to bring about tangible help to Hong Kong's protest, precisely because it seemed to substantiate Beijing's perception of the Umbrella Movement as a foreign-aided plot. U.S. President Barack Obama personally told Chinese President Xi Jinping in a private meeting that the United States had "no involvement in fostering the protests" in Hong Kong (Bush 2016: 259). Apparently, such assurances fell on deaf ears.

By contrast, there was no comment or mention of the Sunflower Movement by the leaders or spokespersons of major nations, with the notable exceptions of the United States and China. Apparently the dispute over a bilateral free-trade agreement was internationally seen as of a lower priority, at least compared to the issue of democratization, which appeared to be more in sync with the dominant universal values. The American response, in comparison, was intriguing for its cautious neutrality. Traditionally, its official stance has been to encourage cross-strait engagement in the hope of deescalating military tension. Since taking office in 2008, Ma Ying-jeou's rapprochement efforts with Beijing had won Washington's endorsement. Instead of condemning the disruption created by the Sunflower Movement, U.S. State Department officials spoke of it as a sign of a "vibrant democracy" and urged the government to resolve the dispute "peacefully and civilly."[29] Countering the KMT claim that failure to ratify the CSSTA would prevent Taiwan from joining the Trans-Pacific Partnership, a U.S.-led multilateral free-trade agreement during the Barack Obama era, U.S. diplomats clearly stated that these two issues were unrelated.[30] A DPP official who was in constant contact with American diplomats interpreted these responses as a rather friendly understanding, because the emphasis was on democratic procedure rather than protectionism (interview #TW3). As a matter of fact, during the occupation of the legislature, two student leaders flew to meet State Department officials with the intention of downplaying the disruptiveness of the protest by conveying that it was not motivated by the pursuit of Taiwan independence or opposition to free trade.[31] Although it was difficult to measure the result of such international lobbying, it was clear that the U.S. officials responded largely in the way that the student leaders had hoped.

The Sunflower Movement was able to effect milestone changes in Taiwan's politics without the global limelight that Hongkonger activists had enjoyed, whereas post-Umbrella Hong Kong witnessed growing clampdowns and imprisonment of protesters, in glaring contrast with the widespread sympathy and admiration from abroad.

In spite of these differences in terms of domestic and international consequences, the Taiwan–Hong Kong movement nexus, forged before the eruption of massive protests and reinforced during them, began to exert a greater impact on East Asian civil society. In May 2014, a large-scale protest against an overgenerous retirement pension for high-ranking officials in Macao took place, involving around 20,000 participants in a city of less than 600,000 citizens. The largest demonstration in Macao, it took place after Taiwan's Sunflower Movement and before Hong Kong's Umbrella Movement and was clearly affected by the surge of protests in these two places. Sulu Sou, who received his undergraduate and postgraduate education at Taiwan's NTU and was familiar with the Hongkonger student activists, played a key role in bridging three communities of activists. In September 2017, Sou was elected into legislative council, making him Macao's youngest lawmaker (age twenty-six at that time). Yet following the Hong Kong precedent, he was soon deprived of his political status because of a criminal prosecution over a protest incident, thus ending his brief two-month tenure.

In Japan, the opposition to Abe Shinzo's nationalist attempt to revise the pacifist constitution was largely restricted to the traditional leftists until the formation of the Students Emergency Action for Liberal Democracy (SEALDs) in March 2015. Although the SEALDs failed in their attempt to prevent Abe from gaining a constitution-changing majority in the Diet, its advent marked a new beginning of progressive student movement in Japan, which had been dormant after the historical collapse in the 1970s. The SEALDs were substantially inspired by Taiwanese and Hongkonger precedents because they offered a much less violent alternative version of student activism, more palatable to Japan's context, where conservatives had enjoyed hegemony for many decades.[32]

An East Asian student movement network emerged with the formation of the Network of Young Democratic Asians (NOYDA), which involved student participants from Hong Kong, Taiwan, Japan, South Korea, the Philippines, Vietnam, and Thailand. In October 2016, as Joshua Wong was denied entry at the Bangkok airport to prevent him from attending an event held by Thai student activists, NOYDA issued a joint protest statement.[33] The East Asian region had never witnessed a transborder nexus among student activists like NOYDA, and so far a regional protest wave comparable in scale to the Arab Spring and the Europe Summer of 2011 was not on the horizon. Nevertheless, the emergence of an international movement network in a region riven by linguistic barriers and nationalistic antagonisms constituted a tangible legacy of the Sunflower Movement and the Umbrella Movement.

Beijing's Reactions

For Chinese rulers, the eruption of two major protests in the same year represented a major setback to their intentions of implementing firmer control of Hong Kong and Taiwan. It symbolized the failure of economic united front work that relied on monetary incentives, including the CSSTA, to cultivate goodwill among Taiwanese, whereas Hongkongers' courageous defiance of the restrictive August 31 Framework indicated their pro-democracy determination over the reinforced patriotic indoctrination from above. Beijing has adopted different approaches in dealing with these two challenges: more conciliatory and tolerant toward the Sunflower Movement, and harsher and more repressive toward the Umbrella Movement.

Like KMT incumbents, Beijing was not prepared for a massive protest against a free-trade agreement that it saw as a major concession of economic benefits. Initially Chinese officials accepted the KMT's interpretation that the opposition party had masterminded the student occupation from behind by insisting on the CSSTA's beneficial effects.[34] As the legislature occupation gained more momentum, there was a belated realization that the KMT's view had failed to capture the whole story. The Chinese officials became aware that their conceded interests profited only a privileged minority. As such, they quickly put forward new preferential policies custom-made for Taiwan's small-and-medium enterprises and youth, who were perceived as having been left out of the CSSTA (Lai and Huang 2016: 213–214). Zhang Zhijun, the minister of China's Taiwan Affairs Office, visited Taiwan in June 2014, the first high-ranking Beijing official to come after the Sunflower Movement. Zhang met a select group of university students as a clear gesture toward alleviating skepticism among young citizens. Zhang's trip attracted a large number of demonstrators everywhere, and his motorcade was blocked and even spattered with paint in protest. On June 28, Zhang skipped some planned trips and took his return flight earlier than scheduled. His abrupt departure from diplomatic decorum aptly symbolized the troubled cross-strait relations after the Sunflower Movement.

Nevertheless, Beijing has shown restraint by refraining from naming or condemning the Sunflower Movement directly. In November 2015, two months before Taiwan's general election, in which the ruling KMT appeared likely to lose its national power, Beijing gave a green light to meeting the Taiwanese leader on an international occasion. On November 7, Xi Jinping met Ma Ying-jeou in Singapore and both concurred on the need to maintain the "one-China consensus," which meant Taiwan was an integral part of China—marking the first meeting between Chinese and Taiwanese leaders since the Nationalists fled China in 1949 during the Civil War. Ma had originally proposed meeting the Chinese leader in Beijing in an effort to secure his place in history. Unexpectedly, Ma was granted the opportunity in a third country, a much better deal for him. In short, before the DPP's Tsai Ing-wen assumed power in May 2016, Beijing had largely adopted a rather conciliatory approach in dealing with post-Sunflower Taiwan.

Beijing's exercise of restraint was not applied to Hong Kong. In the first few days after the explosion of the Umbrella Movement, the official mouthpiece already identified the incident as a "color revolution" instigated by foreign forces and intended to manufacture a regime change. The repeated denials by Umbrella spokespersons apparently failed to disabuse Chinese leaders of their paranoid obsession with a global anti-China conspiracy. Apparently, Beijing saw eye to eye with its local operatives and collaborators that the Umbrella Movement had been instigated as a foreign plot, so it fully endorsed a repressive response against the "unlawful disturbance," a marked contrast with its skepticism toward the KMT interpretation of the Sunflower Movement as the DDP's puppet show. Leung Chun-ying's subsequent provocations with Hong Kong's civil society as well as the appointment to a prominent PRC political position after his decision not to seek reelection seemed to indicate that he had Beijing's unwavering support.

Seemingly violating the Basic Law promise of a high degree of autonomy, Beijing's direct intervention in Hong Kong affairs increased afterward. The incident of Causeway Bay Bookstore revealed the alarming threat that Hongkonger dissidents faced. The bookstore specialized in political books that were prohibited in China, a popular local product for mainland tourists. Starting in mid-2015, its five managers disappeared one by one in Hong Kong, Thailand, and mainland China; they were detained and interrogated by Chinese security officials. The incident sent a chill, signifying that Beijing was willing to violate Hongkongers' right to personal freedom. Two of the detainees were naturalized British and Swedish citizens, which raised concern in

Europe. Yet Chinese officials defended such state-initiated abductions on the grounds that "all Hong Kong residents who had Chinese blood were Chinese citizens." In other words, Hongkonger dissidents would be subject to China's global manhunt even if they had already renounced their PRC citizenship.

In November 2016, Beijing launched a new round of rubber stamp legal interpretation to require that the swearing-in of elected representatives had to be executed "sincerely and solemnly" and the oath that claimed Chinese sovereignty over Hong Kong needed to be read "accurately, completely, and solemnly." An invalid swearing-in immediately disqualified would-be representatives from exercising their legal capacity. This intervention came as a reaction against the newly elected opposition legislative council members who used the swearing-in ceremony to demonstrate their defiance. Baggio Leung and Yau Wai-ching, two localist legislative council members who used the occasion to convey their pro-independence convictions and made derogatory remarks about China, soon forfeited their political status in a court decision. In July 2017, the court further deprived Leung Kwok-hung, Lau Siu-lai, Nathan Law, and Edward Yiu of their legislative membership. With the exception of veteran activist Leung, five newly elected umbrella soldiers have been thrown out of their office due to technical issues related to the swearing-in ceremony. Less than a month later, Joshua Wong, Alex Chow, and Nathan Law were sentenced to six to eight months in jail for leading the Umbrella Movement, in an appellate ruling at the request of the SAR government, reserving their previous light sentences. In particular, Nathan Law's transition from the youngest lawmaker to one of the youngest political prisoners epitomized Hongkongers' vulnerability as they were exposed to heavy-handed reprisals from a more interventionist, distrustful, and vindictive central government.

Conclusion

Both the Sunflower Movement and the Umbrella Movement were history-making events that brought about far-reaching and transformative consequences. Defiant against the pressures from Beijing, Taiwanese rejected the KMT's more accommodating approach to China and gave the independence-leaning DPP the presidency and a legislative majority. In Hong Kong, a homegrown independence movement came into being that posed a more alarming challenge to Beijing. In both places, a young generation of politicians had come of age, as future leaders of political movements emerged. Jailing these youthful political activists and barring them from joining the election might have thwarted Hong Kong's pro-democracy movement for the moment, but it also bestowed on them the halo effect, a potential asset for their future political careers—just as a number of Taiwan's DPP founding politicians, including Chen Shui-bian, had served time in the KMT's political prison. By contrast, Hong Kong's pioneers, such as Martin Lee and Szeto Wah, had not experienced such repression.

It should be pointed out that these transformative results happened because of the ensuing movement mobilization after the conclusion of the occupy protests. The end of the unprecedented massive civil disobedience represented only a temporary truce, and the contention was prolonged in a less intensive way. This chapter has found that the negative emotional outcomes among occupy participants needed to be treated first in order to maintain continuing protest activism. Taiwanese and Hongkonger activists deployed a number of experimental, collective, and individual strategies to manage their traumatic experiences. The termination of the extraordinary occupation of public space brought back normalcy, and as a result, the subsequent movement politics appeared to be more structured by the existing institutional rules. Taiwan's more democratized politics allowed for more proactive and state-oriented protest movements that had scored some milestone victories, whereas Hong Kong's movements appeared to be defensive and proceeded in different arenas of civil society. The stronger opposition party in Taiwan made it possible for it to absorb young political aspirants and to ensure the emergence of a friendly political force. Hong Kong's fractured and weak opposition parties, by contrast, encountered unexpected competition from new election entrants who appeared to be more attractive to young and increasingly vocal pro-independence voters.

Moving beyond the borders, the two major occupy protests and subsequent activism influenced the triangular relations among China, Taiwan, and Hong Kong. While Beijing had originally intended to implement the one-country-two-systems design in Hong Kong as a demonstration site for Taiwan, a reversal actually took place, as more and more Hongkongers began to admire the self-rule and vibrant democracy that Taiwanese enjoyed. Arguably there emerged a process of Taiwanization of Hong Kong's politics, as the terms of political debate (such as the pro-independence movement and indigenization), as well as the electoral tactics (such as the successful model of the NPP) were increasingly adopted locally. Beijing was rightfully apprehensive of these trends; however, its clumsy interventions were more likely to end up further alienating Hongkongers. An episode on the eve of the twentieth anniversary of Hong Kong's handover to China suffices to illustrate this change. In June 2017, a Taiwan Congressional Hong Kong Caucus was formed with eighteen DPP and NPP lawmakers, and its founding ceremony was attended by three Hong Kong legislative councilors, as well as Umbrella Movement leaders Alex Chow and Joshua Wong. Clearly a Taiwan–Hong Kong resistance network has emerged to counter Beijing's further encroachment.

While Beijing exercised restraint in dealing with the Sunflower Movement and its aftermath, such a conciliatory approach came to an abrupt end with the DPP taking the reins of government in May 2016. The DPP had resisted accepting the "1992 consensus" that maintained that Taiwan was a part of China. From the time Tsai Ing-wen took office, Beijing unilaterally suspended official exchange channels, pressured international organizations (such as the World Health Assembly and the International Civil Aviation Organization) to impose more restrictions on Taiwan's participation, insisted on "repatriating" Taiwanese suspects arrested in third countries to China for criminal prosecution, discouraged Taiwan-bound tourists from China, lured Taiwan's foreign allies to sever diplomatic ties with money, and launched its air force and naval fleet for military exercises near Taiwan. In early January 2017, Joshua Wong and Nathan Law flew to Taiwan to attend a discussion forum staged by the NPP. They experienced violent assault by gangsters, who apparently knew the details of Wong and Law's unannounced itinerary, and Law was personally injured in a melee when he stepped out of the Hong Kong airport. Apparently, state-level orchestration of simultaneous gangster violence in Hong Kong and Taiwan was involved.[35]

In sum, the long-term consequences of the Sunflower Movement and the Umbrella Movement will unfold in the context of evolving regional and global geopolitics. The final chapter of these two eventful protests could take years or even decades to play out.

Conclusion

On an autumn evening in 2015, I met Andy Leung (a pseudonym) at a trendy pub located in a gentrified neighborhood of Hong Kong Island. Andy was a tall and robust twenty-nine-year-old man, and appeared excited after finishing a hectic day of campaigning for the district council election, which started with greeting elderly citizens in the early morning. As an umbrella soldier, Andy was an interesting fusion of Oriental and Occidental, emblematic of the erstwhile British colony that now found itself a special administrative region of China. After receiving legal training in London, Andy now managed an operation in many provinces in China. Campaigning in an expatriate-heavy district (more than 20 percent), Andy insisted on wearing a shirt and jacket because he did not want to scare upper-middle-class voters with his tattooed arms.

During the Umbrella Movement, Andy volunteered as a "frontiersman" (*fangxian*) who took shifts patrolling the Admiralty occupation zone. He was pepper-sprayed in the face many times and his limbs were badly swollen from beatings by police batons; nevertheless, he relished the unusual camaraderie with his fellow frontiersmen, who were determined to provide a safe space for student demonstrators. He particularly loved those moments when he and his brothers vented their anger by beating up pro-regime gangsters. Andy did not care much about politics before his involvement in the occupy protest and, in fact, he acknowledged having a strong identity with China. Upon seeing the police's harsh treatment of the peaceful demonstrators, he found it necessary to do something, because of a strong feeling that Hong

Kong was his home. Afterward, he financed a post–Umbrella Movement organization in order to continue his engagement in activism. On his campaign fliers, Andy placed a picture of his fiancée and two dogs to emphasize that he was determined to promote a family-friendly and pet-friendly community. Andy did not succeed in toppling the entrenched pro-regime incumbent in his electoral attempt. Despite the failure, he remained active in the post-Umbrella Community Charter Movement in exploring new ways to engage with the people.

Six months later, I interviewed A-Fang (a pseudonym) in a cafe on the ground floor of Taipei City Hall, where she was doing a stint as a media aide to the nonpartisan mayor Ko Wen-je. Born in 1991, A-Fang was originally an undergraduate student in sociology who became involved in the protest activism that was sweeping Taiwan's universities. She joined the BIY and experienced its low tide in late 2013, when that student organization was on the brink of collapse. A-Fang was among the student demonstrators who broke into the legislature on the eventful evening of March 18, 2014. She was one of those young faces that became recognizable nationwide after taking part in television talk shows, representing the students' voice.

Although in her appearances on television A-Fang was eloquent and calm, she experienced great emotional upheavals during the Sunflower Movement. She had a bitter fight with the student leaders after learning that they had attempted to dissociate themselves from the participants of the Executive Yuan incident. She felt deeply frustrated that their peaceful rally was not able to elicit a government concession. A-Fang sustained a devastating movement injury as she grew distrustful of her erstwhile fellow activists. She experienced difficulties in adjusting to life as a regular student and avoided contact with others by suspending her undergraduate studies for several months. Her everyday life returned to a semblance of normalcy with a sudden marriage, and she appreciated the companionship of her husband as she overcame depression. Soon she became involved in post–Sunflower Movement activism, for which she gave up admission to a master's degree program. Later she decided to use the dowry that her parents had prepared for her to stand in the 2016 legislative election in a New Taipei City district, which DPP candidates had never won. She represented the GPT in this KMT stronghold, but failed to secure the DPP's endorsement. In the three-way competition, she ended up in third place, receiving 12.2 percent of the vote, actually a very decent performance by a first-timer in a two-front battle. Undaunted by the unsuccessful trial, A-Fang remained committed to public engagement, as she accepted the invitation to take part in city administration and regrouped her electoral team into a new local organization devoted to community issues. She later joined the 2018 councilor election, registered as an NPP candidate.

Conclusion

The stories of Andy and A-Fang demonstrate the fascinating intertwining of individual biographies and collective histories during the eventful protests. With its increasing economic and military strength, China became more able to intervene in the domestic politics of Hong Kong and Taiwan over the years, resulting in growing state-civil society tensions. The rising wave of social protests attracted more and more participation from young people like Andy and A-Fang. Prior to the eruption of the Sunflower Movement and the Umbrella Movement, a young generation's distinctive outlook was forged in the crucible of their rising protest activism. The intensive participation in the prolonged occupy protests turned out to be an acute and transformative experience. Andy and A-Fang were physically or psychologically injured, their study and career plans disrupted, and intimate relationships swerved in an unexpected direction. Like many other young Hongkongers and Taiwanese, they relaunched their participation in public issues in spite of their negative emotional outcomes and the seeming lack of concrete achievements when the two protests ended. By their attempts to run for public office, electoral politics was injected with a fresh dose of youthful idealism. In the years to come, Andy's peers are very likely to lead Hong Kong's pro-democracy movement, whereas A-Fang and her like-minded young people will be the driving force in the deepening of Taiwan democracy.

C. Wright Mills (1959) defines "sociological imagination" as a particular mental capacity to understand the reciprocal relationship between personal troubles and public issues. It is during the exceptional moments of eventful protests that mutual interaction between the personal and the public becomes dramatic, intense, and apparent. For this reason, social movement study offers a unique vantage point, because one of its central tasks is to explain how individual efforts accumulate into a collective force capable of generating social changes. Clearly an effective social movement cannot come into being without a sufficient number of people being converted to its cause in first place. And as these people contribute their time and effort to the desired goal, their identity, career, and personal life are also changed by their participation. In other words, social movement research cannot be completed without paying attention to the transformations occurring simultaneously at the individual and the collective levels, as well as their mutual interactions.

I believe this valuable insight is precisely what Karl Marx hinted at in his aphoristic *Theses on Feuerbach,* in which he defines "revolutionary practice" as "the coincidence of the changing of circumstances and of human activity" (Marx 1975: 422). In other words, you cannot change an unacceptable circumstance without having to remake yourself as a new person. This dialectic perspective helps us connect the often-neglected dots between macrolevel social changes and microlevel personal experiences. China's ascendancy as a new world power certainly engenders great and far-reaching consequences in international politics and global economics; nevertheless, through the mediation of domestic institutions, it also stimulates the birth of a cohort of young activists who will become future political leaders in Taiwan and Hong Kong. Their formative experiences during the Sunflower Movement and the Umbrella Movement are very likely to shape further Taiwan-China and Hong Kong–China relations in the decades to come.

A Recapitulation

This book opened with six intellectual puzzles concerning the Sunflower Movement and the Umbrella Movement. Both incidents took place unexpectedly, and even the most attentive participants were surprised by their sudden emergence and subsequent turns. They also marked a major turning point in history, as post-Sunflower Taiwan and post-Umbrella Hong Kong were violently jolted onto a new and uncharted trajectory. Here I summarize the research findings by explaining these six puzzles.

First, why did massive disruptive protests take place in politically conservative Taiwan and Hong Kong, where civil disobedience remained an outlandish idea? The global wave of eventful protests in the new millennium, as manifested in the global justice movement and the 2011 occupy protests in the Middle East and Europe did not generate a perceivable effect here. Faint echoes of the Occupy Wall Street Movement existed, but they did not transcend the tiny circles of movement veterans. The Sunflower Movement and the Umbrella Movement shared many similarities with the eventful protests elsewhere in the world, including occupying public space, participation by young people with economic grievances, and independence from political parties. Yet a distinctive root cause lay in geopolitics. Both movements represented collective challenges to Beijing's imperialistic political project to bring the two societies under firmer control. Chapter 2 documents the growing apprehension and agitation over the larger presence of China in Hong Kong and Taiwan. While Beijing's economic united front strategy succeeded in cultivating a privileged group of local collaborators, it also deepened the existing cleavage between the winners and the losers of "the China opportunity." There were pernicious effects on political institutions and political rights. Hong Kong's autonomy, rule of law, and press freedom deteriorated, and the prospect of democratization was put off indefinitely, whereas Taiwan's nascent democracy was undermined and its self-rule threatened. Hongkongers mounted self-defensive actions against the coercive mainlandization, and at the same time, Taiwanese resisted the looming fate of Hongkongization. Fundamentally it was due to these existential risks that Hongkongers and Taiwanese came to join and support the Umbrella Movement and the Sunflower

Movement, which clearly deviated from the previously accepted norms of protest making.

Second, why did protest actions emerge at the moment when the prospects for a government concession appeared low? The official announcement of the August 31 Framework amounted to a disheartening moment of truth, smashing Hongkongers' expressed hope for a fair top leader election. The proposed formula practically eliminated any meaningful participation by the opposition, a more hardliner response from Beijing than expected. In Taiwan, the anti-CSSTA activists did not gain traction because of the failure to attract public attention to the issue of free trade with China. They also appeared to have exhausted every institutional means available to delay the imminent ratification, and to make matters worse, the main opposition party did not endorse their demand because it was adjusting its existing cross-strait policy in order to appear more palatable to moderate voters.

Chapters 4 and 5 maintain that the Umbrella Movement and the Sunflower Movement did not come about because of favorable political opportunities that reduced the cost of collective action or increased the likelihood of success. An analysis of regime orientation, stability of elite alignment, and political allies on the eve of the two protests indicated a neutral, if not adverse, situation. Both regimes subsequently made fatal mistakes that dramatically increased the sense of threat among citizens. The Hong Kong police's indiscriminate use of tear gas against a peaceful crowd brought about widespread indignation and a road occupation emerged. In Taiwan, the ruling party's heavy-handed attempts to push the CSSTA bill brought national attention, and the students' successful break-in into the legislature, as well as their vulnerable situation as they were besieged by policemen, quickly drew supporters to the scene. In other words, many Hongkongers and Taiwanese suddenly realized the grave consequences of their inaction. Both protests happened as a last resort and a desperate intervention to protect the endangered students, which clearly deviated from the previous dispute over the electoral design or the free-trade agreement with China.

Third, why did students become the recognized leaders of these two major protests instead of more established opposition politicians or movement leaders? True, the Confucian political culture bestowed an elevated social status on university students, the modern inheritors of classical literati, as they tended to be seen as society's conscience. As such, their protests represented a moral force against the power holders, and they were more likely to be perceived as idealistic and nonpartisan. While not denying the legacy of traditional culture, Chapter 3 argues that a generational youth revolt surfaced both in pre-Umbrella Hong Kong and pre-Sunflower Taiwan. Hongkongers and Taiwanese born in the 1980s experienced economic deprivation in the new millennium and spearheaded a new wave of protest activism. University campuses became a hotbed for recruiting younger movement participants and their linkages with NGOs and opposition parties became denser. The network of student activists underwent considerable expansion, and they simultaneously became more sophisticated and experienced in mobilization and more emboldened to launch radical protests. In other words, activist students were able to obtain the movement leadership not only because of their privileged status but even more so because they became numerous, connected, and skillful.

Fourth, how is it that better preparation, stronger organization, and more abundant resources in Hong Kong gave rise to weak movement leadership, whereas the Taiwanese protest generated an effective decision-making core in spite of its earlier rudimentary conditions? Chapters 4 and 5 contend that both large-scale protests engendered exceptional movement-government standoffs that suspended the normal functioning of routine politics. As a sui generis situation, the standoff dynamics were structured by a number of contingencies that no one was able to predict before the onset of movement activism. Hong Kong's movement management was crippled from the very beginning by the simultaneous emergence of three noncontiguous occupation zones and the lack of a spatial center to ensconce and protect the leadership, whereas, in Taiwan, the occupied legislature besieged and protected by policemen turned out to be an ideal arrangement for attracting the national spotlight to the core participants, while at the same time not exposing them to internal dissidents. In addition, the existence of prior organizations with clear command channels and boundaries turned out to be a liability in the Hong Kong standoff because it impeded the post hoc construction of new leadership. In Taiwan, there were no preexisting equivalents to Hong Kong's OCLP and HKFS; however, the Sunflower Movement engendered effective leadership and unfolded in an orderly manner, a scenario for which the OCLP leaders had planned for more than one year without being able to achieve it.

Fifth, how was it possible to sustain a prolonged mass protest when the movement leadership appeared unprepared and unable to provide the necessary resources? As indicated in Chapter 6, the answer is that the unsolicited contributions of movement participants made it possible with their on-the-spot and decentralized decisions, a mechanism I called "improvisation." In practice, no matter how resourceful and prepared a movement organization might be, a sustained standoff with the government always needed initiative from the participants. Improvisation, however, was far from a cure-all solution to the challenges faced by the large-scale movements. Not every participant was equally able to contribute to the movement, because seasoned activists were better able to play an executive role. Moreover, there remained multiple contradictions in improvisation because of the inherent difficulties in reconciling the instrumental and the expressive demands. The existence of improvisation in no way lent credence to the ideal of a leaderless movement, horizontalism, or the "multitude." Particularly in the situation without a coherent and overlapping movement network, improvisation may have actually exacerbated internal strife.

Finally, why did the Umbrella Movement end up further dividing Hong Kong's opposition, whereas the Sunflower Movement helped Taiwan's opposition party gain national power? As discussed in Chapter 7, both Hong Kong and Taiwan witnessed subsequent activism following the end of the occupy episodes. However, the consequences were mediated through a number of institutional factors as the exceptional standoff period concluded. Due to its stronger organization, Taiwan's DPP appeared better able to attract the new young activists and foster the growth of a friendly political force. In contrast, Hong Kong's fractured and weak pan-democratic parties faced competition from umbrella soldiers and localists, whose political ascendancy came at the expense of the preexisting opposition.

My observation ends immediately before the fourth anniversary of the Umbrella Movement, in August 2018. At the moment, Tsai Ing-wen's DPP government is deeply mired in a two-front battle, as the Sunflower generation presses for legalization of same-sex marriage (which was supported in a landmark decision by justices of the Constitutional Court in May 2017, making Taiwan the first Asian country to achieve this breakthrough), abolition of nuclear energy, and progressive reforms in pensions, labor law, and transitional justice, whereas the KMT conservatives launched a last-ditch effort to preserve the status quo. In Hong Kong, the small-circle election of its chief executive by an unrepresentative election committee of 1,200 members was held in March 2017, with the result, as expected, of a victory for Beijing's handpicked Carrie Lam. After the imprisonment of Joshua Wong and his comrades, many Umbrella Movement leaders and those who were involved in the Fishball Revolution were given heavier punishment. For instance, Edward Tin-kei Leung, a charismatic young leader in post-Umbrella activism, was sentenced to six years in jail. Beijing clearly ratcheted up its control over the former British colony. Agnes Chow of Demosisto was barred from joining the by-election in March 2018 for the legislative seat taken away from Nathan Law. Benny Tai sustained a savage round of criticisms from the pro-Beijing camp for his alleged advocacy of political independence. He and other OCLP leaders are facing a likely guilty verdict from the court that will put them behind bars for years. The police proposed to disband Hong Kong National Party, a post-Umbrella organization with noted pro-independence demands. Reporters without Borders, an international watchdog for press freedom, relocated its Asian Bureau office from Hong Kong to Taiwan in April 2017—a decision clearly indicating the contrasting development in press freedom in the wake of the two eventful protests. While a new chapter of social reforms and democratic deepening was being written in Taiwan,

Hong Kong continued to be deeply mired in the unfinished project of democratization.

Implications for Social Movement Study

Social movements in East Asia have not enjoyed a prominent place in the field of social movement study, even though this dynamic region has witnessed revolutions, civil wars, democratizations, and all sorts of social protests over the past century. When East Asian scholars began to develop their movement research in the 1990s, they first imported the existing conceptual tools from the West. Although there have been subsequent local adjustments and revisions, they failed to surface in the international discussion (Broadbent 2011). In other words, East Asian social movements have been on the periphery of international research, whose theoretical development continues to focus on movements in the United States and European countries (see Boudreau 1996; Cox, Nilsen, and Pleyers 2017; Ferree and Merrill 2004). As pointed out by Eitan Alimi (2016: 7–10), there has been a persistent "fruitful tension" between Western theories and non-Western cases in social movement study.

In this book, I have adopted a mixed writing strategy. On the one hand, I relied extensively on the available conceptual tools, such as networks, generation, and identity, to structure my narrative in Chapter 3 and political opportunities and threat in Chapters 4 and 5. On the other hand, I worked on theorization in order to shed light on some particular aspects of the Taiwanese and Hongkonger eventful protests. Chapters 4 and 5 conceptualize "standoff" as an exceptional and intensive interaction between protesters and the government, whereas Chapter 6 presents "improvisation," defined as decentralized decision making, as an alternative to the existing concept "mobilization." How can these research findings on the periphery contribute to social movement study? Can the analysis of movements in Taiwan and Hong Kong shed light on contemporary theoretical issues?

Social movement study has become a highly institutionalized research field with a community of practitioners employing a similar set of conceptual tools and consensually referencing a list of classical works. The era of paradigm warfare, such as the battle between resource mobilization theory and new social movement theory in the 1980s and the 1990s, is clearly over and has been replaced by a more synthetic approach that simultaneously examines movements' strategic and cultural dimensions. Theoretical debates continue, for instance on whether the term "political opportunity" is too structuralistic, but the degree of divergence has considerably narrowed. The theoretical movement pioneered by Charles Tilly, Sidney Tarrow, and Doug McAdam to incorporate those previously separated research areas of social movements, revolutions, nationalism, industrial disputes, and ethnic conflicts into a single paradigm of contentious politics has attracted considerable attention. Their attempt to codify a universally applicable vocabulary of mechanisms and processes indicates the existence of a broad consensus among researchers (McAdam, Tarrow, and Tilly 1996, 1997, 2001; McAdam and Tarrow 2010; Tilly and Tarrow 2007). Furthermore, the establishment of specialized journals like *Mobilization* (in 1996) and *Social Movement Studies* (in 2002), now flagship publication outlets in this field, helps to define the boundaries of social movement study.

While specialization and the emergence of a common research agenda make possible the cumulative efforts to deepen social movement study, there are also worries of increased narrowing of the intellectual horizon. Andrew Walder (2009) criticized the exclusive focus on mobilization, which tended to ignore the larger questions in political sociology, such as formation of identities. McAdam and Boudet raised similar concerns over what they call the "Ptolemaic view of social movements": "movements substituting for the Earth as center of the political universe" (2012: 2). Such a movement-centric perspective led to the neglect of the role of nonmovement actors and of other similar events that did not generate movements. In other words, institutionalization might inadvertently create a filter bubble to the extent that social movement study became more self-referential and irrelevant to other intellectual fields. In fact, when first proposing the perspective of resource mobilization theory in the 1970s, McCarthy and Zald (1987: 16) took care to frame their closer look at mobilization process as "a partial theory" because they deliberately shelved the discussion of larger structural issues. Unfortunately, what was clearly intended as a temporarily designated research focus turned out to nearly monopolize subsequent scholarly attention.

Echoing these concerns, I offer the following three methodological suggestions, based on my research on social movements in Taiwan and Hong Kong.

Embedding Mobilization Research in a Larger Context of Social Change

Social movements become an intellectual concern because of their potential to generate social transformation. Social movements are different from other sources of change (for example, technological advance, state building, and economic development) precisely because they come into being as a result of intentional effort by those who are underprivileged or do not possess the means to effect the desired change individually. Therefore, the emergence of social movements is predicated on the prior changes that make possible their rise in the first place. It follows, then, that a narrowly conceived mobilization-centric study easily overemphasizes the short episode of contention without paying sufficient attention to the long-term causes that lead to the flare-up of protests.

In any explanation of the origin of the Sunflower Movement and the Umbrella Movement, it is impossible not to mention the hegemonic project of Chinese rulers who have intentionally created economic dependence for both Taiwan and Hong Kong for political purposes. Over the years, pro-Beijing collaborators became influential and pro-democracy political parties became fractured or tamed, but civil society became more defiant, agitated, and empowered by the rise of discontented youth who have been left out of Beijing's economic united front work. Therefore, we cannot understand the rise of these two highly exceptional protests without looking at the multiple and associated contradictions generated by China's political agenda. Thus, to set the analysis of the actual period of mobilization within a larger and longer framework is a critical task for social movement students.

Extending the Observation to Include the Post-mobilization Period

No matter how routinized or expected it might be, a protest always carries some extraordinary qualities that most citizens would prefer to avoid. Cycles of protest are the norm, since no society can permanently endure sustained mobilization without experiencing systemic crises. With the exception of social revolutions, major social changes are rarely achieved while demonstrators still remain in the streets. Far-reaching transformations are likely to take years or even decades of fermentation, and when people begin to recognize these changes, the passion to protest might have already dimmed.

When the Sunflower Movement and the Umbrella Movement ended, there was no clear indication of who was the winner. While the government incumbents might claim to have solved major political crises with zero casualties, the movement leaders stayed as defiant as before. However, as a result of the subsequent activism, significant changes came about, such as the abolition of nuclear power in Taiwan and a surge in the pro-independence sentiment in Hong Kong, which testified to the enduring legacy of these two exceptional protest events.

Reconnecting Protests and Institutional Politics

There has been a time-honored division of intellectual labor where political scientists focus on elections and sociologists look at protest behaviors. Such a demarcation not only is artificial but also fails to examine the multiple interactions of institutional and extra-institutional political participation. Citizens do not make this distinction; nor do movement activists and politicians avoid the less familiar territory. Consequently, both protests and more institutionalized venues for promoting social changes should be examined simultaneously.

The Sunflower Movement and the Umbrella Movement took place more or less because of the failure of the opposition parties to represent genuine citizen preferences. Taiwan's DPP appeared too absorbed in modifying its pro-independence stance to register and respond to the widespread fear over economic integration with China, whereas Hong Kong's pan-democrats were too disunited to present a common front. Hence, civil-society actors grasped the opportunity of the political vacuum and initiated their unprecedented protests. Moreover, both Taiwanese and Hongkonger activists subsequently redirected their attention to elections. The successful entrance of Taiwan's NPP and Hong Kong's localists and movement activists into the legislative organs turned out to be a vivid reminder of the institutional outcomes of extra-institutional participation.

In short, at its core social movement study is an intellectual project to make sense of the dialectics of social structure and collective human agency, or what Karl Marx has referred to as "making history under circumstances existing already, given and transmitted from the past" in the opening paragraphs of *The Eighteenth Brumaire of Louis Bonaparte* (Marx 1974: 146). While more than two decades of institutionalization has enriched our understanding of the internal process of movement mobilization, now it is time to reconnect social movement study with other parallel fields of intellectual investigation by extending its analytical scope from the micro- or mesolevel to the macrolevel, broadening the time horizon, and raising more ambitious questions related to what the late Charles Tilly (1984) characterized as "big structures, large processes, and huge comparisons."

China's Rise Viewed from Its Peripheral Civil Societies

My final reflection is about China's spectacular ascendancy in the global arena, which has justifiably attracted universal attention. Most existing comments focus on economic or military aspects. Questions such as when China's GDP will surpass that of the United States and how China's foreign reserves and outward investment will reshape global economics are often asked. The monumental "One Belt, One Road" venture, which encompasses massive building and construction projects in sixty countries, is seen as an attempt to build a Sino-centric co-prosperity zone, whereas the Asian Infrastructure Investment Bank aims to create a China-controlled international financial institution in a challenge to the leading roles of the World Bank and the Asian Development Bank. Around the globe, there has been discussion of China's "sharp power," or the intensive use of economic strength to censor unfavorable information by targeting structural weakness in the democratic West. China's international application of sharp power was predated by the economic united front strategy in Hong Kong and Taiwan, as diagnosed in Chapter 2. While Hongkonger and Taiwanese businesspersons have been converted into Beijing's collaborators, their growing political influence has also sowed the seeds for popular protests. It remains to be seen how the dynamic of resistance to China's sharp power evolves in a larger context.

So far China's fast growth and expanding economic influence have drawn contrasting appraisals. Giovanni Arrighi (2007) anticipates a new Chinese model of market-based development without replicating the Western experience of dispossession, wastefulness, and overseas expansion. Stefan Halper (2012) contends that China has successfully demonstrated an authoritarian path to prosperity and power with the "Beijing Consensus." Martin Jacques (2012) maintains that China's growing economic might will eventually enable an attempt to craft a new world order based on the Confucian "civilization state." On the other hand, there are skeptics of China's economic power. Ho-fung Hung (2015) points out that China remains dependent on low-cost exports and is trapped by its inability to address widening regional and class disparities without a fundamental political change. In a more popularized form, the documentary film *Death by China,* produced by Peter Navarro in 2011, raises a litany of accusations of how China made illicit profits via currency manipulation, labor repression, environmental pollution, and disregard for consumer safety.

The "Thucydides Trap" anticipates armed conflicts following the rise of a new world power. Geopolitical tensions have become more intensified, as China's more assertive role and its military buildup have given rise to security responses in neighboring countries, including Japan, South Korea, Vietnam and the Philippines. On both sides of the Pacific, a pessimistic estimation is emerging that a China-U.S. military confrontation is becoming inevitable. In an official visit to Japan in February 2017, the U.S. defense secretary, James Mattis, warned against the Chinese attempt to restore a tribute system of the Ming Dynasty, which coerced neighboring countries to follow a China-centered regional order. This remark clearly demonstrates heightened military tensions in this region.

It is true that economic strength, military power, and geopolitical rivalry continue to be driving forces that shape the current international order, which is undergoing a fundamental change due to China's rise as a new world power. In contrast, however, civil society, understood as bottom-up efforts to organize and advocate for changes, appears powerless when facing these larger and more compelling forces. Nevertheless there are some historical moments when civil-society actors are able to generate certain regional or international consequences independently. Poland's Solidarity

Movement of 1980–1981 serves as a relevant precedent. Although the Polish opposition was put down by a martial-law rule, it inspired the subsequent pro-democracy movements in Eastern Europe and laid the foundations for the dissolution of the Soviet Union and its control over the peripheral satellite states. Certainly it would be fallacious to see a revolt on its rim as the main cause of the decline of the Soviet Union, but it is no less erroneous and incomplete if we fail to examine how the resuscitation of eastern European civil society contributed to the transition away from communism.

Currently, China's civil society appears too fragile and weak to initiate changes on its own. Xi Jinping has eliminated political rivals, strengthened ideological control, silenced dissidents, jailed human rights activists, and instituted a one-man rule for life. Numerous studies point out that the Chinese state has mastered the art of managing the increasingly frequent social protests by defusing their political potential (Cai 2010; X. Chen 2012; Feng and Su 2012; Friedman 2014; Lee and Zhang 2013; Perry 2008). Instead of heralding more progressive changes, Chinese NGOs have become more and more dependent on governmental resources (Fulda 2015; Spires 2011). The online public sphere, once active and contentious, is now being contained by a more digitally sophisticated party-state (Lei 2018).

In view of the demoralized status of civil society in China proper, protests and continuing agitations on China's periphery particularly merit attention. Prasenjit Duara characterizes Hong Kong as a "global frontier," fully embodying its dual sense of being "a periphery" of China as well as "a liminal space, a zone of openness, indeterminacy, and absence of relatively fixed identity" (2016: 211). Moreover, as Ching Kwan Lee (2017: 163–166) has demonstrated the importance of analyzing the rise of China from its distant investment in Africa, a peripheral survey from its zone of influences helps us to understand how an ascending China will restructure the global order. As Taiwan is rapidly drawn into a China-centered geopolitical order, such description is equally applicable. The Sunflower Movement and the Umbrella Movement failed to elicit a favorable response in China because of the censorship and the official labeling of secessionism, as a study found that both Chinese in the mainland and overseas oppose these two protests (Zhu 2017). Dozens of human rights activists in Beijing were rounded up during the Umbrella Movement. Among them, Kou Yanding was arrested and held for four months for her avowed support for the Hong Kong protest (S. Zhao 2017: 293–300). Nevertheless, the subsequent civil-society activism in Taiwan and Hong Kong remains bound to impact the center-periphery relations with probable spillover reverberations. In short, like Soviet leaders three decades ago, Xi Jinping is now facing a "Polish problem" in his backyard as a result of the two eventful protests in Taiwan and Hong Kong.

Appendix 1

In-depth Interviews

In-depth interviews with people related to the Sunflower Movement and the Umbrella Movement provided considerable insider information. In Taiwan, I began to collect oral data immediately after the conclusion of the legislature occupation, whereas my interviews with Hong Kong participants started before the outbreak of the Umbrella Movement. Most of the interviews were recorded with the permission of interviewees and then transcribed. Their length varied from thirty minutes to two hours. My samples in both places include student participants and leaders, NGO activists, politicians and their aides, party workers, journalists, and university professors. In total, I documented interviews with 71 Hongkongers, 66 Taiwanese, and one Macanese, some of whom were interviewed more than one time. Nine interviews with Hongkongers and 11 with Taiwanese were completed by my research assistants and friends. Aside from them, I personally carried out the rest of the interviews face-to-face. The research relied on a grant from Taiwan's Ministry of Science and Technology, and proceeded with permission from National Taiwan University's Research Ethics Committee issued in August 2016.

I have decided to preserve the anonymity of my interviewees by referencing them by code numbers in the text, partly because a number of the participants in Taiwan and Hong Kong were still awaiting criminal trials over their involvement at the time of writing. More importantly, some of my interviewees expressed the desire that their true identity not be revealed. Tables A.1 and A.2 present my Taiwanese and Hongkonger interviewees. For brevity's sake, I have listed only their position or status at the time of the interview and the selected background information as related to the citation. In the text, "interview #HK4-2" means that the source comes from the second interview with the person identified as HK4.

In English, there exists a useful online archive, the Daybreak Project, that documents the in-depth interviews with Sunflower Movement participants and observers (see the Daybreak Project, https://goo.gl/dG5xxn, accessed July 21, 2018).

TABLE A.1. TAIWANESE INTERVIEWEES

Code	Positions or experiences	Date
TW1	A Shih Hsin University student, a Black Island Nation Youth Front (BIY) member	April 10, 2014
TW2	A National Chengchi University doctoral student, the Democratic Front against Cross-strait Trade in Services (DF) secretary, the spokesperson of Social Democratic Party	April 15, 2015; April 18, 2015; May 6, 2016
TW3	The Democratic Progressive Party (DPP) director of Chinese Affairs Department	April 17, 2014
TW4	The DPP director of Department of Social Movements	April 17, 2014
TW5	A Tunghai University graduate student	April 18, 2014
TW6	An New Society for Taiwan editor	April 21, 2014
TW7	A DPP legislator aide	April 21, 2014
TW8	A DPP legislator	April 22, 2014
TW9	A Taiwan Labor Front staff member	April 22, 2014
TW10	The Taiwan Labor Front secretary-general	April 22, 2014
TW11	A National Taiwan University (NTU) graduate student	April 24, 2014; April 11, 2017
TW12	A Tunghai University graduate student	April 29, 2014
TW13	A National Yang-ming University student	April 30, 2014
TW14	A National Yang-ming University student	April 30, 2014
TW15	A Citizen 1985 Action Coalition member, a Watchout member	May 1, 2014; May 19, 2016
TW16	An NTU graduate student	May 1, 2014
TW17	An NTU student, a Pariah Liberation Area participant	May 5, 2014
TW18	A National Taiwan University of Science and Technology student, a Beez member	May 5, 2014
TW19	An NTU graduate student, a Sunflower Movement International Department member	May 8, 2014
TW20	An NTU graduate student, a Sunlightseeker member	May 13, 2014
TW21	A National Dong Hwa University student	May 29, 2014
TW22	A Citizen 1985 Action Coalition member	June 6, 2014
TW23	An Asia University student	May 16, 2014
TW24	A Tunghai University student	June 5, 2014
TW25	An activist coffee shop owner	June 6, 2014
TW26	A Providence University student	June 12, 2014
TW27	The Taiwan Environmental Protection Union secretary-general, a National Chung Hsing University professor	June 13, 2014
TW28	A National Dong Hwa University doctoral student	June 26, 2014
TW29	A National Cheng Kung University student	August 28, 2014
TW30	An RMIT University (Australia) doctoral student	March 6, 2015
TW31	The DF convener, the Economy Democracy Union convener	May 15, 2015; September 11, 2015
TW32	A National Chengchi University professor, a former deputy minister of the Mainland Affairs Council	December 12, 2015

Code	Positions or experiences	Date
	TABLE A.1. TAIWANESE INTERVIEWEES (continued)	
TW33	A New School for Democracy staff member	March 14, 2016
TW34	An NTU graduate student, a Democracy Tautin convener	April 6, 2016
TW35	An NTU student	April 8, 2016
TW36	A New Power Party (NPP) presidium member	April 12, 2016
TW37	An NTU student	April 29, 2016
TW38	An NTU student	May 4, 2016
TW39	A BIY member, a Taiwan Green Party legislative election candidate	May 11, 2016
TW40	An NTU graduate student, an Economy Democracy Union staff member	May 23, 2016
TW41	An NTU graduate student	May 25, 2016
TW42	An Appendectomy Project member, an NPP legislative election candidate	June 3, 2016
TW43	A BIY member, the leader of security members in the plenary chamber	June 7, 2016
TW44	The secretary-general of the Association of Parents Participating in Education in Taiwan	June 8, 2016
TW45	A Taiwan Green Party legislative election candidate	June 10, 2016
TW46	A former NTU labor union staff member	June 14, 2016
TW47	A DPP legislator aide	June 29, 2016
TW48	A National Chiao Tung University graduate student	July 12, 2016
TW49	A former Taiwan Green Party central committee member	July 13, 2016
TW50	A former Praxis in South president	July 15, 2016
TW51	A BIY member, a DPP legislator aide	July 18, 2016
TW52	A Taiwan Publication Freedom Front member	July 20, 2016
TW53	An Island March staff member, an NPP legislator aide	August 10, 2016
TW54	The DPP Director of Youth Department, a former NTU labor union staff member	August 17, 2016
TW55	A Democracy Tautin convener	August 24, 2016
TW56	The Youth against Oppression in Taiwan president	October 2, 2016
TW57	An NTU graduate student, the Island March president	October 4, 2016
TW58	A Citizen 1985 Action Coalition member	October 4, 2016
TW59	A former NTU labor union staff member	October 31, 2016
TW60	The Formoshock convener, a former Youth Alliance against Media Monster deputy convener	December, 21 2016
TW61	A former Youth Alliance against Media Monster staff member, a National Tsing Hua University graduate student	December, 23 2016
TW62	A former Green Party Taiwan (GPT) convener	September, 26 2017
TW63	A DPP legislator aide	September 28, 2017
TW64	A Taiwan Pride convener	November 14, 2017
TW65	An EyeCTV co-producer	December 4, 2017
TW66	A former Trees Party secretary-general	December 7, 2017

Code	Positions or status	Date
	TABLE A.2. HONGKONGER AND MACANESE INTERVIEWEES	
HK1	An Occupy Central with Love and Peace (OCLP) co-founder, a Chinese University of Hong Kong (CUHK) professor	March 24, 2014; November 17, 2015; January 5, 2017
HK2	A Civic Party vice-chairperson	March 25, 2014
HK3	A Hong Kong Institute of Education professor	October 10, 2014
HK4	A Lingnan University professor, the Mobile Democracy Classroom convener	March 14, 2015; November 15, 2015; January 5, 2017
HK5	A Hong Kong Baptist University professor	April 4, 2015; December 15, 2016
HK6	A Yazhou Zhoukan journalist	April 15, 2015
HK7	A CUHK staff member	May 16, 2015
HK8	A CUHK student	May 18, 2015; May 26, 2015
HK9	A CUHK student	May 18, 2015
HK10	A CUHK student	May 18, 2015
HK11	A CUHK student	May 18, 2015
HK12	A CUHK student	May 20, 2015
HK13	A CUHK student	May 20, 2015
HK14	A CUHK student	May 20, 2015
HK15	A University of Hong Kong (HKU) student	May 27, 2015; November 16, 2015
HK16	A former president of the CUHK Student Union, a former Hong Kong Federation of Students (HKFS) standing director	June 1, 2015; May 3, 2016
HK17	A former HKFS secretary-general, a staff member of the Justice and Peace Commission of the Hong Kong Catholic Diocese	June 5, 2015
HK18	A staff member of the Justice and Peace Commission of the Hong Kong Catholic Diocese	June 5, 2015
HK19	The HKFS secretary-general	June 5, 2015
HK20	The chair of the Network for Women in Politics, a former aide to legislative council member Emily Lau	October 19, 2015; March 17, 2016; November 1, 2016
HK21	An editor of HKU's Undergrad	November 14, 2015
HK22	A Labour Party legislative council member	November 14, 2015
HK23	A CUHK student	November 15, 2015
HK24	Scholarism convener, the Demosisto secretary-general	November 15, 2015; October 2, 2016
HK25	A former HKFS secretary-general	November 15, 2015
HK26	A Hong Kong Democratic Party (DP) district councilor	November 15, 2015
HK27	A DP central committee member	November 15, 2015
HK28	A Youngspiration district council election candidate	November 15, 2015
HK29	A Hong Kong Institute of Education professor	November 16, 2015
HK30	A Lingnan University professor	November 16, 2015
HK31	An Island West Dynamic Movement district council election candidate	November 16, 2015

Code	Positions or status	Date
	TABLE A.2. HONGKONGER AND MACANESE INTERVIEWEES (continued)	
HK32	An editor of HKU's Undergrad	November 14, 2015
HK33	A former editor-in-chief of HKU's Undergrad	November 16, 2015
HK34	A Mei Foo Home and Public Affairs staff member, a Financier Conscience member	March 15, 2016
HK35	A Progressive Lawyer Group core member	March 19, 2016
HK36	A League of Social Democrats (LSD) vice-chairperson	May 26, 2016
HK37	An HKU student, a Left 21 member	May 30, 2016
HK38	A Hong Kong Institute of Education post-doctoral researcher	June 15, 2016
HK39	A staff member of the Justice and Peace Commission of the Hong Kong Catholic Diocese, an OCLP security brigade leader	June 15, 2016
HK40	A City University of Hong Kong student	June 28, 2016
HK41	An HKU student	June 28, 2016
HK42	A Macao Conscience member	June 29, 2016
HK43	A Youngspiration legislative council election candidate	July 22, 2016
HK44	A former general editor of Chinese University of Hong Kong (CUHK) Student Press	July 28, 2016
HK45	A CUHK student	July 28, 2016
HK46	A former Scholarism member	August 1, 2016
HK47	A National Chengchi University graduate student	August 12, 2016
HK48	A former Civic Party member	August 14, 2016
HK49	A Hong Kong Psychologists Concern member	August 14, 2016
HK50	A former HKU Students' Union (HKUSU) president	August 15, 2016
HK51	A Hong Kong Policy Research Institute researcher	August 15, 2016
HK52	A former HKUSU president, a former HKFS standing director	August 16, 2016
HK53	A former HKFS secretary-general, a former Civil Human Rights Front (CHRF) convener	August 16, 2016
HK54	A former editor of HKU's Undergrad	August 16, 2016
HK55	A former president of CUHK Student Union, a former HKFS deputy secretary-general, a former CHRF convener	August 17, 2016
HK56	A former staff member of CUHK Representative Council	August 17, 2016
HK57	A former president of CUHK Student Union, a member of DP's central committee	September 1, 2016
HK58	A former HKFS secretary-general	September 1, 2016
HK59	An aide to legislative council member Cyd Ho, a former HKFS secretary-general	September 2, 2016
HK60	An aide to legislative council member Ip Kin-yuen, a former CHRF deputy convener	September 2, 2016
HK61	The Professional Commons chair	September 3, 2016
HK62	A former HKFS secretary-general, a University 2012 legislative council election candidate	September 3, 2016

TABLE A.2. HONGKONGER AND MACANESE INTERVIEWEES *(continued)*		
Code	Positions or status	Date
HK63	A Hong Kong Academy for Performing Arts lecturer	September 12, 2016
HK64	A Lingnan University professor	October 17, 2016
HK65	A former president of CUHK Student Union, a former CHRF convener	December 27, 2016
HK66	A former HKUSU president, a former Left 21 member	January 5, 2017
HK67	A former HKUSU vice-president	January 5, 2017
HK68	An Insurance Arise core member	January 6, 2017
HK69	A spokesperson of Umbrella Parents	January 6, 2017
HK70	The Hong Kong Indigenous spokesperson	July 13, 2017
HK71	A Liber Research Community participant	July 15, 2017
HK72	A former Labour Party legislative council member	March 9, 2018

Appendix 2

Methodology of Protest Event Analysis

Protest event analysis has emerged as one of the most commonly used methods in social movement study to understand the trajectories of contentious politics. Here a protest event is operationally defined as a public and confrontational act mounted by an intentional group of people whose claim involves a conflict of interest with their opponents. A social movement or campaign usually involves more than one protest event. As the basic unit, a protest event has certain spatial and temporal boundaries. Activities that take place in different localities at the same time are counted as different protest events, whereas activities that persist longer than one day are seen as one. However, in a prolonged protest event, such as a sit-in occupation, other participants might also mount supportive activities independently, which then are defined as new protest events.

I relied on electronic journalistic databases to collect information on the protest events. For Taiwan, I used the database of the *United Daily News* (*lianhe zhishiku*) as my data set (https://goo.gl/351R6G), which contains data from two newspapers (*United Daily* and *United Evening News*), which are ideologically KMT-leaning. *Mingpao* is my source for Hong Kong, which was traditionally neutral in terms of political stance until the change in editorial team in early 2014. *Mingpao*'s reports were accessed via WiseNews (https://goo.gl/YsoRPk). In spite of the ideological colors, both are the most frequently used e-data sources for reliability.

The observation period is set from 2006 to 2013 in order to include two tenures of top political leaders, Chen Shui-bian (2000–2008) and Ma Ying-jeou (2008–2016) in Taiwan, and Donald Tsang (2005–2012) and Leung Chun-yin (2012–2017) in Hong Kong. Since the protest analysis in this book is primarily designed to understand the preceding mobilizations, I set December 31, 2013, as the terminus of my observation, three months and nine months before the eruption of the two major occupy protests in the two places, respectively.

Operationally, I searched the electronic databases by using twenty-four keywords that are often used to describe protest events. They are "petition" (*chenqing, qingyuan*), "protest" (*kangyi*), "contention" (*kangzheng*), "sit-in" (*jingzuo*), "demonstration" (*youx-*

ing, shiwei), "lobbying" (*youshui*), "advocacy" (*changyi*), "gathering" (*jihui*), "collecting signatures" (*lianshu*), "strike" (*bagong*), "slow-down" (*daigong*), "taking leave collectively" (*jiti qingjia*), "hunger strike" (*jueshi*), "barricade" (*weidu, weichang*), "filing a lawsuit" (*susong*), "press conference" (*jizhehui*), "protest drama" (*xingdongju*), "occupying" (*zhanling*), "throwing stones" (*diushikuai*), "clash" (*chongzhuang*), "vandalism" (*pohuai gongwu*), "bitter march" (*kuxing, yixing*), "deliberation" (*shangtao*), and "retake" (*guangfu*). These selected journalistic reports were then manually winnowed for irrelevancy and redundancy, generating 4,644 and 698 protest events in Taiwan and Hong Kong, respectively.

In Taiwan, environmental (43.3 percent), labor (12.4 percent), and land and residency (11.7 percent) protests are the top three issues, whereas protests over labor (27.8 percent), human rights and law (14.5 percent), and land and residency (12 percent) issues are more commonly seen in Hong Kong.

Notes

INTRODUCTION

1. NOWnews, https://goo.gl/cn32Fx, accessed July 15, 2018. Author's translation.
2. The World Values Survey, https://goo.gl/BHzrXk, accessed November 2, 2016.
3. Taiwan's Bureau of Foreign Trade, https://goo.gl/Ug6jck, accessed October 7, 2016.
4. Hong Kong's Census and Statistics Department, https://goo.gl/CpTmDm, accessed October 7, 2016.
5. Taiwan's Tourism Bureau, https://goo.gl/p7ZGfe, accessed October 7, 2016.
6. Hong Kong's Tourism Board, https://goo.gl/3aXX3w, accessed October 10, 2016.

CHAPTER 1

1. This term is inspired by the revisionist interpretation of John Carroll (2005), which sheds light on how Hong Kong's Chinese business leaders helped to build the colony. In a similar vein, a group of Taiwanese researchers published an edited volume to explore how Taiwan experienced different forms of modernity through historical contacts with Dutch, Chinese, and Japanese empires; see also Hwang, Wang, and Huang 2010. Explicitly or not, both works question the conventional China-centered perspective.
2. Before the rise of officially permitted anti-Japan protests in China in 2000s, "Hong Kong was the only place in which the Chinese manifested strong national feelings and reactions to the publicity of the Japanese government" (Sze 1999: 199).
3. *People's Daily,* https://goo.gl/2fiuHz, accessed October 5, 2016.

CHAPTER 2

1. HK01, https://goo.gl/pywByf, accessed December 15, 2017.
2. Data for China and Hong Kong are based on World Bank, https://goo.gl/bLmAUK, and data for Taiwan are from Taiwan's National Statistics, https://goo.gl/jRlqHS, accessed October 6, 2016. The comparison is based on the author's calculations.

3. Taiwan data are based on Ministry of Economic Affairs Investment Commission, https://goo.gl/MhByc8, and Hong Kong data are from Census and Statistics Department, https://goo.gl/GIWDfm, accessed October 7, 2016. The figures are based on the author's calculations.

4. Data are from Taiwan's Ministry of Economic Affairs Bureau of Foreign Trade, https://goo.gl/N6k5YU, accessed October 7, 2016.

5. Data are from Hong Kong's Census and Statistics Department, https://goo.gl/YoIBE7, accessed October 12, 2016.

6. *The Economist,* https://goo.gl/FwPHTT, accessed October 13, 2016.

7. Statistics from Taiwan's Council of Agriculture, http://goo.gl/DZbvel, accessed January 12, 2016. Author's calculation.

8. Data are from Hong Kong Tourism Board, https://goo.gl/QONMlo, accessed October 14, 2016.

9. *Liberty Times,* http://goo.gl/J6GiqI, accessed June 28, 2016.

10. Ranking by Reporters without Borders, https://rsf.org/en, accessed October 6, 2016.

11. For the full text in Chinese, see https://goo.gl/0hMMLz, accessed October 14, 2016.

12. For the full text, see https://goo.gl/HZSPFG, accessed October 17, 2016.

13. The dispute over television licensing was framed as a fight between the Hong Kong spirit and the pro-Beijing government. See Y. Leung 2015.

14. See the full text, Public Television Service, https://goo.gl/TLvXvD, accessed October 19, 2016.

15. *Liberty Times,* https://goo.gl/Rw8pcy, accessed October 19, 2016.

16. Initium Media, https://goo.gl/gQW4jK, accessed June 6, 2016.

17. Chen Wei-ting's talk at National Chiao Tung University, Hsinchu, September 23, 2014.

18. For the full text in Chinese, see http://goo.gl/q0702x, accessed June 30, 2015.

19. According to the TVBS poll, the percentages of Taiwanese people in their twenties who chose the indigenous identity were 76 percent (2008), 83 percent and 87 percent (2012), and 89 percent (2013). See https://goo.gl/PVv2fi, accessed October 21, 2016.

20. The HKUPOP, https://goo.gl/uFFAJW, accessed October 20, 2016.

21. These laid-off workers were victims of the factory-closure wave in the mid-1990s as Taiwan's labor-intensive industries were relocating to Southeast Asia and China. Most of them worked in textile or microelectronic assembly plants. Due to the insufficient protection by the labor laws at that time, their employers simply walked away without paying workers' delayed wages, severance, and retirement pay.

22. In 1997, around one thousand laid-off workers received a loan from the government, with the total sum amounting to NT$440 million. Legally, it was called "subrogation" because Taiwan's government had become the creditor to the responsible employers.

23. *Apple Daily* (Taiwan), https://goo.gl/rbQojt, accessed December 22, 2016.

CHAPTER 3

1. *The Time,* https://goo.gl/wFISwA, accessed October 26, 2016.
2. The BBC, https://goo.gl/3v8Ss2, accessed October 26, 2016.

Notes to Chapter 5

3. Taiwan's data are from Directorate-General in Budget, Accounting and Statistics (https://goo.gl/j7dpE7), and Hong Kong's is from Census and Statistics Department (https://goo.gl/R4Z0H6), accessed December 26, 2016. Author's calculations.

4. All of the above-mentioned data are from Taiwan's National Statistics (https://goo.gl/5bkikU) and the World Bank (https://goo.gl/jedn9s), accessed October 16, 2016. Author's calculations.

5. For the full text, see https://goo.gl/mFvFVi, accessed December 27, 2016.

6. For the full lyrics, see https://goo.gl/eLqHRy, accessed December 27, 2016.

7. See its official website, https://goo.gl/9b4PhV, accessed December 28, 2016.

8. See its official website, https://goo.gl/dJGkic, accessed December 28, 2016.

9. Storm Media, https://goo.gl/e9N5Pf, accessed January 9, 2017.

10. See the comments by Ho Fu-hung in *Passion Times,* https://goo.gl/4A3V5g, accessed January 16, 2017.

11. House News, https://goo.gl/T6Rlbh, accessed January 15, 2017.

CHAPTER 4

1. The following sections are adapted in part from M. Ho 2015b.

2. The DPP's news release dated February 22, 2012, https://goo.gl/L8bkvg, accessed November 14, 2015.

3. *Apple Daily* (Taiwan), https://goo.gl/XeIOC7, accessed November 6, 2016.

4. *Liberty Times,* http://goo.gl/xbn9iI, accessed September 22, 2014.

5. Central News Agency, http://goo.gl/Yu9zpS, accessed September 22, 2014.

6. The Presidential Office's news release, https://goo.gl/UR8mwo, accessed November 8, 2016.

7. *Liberty Times,* http://goo.gl/2xwJ64, accessed September 22, 2014.

8. *Liberty Times,* http://goo.gl/WMwxUK, accessed September 22, 2014.

9. A student activist expressed this remark in a forum in Taipei, September 20, 2014.

10. *Liberty Times,* https://goo.gl/g9kV86, accessed November 19, 2016.

11. *Epoch Time,* https://goo.gl/KlVjNq, accessed November 19, 2016.

12. For a detailed account of the Executive Yuan Incident, see Chuan-kai Lin 2016.

13. For the full text, the see Mainland Affairs Council, https://goo.gl/gr5NEJ, accessed November 21, 2016.

14. *Apple Daily* (Taiwan), https://goo.gl/eJGRMi, accessed November 21, 2016.

15. Central News Agency, https://goo.gl/E11bdQ, accessed November 21, 2016.

CHAPTER 5

1. The OCLP's Facebook page, https://goo.gl/, accessed November 11, 2016.

2. Chan Kin-man's talk, Institute of Sociology, Academia Sinica, December 5, 2013.

3. Storm Media, https://goo.gl/4fe6b4, accessed June 18, 2015.

4. Storm Media, https://goo.gl/Tl2tNk, accessed August 24, 2015.

5. *South China Morning Post,* https://goo.gl/HOvQLC, accessed November 11, 2016.

6. The author is grateful to Hsu Jen Shuo for sharing the information.

7. The HKUPOP, https://goo.gl/EtZvlo, accessed November 7, 2016.

8. Storm Media, https://goo.gl/yeQc74, accessed November 9, 2016.

9. *Mingpao,* https://goo.gl/bawtGW, accessed November 9, 2016.

10. *Apple Daily* (Hong Kong), https://goo.gl/MxHhOs, accessed November 9, 2016.
11. *Apple Daily* (Hong Kong), https://goo.gl/zpfH6z, accessed November 9, 2016.
12. *Apple Daily* (Hong Kong), https://goo.gl/EpTGqa, accessed November 16, 2016.
13. *Mingpao,* https://goo.gl/SIEICj, accessed November 17, 2016.
14. *Apple Daily* (Hong Kong), https://goo.gl/Xn3Oky, accessed November 19, 2016.
15. *Mingpao,* https://goo.gl/cfOohG, accessed November 19, 2016. For an analysis of why Hong Kong's working class failed to respond to the students' call for a general strike, see Chan and Yeung 2016: 119–134.
16. *Mingpao,* https://goo.gl/uwQRuS, accessed November 21, 2016.
17. *Mingpao,* https://goo.gl/99Xt8J, accessed November 21, 2016.
18. *Mingpao,* https://goo.gl/ehfjU9, accessed November 21, 2016.
19. Indiemedia, https://goo.gl/eHCwCv, accessed November 21, 2016.
20. *Mingpao,* https://goo.gl/a0XCBY, accessed November 21, 2016.
21. *Mingpao,* https://goo.gl/KuwrXM, accessed November 21, 2016.
22. Storm Media, https://goo.gl/VlA2wA, accessed August 28, 2015.
23. Stand News, https://goo.gl/H3TBp8, accessed November 17, 2016.
24. Chinese University Student Press, https://goo.gl/oc4bgd, accessed November 17, 2016.
25. *Apple Daily* (Hong Kong), https://goo.gl/lJaj9f, accessed November 18, 2016.
26. *Apple Daily* (Hong Kong), https://goo.gl/Hhxh0S, accessed November 23, 2016.
27. *Liberty Times,* https://goo.gl/FbqZzH, accessed November 23, 2016.

CHAPTER 6

1. The following sections are in part reused and rearranged from M. Ho 2017.
2. *Oxford English Dictionary,* http://goo.gl/x0UCOf, accessed August 25, 2014.
3. Chan Kin-man's talk in Taipei, August 2, 2015. Chan went on to say the "parasol" movement would have been a more appropriate name because most of the supporters who threw them were women carrying them on that sunny day.
4. *Liberty Times,* https://goo.gl/0ruKUH, accessed November 30, 2016.
5. *Liberty Times,* https://goo.gl/gCSvAV, accessed November 30, 2016.
6. See the official webpage, https://goo.gl/oewmLC, accessed November 30, 2016.
7. See the official webpage, https://goo.gl/2FnF7m, accessed November 30, 2016.
8. See the official website, https://goo.gl/frDe3a, accessed December 3, 2016.
9. *Liberty Times,* https://goo.gl/blUMml, accessed December 1, 2016.
10. Indee DaaDee's talk in a forum organized by Institute of Sociology, Academia Sinica, October 11, 2014.
11. *New York Times,* https://goo.gl/2mcPti; BBC, https://goo.gl/DCy79W; *The Independent,* https://goo.gl/OTRVYg; all accessed December 3, 2016.
12. *The Epoch Time,* https://goo.gl/WVBqUq, accessed December 7, 2016.
13. Storm Media, https://goo.gl/nZqJxF, accessed December 5, 2016.
14. For the full text, see https://goo.gl/Y6fHUn, accessed December 5, 2016.
15. Storm Media, https://goo.gl/TpCKdq, accessed December 5, 2016.
16. *Apple Daily* (Taiwan), http://goo.gl/df3c6o, accessed September 11, 2014.
17. TVBS, https://goo.gl/SJgMJn, accessed December 5, 2015.
18. For the English translation of Lin's speech, see https://goo.gl/f5pIYo, accessed December 5, 2015.

CHAPTER 7

19. Newtalk, https://goo.gl/fT13Qv, accessed December 6, 2016.
20. See the video clip, https://goo.gl/hnaM5X, accessed December 7, 2016.

CHAPTER 7

1. For the full text of the statement, see http://goo.gl/QoLuno, accessed May 13, 2016.
2. See the Presidential Office, http://goo.gl/6SKrxr, accessed March 31, 2016.
3. See the Chief Executive Office, https://goo.gl/oaDtUS, accessed January 20, 2017.
4. *Apple Daily* (Hong Kong), https://goo.gl/fwRSvg, accessed January 20, 2017.
5. *Apple Daily* (Hong Kong), https://goo.gl/bG2ds1, accessed January 20, 2017.
6. Stand News, https://goo.gl/NJD655, accessed January 20, 2017.
7. *Apple Daily* (Taiwan), https://goo.gl/4kFbJK, accessed January 20, 2017.
8. Stand News, https://goo.gl/qbxKfd, accessed January 20, 2017.
9. *Apple Daily* (Taiwan), https://goo.gl/YDd6rO, accessed June 15, 2017.
10. The NTU Consciousness Paper, https://goo.gl/Rc0ghg, accessed February 6, 2017.
11. Initium Media, https://goo.gl/Yda5IF, accessed February 6, 2017.
12. Initium Media, https://goo.gl/tF0Czq, accessed February 6, 2017.
13. Initium Media, https://goo.gl/9hjvxd, accessed February 6, 2017.
14. *Apple Daily* (Taiwan), https://goo.gl/628w2a, accessed February 2, 2017.
15. *Liberty Times,* https://goo.gl/1ffkAf, accessed February 2, 2017.
16. *Epoch Times,* https://goo.gl/H3x0Z8, accessed February 2, 2017.
17. *Apply Daily* (Hong Kong), https://goo.gl/YEKCNN, accessed February 2, 2017.
18. *Apple Daily* (Hong Kong), http://goo.gl/BlrEhk, accessed May 25, 2016.
19. *Apple Daily* (Hong Kong), https://goo.gl/BT4MkD, accessed February 3, 2017.
20. Stand News, https://goo.gl/GB8h4b, accessed May 23, 2016.
21. *Apple Daily* (Hong Kong), https://goo.gl/JpXBhB, accessed June 1, 2016.
22. *Apple Daily* (Taiwan), http://goo.gl/AdjXow, accessed April 11, 2016.
23. The KMT, https://goo.gl/qykKrl, accessed February 25, 2016.
24. The *Undergrad,* https://goo.gl/kUVThZ, accessed February 9, 2017.
25. For their reflections on political involvement, see Lu et al. 2016.
26. The Democracy Grassroots, http://grass.tw/, accessed December 31, 2014.
27. *Apple Daily* (Hong Kong), https://goo.gl/NdRGp5, accessed February 10, 2017.
28. For the full text, see https://goo.gl/IUms2X, accessed February 10, 2017.
29. Storm Media, https://goo.gl/fMbEQa, accessed February 10, 2017.
30. Storm Media, https://goo.gl/z6uPkt, accessed February 10, 2017.
31. Field note, a discussion forum on student movements organized by the Institute of Sociology, Academia Sinica, March 14, 2015.
32. A discussion with Tominaga Kyoko, November 27, 2016.
33. *Time,* https://goo.gl/BhMqHI, accessed February 10, 2017.
34. *Liberty Times,* https://goo.gl/uwpmYX, accessed February 10, 2017.
35. For China's involvement with organized crime in Taiwan for political purposes, see Cole 2017: 82–86.

References

Alberoni, Francesco. 1984. *Movement and Institution*. New York: Columbia University Press.
Alexander, Jeffrey C. 2011. *Performative Revolution in Egypt: An Essay in Cultural Power*. London: Bloomsbury.
Alimi, Eitan Y. 2016. "Introduction." In *Popular Contention, Regime, and Transition: Arab Revolts in Comparative Global Perspective*, edited by Eitan Y. Alimi, Avraham Sela, and Mario Sznajder, 1–14. Oxford: Oxford University Press.
Almeida, Paul D. 2003. "Opportunity Organizations and Threat-Induced Contention." *American Journal of Sociology* 109 (2): 345–400.
Amenta, Edwin, Neal Caren, Elizabeth Chiarello, and Yang Su. 2010. "The Political Consequences of Social Movements." *Annual Review of Sociology* 36:287–307.
Amenta, Edwin, Neal Caren, and James E. Stobaugh. 2012. "Political Reform and the Historical Trajectories in the Twentieth Century." *Social Forces* 90 (4): 1073–1100.
Amenta, Edwin, and Drew Halfmann. 2012. "Opportunity Knocks." In *Contention in Context: Political Opportunities and Emergence of Protest*, edited by Jeff Goodwin and James M. Jasper, 227–239. Stanford, CA: Stanford University Press.
Amenta, Edwin, Drew Halfmann, and Michael P. Young. 1999. "The Strategies and Context of Social Protest: Political Mediation and the Impact of the Townsend Movement in California." *Mobilization* 4 (1): 1–23.
Aminzade, Ron, and Doug McAdam. 2002. "Emotions and Contentious Politics." *Mobilization* 7 (2): 107–109.
Andrews, Kenneth T. 2004. *Freedom Is a Constant Struggle: The Mississippi Civil Rights Movement and Its Legacy*. Chicago: University of Chicago Press.
Arrighi, Giovanni. 2007. *Adam Smith in Beijing: Lineages of the Twenty-First Century*. London: Verso.

Babones, Salvatore. 2017. *American Tianxia: Chinese Money, American Power and the End of History*. Bristol: Policy Press.

Baumgarten, Britta. 2013. "Geração à Rasca and Beyond: Mobilizations in Portugal after 12 March 2011." *Current Sociology* 61 (4): 457–473.

Bayat, Asef. 2017. *Revolution without Revolutionaries: Making Sense of the Arab Spring*. Stanford, CA: Stanford University Press.

Beissinger, Mark R. 2011. "Mechanisms of Maidan: The Structure of Contingency in the Making of the Orange Revolution." *Mobilization* 16 (1): 25–43.

———. 2013. "The Semblance of Democratic Revolution: Coalitions in Ukraine's Orange Revolution." *American Political Science Review* 107 (3): 574–592.

Bellin, Eva. 2012. "Reconsidering the Robustness of Authoritarianism in the Middle East: Lessons from the Arab Spring." *Comparative Politics* 44 (2): 127–149.

Bennett, W. Lance, and Alexandra Segerberg. 2013. *The Logic of Connective Action: Digital Media and the Personalization of Contentious Politics*. Cambridge: Cambridge University Press.

Boudreau, Vincent. 1996. "Northern Theory, Southern Protest: Opportunity Structure Analysis in Cross-National Perspective." *Mobilization* 1 (2): 175–189.

Broadbent, Jeffrey. 2011. "Introduction: East Asian Social Movements." In *East Asian Social Movements: Power, Protest and Change*, edited by Jeffrey Broadbent and Vickie Brockman, 1–29. New York: Springer.

Brown, Melissa J. 2004. *Is Taiwan Chinese? The Impact of Culture, Power, and Migration on Changing Identities*. Berkeley: University of California Press.

Bunce, Valerie. 2016. "The Drivers of Diffusion: Comparing 1989, the Color Revolutions, and the Arab Spring." In *Popular Contention, Regime, and Transition: Arab Revolts in Comparative Global Perspective*, edited by Eitan Y. Alimi, Avraham Sela, and Mario Sznajder, 115–133. Oxford: Oxford University Press.

Bunce, Valerie, and Sharon Wolchik. 2011. *Defeating Authoritarian Leaders in Post-Communist Countries*. Cambridge: Cambridge University Press.

Bush, Richard C. 2016. *Hong Kong in the Shadow of China: Living with the Leviathan*. Washington, DC: Brooking Institution Press.

Cai, Yongshu. 2010. *Collective Resistance in China Why Popular Protests Succeed or Fail*. Stanford, CA: Stanford University Press.

———. 2017. *The Occupy Movement in Hong Kong: Sustaining Decentralized Protest*. London: Routledge.

Calhoun, Craig. 1997. *Neither Gods nor Emperors: Students and the Struggle for Democracy in China*. Berkeley: University of California Press.

Carroll, John M. 2005. *Edge of Empires: Chinese Elites and British Colonials in Hong Kong*. Hong Kong: Hong Kong University Press.

———. 2007. *A Concise History of Hong Kong*. Hong Kong: Hong Kong University Press.

———. 2009. "A Historical Perspective: The 1967 Riots and the Strike-Boycott of 1925–1926." In *May Days in Hong Kong: Riot and Emergency in 1967*, edited by Robert Bickers and Ray Yep, 69–85. Hong Kong: Hong Kong University Press.

Castells, Manuel. 2009. *Communication Power*. Oxford: Oxford University Press.

———. 2012. *Network of Outrage and Hope: Social Movements in the Internet Age*. Oxford: Polity Press.

Chan, Joseph M., and Francis L. F. Lee. 2010. "Xianggangren buneng wangji liusi zhi mi: Chuanmei shehuizuzhi minzuguojia he jitijiyi [Why Can't Hong Kong Forget the June

4th Incident? Media, Social Organization, Nation-State and Collective Memory]." *Xinwenxue yanjiu* [Mass Communication Research] 103:215–259.
———. 2012. "Mass Media and Public Opinion." In *Contemporary Hong Kong Government and Politics,* edited by Wai-man Lam, Percy Luen-tim Lui, and Wilson Wong, 223–246. Hong Kong: Hong Kong University Press.
Chan, King Chi Chris, and Julian Wing Yan Yeung. 2016. "*Yusan yundong zhihou: Xunzhao xin kangzheng moshi* [After the Umbrella Movement: In Search of a New Model of Resistance]." In *Minzhu yu xianggang guanzhi* [Democracy and Governance in Hong Kong], edited by Ming Sing, 119–134. Hong Kong: Jinyibu.
Chan, King-fai, Petula S. Y. Ho, Xiao Xiao, and Anthony. 2015. *Yusan zhengzhi sizhongzou* [A Quartet of Umbrella Politics]. Hong Kong: Jinyibu.
Chan, Koonchung. 2008. *Xiayige shinian: Xianggang de guangrong niandai* [The Next Decade: Hong Kong's Glorious Era?]. Hong Kong: Oxford University Press.
———. 2012. *Zhongguo tianchao zhuyi yu xianggang* [China's Doctrine of Celestial Dynasty and Hong Kong]. Hong Kong: Oxford University Press.
Chan, Shun-hing. 2015. "The Protestant Community and the Umbrella Movement in Hong Kong." *Inter-Asia Cultural Studies* 16 (3): 380–395.
Chang, Han-Yu, and Ramon H. Myers. 1963. "Japanese Colonial Development Policy in Taiwan, 1895–1906: A Case of Bureaucratic Entrepreneurship." *Journal of Asian Studies* 22 (4): 433–449.
Chang, Sheng-Han. 2015. "*Shuilai zuozuzhi: Qingnian lesheng lianmeng de zuzhi licheng* [Becoming Organizers: The Case of the Youth for Lo-Sheng Sanatorium]." Master's thesis, National Taiwan University Department of Sociology.
Chang, Sheng-Han, Shou-ta Huang, and Chung-jen Yu. 2014. *Lushe zhi chun: Xueyun qingnian zhan dou shouce* [The Spring of Losers: A Combat Manual for Activist Students]. Taipei: Libratory.
Chang, Wen-chen. 2017. "The Right to Free Assembly and the Sunflower Movement." In *Law and Politics of Taiwan Sunflower and Hong Kong Umbrella Movements,* edited by Brian Christopher Jones, 30–48. London: Routledge.
Chen, Dung-sheng, and Kuo-ming Lin. 2008. "The Prospects of Deliberative Democracy in Taiwan." In *Asian New Democracies: The Philippines, South Korea and Taiwan Compared,* edited by Michael Hsin-huang Hsiao, 289–304. Taipei: Taiwan Foundation for Democracy.
Chen, Feng. 2008. "Worker Leader and Framing Factory-Based Resistance." In *Popular Protest in China,* edited by Kevin J. O'Brien, 88–107. Cambridge, MA: Harvard University Press.
Chen, Feng, and Yi Kang. 2016. "Disorganized Popular Contention and Local Institutional Building in China: A Case Study in Guangdong." *Journal of Contemporary China* 25 (100): 596–612.
Chen, I-ting. 2015. *Sanli sanwai: Minzhu qianxi de xianggang gushi* [Inside and Outside of the Umbrella: Hong Kong's Stories on the Eve of Democracy]. Taipei: Shuiniu.
Chen, Ketty W. 2017. "This Land Is your Land? This Land Is *MY* Land: Land Expropriation during Ma Ying-jeou Administration and Implications on Social Movements." In *Taiwan's Social Movements under Ma Ying-jeou,* edited by Dafydd Fell, 92–112. London: Routledge.
Chen, Wan-chi, and Su-Jen Huang. 2015. "*Lifayuan wai de chunna: Taiyanghua yundong jingzuozhe zhi renkou ji canyu tuxiang* [Outcry outside the Legislature: A Portrait of

Sunflower Movement Sit-In Demonstrators." *Taiwan shehuixue* [Taiwanese Sociology] 30:141–179.
Chen, Xi. 2008. "Collective Petitioning and Institutional Conversion." In *Popular Protest in China*, edited by Kevin J. O'Brien, 54–70. Cambridge, MA: Harvard University Press.
———. 2012. *Social Protest and Contentious Authoritarianism in China*. Cambridge: Cambridge University Press.
Chen, Yun-chung. 2014. "*Xianggang de tudi zhengyi yundong: Baowei jiayuan yu baowei guozu shi buxiangrong de* [Land Justice Movement in Hong Kong: Why Defending the Community Is Incompatible with Defending the Nation]." *Wenhua yanjiu* [Router: A Journal of Cultural Studies] 18:188–199.
Chen, Yun-chung, and Mirana M. Szeto. 2015. "The Forgotten Road of Progressive Localism: New Preservation Movement in Hong Kong." *Inter-Asia Cultural Studies* 16 (3): 436–453.
Cheng, Chung-tai. 2013. "*Zuoyou jiao zhi mi: Xianggang kangzheng de bentu zhuan xiang* [The Puzzles of Lefttards and Rightards: The Indigenous Transition of Hong Kong's Resistance]." *New Society* [*Xinshehui*] 31:36–38.
Cheng, Edmund W. 2016. "Street Politics in a Hybrid Regime: The Diffusion of Political Activism in Post-colonial Hong Kong." *China Quarterly* 226:383–406.
———. 2018. "Master Frames, Transformative Events and the Repertoires of Contention." In *Routledge Handbook of Contemporary Hong Kong*, edited by Tai-lok Lui, Stephen Wing Chiu, and Ray Yep, 210–226. London: Routledge.
Cheng, Edmund W., and Wai-Yin Chan. 2017. "Explaining Spontaneous Occupation: Antecedents, Contingencies and Spaces in the Umbrella Movement." *Social Movement Studies* 16 (2): 222–239.
Cheng, Edmund W., and Samson Yuen. 2017. "Neither Repression nor Concession? A Regime's Attrition against Massive Protests." *Political Studies* 65 (1): 1–20.
Cheng, Joseph Yu-shek, ed. 2005. *The July 1 Protest Rally: Interpreting a Historic Event*. Hong Kong: City University of Hong Kong Press.
———. 2014. "The Emergence of Radical Politics in Hong Kong: Causes and Impact." *China Review* 14 (1): 199–232.
Chin, Wan. 2011. *Xianggang chengbang lun* [Hong Kong as a City-State]. Hong Kong: Enrich Publishing.
Ching, Leo T. S. 2001. *Becoming "Japanese": Colonial Taiwan and the Politics of Identity Formation*. Berkeley: University of California Press.
Chiu, Eugene W. 2003. *Taiwan xuesheng yundong* [Taiwan's Student Movements]. Taipei: Daoxiang.
Chiu, Hua-Mei. 2011. "The Dark Side of Silicon Island: High-Tech Pollution and the Environmental Movement in Taiwan." *Capitalism Nature Socialism* 22 (1): 40–57.
Chiu, Kuei-fen, Dafydd Fell, and Lin Ping. 2014. "Migration to and from Taiwan: Identities, Politics and Belonging." In *Migration to and from Taiwan*, edited by Chiu Kuei-fen, Dafydd Fell, and Lin Ping, 1–11. London: Routledge.
Chiu, Stephen Wing Kai. 2016. "*Jiedu gangren renxin beili zhi mi* [Solving the Puzzle of Hongkongers' Alienation]." *Mingpao*, April 19, 2016. https://goo.gl/4yhl29, accessed October 21, 2016.
Chiu, Yubin. 2011. "*Taiwan zizhu gongyun zuzhi celue de lishi juxian* [The Historical Limit of Organizing Strategy in Independent Unionism]." In *Shehui yundong de ni-*

andai [The Era of Social Movements], edited by Ming-sho Ho and Hsiu-hsin Lin, 83–125. Taipei: Qunxue.

Choi Yuen Village Support Team. 2013. *Caiyuan liufu wanglairen* [Choi Yuen Village Accommodates the Passengers]. Hong Kong: V-Artivist.

Chou, Wan-yao. 1989. *Rijushidai taiwan yihui shezhi qingyuan yundong* [The Petition Movement for Taiwanese Parliament during Japanese Occupation]. Taipei: Daoxiang.

———. 2003. *Haixingxi de niandai: riben zhimin tungzhi mouqi lunwenji* [The Era of Seafaring: A Collection of Essays on Taiwan History during the Late Period of Japanese Colonialism]. Taipei: Yunchen.

———. 2017. "*Zhanhou taiwan de lishi jiaoyu kegang zhengyi yiji fan weidiao yundong* [The History Education in Postwar Taiwan, Curriculum Controversies, and Anti-Revisionism Movement]." In *Jiyi de zhanzheng fan weidiao kegang jishi* [The War over Memory: A History of Opposing Curriculum Revisionism], edited by Chou Fu-yi, 8–33. Taipei: Youth Synergy Taiwan Foundation.

Choy, Ivan Chi-keung, Yan-yin Paul Wong, Yiu Cheong Richard Tsoi, Yiu Kwong Chong. 1998. *Tongtu shugui: Qiantu tanpan yilai de xianggang xueyun* [From Identity to Indifference: Hong Kong's Student Movement since 1981]. Hong Kong: Xianggang Renwen Kexue Chubanshe.

Chua, Beng Huat. 2017. "Introduction: Inter-referencing East Asian Occupy Movements." *International Journal of Cultural Studies* 20 (2): 121–126.

Chun, Allen. 2017. *Forget Chineseness: On the Geopolitics of Cultural Identification*. Albany: State University of New York Press.

Chung, Sze-yuen. 2001. *Xianggang huigui licheng: Zhong shiyuan huiyilu* [Hong Kong's Journey to Reunification: Memoirs of Sze-yuen Chung]. Hong Kong: Chinese University Press.

Chuoshui River Club Editorial Team, ed. 2016. *Zhuoshui zhangliu* [The Long River of Chuoshui]. Taipei: Avanguard.

Clarke, Killian. 2014. "Unexpected Brokers of Mobilization: Contingency and Networks in the 2011 Egyptian Uprising." *Comparative Politics* 46 (4): 379–394.

Cole, J. Michael. 2015. *Black Island: Two Years of Activism in Taiwan*. Charleston, SC: CreateSpace Independent Publishing Platform.

———. 2017. *Convergence or Conflict in the Taiwan Strait: The Illusion of Peace?* London: Routledge.

Cox, Laurence, Alf Nilsen, and Geoffrey Pleyers. 2017. "Social Movement Thinking beyond the Core: Theories and Research in Post-colonial and Postsocialist Societies." *Interface* 9 (2): 1–36.

Cumings, Bruce. 1987. "The Origin and Development of the Northeast Asian Political Economy: Industrial Sectors, Product Cycles and Political Consequences." In *The Political Economy of the New Asian Industrialism*, edited by Frederic C. Deyo, 44–83. Ithaca, NY: Cornell University Press.

deLisle, Jacques. 2017. "Democracy and Constitutionalism in China's Shadow: Sunflowers in Taiwan and Umbrellas in Hong Kong." In *Law and Politics of Taiwan Sunflower and Hong Kong Umbrella Movements*, edited by Brian Christopher Jones, 205–230. London: Routledge.

della Porta, Donatella. 2014. *Mobilizing for Democracy: Comparing 1989 and 2011*. Oxford: Oxford University Press.

della Porta, Donatella, and Lorenzo Mosca. 2005. "Global-net for Global Movements? A Network of Networks for a Movement of Movements." *Journal of Public Policy* 25 (1): 165–190.

della Porta, Donatella, and Dieter Rucht. 1995. "Left-Libertarian Movements in Context: A Comparison of Italy and West Germany." In *The Politics of Social Protest: Comparative Perspectives on States and Social Movements,* edited by J. Craig Jenkins and Bert Klandermans, 229–272. London: UCL Press.

Democratic Progressive Party. 2014. *The 2014 China Policy Review: Summary Report.* Taipei: Democratic Progressive Party.

Diani, Mario. 2003. "Introduction: Social Movements, Contentious Actions, and Social Networks: 'From Metaphor to Substance'?" In *Social Movements and Networks: Relational Approaches to Collective Action,* edited by Mario Diani and Doug McAdam, 1–17. Oxford: Oxford University Press.

Dirlik, Arif. 2016. "The Mouse That Roared: The Democratic Movement in Hong Kong." *Contemporary Chinese Political Economy and Strategic Relations* 2 (2): 665–681.

———. 2018. "Taiwan: The Land Colonialisms Made." *boundary 2: an international journal of literature and culture* 45 (3): 1–25.

Duara, Prasenjit. 2016. "Hong Kong as a Global Frontier: Interface of China, Asia, and the World." In *Hong Kong in the Cold War,* edited by Priscilla Roberts and John M. Carroll, 211–230. Hong Kong: Hong Kong University Press.

Editorial Committee for the Sixtieth Anniversary of Undergrad. 2015. *Xueyuan liushi* [The Sixtieth Anniversary of Undergrad]. Hong Kong: Undergrad.

Einwohner, Rachel L. 2003. "Opportunity, Honor and Action in the Warsaw Ghetto Uprising of 1943." *American Journal of Sociology* 109 (3): 650–675.

Esherick, Joseph W., and Jeffrey N. Wasserstrom. 1994. "Acting Out Democracy: Political Theater in Modern China." In *Popular Protest and Political Culture in Modern China,* edited by Jeffrey N. Wasserstrom and Elizabeth J. Perry, 21–70. Boulder, CO: Westview.

Feng, Wang, and Yang Su. 2012. "Communist Resilience: Institutional Adaptations in Post-Tiananmen China." In *Socialism Vanquished, Socialism Challenged: East Europe and China, 1989–2009,* edited by Nina Bandelj and Dorothy J. Solinger, 219–237. Oxford: Oxford University Press.

Fernández-Savater, Amador, and Cristina Flesher Fominaya. 2017. "Life after the Squares: Reflections on the Consequences of the Occupy Movements." *Social Movement Studies* 16 (1): 119–151.

Ferree, Myra Marx, and David A. Merrill. 2004. "Hot Movements, Cold Cognition: Thinking about Social Movements in Gendered Frames." In *Rethinking Social Movements: Structure, Meaning and Emotion,* edited by Jeff Goodwin and James M. Jasper, 247–261. Lanham, MD: Rowman and Littlefield.

Fleischauer, Stefan. 2016. "Taiwan's Independence Movement." In *Routledge Handbook of Contemporary Taiwan,* edited by Gunter Schubert, 68–84. London: Routledge.

Flesher Fominaya, Christina. 2014a. "Debunking Spontaneity: Spain's 15-M/Indignados as Autonomous Movement." *Social Movement Studies* 14 (2): 142–163.

———. 2014b. *Social Movements and Globalization.* New York: Palgrave Macmillan.

Fligstein, Neil, and Doug McAdam. 2012. *A Theory of Fields.* Oxford: Oxford University Press.

Fong, Brian C. H. 2013. "State-Society Conflicts under Hong Kong's Hybrid Regime:

Governing Coalition Building and Civil Society Challenges." *Asian Survey* 53 (5): 854–882.

———. 2014. "The Partnership between the Chinese Government and Hong Kong's Capitalist Class: Implications for HKSAR Governance, 1997–2012." *China Quarterly* 217:165–220.

———, ed. 2015. *Xianggang gexinlun* [Discourse on Reforming Hong Kong]. Taipei: Azoth Books.

———. 2017. "One Country, Two Nationalisms: Center-Periphery Relations between Mainland China and Hong Kong, 1997–2016." *Modern China* 43 (5): 523–556.

Friedman, Edward. 2013. "China's Ambitions, America's Interests, Taiwan's Destiny, and Asia's Future." *Asian Survey* 53 (2): 225–244.

———. 2014. *Insurgency Trap: Labor Politics in Postsocialist China*. Ithaca, NY: Cornell University Press.

Fu, Yang-chih, Ying-Hwa Chang, Su-hao Tu, and Pei-shan Liao. 2014. *Taiwan shehui bianqian jiben diaocha jihua diliu qidi sici diaocha jihua zhihang baogao* [Summary Report of Taiwan Social Change Survey: The Sixth Round, the Fourth Year]. Taipei: Institute of Sociology, Academia Sinica.

Fulda, Andreas, ed. 2015. *Civil Society Contributions to Policy Innovation in PR China*. New York: Palgrave Macmillan.

Fuller, Douglas B. 2008. "The Cross-Strait Economic Relationship's Impact on Development in Taiwan and China: Adversaries and Partners." *Asian Survey* 48 (2): 239–267.

———. 2014. "ECFA's Empty Promise and Hollow Threat." In *Political Changes in Taiwan under Ma Ying-jeou: Partisan Conflict, Policy Choices, External Constraints and Security Challenges*, edited by Jean-Pierre Cabestan and J. deLisle, 85–99. London: Routledge.

Gan, Wendy. 2017. "Puckish Protesting in the Umbrella Movement." *International Journal of Cultural Studies* 20 (2): 162–176.

Ganz, Marshall. 2000. "Resources and Resourcefulness: Strategic Capacity in the Unionization of California Agriculture, 1959–1966." *American Journal of Sociology* 105 (4): 1003–1062.

Gerbaudo, Paolo. 2012. *Tweets and the Streets: Social Media and Contemporary Activism*. New York: Pluto Press.

Gerlach, Luther P. 1999. "The Structure of Social Movements: Environmental Activism and Its Opponents." In *Waves of Protest: Social Movements since the Sixties*, edited by Jo Freeman and Victoria Johnson, 85–98. New York: Rowman and Littlefield.

Ghonim, Wael. 2012. *Revolution 2.0: The Power of the People Is Greater Than the People in Power*. New York: Houghton Mifflin Harcourt.

Gitlin, Todd. 2012. *Occupy Nation: The Roots, the Spirit, and the Promise of Occupy Wall Street*. New York: Harper Collins.

———. 2013a. "Occupy's Predicament: The Moment and the Prospects for the Movement." *British Journal of Sociology* 64 (1): 3–25.

———. 2013b. "Reply to Craig Calhoun." *British Journal of Sociology* 64 (1): 39–45.

Goffman, Erving. 1967. *Interaction Ritual*. New York: Doubleday.

Goldstone, Jack A. 2004. "More Social Movements or Fewer? Beyond Political Opportunity Structures to Relational Field." *Theory and Society* 33 (3–4): 333–365.

Goldstone, Jack A., and Doug McAdam. 2001. "Contention in Demographic and Life-Course Context." In *Silence and Voice in the Study of Contentious Politics*, Cam-

bridge Studies in Contentious Politics, 195–221. Cambridge: Cambridge University Press.
Goldstone, Jack A., and Charles Tilly. 2001. "Threat (and Opportunity): Popular Action and State Response in the Dynamics of Contentious Action." In *Silence and Voice in the Study of Contentious Politics*, Cambridge Studies in Contentious Politics, 179–194. Cambridge: Cambridge University Press.
Goodstadt, Leo F. 2005. *Uneasy Partners: The Conflict of Public Interest and Private Profit in Hong Kong*. Hong Kong: Hong Kong University Press.
———. 2014. *Poverty in the Midst of Affluence: How Hong Kong Mismanaged Its Prosperity*. Hong Kong: Hong Kong University Press.
Goodwin, Jeff. 2001. *No Other Way Out: States and Revolutionary Movements, 1945–1991*. Cambridge: Cambridge University Press.
———. 2012. "Conclusion." In *Contention in Context: Political Opportunities and Emergence of Protest*, edited by Jeff Goodwin and James M. Jasper, 277–300. Stanford, CA: Stanford University Press.
Goodwin, Jeff, and James M. Jasper. 1999. "Caught in a Winding, Snarling Vine: The Structural Bias of Political Process Theory." *Sociological Forum* 14 (1): 27–55.
———. 2004. "Introduction." In *Rethinking Social Movements: Structure, Meaning, and Emotion*, edited by Jeff Goodwin and James M. Jasper, vii–x. Lanham, MD: Rowman and Littlefield.
Goodwin, Jeff, James M. Jasper, and Francesca Polletta, eds. 2001. *Passionate Politics: Emotion and Social Movements*. Chicago: University of Chicago Press.
Graeber, David. 2002. "The New Anarchists." *New Left Review* 13:61–73.
———. 2009. *Direct Action: An Ethnography*. Oakland, CA: AK Press.
———. 2013. *The Democracy Project: A History, a Crisis, a Movement*. New York: Allen Lane.
Granovetter, Mark. 1973. "The Strength of Weak Ties." *American Journal of Sociology* 78 (6): 1360–1380.
Green, Jasper K. 2015. "Rising Powers and Regional Orders: China's Strategy and Cross-Strait Relations." *Globalizations* 13 (2): 129–142.
Grinberg, Lev Luis. 2013. "The J14 Resistance Mo(ve)ment: The Israeli Mix of Tahrir Square and Puerta del Sol." *Current Sociology* 61 (4): 491–509.
Gunning, Jeroen, and Ilan Zvi Baron. 2014. *Why Occupy a Square: People, Protests and Movements in the Egyptian Revolution*. Oxford: Oxford University Press.
Guthrie, Doug. 2002. *Dragon in a Three-Piece Suit: The Emergence of Capitalism in China*. Princeton, NJ: Princeton University Press.
Halfmann, Drew. 2011. *Doctors and Demonstrators: How Political Institutions Shape Abortion Law in the United States, Britain, and Canada*. Chicago: University of Chicago Press.
Halper, Stefan. 2012. *The Beijing Consensus: Legitimizing Authoritarianism in Our Time*. New York: Basic Books.
Hardt, Michael, and Antonio Negri. 2017. *Assembly*. Oxford: Oxford University Press.
Hase, Patrick H. 2008. *The Six-Day War of 1899: Hong Kong in the Age of Imperialism*. Hong Kong: Hong Kong University Press.
He, Ping. 2016. *Xu jiatun liuxia de bimi* [The Secrets Left Behind by Xu Jiatun]. Hong Kong: Mirror Books.
Heaney, Michael T., and Fabio Rojas. 2015. *Party in the Street: The Antiwar Movement and the Democratic Party after 9/11*. New York: Cambridge University Press.

Ho, Albert 2010. *Qianbei de fendou* [A Humble Struggle]. Hong Kong: Hong Kong University Press.
Ho, Denny Kwok Leung. 2000. "The Rise and Fall of Community Movement: The Housing Movement in Hong Kong." In *The Dynamics of Social Movements in Hong Kong*, edited by Stephen Wing Kai Chiu and Tai-lok Lui, 185–208. Hong Kong: Hong Kong University Press.
Ho, Jung-hsin. 2001. *Xueyun shidai: Zhongsheng xuanhua de shinian* [The Student Movement Generation: A Boisterous Decade]. Taipei: China Times Publisher.
Ho, Ming-sho. 2010. "Understanding the Trajectory of Social Movements in Taiwan (1980–2010)." *Journal of Current Chinese Affairs* 39 (3): 3–22.
———. 2014a. "The Fukushima Effect: Explaining the Recent Resurgence of the Antinuclear Movement in Taiwan." *Environmental Politics* 23 (6): 965–983.
———. 2014b. "The Resurgence of Social Movements under the Ma Ying-jeou Government: A Political Opportunity Structure Perspective." In *Political Changes in Taiwan under Ma Ying-jeou: Partisan Conflict, Policy Choices, External Constraints and Security Challenges*, edited by Jean-Pierre Cabestan and Jacques deLisle, 100–119. London: Routledge.
———. 2014c. "A Revolt against Chinese Intellectualism: Understanding the Protest Script in Taiwan's Sunflower Movement of 2014." *Mobilizing Ideas*. http://goo.gl/isGj6L, accessed November 11, 2016.
———. 2014d. *Working Class Formation in Taiwan: Fractured Solidarity in State-Owned Enterprises, 1945–2012*. New York: Palgrave Macmillan.
———. 2015a. "The Dialectic of Institutional and Extra-institutional Tactics: Explaining the Trajectory of Taiwan's Labor Movement." *Development and Society* 44 (2): 247–274.
———. 2015b. "Occupy Congress in Taiwan: Political Opportunity, Threat and the Sunflower Movement." *Journal of East Asian Studies* 15 (1): 69–97.
———. 2016. "Making an Opportunity: Strategic Bipartisanship in Taiwan's Environmental Movement." *Sociological Perspectives* 59 (3): 543–560.
———. 2017. "From Mobilization to Improvisation: The Lessons from Taiwan's 2014 Sunflower Movement." *Social Movement Studies* 17 (2): 189–202.
———. 2018. "Taiwan's Anti-nuclear Movement: The Making of a Militant Citizen Movement." *Journal of Contemporary Asia* 48 (3): 445–464.
Ho, Ming-sho, and Chunhao Huang. 2017. "Movement Parties in Taiwan (1987–2016): A Political Opportunity Explanation." *Asian Survey* 57 (2): 343–367.
Ho, Petula S. Y. 2015. *Kangming shidai de richang* [Daily Life during a Time of Disobedience]. Hong Kong: Red-Publish.
Holmes, Amy Austin. 2012. "There Are Weeks When Decades Happen: Structure and Strategy in the Egyptian Revolution." *Mobilization* 17 (4): 391–410.
Hong Kong Christian Institute, ed. 2015. *San yuan wei yuan* [Unfinished Umbrella Movement]. Hong Kong: Hong Kong Christian Institute.
Howard, Philip N. 2010. *The Digital Origins of Dictatorship and Democracy*. Oxford: Oxford University Press.
Hsiao, Michael Hsin-huang. 1990. "Emerging Social Movements and the Rise of a Demanding Civil Society in Taiwan." *Australian Journal of Chinese Affairs* 24:163–180.
Hsiao, Michael Hsin-huang, and Ming-sho Ho. 2010. "Civil Society and Democracy-Making in Taiwan: Reexamining the Link." In *East Asia's New Democracies: Deep-*

ening, Reversal, and Non-liberal Alternatives, edited by Yin-wah Chu and Siu-lun Wong, 43–64. London: Routledge.

Hsiao, Michael Hsin-huang, and Po San Shirley Wan. 2016. "*Erling yisi xuesheng yundong yu minyi: Taiwan yu xianggang de bijiao* [The 2014 Student Movements and the Public Opinions: A Comparison of Taiwan and Hong Kong]." In *Taiwan yu xianggang de qingnian yu shehui bianqian* [Youth and Social Changes in Taiwan and Hong Kong], edited by Michael Hsin-huang Hsiao, Stephen Wing Kai Chiu, and Po-san Wan, 119–159. Hong Kong: Hong Kong Institute of Asia-Pacific Studies, Chinese University of Hong Kong.

Hsiao, Yuan. 2017. "Virtual Ecologies, Mobilization and Democratic Groups without Leaders: Impacts of Internet Media on the Wild Strawberry Movement." In *Taiwan's Social Movements under Ma Ying-jeou,* edited by Dafydd Fell, 34–53. London: Routledge.

Hsiau, A-Chin. 2008. *Huigui xianshi: Taiwan yijiu qiling niandai zhanhou shidai yu wenhua zhengzhi bianqian* [Political and Cultural Change in 1970s Taiwan and the Postwar Generation]. Taipei: Institute of Sociology, Academia Sinica.

Hsieh, Shuo-yuan, ed. 2016. *Jianmin jiefang qu* [Pariah Liberation Area]. Taipei: Pariah Liberation Area.

Hsu, Szu-chien. 2017. "The China Factor and Taiwan's Civil Society: Organizations in the Sunflower Movement. The Case of the Democratic Front against Cross-Strait Service Trade Agreement." In *Taiwan's Social Movements under Ma Ying-jeou,* edited by Dafydd Fell, 134–153. London: Routledge.

Huang, Mab. 1976. *Intellectual Ferment for Political Reform in Taiwan, 1971–1973.* Ann Arbor, MI: Center for Chinese Studies, University of Michigan.

Huang, Shu-mei. 2018. "Liminal Space and Place-Fixing in Urban Activism." *Inter-Asia Cultural Studies* 19 (3): 1–13.

Huang, Shu-mei, and Ian Rowen. 2015. "*Chengqi yusan de feichang chengshi: Yujian tazhe de yuxian kongjian* [Raising Umbrellas in the Exceptional City: Encounters with the 'Other' in Liminal Spaces]." *Kaogu renlei xuekan* [Journal of Archaeology and Anthropology] 83:25–56.

Hughes, Christopher R. 1997. *Taiwan and Chinese Nationalism: National Identity and Status in International Society.* London: Routledge.

———. 2014. "Revisiting Identity Politics under Ma Ying-jeou." In *Political Changes in Taiwan under Ma Ying-jeou: Partisan Conflict, Policy Choices, External Constraints and Security Challenges,* edited by Jean-Pierre Cabestan and Jacques deLisle, 120–136. London: Routledge.

Hui, Po-keung. 1999. "Comprador Politics and Middleman Capitalism." In *Hong Kong's History: State and Society under Colonial Rule,* edited by Tak-wing Ngo, 30–45. London: Routledge.

Hung, Chen-ling, ed. 2015. *Woshi gongmin yeshi meiti* [Sunflower Movement, New Citizens, and New Media]. Taipei: Locus Publishing.

Hung, Ho-fung. 2011. "*Zai weigang faxian yushan: Taigang bentuyishi de gongzhen* [Discovering Mountain Jade in Victoria Harbor: The Resonance of Indigenous Consciousness in Hong Kong and Taiwan]." In *Bentu lunshu* [Journal of Local Discourse] 2010, edited by the Editorial Committee of Local Discourse, 115–122. Hong Kong: Azoth Books.

———. 2015. *The China Boom: Why China Will Not Rule the World.* New York: Columbia University Press.

———. 2016. "From Qing Empire to the Chinese Nation: An Incomplete Project." *Nations and Nationalism* 22 (4): 660–665.
Hung, Ho-fung, and Iam-chong Ip. 2012. "Hong Kong's Democratic Movement and the Making of China's Offshore Civil Society." *Asian Survey* 52 (3): 504–527.
Hwang, Jinlin, Horng-Luen Wang, and Chung-hsien Huang, eds. 2010. *Diguo bianyuan: Taiwan xiandaixing de kaocha* [At Periphery of Empires: An Investigation of Taiwan's Modernities]. Taipei: Socio.
Inmediahk. 2016. *Women de yusan shidai* [Our Umbrella Time]. Hong Kong: Culture and Media Education Foundation.
Invisible Committee. 2009. *The Coming Insurrection*. Los Angeles: Semiotext(e).
Ip, Chung-yan Joanne, and Stephen Wing Kai Chiu. 2016. "*Xi liu qingnian keguan zhuangkuang yu zhuguan ganshou* [Downward Youth? Objective Conditions and Subjective Perception]." In *Zaodong qingchun: Xianggang xinshidai chujing guancha* [Agitated Youth: An Observation of Hongkonger Young Generation's Situations], edited by Stephen Wing Kai Chiu, Chung-yan Joanne Ip, and Hang Li, 54–67. Hong Kong: Chunghwa.
Ip, Iam-Chong. 2015. "Politics of Belonging: A Study of the Campaign against Mainland Visitors in Hong Kong." *Inter-Asia Cultural Studies* 16 (3): 410–421.
Israel, John. 1966. *Student Nationalism in China, 1927–1936*. Stanford, CA: Stanford University Press.
Jacobs, J. Bruce. 2005. "'Taiwanization' in Taiwan's Politics." In *Cultural, Ethnic, and Political Nationalism in Contemporary Taiwan*, edited by John Makeham and A-Chin Hsiau, 17–54. London: Palgrave Macmillan.
Jacques, Martin. 2012. *When China Rules the World: The End of the Western World and the Birth of a New Global Order*. 2nd ed. New York: Penguin Books.
Jasper, James M. 1997. *The Art of Moral Protest*. Chicago: University of Chicago Press.
———. 1999. "Recruiting Intimates, Recruiting Strangers: Building the Contemporary Animal Rights Movement." In *Waves of Protest: Social Movements since the Sixties*, edited by Jo Freeman and Victoria Johnson, 65–82. New York: Rowman and Littlefield.
———. 2004. "A Strategic Approach to Collective Action: Looking for Agency in Social-Movement Choices." *Mobilization* 9 (1): 1–16.
———. 2011. "Emotions and Social Movements: Twenty Years of Theory and Research." *Annual Review of Sociology* 37:285–303.
———. 2012. "Introduction." In *Contention in Context: Political Opportunities and Emergence of Protest*, edited by Jeff Goodwin and James M. Jasper, 1–31. Stanford, CA: Stanford University Press.
———. 2014. *Protest: A Cultural Introduction to Social Movements*. Oxford: Polity Press.
Jenkins, Craig J., and Charles Perrow. 1977. "Insurgency of the Powerless: Farm Worker Movement (1946–1972)." *American Sociological Review* 42 (2): 249–268.
Jhuang, Cheng-Yang. 2015. "*Dangdai xuesheng xindongzhe de zuzhi tuxiang* [A Picture of the Contemporary Student Activists and Their Organizations]." Master's thesis, National Sun Yat-sen University Institute of Sociology.
Jiao, Jun. 2015. *Shuiguo zhengzhixue* [The Politics of Fruit]. Taipei: Juliu.
Juris, Jeffrey S. 2005. "The New Digital Media and Activist Networking within Anti-corporate Globalization Movements." *Annals of the American Academy of Political and Social Science* 597 (1): 189–208.

Kaeding, Malte Philipp. 2011. "Identity Formation in Taiwan and Hong Kong: How Much Difference, How Many Similarities?" In *Taiwanese Identity in the Twenty-First Century: Domestic, Regional and Global Perspectives*, edited by Gunter Schubert and Jens Damm, 258–279. London: Routledge.

———. 2014. "Challenging Hongkongisation: The Role of Taiwan's Social Movements and Perceptions of Post-handover Hong Kong." *Taiwan in Comparative Perspective* 5:120–133.

———. 2015. "Resisting Chinese Influence: Social Movements in Hong Kong and Taiwan." *Current History* 114:209–215.

———. 2017. "The Rise of 'Localism' in Hong Kong." *Journal of Democracy* 28 (1): 157–171.

Karatzogianni, Athina, and W. Andrew Robinson. 2010. *Power, Resistance and Conflict in the Contemporary World*. London: Routledge.

Kastner, Scott L. 2009. *Political Conflict and Economic Interdependence across the Taiwan Strait and Beyond*. Stanford, CA: Stanford University Press.

Keng, Shu, and Gunter Schubert. "Agents of Taiwan-China Unification? The Political Roles of Taiwanese Business People in the Process of Cross-Strait Integration." *Asian Survey* 50 (2): 287–310.

Kitschelt, Herbert. 1991. "Resource Mobilization Theory: A Critique." In *Research on Social Movements: The State of the Art in Western Europe and the USA*, edited by Dieter Rucht, 323–347. Boulder, CO: Westview Press.

Krastev, Ivan. 2014. *Democracy Disrupted: The Politics of Global Protest*. Philadelphia: University of Pennsylvania Press.

Kriesi, Hanspeter. 2004. "Political Context and Opportunity." In *The Blackwell Companion to Social Movements*, edited by David A. Snow, Sarah A. Soule, and Hanspeter Kriesi, 67–90. Oxford: Oxford: Blackwell Press.

Ku, Agnes Shuk-mei. 2009. "Civil Society's Dual Impetus: Mobilization, Representations and Contestations over the July 1 March in 2003." In *Politics and Government in Hong Kong: Crisis under Chinese Sovereignty*, edited by Ming Sing, 38–57. London: Routledge.

———. 2012. "Remaking Places and Fashioning an Opposition Discourse: Struggle over the Star Ferry Pier and the Queen's Pier in Hong Kong." *Environment and Planning D* 30 (1): 5–22.

Kurzman, Charles. 1996. "Structural Opportunity and Perceived Opportunity in Social Movement Theory." *American Sociological Review* 61 (1): 153–170.

———. 2004a. "The Poststructuralist Consensus in Social Movement Theory." In *Rethinking Social Movements: Structure, Meaning, and Emotion*, edited by Jeff Goodwin and James M. Jasper, 111–120. Lanham, MD: Rowman and Littlefield.

———. 2004b. *The Unthinkable Revolution in Iran*. Cambridge, MA: Harvard University Press.

Kwong, Ying-ho. 2016. "State-Society Conflict Radicalization in Hong Kong: The Rise of 'Anti-China' Sentiment and Radical Localism." *Asian Affairs* 47 (3): 428–442.

Lai, Tse-han, Ramon H. Myers, and Wou Wei. 1991. *A Tragic Beginning: The Taiwan Uprising of February 28, 1947*. Stanford, CA: Stanford University Press.

Lai, Yu-an, and In-an Huang. 2016. "*Duinei jiaodai shiya taiwan: Xi jinping quanqiu zhanlue xia de duitaiwan zhengce* [Playing Hardball with Taiwan for Domestic Purposes: Xi Jinping's Policy toward Taiwan under the Global Strategy]." In *Xi jinping da qiju* [A Great Chessboard for Xi Jinping], edited by Szu-chien Hsu, 203–242. Taipei: Rive Gauche.

Lam, Jermian T. M. 2012. "District Councils, Advisory Bodies and Statutory Bodies." In *Contemporary Hong Kong Government and Politics*, edited by Wai-man Lam, Percy Luen-tim Lui, and Wilson Wong, 111–131. Hong Kong: Hong Kong University Press.

Lam, Maan Wing, ed. 2015. *Xiaoshi de qishijiu tian* [The Vanished Seventy-Nine Days]. Hong Kong: Yisaiya.

Lam, Wai-man. 2004. *Understanding the Political Culture of Hong Kong: The Paradox of Activism and Depoliticization.* New York: M. E. Sharpe.

———. 2017. "Changing Political Activism: Before and after the Umbrella Movement." In *Hong Kong 20 Years after the Handover: Emerging Social and Institutional Fractures after 1997*, edited by Brian Fong and Tai-lok Lui, 73–102. New York: Palgrave Macmillan.

Lamley, Harry J. 1970. "The 1895 Taiwan War of Resistance: Local Chinese Efforts against a Foreign Power." In *Taiwan: Studies in Chinese Local History*, edited by Leonard H. D. Gordon, 23–70. New York: Columbia University Press.

Lau, Simon. 2015. *Qing yu yi: Jinzhong cunmin de shenghuo shijian* [Affection and Righteousness: The Life Practice of Admiralty Villagers]. Hong Kong: UP Publications.

Lau, Tracy. 2013. "State Formation and Education in Hong Kong: Pro-Beijing Schools and National Education." *Asian Survey* 53 (4): 728–753.

Law, Wing-sang. 2014. *Zhimin jiaguo wai* [Beyond Colonialism and The Homeland-State]. Hong Kong: Oxford University Press.

Lee, Ching Kwan. 2017. *The Specter of Global China: Politics, Labor and Foreign Investment in Africa.* Chicago: University of Chicago Press.

Lee, Ching Kwan, and Yonghong Zhang. 2013. "The Power of Instability: Unraveling the Microfoundations of Bargained Authoritarianism in China." *American Journal of Sociology* 118 (6): 1475–1508.

Lee, Francis L. F. 2015. "Social Movement as Civic Education: Communication Activities and Understanding of Civil Disobedience in the Umbrella Movement." *Chinese Journal of Communication* 8 (4): 393–411.

———. 2017. "Introduction: Media Communication and the Umbrella Movement." In *Media Mobilization and the Umbrella Movement*, edited by Francis L. F. Lee, 1–5. London: Routledge.

Lee, Mei-chun. 2015. "Occupy on Air: Transparency and Surveillance in Taiwan's Sunflower Movement." *Anthropology Now* 7 (3): 32–41.

Lee, Teng-hui. 2015. *Shin taiwan de zhuzhang* [New Taiwan's Demands]. Taipei: Yuanzhu Wenhua.

Lei, Ya-wen. 2018. *The Contentious Public Sphere: Law, Media and Authoritarian Rule in China.* Princeton, NJ: Princeton University Press.

Leung, Benjamin K. P. 2000. "The Student Movement in Hong Kong: Transition to a Democratizing Society." In *The Dynamics of Social Movements in Hong Kong*, edited by Stephen Wing Kai Chiu and Tai-lok Lui, 209–226. Hong Kong: Hong Kong University Press.

———. 2011. "Social Movement as Cognitive Praxis: The Case of Student Movement and the Labor Movement in Hong Kong." In *East Asian Social Movements: Power, Protest, and Change in a Dynamic Region*, edited by Jeffrey Broadbent and Vicky Brockman, 347–364. London: Springer.

Leung, Man-tao. 2010. "*Shijian zhanzai women zhebian* [Time Is on Our Side]." In

Xianggang bashihou zhanzai dande yibian [Hong Kong's Post-80: Standing on the Side of the Eggs], edited by Carmen Kwong. Hong Kong: Up Publications.

Leung, Yuk-ming Lisa. 2015. "(Free) TV Cultural Rights and Local Identity: The Struggle of HKTV as a Social Movement." *Inter-Asia Cultural Studies* 16 (3): 422–435.

Li, Chih-te. 2014. *Wuan de lutu* [A Journey in the Strait]. Taipei: Baqi Wenhua.

Li, Hang. 2013. "Contentious Politics in Two Villages: Comparative Analysis of Anti-High-Speed-Rail Campaigns in Hong Kong and Taiwan." PhD diss., Chinese University of Hong Kong.

Li, Man-Kong. 2015. "*Zhongda xueshenghui: shinian pingdian* [The Chinese University Student Union: A Decade's Review]." In *Zhongda wushinian* [Fifty Years of the Chinese University of Hong Kong], edited by the Editorial Committee of Fifty Years of the Chinese University of Hong Kong, 347–356. Hong Kong: Chinese University Student Union.

Lin, Chi-hua. 2013. "*Yiguo liangzhi xia xianggang zhengzhi de bianqian* [The Political Changes in Hong Kong under 'One Country, Two Systems']." PhD diss., Soochow University Department of Political Science.

Lin, Chuan-kai. 2016. "*Erlingyisi nian sanersan zhengyuan kangzheng shifa guocheng chenshu* [A Statement of the Incident of Executive Yuan Protest and its Process]." An Investigative Report, https://goo.gl/BajNZ5, accessed November 21, 2016.

Lin, Syaru Shirley. 2016. *Taiwan's China Dilemma: Contested Identities and Multiple Interests in Taiwan's Cross-Strait Economic Policy*. Stanford, CA: Stanford University Press.

Lin, Thung-hong. 2009. "*Taiwan de hougongyehua: Jiejijiegou de zhuanxing yu shehui bupingdeng* [Post-industrializing Taiwan: Changing Class Structure and Social Inequality]." *Taiwan shehui xuekan* [Taiwanese Journal of Sociology] 43:93–158.

Lin, Thung-hong, Ching-shu Hung, Chien-hung Lee, Chao-ching Wang, and Feng-yih Chang. 2011. *Bengshidai: Caituanhua pinqionghua yu shaozin hua de wei ji* [The Collapsing Generation: The Crises of Corporate Domination, Pauperization and Low Fertility Rate]. Taipei: Taiwan Labor Front.

Lo, Sonny Shiu-Hing. 2008a. "Can Taipei Influence Beijing's Policy toward Hong Kong?" In *China's Hong Kong Transformed: Retrospect and Prospect beyond the First Decade*, edited by Ming K. Chan, 287–314. Hong Kong: City University of Hong Kong Press.

———. 2008b. *The Dynamics of Beijing–Hong Kong Relations: A Model for Taiwan?* Hong Kong: Hong Kong University Press.

Loh, Christine. 2010. *Underground Front: The Chinese Communist Party in Hong Kong*. Hong Kong: Hong Kong University Press.

Lu, Jennifer, et al. 2016. *Zhengzhi gongzuo zaiganma: Yi qun nian qing shi dai de li xian gao bai* [What Is Political Work Really About? The Confessions of a Young Generations' Adventure]. Taipei: Locus Publishing.

Lui, Tai-lok. 2007. *Sidai xiangganren* [Four Generations of Hongkongers]. Hong Kong: Duoyibu Meiti.

———. 2012. *Na siceng xiangshi de qiling niandai* [The Memorable 1970s]. Hong Kong: Chunghwa.

———. 2014. "Getting Uneasy: The Changing Psychology of Hong Kong's Middle Classes." In *Chinese Middle Classes: Taiwan, Hong Kong, Macau and China*, edited by Michael Hsin-huang Hsiao, 97–119. London: Routledge.

———. 2015a. "A Missing Page in the Grand Plan of 'One Country, Two Systems': Regional Integration and Its Challenges to Post-1997 Hong Kong." *Inter-Asia Cultural Studies* 16 (3): 396–409.

———. 2015b. *Xianggang moshi: Cong xianzaishi dao guoqushi* [The Hong Kong Model: From the Present Tense to the Past Tense]. Hong Kong: Chunghwa.

Lui, Tai-lok, and Stephen Wing Kai Chiu. 2000. "Introduction." In *The Dynamics of Social Movements in Hong Kong*, edited by Stephen Wing Kai Chiu and Tai-lok Lui, 1–20. Hong Kong: Hong Kong University Press.

Ma, Ngok. 2007. *Political Development in Hong Kong: State, Political Society, and Civil Society*. Hong Kong: Hong Kong University Press.

———. 2011a. "Hong Kong's Democrats Divide." *Journal of Democracy* 22 (1): 54–67.

———. 2011b. "Value Changes and Legitimacy Crisis in Post-industrial Hong Kong." *Asian Survey* 51 (4): 683–712.

———. 2012. "Political Parties and Elections." In *Contemporary Hong Kong Government and Politics*, edited by Wai-man Lam, Percy Luen-tim Lui, and Wilson Wong, 159–178. Hong Kong: Hong Kong University Press.

MacDonald, Kevin. 2002. "From Solidarity to Fluidarity: Social Movements beyond 'Collective Identity.'" *Social Movement Studies* 1 (2): 109–128.

Maeckelbergh, Marianne. 2013. "Learning from Conflict: Innovating Approaches to Democratic Decision Making in the Alterglobalization." *Transforming Anthropology* 21 (1): 27–40.

Maher, Thomas V. 2010. "Threat, Resistance, and Collective Action: The Cases of Sobibór, Treblinka and Auschwitz." *American Sociological Review* 75 (2): 252–272.

Marx, Gary T., and Douglas McAdam. 1994. *Collective Behavior and Social Movements: Process and Structure*. Englewood Cliffs, NJ: Prentice Hall.

Marx, Karl. 1974. *Surveys from Exile*. Edited by David Fernbach. New York: Vintage.

———. 1975. *Early Writings*. Edited by Rodney Livingstone. New York: Vintage.

Mason, Paul. 2012. *Why It's Kicking Off Everywhere: The New Global Revolutions*. London: Verso.

Matthews, Gordon, Eric Kit-wai Ma, and Tai-lok Lui. 2008. *Hong Kong, China: Learning to Belong to a Nation*. London: Routledge.

McAdam, Doug. 1982. *Political Process and the Development of Black Insurgency 1930–1970*. Chicago: University of Chicago Press.

———. 1983. "Tactical Innovation and the Pace of Insurgency." *American Sociological Review* 48 (6): 735–754.

———. 1989. "Biographical Consequences of Activism." *American Sociological Review* 54 (5): 744–760.

———. 1996. "Conceptual Origins, Current Problems, Future Directions." In *Comparative Perspectives on Social Movements*, edited by Doug McAdam, John D. McCarthy, and Mayer N. Zald, 23–40. Cambridge: Cambridge University Press.

McAdam, Doug, and Hilary Schaffer Boudet. 2012. *Putting Social Movements in Their Place: Explaining Opposition to Energy Projects in the United States, 2000–2005*. Cambridge: Cambridge University Press.

McAdam, Doug, and Karina Kloos. 2014. *Deeply Divided: Racial Politics and Social Movements in Post-war America*. Oxford: Oxford University Press.

McAdam, Doug, and William H. Sewell Jr. 2001. "It's about Time: Temporality in the

Study of Social Movements and Revolution." In *Silence and Voices in the Study of Contentious Politics,* Cambridge Studies in Contentious Politics, 89–125. Cambridge: Cambridge University Press.

McAdam, Doug, and Sidney Tarrow. 2010. "Ballots and Barricades: On the Reciprocal Relationship between Elections and Social Movements." *Perspectives on Politics* 8 (2): 529–542.

———. 2011. "Introduction: Dynamics of Contention Ten Years On." *Mobilization* 16 (1): 1–10.

McAdam, Doug, Sidney Tarrow, and Charles Tilly. 1996. "To Map Contentious Politics." *Mobilization* 1 (1): 17–34.

———. 1997. "Toward an Integrated Perspective on Social Movements and Revolution." In *Comparative Politics: Rationality, Culture, and Structure,* edited by Mark Irving Lichbach and Alan S. Zuckerman, 143–173. Cambridge: Cambridge University Press.

———. 2001. *Dynamics of Contention.* Cambridge: Cambridge University Press.

McCarthy, John D. 1987. "Pro-life and Pro-choice Mobilization: Infrastructure Deficits and New Technologies." In *Social Movements in an Organizational Society,* edited by Mayer N. Zald and John D. McCarthy, 49–66. New Brunswick, NJ: Transaction.

McCarthy, John D., and Mayer N. Zald. 1987. "Resource Mobilization and Social Movements: A Partial Theory." In *Social Movement in an Organizational Society,* edited by Mayer N. Zald and John D. McCarthy, 15–42. New Brunswick, NJ: Transaction Books.

McConnaughy, Corrine M. 2013. *The Woman Suffrage Movement in America: A Reassessment.* Cambridge: Cambridge University Press.

McPhail, Clarke. 1991. *The Myth of the Madding Crowd.* New York: A. de Gruyter.

Mearsheimer, John J. 2014. "Taiwan's Dire Straits." *National Interest* 130:29–39.

Melucci, Alberto. 1985. "The Symbolic Challenge of Contemporary Movements." *Social Research* 52 (4): 789–816.

Mendel, Douglas. 1970. *The Politics of Formosan Nationalism.* Berkeley: University of California Press.

Mengin, Françoise. 2015. *Fragments of an Unfinished War: Taiwanese Entrepreneurs and the Partition of China.* London: Hurst.

Meyer, David S. 1990. *A Winter of Discontent: The Nuclear Freeze and American Politics.* New York: Praeger.

———. 2004. "Protest and Political Opportunities." *Annual Review of Sociology* 30:125–145.

Meyer, David S., and Debra C. Minkoff. 2004. "Conceptualizing Political Opportunity." *Social Forces* 82 (4): 1457–1492.

Meyer, David S., and Sidney Tarrow. 1998. "A Social Movement Society." In *The Social Movement Society: Contentious Politics for a New Century,* edited by David S. Meyer and Sidney Tarrow, 1–28. New York: Rowman and Littlefield.

Mills, C. Wright. 1959. *The Sociological Imagination.* Oxford: Oxford University Press.

Momesso, Lara, and Isabelle Cheng. 2017. "A Team Player Pursuing Its Own Dreams: Rights-Claim Campaign of Chinese Migrant Spouses in the Migrant Movement before and after 2008." In *Taiwan's Social Movements under Ma Ying-jeou,* edited by Dafydd Fell, 219–235. London: Routledge.

Morris, Aldon D., and Susan Staggenborg. 2004. "Leadership in Social Movements." In *The Blackwell Companion to Social Movements,* edited by David A. Snow, Sarah Soule, and Hanspeter Kriesi, 171–196. Oxford: Blackwell.

Mudge, Stephanie L., and Anthony S. Chen. 2014. "Political Parties and the Sociological Imagination: Past, Present and Future Directions." *Annual Review of Sociology* 40:305–330.

Ng, Jason Y. 2016. *Umbrellas in Bloom: Hong Kong's Occupy Movement Uncovered*. Hong Kong: Blacksmith Books.

Ng, Kai Hon. 2013. "Social Movements and Policy Capacity in Hong Kong: An Alternative Perspective." *Issues and Studies* 49 (2): 179–214.

Ng, Margaret. 2008. "Democratization of Hong Kong SAR: A Pro-democracy View." In *China's Hong Kong Transformed: Retrospect and Prospects beyond the First Decade*, edited by Ming K. Chan, 59–96. Hong Kong: City University of Hong Kong Press.

Ng, Michael H. K. 2017. "Rule of Law in Hong Kong History Demythologised: Student Umbrella Movement of 1919." In *Civil Unrest and Governance in Hong Kong*, edited by Michael H. K. Ng and John D. Wong, 11–25. London: Routledge.

Notes from Nowhere. 2003. *We Are Everywhere: The Irresistible Rise of Global Anticapitalism*. London: Verso.

Noueihed, Lin, and Alex Warren. 2012. *The Battle for the Arab Spring: Revolution, Counter-Revolution and the Making of a New Era*. New Haven, CT: Yale University Press.

O'Brien Kevin J. 1996. "Rightful Resistance." *World Politics* 49 (1): 31–55.

One More Story Voice Citizen Team, ed. 2014. *Nashi wozai* [I Was There]. Taipei: Yuanzu Wenhua.

Ortmann, Stephan. 2012. "Hong Kong: Problems of Identity and Independence." In *Student Activism in Asia: Between Protest and Powerlessness*, edited by Meredith L. Weiss and Edward Aspinall, 79–100. Minneapolis: University of Minnesota Press.

Osa, Maryjane. 2003. *Solidarity and Contention: Networks of Polish Opposition*. Minneapolis: University of Minnesota Press.

Passion Times, ed. 2016. *Yusan shibailu* [A Chronicle of Umbrella Failure]. Hong Kong: Passion Times.

Peng, Jen-Yu. 2016. "*Fanpan zhong jiangou de zhuti* [The Subjectivity Constructed by Rebellion]." In *Zhaopo: Taiyanghua yundong de zhenfu zongshen yu shiyu* [Shining Through: The Scope, Depth and Horizon of the Sunflower Movement], edited by Hsiu-hsin Lin and Rwei-ren Wu, 321–368. Taipei: Rive Gauche Publishing.

Perry, Elizabeth J. 1992. *Challenging the Mandate of Heaven: Social Protest and State Power in China*. New York: M. E. Sharpe.

———. 2008. "Permanent Rebellion? Continuities and Discontinuities in Chinese Protest." In *Popular Protest in China*, edited by Kevin J. O'Brien, 205–215. Cambridge, MA: Harvard University Press.

———. 2010. "Popular Protest: Playing by the Rules." In *China Today, China Tomorrow: Domestic Politics, Economy and Society*, edited by Joseph Fewsmith, 11–28. Lanham, MD: Rowman and Littlefield.

Philips, Steven E. 2003. *Between Assimilation and Independence: The Taiwanese Encounter Nationalist China, 1945–1950*. Stanford, CA: Stanford University Press.

———. 2007. "Between Assimilation and Independence: Taiwanese Political Aspirations under Nationalist Chinese Rule, 1945–1948." In *Taiwan: A New History*, edited by Murray A. Rubinstein, 275–319. New York: M. E. Sharpe.

Pickerill, Jenny, and John Krinsky. 2012. "Why Does Occupy Matter?" *Social Movement Studies* 11 (3–4): 279–287.

Piven, Frances Fox, and Richard A. Cloward. 1992. "Normalizing Collective Protest." In

Frontiers of Social Movement Theory, edited by Aldon D. Morris and Carol McClurg Mueller, 301–325. New Haven, CT: Yale University Press.

Polletta, Francesca. 2002. *Freedom Is an Endless Meeting: Democracy in American Social Movement.* Chicago: University of Chicago Press.

Poon, Alice. 2010. *Dichan Baquan* [The Hegemony of Landed Property]. Hong Kong: Enrich Publishing.

Post-80 Self-Studying Youth, ed. 2012. *Jixu yundong* [The Continuing Movement]. Hong Kong: Student Christian Movement for Hong Kong.

Protesters in Occupation Zones. 2015. *Jietou shang zhangpeng ren* [On the Streets, People with Tents]. Hong Kong: Jinyibu.

Ramos, Howard. 2008. "Opportunity for Whom?" *Social Forces* 87 (2): 795–823.

Rand, Dafna Hochman. 2013. *Roots of the Arab Spring: Contested Authority and Political Change in the Middle East.* Philadelphia: University of Pennsylvania Press.

Rawnsley, Ming-yeh T., and Chien-san Feng. 2014. "Anti-Media-Monopoly Policies and Further Democratization in Taiwan." *Journal of Current Chinese Affairs* 43 (3): 105–128.

Rigger, Shelley. 2011. *Why Taiwan Matters: Small Island, Global Powerhouse.* Lanham, MD: Rowman and Littlefield.

———. 2016. "The China Impact on Taiwan's Generational Politics." In *Taiwan and the "China Impact": Challenges and Opportunities,* edited by Gunter Schubert, 70–90. London: Routledge.

Rucht, Dieter. 1996. "German Unification, Democratization, and the Role of Movements." *Mobilization* 1 (1): 35–62.

Schedler, Andreas. 2007. "Mapping Contingency." In *Political Contingency: Studying the Unexpected, the Accidental, the Unforeseen,* edited by Ian Shapiro and Sonu Bedi, 54–78. New York: New York University Press.

Schubert, Gunter. 2016. "Facing the Dragon and Riding the Tiger: Assessing the Mainland Taishang as an 'Implicit Factor' in Cross-Strait Relations." In *Taiwan and the "China Impact": Challenges and Opportunities,* edited by Gunter Schubert, 91–109. London: Routledge.

Sewell, William H., Jr. 1996. "Historical Events as Transformations of Structures: Inventing Revolution at the Bastille." *Theory and Society* 25 (6): 841–881.

———. 2001. "Space in Contentious Politics." In *Silence and Voice in the Study of Contentious Politics,* Cambridge Studies in Contentious Politics, 51–88. Cambridge: Cambridge University Press.

Shepherd, John. 1993. *Statecraft and Political Economy on the Taiwan Frontier, 1600–1800.* Stanford, CA: Stanford University Press.

Shirky, Clay. 2008. *Here Comes Everybody: The Power of Organizing without Organizations.* New York: Penguin.

Sing, Ming. 2004. *Hong Kong's Tortuous Democratization: A Comparative Analysis.* London: Routledge.

Sing, Ming, and Yuen-sum Tang. 2012. "Mobilization and Conflicts over Hong Kong's Democratic Reform." In *Contemporary Hong Kong Government and Politics,* edited by Wai-man Lam, Percy Luen-tim Lui, and Wilson Wong, 137–158. Hong Kong: Hong Kong University Press.

Skocpol, Theda, and Vanessa Williamson, 2012. *The Tea Party and the Remaking of Republican Conservatism.* Oxford: Oxford University Press.

Smith, Jackie. 2002. "Bridging Global Divides? Strategic Framing and Solidarity in Transnational Social Movement Organizations." *International Sociology* 17 (2): 505–528.

Snow, David A., and Dana M. Moss. 2014. "Protest on the Fly: Toward a Theory of Spontaneity in the Dynamics of Protest and Social Movements." *American Sociological Review* 79 (6): 1122–1143.

So, Alvin Y. 1999. *Hong Kong's Embattled Democracy: A Societal Analysis*. Baltimore, MD: Johns Hopkins University Press.

———. 2008. "Social Conflict in Hong Kong after 1997: The Emergence of a Post-modern Mode of Social Movements?" In *China's Hong Kong Transformed: Retrospect and Prospect beyond the First Decade*, edited by Ming K. Chan, 233–251. Hong Kong: City University of Hong Kong Press.

Spires, Anthony. 2011. "Contingent Symbiosis and Civil Society in an Authoritarian State: Understanding the Survival of China's Grassroots NGOs." *American Journal of Sociology* 117 (1): 1–45.

Staggenborg, Suzanne. 1988. "The Consequences of Professionalization and Formalization in the Pro-choice Movement." *American Sociological Review* 53 (4): 585–605.

———. 1998. "Social Movement Communities and Cycles of Protest: The Emergence and Maintenance of a Local Women's Movement." *Social Problems* 45 (2): 180–204.

Su, I-jen. 2014. "*Xinli chuyu dexin changyu: Taiyanghua xueyun de linchuang xinli fuwu* [A New Field of Mental Care: The Service of Clinical Psychology during the Sunflower Movement]." *Linchuang xinli tongxun* [Newsletter of Clinical Psychology] 61:24–37.

Su, Kuo-hsien. 2008. "*Taiwan de suode fenpei yu shehui liudong zhi zhangqi qushi* [The Long Term Trends of Taiwan's Income Distribution and Class Mobility]." In *Kuajie: Liudong yu jianchi de taiwan shehui* [Crossing the Boundaries: The Changes and Persistence of Taiwan's Society], edited by Hong-zen Wang, Kuan-chun Li, and I-chu Kung, 187–217. Taipei: Socio.

Sze, Stephen Man Hung. 1999. "Media, Subculture and the Political Participation: Characteristics of Political Populism on Hong Kong." In *Political Participation in Hong Kong: Theoretical Issues and Historical Legacy*, edited by Joseph Y. S. Cheng, 175–206. Hong Kong: City University of Hong Kong Press.

Szeto, Mirana M. 2011. "*Sikao xianggang xin shehui yundong* [Thinking Hong Kong's New Social Movements]." In *Bentu lunshu* [Journal of Local Discourse] 2010, edited by the Editorial Committee of Local Discourse, 47–55. Hong Kong: Azoth Books.

Szeto, Wah. 2011. *Dajing dongqu: Situ hua huiyilu* [The Great River Flows to the East: Szeto Wah's Memoir]. Hong Kong: Oxford University.

Sznajder, Mario. 2016. "Chile's Winter of Discontent: Is Protest Achieving Deeper Democratization?" In *Popular Contention, Regime, and Transition: Arab Revolts in Comparative Global Perspective*, edited by Eitan Y. Alimi, Avraham Sela, and Mario Sznajder, 227–253. Oxford: Oxford University Press.

Tai, Benny. 2013. *Zhanling zhonghuan* [Occupy Central]. Hong Kong: Enrich Publishing.

Taipei Documentary Filmmakers' Union. 2014. *Sunflower Occupation*. Taipei: Tianmaxingkong.

Talshir, Gayil. 2016. "The 2011 Israeli Protest Movement between the 'Arab Spring' and the 'Occupy' Movement: A Hybrid Model." In *Popular Contention, Regime, and Transition: Arab Revolts in Comparative Global Perspective*, edited by Eitan Y. Alimi, Avraham Sela, and Mario Sznajder, 254–276. Oxford: Oxford University Press.

Tang, Gary. 2015. "Mobilization by Images: TV Screen and Mediated Instant Grievances in the Umbrella Movement." *Chinese Journal of Communication* 8 (4): 338–355.

Tang, Yen-chen. 2013. "*Liangan guanxi yinsu zhende yingxiang le erlingyiernian de tai wan zongtong da xuan ma* [Did the Cross-Strait Relations Really Affect the 2012 Presidential Election in Taiwan]?" *Taiwan minzhu jikan* [Taiwan Democracy Quarterly] 10 (3): 91–130.

Tarrow, Sidney. 1989. *Democracy and Disorder: Protest and Politics in Italy 1965–75.* Oxford: Clarendon Press.

———. 1994. *Power in Movement: Social Movements, Collective Action and Politics.* Cambridge: Cambridge University Press.

———. 1996. "States and Opportunities: The Political Structuring of Social Movements." In *Comparative Perspectives on Social Movements*, edited by Doug McAdam, John D. McCarthy, and Mayer N. Zald, 41–61. Cambridge: Cambridge University Press.

———. 2011. *Power in Movement: Social Movements and Contentious Politics,* 3rd ed. Cambridge: Cambridge University Press.

———. 2013. *The Language of Contention: Revolutions in Words, 1688–2012.* Cambridge: Cambridge University Press.

Tejerina, Benjamin, Ignacia Perugorría, Tova Benski, and Lauren Langman. 2013. "From Indignation to Occupation: A New Wave of Global Mobilization." *Current Sociology* 61 (4): 377–392.

Tilly, Charles. 1978. *From Mobilization to Revolution.* Reading, MA: Addison-Wesley.

———. 1984. *Big Structures, Large Processes, Huge Comparisons.* New York: Russell Sage Foundation.

———. 2004. *Social Movements, 1768–2004.* Boulder, CO: Paradigm Publishers.

Tilly, Charles, and Sidney Tarrow. 2007. *Contentious Politics.* New York: Paradigm.

Ting, Yun-kung, ed. *Daoguo guanjianzi* [Island Nation's Keywords]. Taipei: Rive Gauche.

Tominaga, Kyoko. 2014. "Social Movements and the Diffusion of Tactics and Repertoires: Activists' Network in Anti-globalism Movement." *International Journal of Social, Behavioral, Educational, Economic, Business and Industrial Engineering* 8 (6): 1783–1789.

———. 2017. "Social Reproduction and the Limitation of Protest Camps: Openness and Exclusion of Social Movements in Japan." *Social Movement Studies* 16 (3): 269–282.

Torne, Matthew. 2014. *Lessons in Dissent.* Hong Kong: Torne Films.

Ts'ai, Hui-yu Caroline. 2009. *Taiwan in Japan's Empire Building: An Institutional Approach to Colonial Engineering.* London: Routledge.

Tsai, Jung-fang. 1993. *Hong Kong in Chinese History: Community and Social Unrest in the British Colony, 1842–1913.* New York: Columbia University Press.

Tsai, Yen-ling. 2014. "*Nongzuo wei fangfa: Yi nong wei ben de di kang zheng zhi* Wenhua yanjiu [Farming Life, Farming Resistance]." *Wenhua yanjiu* [Router: A Journal of Cultural Studies] 18:217–226.

Tsang, Steve. 2004. *A Modern History of Hong Kong.* Hong Kong: Hong Kong University Press.

Tsui, Lokman. 2017. "The Coming Colonization of Hong Kong Cyberspace: Government Responses to the Use of New Technologies by Umbrella Movement." In *Media Mobilization and the Umbrella Movement*, edited by Francis L. F. Lee, 115–123. London: Routledge.

Tsui, Sing Yan. 2015. *Yuzao de chengbang: Xianggang minzu yuanliu shi* [A National History of Hong Kong]. Hong Kong: Red-Publish.

Tung, Chen-yuan. 2003. "Cross-Strait Economic Relations: China's Leverage and Taiwan's Vulnerability." *Issues and Studies* 39 (3): 137–175.
Turner, Ralph H., and Lewis M. Killian. 1957. *Collective Behavior.* Englewood Cliffs, NJ: Prentice-Hall.
Umbrella People. 2015. *Bei shidai xuanzhong de women* [We Are Chosen by the Time]. Hong Kong: Baijuan.
Useem, Bert. 1980. "Solidarity Model, Breakdown Model, and the Boston Anti-busing Movement." *American Sociological Review* 45 (3): 357–369.
van Slyke, Lyman P. 1967. *Enemies and Friends: The United Front in Chinese Communist History.* Stanford, CA: Stanford University Press.
Veg, Sebastian. 2016. "Creating a Textual Public Space: Slogans and Texts from Hong Kong's Umbrella Movement." *Journal of Asian Studies* 75 (3): 673–702.
——— . 2017. "The Rise of 'Localism' and Civic Identity in Posthandover Hong Kong: Questioning the (Chinese) Nation-State." *China Quarterly* 230:323–347.
Wachman, Alan M. 1994. *Taiwan: National Identity and Democratization.* New York: M. E. Sharpe.
Wagner-Pacifici, Robin. 2000. *Theorizing the Standoff: Contingency in Action.* Cambridge: Cambridge University Press.
Walder, Andrew G. 2009. "Political Sociology and Social Movements." *Annual Review of Sociology* 35:393–412.
Wan, Po San Shirley, and Wan Tai Victor Zheng. 2016. "*Shenfen rentong: Dui zhongguo de zhongxin xiangxiang* [Identities: Re-imagining China]." *Zaodong qingchun: Xianggang xinshidai chujing guancha* [Restless Youth: An Observation of the Situation of Hong Kong's Young Generation], edited by Stephen Wing Kai Chiu, Chung-yan Joanne Ip, and Hang Li, 127–142. Hong Kong: Chunghwa Books.
Wang, Jie Ying. 2015. "Mobilizing Resources in Networked Social Movements: Cases in Hong Kong and Taiwan." PhD diss., Hong Kong Baptist University.
——— . 2017. "Mobilizing Resources to the Square: Hong Kong's Anti-moral and National Education Movement as Precursor to the Umbrella Movement." *International Journal of Cultural Studies* 20 (2): 127–145.
Way, Lucan. 2008. "The Real Causes of the Color Revolutions." *Journal of Democracy* 19 (3): 55–69.
Wei, Shuge. 2016. "Recover from 'Betrayal': Local Anti-nuclear Movements and Party Politics in Taiwan." *Asia-Pacific Journal* 8 (3): 1–21.
Wei, Yang. 2016. "Taiyanghua shengkai hou huikan zaodong niandai: Qingnian sheyun xingdongzhe shequn wangluo de shengcheng yu shijian [The Restless Decade before the Sunflower Movement: The Emergence and Practices of Networks of Social Movement Youth Activists]." Master's thesis, National Tsing Hua University.
Wong, Joshua. 2015. *Wo bushi xilu* [I Am Not a Kid]. Hong Kong: Baijuan.
——— . 2017. "Hong Kong's Youth Must Fight for a Free Future." *Financial Times,* July 1, 2017. https://goo.gl/BPF4yq, accessed July 2, 2017.
Wong, K.T.W., and Stephen Wing Kai Chiu. 2016. "*Hou wuzhizhuyi de xinshidai* [A Post-materialistic New Generation?" In *Zaodong qingchun: Xianggang xinshidai chujing guancha* [Agitated Youth: An Observation of Hongkonger Young Generation's Situations], edited by Stephen Wing Kai Chiu, Chung-yan Joanne Ip, and Hang Li, 110–125. Hong Kong: Chunghwa.
Wong, K.T.W., and Jackson K. H. Yeh. 2013. "*Xianggang yu taiwan minzhong de zhuguan*

pinfuchaju ji zhengzhi houguo [Perceived Income Inequality and its Political Consequences in Hong Kong and Taiwan]." In *Miandui tiaozhan: Taiwan yu xianggang zhi bijiao yanjiu* [Facing Challenges: A Comparison of Taiwan and Hong Kong], edited by Wen-shan Yang and Po-san Wan, 237–266. Taipei: Institute of Sociology, Academia Sinica.

Wong, Pik Wan. 2000. "The Pro-Chinese Democracy Movement in Hong Kong." In *The Dynamics of Social Movement in Hong Kong,* edited by Stephen Wing Kai Chiu and Tai-lok Lui, 55–90. Hong Kong: Hong Kong University Press.

Wong, Shiau Ching. 2016. "Mediated Opportunities of Social Movements in Hong Kong and Taiwan: The Interplay of Agencies and Hybrid Media Engagement within Media System." PhD diss., University of Melbourne.

Wong, Shiau Ching, and Scott Wright. 2018. "Generating a 'Voice' among 'Media Monsters': Hybrid Media Practices of Taiwan's Anti-Media Monopoly Movement." *Australian Journal of Political Science* 53 (1): 89–102.

Wright, Teresa. 2001. *The Perils of Protest: State Repression and Student Activism in China and Taiwan.* Honolulu: University of Hawai'i Press.

———. 2012. "Taiwan: Resisting Control of Campus and Polity." In *Student Activism in Asia: Between Protest and Powerlessness,* edited by Meredith L. Weiss and Edward Aspinall, 101–124. Minneapolis: University of Minnesota Press.

Wu, Jieh-min. 2016. "The China Factor in Taiwan." In *Routledge Handbook of Contemporary Taiwan,* edited by Gunter Schubert, 426–446. London: Routledge.

Wu, Jieh-min, Hung-Jeng Tsai, and Tsu-bang Cheng, eds. 2017. *Diaodeng li de jumang zhongguo yinsu zuoyongli yufan zuoyongli* [The Anaconda in the Chandelier: Forces and Reactions of the China Factor]. Taipei: Rive Gauche.

Wu, Nai-teh, and Ming-tong Chen. 1996. "*Zhengquan zhuanyi he jingying liudong* [The Regime Shift and the Circulation of Elites]." In *Taiwan shi lunwen jingxuan* [A Collection of Essays on Taiwan's History], edited by Yen-hsien Chang, Hsiao-feng Lee, and Pao-tsum Tai, 351–386. Taipei: Yushanshe.

Wu, Rwei-ren. 2016. "The Lilliputian Dreams: Preliminary Observations of Nationalism in Okinawa, Taiwan and Hong Kong." *Nations and Nationalism* 22 (4): 683–705.

Xu, Huizhi, ed. 2014. *Cong women yanjing kanjian daoyu tianguang* [Seeing the Island Sunrise with Our Eyes]. Taipei: Unique Route.

Xu, Jiatun. 1993. *Xianggang huiyilu* [A Hong Kong Memoir]. Taipei: Lianjing.

Yang, Chia-ling. 2017. "The Political Is the Personal: Women's Participation in Taiwan's Sunflower Movement." *Social Movement Studies* 16 (6): 660–671.

Yang, Tsui. 2014. *Yabubian de meigui: Yiwei muqin de sanyiba yundong shijianbao* [Uncrushable Roses: A Mother's Notebook of the March Eighteenth Movement]. Taipei: Libratory.

Yen, Shan-nung, Huei-wen Lo, Chiu-hung Liang, and Ping-lun Chiang. 2015. *Zhebushi taiyanghua xueyun* [This Is Not a Sunflower Student Movement]. Taipei: Yunchen Wenhua.

Yep, Ray. 2014. "*Liuqi baodong de zui yu fa: Jingji faling yu guojia baoli* [The Crime and Punishment of the 1967 Riot: Emergency Regulations and State Violence]." In *Xionghai tsuguo: Xianggang de aiguo zuopai* [Embracing the Fatherland: Patriotic Leftist Movement in Hong Kong], edited by Wing Kai Chiu, Tai-lok Lui, and Sai-shing Yung, 13–32. Hong Kong: Oxford University Press.

Yick, Ronald. 2015. "*Hanwei guoji jinrong zhongxin diwei jiushi hanwei xianggang* [Defending the Status of International Financial Center Is Defending Hong Kong]." In *Xianggang gexinlun* [Discourse on Reforming Hong Kong], edited by Brian C. H. Fong, 181–192. Taipei: Azoth Books.

Yu, Wen-cheng. 2016. *Women zheyidai: Qinianji zuojia* [Our Generation: The Seventh Grader Writers]. Taipei: Rye Field Publishing.

Yu, Wing-yat. 2005. "Dynamics of Party-Mass Relations: The Organizational Failure of Hong Kong's Political Parties." In *The July 1 Protest Rally: Interpreting a Historic Event*, edited by Joseph Y. S. Cheng, 249–276. Hong Kong: City University of Hong Kong Press.

Yu, Yi-wen, Ko-chia Yu, and Tse-chun Lin. 2016. "Political Economy of Cross-Strait Relation: Is Beijing's Patronage Policy on Taiwanese Businesses Sustainable." *Journal of Contemporary China* 25 (99): 372–388.

Yuen, Samson. 2014. "Under the Shadow of China: Beijing's Policy towards Hong Kong and Taiwan in Comparative Perspective." *China Perspectives* 2014 (2): 69–76.

———. 2015. "*Yusan yundong de dongyuan luoji* [The Mobilizing Logic of the Umbrella Movement]. Conference paper presented at New Communication, New Subjects, and New Civil Society, Taipei, National Taiwan Normal University, October 17–18.

Zhao, Dingxin. 1998. "Ecologies of Social Movements: Student Mobilization during the 1989 Prodemocracy Movement in Beijing." *American Journal of Sociology* 103 (6): 1493–1529.

———. 2001. *The Power of Tiananmen: State-Society Relations and the 1989 Beijing Student Movement*. Chicago: University of Chicago Press.

Zhao, Sile. 2017. *Tamen de zhengtu* [Their Fights]. Taipei: Baqi.

Zheng, Wan, Tai Victor, and Po-san Wan. 2013. "*Ziyouxing shinian huigu* [The Individual Visit Scheme: A Decade in Review]." Occasional paper, Hong Kong, Hong Kong Institute of Asia-Pacific Studies, Chinese University of Hong Kong.

———. 2016. "*Renren xinzhong you gancheng: Cong taigang minyi jiaodu kan shehui gongping* [Everyone Has a Measurement: Social Fairness Seen in Public Opinions in Taiwan and Hong Kong]." In *Taiwan yu xianggang de qingnian yu shehui bianqian* [Youth and Social Changes in Taiwan and Hong Kong], edited by Michael Hsin-huang Hsiao, Stephen Wing Kai Chiu, and Po-san Wan, 267–296. Hong Kong: Hong Kong Institute of Asia-Pacific Studies, Chinese University of Hong Kong.

Zhu, Han. 2017. "A Divided Society: Chinese Public Opinion on Resistance Movements, Democracy, and Rule of Law." In *Law and Politics of Taiwan Sunflower and Hong Kong Umbrella Movements*, edited by Brian Christopher Jones, 161–188. London: Routledge.

Index

Alberoni, Francesco, 98
Alexander, Jeffrey C., 12
Alimi, Eitan, 216
Alliance for Supervision over Cross-Strait Agreements (Taiwan), 58
Alliance for True Democracy (Hong Kong), 120, 126
Alliance of Referendum for Taiwan, 110
Anti-curriculum Revision Campaign, 184–185. See also Taiwan's post-Sunflower activism
Anti–Express Rail Movement (Hong Kong), 53, 55, 74, 78–80, 84–85, 87, 163
Anti–Kuokuang Petrochemical Park Movement (Taiwan), 75
Anti–Media Monopoly Movement (Taiwan), 56, 58–59, 75, 82, 88, 91–92, 162
Anti–National Education Movement (Hong Kong), 55, 67, 86, 92, 139
Antinuclear movement (Taiwan), 64–65, 183–184; scheduled nuclear phaseout in 2025, 184. See also Taiwan's post-Sunflower activism
Anti-Secession Law, 47, 50
Anti-WTO protest in Hong Kong, 7, 92
Appendectomy Project, 186. See also Taiwan's post-Sunflower activism
Arab Spring, 6, 71–72, 202, 204

Arrighi, Giovanni, 220
Asian financial crisis, 50, 75, 77
Asian Infrastructure Investment Bank, 177, 219
August 31 Framework, 122, 124–125, 127, 133–135, 177, 204, 213

Baron, Ilan Zvi, 12, 180
Basic Law of Hong Kong, 37, 40, 118, 120, 133, 178, 191, 205
Bayat, Asef, 71
Beez (Taiwan), 161–162
Beissinger, Mark, 6
Bennett, W. Lance, 151
Black Forest (National Chung Hsing University), 80
Black Island Nation Youth Front, 75, 101–102, 107, 109, 139, 143, 210
Bunce, Valerie, 93

Cai, Yongshu, 9, 144
Calhoun, Craig, 14
Cameron, David, 3
Carroll, John, 231n1
Castells, Manuel, 6, 72, 193
Causeway Bay Bookstore Incident (Hong Kong), 205
Central Government Complex (Hong Kong), 2, 123

Chan, Ho-tin, 197. See also Hong Kong National Party
Chan, Johannes Man-mun, 188
Chan, Kin-man, 119–120, 138, 234n3. See also Occupy Trio
Chan, Koonchung, 32–33, 52
Chang, Ching-chung, 101, 103, 107
Chavez, Cesar, 138
Chen, Deming, 101
Chen, Wei-ting, 82, 109, 131, 142, 186; in anti–Media Monopoly Movement, 58–59, 88; on decision making, 148; and movement injuries, 182–183; supporting Taiwan independence, 159, 171; "Wei-ting-the-Pooh," 15, 155
Chen, Yunlin, 57
Cheng, Chung-tai, 55, 197
Cheng, Edmund W., 67
Cheng, Li-chiun, 83
Chiang, Kai-shek, 26, 81
Chile's student movement, 193
Chimei Incident (China), 47
Chin, Wan, 89–90, 188, 197
China: "Celestial Dynasty doctrine," 52; economic and global ascendancy, 36, 44–45, 201, 211, 219; legal interpretations of Basic Law, 118, 206; policy toward Hong Kong, 40–44, 49; policy toward Taiwan, 41, 47–49; relationship with United States, 220; responses to Sunflower Movement, 205; sharp power, 42, 70, 219–220; Umbrella Movement as intervention of foreign forces, 202, 205
China factor: China-related protests in Hong Kong and Taiwan, 68–69; definition, 41–42
Chinese Communist Party, 17, 28, 32, 38, 47–49, 134; activities in Hong Kong, 25, 29, 42–44, 46, 49
Chinese intellectual protests: origin, 14–15; replacement by youth popular culture, 15–16
Chinese University of Hong Kong, 85, 129, 139
Chinese University Student Union, 84–85, 87
Choi Yuen village (Hong Kong), 53, 85, 92. See also Anti–Express Rail Movement
Chow, Agnes, 215. See also Demosistō
Chow, Alex Yong-kang, 123, 131, 147, 178, 197, 207; "Alexter," 15; imprisonment, 206; movement injuries, 181

Chronicle of Umbrella Failure, A., 171. See also Civic Passion
Chu, Eddie Hoi-dick, 197
Chu, Eric Li-luan, 104
Chu, Yiu-ming, 119. See also Occupy Trio
Chungli Incident (Taiwan), 32
Chuoshui River Club (National Taiwan University), 83
Citizen Charter Movement, 187. See also Hong Kong's post-Umbrella activism
Citizen 1985 Action Coalition (Taiwan), 168
City University of Hong Kong Students' Union, 162
Civic Party (Hong Kong), 53, 118, 174, 190. See also Pan-democrats
Civic Passion (Hong Kong), 54, 90, 142–143, 171, 196–197; in Mong Kok occupation, 143. See also Localists
Civic Square (Hong Kong), 2, 15, 89, 93, 127, 130, 137, 155; police reactions, 122–123
Civil disobedience, 4, 16, 180, 207, 212; in Hong Kong, 68, 119–122, 126, 129, 135, 139, 174; in Taiwan, 66–67, 163, 174, 179, 195
Civil Human Rights Front (Hong Kong), 64–65, 69, 87
Civil Movement for Constitutional Reform, 186. See also Taiwan's post-Sunflower activism
Civil nomination, 120–122, 126
Class boycott campaign (Hong Kong), 122, 131–133, 139, 163, 188
Closer Economic Partnership Arrangement (Hong Kong), 40–41, 49
Collapsing Generation, The, 77
College-of-Social-Sciences Faction (Taiwan), 112–113
Community Charter Movement, 187, 210. See also Hong Kong's post-Umbrella activism
Conservative political culture, 4, 8, 169–170.
Cross-Strait Service Trade Agreement (Taiwan), 1, 41, 99–116 passim, 157, 164, 166, 177, 192, 204, 213; the "black-box" criticism, 101, 106; relationship with the Trans-Pacific Partnership, 202–203; signing of, 99
Cross-Strait Trade in Goods Trade Agreement (Taiwan), 177

Dark Corner Incident (Hong Kong), 161, 173–174
Death by China, 220
Declaration of Core Values (Hong Kong), 54
Declaration of Free Persons (Taiwan), 59
della Porta, Donatella, 3, 6, 73
Democracy Kuroshio (Taiwan), 161, 186. *See also* Taiwan's post-Sunflower activism
Democracy Tautin, 186, 192. *See also* Taiwan's post-Sunflower activism
Democratic Alliance for the Betterment of Hong Kong, 37
Democratic Front against Cross-Strait Service Trade Agreement (Taiwan), 100–102, 107, 110, 131, 139–140
Democratic Progressive Party (Taiwan), 40–41, 47–48, 51, 57–59, 64–65, 171–172, 198–199, 205–208; coping strategy with third forces, 195, 200, 215; Democracy Grassroots project, 201; independence clause, 35–36; involvement in Sunflower Movement, 109, 141; mobilizing supporters on March 21, 142–143, 166; relationship with social movements, 83–84, 91, 131; responses to post-Sunflower activism, 184–186; revision of China policy, 59–60, 99–102, 104–105, 219
Demosisto, 197, 215. *See also* Hong Kong's post-Umbrella activism
Deng, Xiaoping, 21, 43
Diaoyutai (Senkaku Islands) Movement, 31–32, 34
Dirlik, Arif, 23, 62
Discourse on Reforming Hong Kong, 187. *See also* Hong Kong's post-Umbrella activism
"Dstreet" (Deliberative Democracy on the Street, Taiwan), 157
Duara, Prasenjit, 221

Economic Cooperation Framework Agreement (Taiwan), 41, 48, 56, 58, 99–100
Economic united front, 42–44, 46–49, 59, 70; conceding benefits, 47–48, 50; opposition to, 204, 212, 218
Euromaidan Revolution (Ukraine), 98
Eventful protests, 3–8, 12–13, 71, 75, 151–152, 180, 211–212
Executive Yuan Incident (Taiwan), 111–114, 133, 158, 178, 181, 210

Facebook, 58, 72, 88–90, 107, 188
February 28 Incident (Taiwan), 27–28, 35, 120
Financier Conscience, 190. *See also* Hong Kong's post-Umbrella activism
Fishball Revolution, 187–189, 193, 215. *See also* Hong Kong's post-Umbrella activism
Five-District Referendum (Hong Kong), 118
Fixing HK, 192. *See also* Hong Kong's post-Umbrella activism
Flash-mob protests, 7, 131
Formoshock, 186. *See also* Taiwan's post-Sunflower activism
Fourth Nuclear Power Plant (Taiwan), 104, 183–184. *See also* Antinuclear Movement
Fukushima Accident, 65, 184
Fung, Billy Jing-en, 188

g0v (Taiwan), 157
Ganz, Marshall, 138
General Strike and Boycott of 1925–1926 (Hong Kong), 29
Gerbaudo, Paolo, 173, 180
Ghonim, Wael, 72. *See also* Arab Spring
Gitlin, Todd, 72, 171
Goffman, Erving, 154
Golden Forum (Hong Kong), 89
Goldstone, Jack, 75, 96, 193
Graeber, David, 71
Green Party Taiwan, 194–195, 199–200, 210
Guangzhou–Shenzhen–Hong Kong Express Rail, 50. *See also* Anti-Express Rail Movement
Gunning, Jeroen, 12, 180

Halper, Stefan, 220
Hao, Ming-i, 100, 105
Hardt, Michael, 152. *See also* Multitude
Hatta, Yoichi, 26
Hau, Lung-pin, 103–104
Ho, Albert Chun-yan, 34, 39
Hong Kong: anticolonial movements, 25; British colonialism, 24; as China's periphery, 22; Chinese nationalism, 33–35; colonial nostalgia, 28; economic miracle, 76; emigration, 38; fading of "Hong Kong Dream," 76; handover to China, 21; indigenous people, 22; mainlandization, 40–41; one country, two systems, 21, 42, 68, 133, 191, 198–199, 207; postwar continuity, 26; press freedom, 51; pro-democracy movement, 35–38; Taiwanization, 207

Hong Kong Alliance in Support of Patriotic Democratic Movements in China, 52, 54–55, 64–65, 74, 84, 89
Hong Kong as a City-State, 89. *See also* Chin, Wan
Hong Kong Democratic Party, 34, 37–39, 54, 117, 126, 179, 200; negotiation with the Liaison Office, 118–119. *See also* Pan-democrats
Hongkonger identity, 33, 38, 40, 60–62, 70, 207
Hong Kong Federation of Students, 84–86, 89–90, 133–144 passim, 171, 173–174, 193, 197, 214; disintegration of, 182; leadership in Umbrella Movement, 122–123; student proposal for suffrage, 121
Hong Kong Indigenous, 189. 197. *See also* Hong Kong's post-Umbrella activism
Hong Kong National Party, 197, 215. *See also* Hong Kong's post-Umbrella activism
Hong Kong's economic relationship with China, 5, 45, 49, 51
Hong Kong's elections: change of electoral system, 117–118; 2012 legislative council election, 119; 2015 district council election, 196, 198–199; 2016 by-election, 189–190; 2016 legislative council election, 196–199
Hong Kong's 1956 riot, 28
Hong Kong's 1967 riot, 29, 43
Hong Kong special administrative region government, 21, 40–54 passim, 68, 90, 113, 117–127 passim, 177–197 passim, 206
Hong Kong's post-Umbrella activism, 186–191; comparison with Taiwan, 191–193; pro-independence sentiments, 7, 191
Hong Kong's pro-government protests, 132, 137, 208
Hong Kong's youth: 5–6, 19–20, 176, 191; economic grievances, 75–77; expansion of higher education, 16; "Post-80," 74–79; postmaterialism, 78
Hong Kong Television Incident, 90
Hong Kong University Students' Union, 84–85, 188
Horizontalism, 215. *See also* Prefigurative politics
Hsieh, Frank Chang-ting, 98–99, 109
Hsu, Shih-Jung, 88
Hu, Jintao, 47
Huang, Kun-huei, 109

Huang, Kuo-chang, 58, 111, 141, 183, 186, 195, 199–200
Humanity Workshop (Tunghai University), 81
Hung, Ho-fung, 21, 44, 54, 92, 220

Improvisation: by adaptation, 163–164; definition, 153–154; differential contribution, 172–174; feeling of empowerment, 150–151; functions, 152, 154–162, 175; by innovation, 164–165; limitations, 167–170; by replication, 162–163; sense of urgency, 151
Independent Company of Lane Eight (Taiwan), 163–164
Indie DaaDee, 159
Indignados Movement (Spain), 6, 8, 72
Inmediahk (Hong Kong), 139
Intestine Flower Trash Talk Forum (Taiwan), 159
Island Nation's Keywords, 79
Island's Sunrise, 162, 179, 198

Jacques, Martin, 220
Jasper, James M., 140, 145–146, 170, 180
Jiang, Yi-huah, 67, 99, 112, 148
July First demonstrations (Hong Kong), 64–65, 67–68, 87, 93, 117, 121–122
June Fourth candlelight vigil in Hong Kong, 38, 54, 64–65, 67–68, 191
June Fourth candlelight vigil in Taiwan, 57

Kang, Youwei, 24
Kaohsiung Incident (Taiwan), 32, 35
Killian, Lewis, 146
Ko, Wen-je, 210
Kou, Yanding, 221
Kowloon Disturbances of 1966 (Hong Kong), 29, 53
Kuomintang (Chinese Nationalist Party), 21–35 passim, 57–60, 98–116 passim, 161, 179, 186–187, 195–206 passim, 215; activities in Hong Kong, 22, 28; internal division, 103–104; liaison with Chinese government, 41, 47–48, 59
Kurzman, Charles, 145

Labour Party (Hong Kong), 118, 131, 201. *See also* Pan-democrats
Lai, Chung-chiang, 100, 131
Lam Cheng, Carrie Yuet-ngor, 133–134, 138, 177, 215

Lau, Emily Wai-hing, 39
Lau, Siu-lai, 197, 206
Law, Nathan Kwun-chung, 178, 197, 199, 208, 215; imprisonment, 206
League of Social Democrats (Hong Kong), 118, 123, 201. *See also* Pan-democrats
Lee, Cheuk-yan, 131, 197
Lee, Ching Kwan, 221
Lee, Martin Chu-ming, 207
Lee, Teng-hui, 26, 31, 35, 50, 54, 83
Lee Tung Street preservation movement (Hong Kong), 53
Left 21 (Hong Kong), 87, 90
"Leftards," 55, 171
Legislative council (Hong Kong), 50, 86, 93, 118–142 passim, 189–190, 196–206 passim; direct election, 37; dominance of business, 46; resolution against Taiwan independence, 39; vetoing the reform package in 2015, 177
Legislative Yuan (Taiwan), 1, 8, 15, 31–36 passim, 89, 101–106 passim, 113–116, 139, 169
Lenin, Vladimir, 97
Letting-Dogs-Out Club (National Sun Yat-sen University), 80–81
Leung, Baggio Chung-hang, 197, 206
Leung, Chun-ying, 125, 133–134, 178, 188, 198, 205; policy address in 2015, 177
Leung, Edward Tin-kei, 189, 197, 215
Leung, Kwok-hung (the Long Hair), 123, 130–132, 206
Leung, Man-tao, 74
Leung, Yvonne Lai Kwok, 181
Li, Arthur Kwok-cheung, 188
Liaison Office in Hong Kong, 40, 49, 52, 119
Liao, Wen-yi, 28
Liberal Party (Hong Kong), 46, 126
Liberty Square (Taiwan), 80
Lien, Chan, 47
Lin, Fei-fan, 82, 93, 108–109, 112, 131, 142, 148, 159, 183, 186; Harry Potter–style glasses and green overcoat, 15; in Pariah Liberation Area, 171–172; speech on March 30, 1, 166; supporting Taiwan independence, 171
Lin, Yi-hsiung, 83; hunger strike in 2014, 183–184
Local actionists (Hong Kong), 53–54
Localists (Hong Kong), 39, 92, 144, 193, 200, 215, 219; antimainlander protests, 53–55; conflicts with "leftards," 170–172,

182; election, 190, 196–197; Internet origin, 89–90
Lo-Sheng Sanatorium preservation movement (Taiwan), 80, 92
Lui, Tai-lok, 27, 33, 37, 45, 76–77

Ma, Ying-jeou, 41, 48–50, 58–60, 115, 134, 148, 167, 184; debate with Tsai Ing-wen over the ECFA, 56–57, 99; denouncing student protesters, 111–112; meeting with Xi Jinping, 205; New Year speech in 2015, 177; pressing the CSSTA, 103; rivalry with Wang Jin-pyng, 104, 106; support for Umbrella Movement, 202
Macao, 14, 17, 22, 57, 135, 203, 223
Mandate of heaven, 17
Mao, Zedong, 42
Marx, Karl, 24, 211, 219
Mattis, James N., 220
May Day demonstrations (Taiwan), 64–65
McAdam, Doug, 11–13, 73–75, 96–98, 154, 180, 191, 194, 216–217
McLehose, Murray Crawford, 33
Mearsheimer, John J., 46
Merkel, Angela, 3
Mills, C. Wright, 211
Mobile Democracy Classroom (Hong Kong), 132, 156
Mobilization, 154, 166, 170, 173, 216–217; definition, 152–153
Moss, Dana, 153
Movement brinkmanship, 129
Movement Club (National Chung Cheng University), 80–81
Movement injuries, 180–182, 191, 210
Multitude, 152, 175, 215

Nachtwey, James, 71
National security legislation (Hong Kong), 40
National Taiwan University, 30, 57, 81–82, 108, 112
National Taiwan University Student Association, 81
Navarro, Peter, 220
Negri, Antonio, 152. *See also* Multitude
Neo Democrats (Hong Kong), 118. *See also* Pan-democrats
Network of Young Democratic Asians, 204
New Power Party, 186, 195, 199–200, 207–208, 210, 219. *See also* Taiwan's post-Sunflower activism

New School for Democracy, 92–93
Ng, Jason, 127, 155–156, 160, 170
1992 consensus, 47–49, 99, 208
Nonviolence, 9, 89, 135, 139, 164, 170, 189–190, 193
Northeast New Territories Development Plan (Hong Kong), 55

Obama, Barack, 3, 202
Occupy Central with Love and Peace (Hong Kong), 124–134 passim, 144, 164–168 passim, 171, 173, 187–188, 214–215; deliberative democracy, 120–121, 168; July 2 rehearsal, 122; networking with Taiwan activists, 120; relationship with religion, 139; resources, 139–140. *See also* Occupy Trio
Occupy the Ministry of the Interior (Taiwan), 66–67, 88
Occupy trio, 120–124, 130–131, 134, 140, 164, 171; surrender to police, 132
Occupy Wall Street Movement, 6–8, 71–72, 87, 170, 180, 212
One Belt, One Road, 219
"Open Letter to the Taiwanese Government and Taiwanese," 90
Orange Revolution (Ukraine), 6
Osa, Maryjane, 93
Our Post-80 Declaration (Hong Kong), 78

Pan-democrats (Hong Kong), 118–122; involvement in Umbrella Movement, 125–127, 143, 171; relationship with umbrella soldiers, 190, 196–197, 200, 219
Parent Participating Education (Taiwan), 169
Pariah Liberation Area (Taiwan), 169, 171–172
Pattern, Chris, 37
Pearl River Bridge, 50
Peng, Ming-min, 30, 36
People First Party (Taiwan), 200
People Power (Hong Kong), 118–119, 126, 143. *See also* Pan-democrats
People Rule Movement (Taiwan), 83
People's Democratic Front (Taiwan), 194
Podemos (Spain), 193
Poland's Solidarity Movement, 220–221
Political opportunities: definition, 95–97; making opportunities, 97; in Sunflower Movement, 103–106; in Umbrella Movement, 124–127. *See also* Movement brinkmanship; Threat
Praxis in the South (Taiwan), 82
Precariat (precarious proletariat), 75
Prefigurative politics, 152. *See also* Horizontalism
Progressive Lawyers Group, 190, 192. *See also* Hong Kong's post-Umbrella activism
Protest Club (National Cheng Kung University), 80–82

Qiang, Shigong, 52
Queen's Pier preservation movement (Hong Kong), 53

Radical Notes (National Tsing Hua University), 80–82
Rebiya Kadeer Incident (Taiwan), 57
Red-Shirt Army Movement (Taiwan), 63
Rejectionist ethics, 193
Reporters without Borders, 51, 215

Same-sex marriage, 199, 215
Scholarism (Hong Kong), 92, 129, 131–136, 138–140, 142–143, 171; in Anti–National Education Movement, 86–88; leadership in Umbrella Movement, 122–123; student proposal for suffrage, 121. *See also* Wong, Joshua Chi-fung
Segerberg, Alexandra, 151
Severe acute respiratory syndrome (SARS), 49–50, 75–76
Sewell, William, Jr., 3
Shimonoseki Treaty, 23
"Shoppers' revolution" (Hong Kong), 135, 165
Shum, Lester, 123, 131; "Alexter," 15
Sino-British Joint Declaration, 21
Snow, David, 153
Social Democratic Party (Taiwan), 195, 199–200. *See also* Taiwan's post-Sunflower activism
Social movements: classical research agenda, 11–12; debate between constructionists and structuralists, 12–13; definition, 10–11; dilemmas, 175; emergent norm theory, 145–146; emotional aspects, 150–153, 157–159; impact of social media, 72; macro-micro link, 18, 219; movement-party interaction, 166; network, 72–73; relationship with

Index 267

geopolitics, 18; relationship with personal life, 159–160, 211–212, 218; relationship with political parties, 193–194; routinization, 146–147; spontaneity, 152–153, 174; strategy model, 145–146
Social movement study: in East Asia, 216; and electoral study, 218–219; institutionalization, 12, 216–217; movement-centric perspective, 217; and social changes, 211–212, 217–218
Sou, Sulu, 203. See also Macao
Stand by You: Add Oil Machine (Hong Kong), 158
Standoff: contingency, 143–144; declining popular support, 114, 136–137; definition, 97; initial advantage for protesters, 114, 133; perils of sustained standoff, 114–115, 136–137; resources, 9–10, 84, 138–140, 144–146, 153–154, 165; rigidity of prior planning, 140; as a rupture, 139–140, 145; search for an exit strategy, 114–115, 138, 148; vulnerability to pro-government protests, 136
Star Ferry Terminal preservation movement (Hong Kong), 53
Street Democracy Classroom Action (Taiwan), 156
Student role in Chinese culture, 14–15
Students Emergency Action for Liberal Democracy (Japan), 203
Su, Beng, 83
Su, Tseng-chang, 99, 109
Sun, Yat-sen, 17, 24
Sunflower Movement: decision making, 107–108, 115–116; emergency corridor controversy, 168–169; handicraft activities, 158; housewives, 160; indigenous peoples, 160; infographics, 157; isolated island effect, 141–142; leadership structure, 7, 109–111, 131, 140–144, 152, 175; as a lesson to Hong Kong, 121, 134; LGBT, 169; logistic support, 108, 154–156; on-site survey of participants, 5; origin of the name, 2, 155; passing-by protests, 165; perceived spontaneity, 102, 108, 174–175; problems in maintaining order, 110; prosecution, 178; protest on April 11, 165, 178; quick tactical decision on March 18–19, 102, 117–119; security brigade, 110, 144, 168; sit-ins at KMT branch offices, 111–112, 134; support in poll, 114, 179; "team of 3,621," 164, 173; Wang Jin-pyng's announcement, 115; weak response from labor, 111
Syriza (Greece), 193
Szeto, Wah, 25, 33, 207

Tahrir Revolution (Egypt), 8, 12, 72, 98, 180. See also Arab Spring
Tai, Benny Yiu-ting, 119–121, 124, 126, 130, 188, 215. See also Occupy Trio
Taiwan: anticolonial movements, 24–25; challenged statehood, 4, 17; as China's periphery, 22; Chinese nationalism, 34; colonial nostalgia, 31; economic miracle, 76; end of high social mobility era, 76; Hongkongization, 41; independence movement, 27; indigenous people, 22–23; Japanese colonialism, 24; martial law, 28, 30, 35, 42, 184; postwar continuity, 27; pro-democracy movement, 31–32, 35–36; Republic of Formosa, 23–24; returning to reality in the 1970s, 31–32
Taiwan Citizen Union, 195, 199. See also New Power Party; Social Democratic Party
Taiwan Confederation of Trade Unions, 65, 92
Taiwan Congressional Hong Kong Caucus, 207
Taiwanese Communist Party, 25
Taiwanese identity, 31, 35–38, 40, 50, 58, 60–62
Taiwan March, 186. See also Taiwan's post-Sunflower activism
Taiwan Publishing Freedom Front, 192. See also Taiwan's post-Sunflower activism
Taiwan Rural Front, 66, 83, 88
Taiwan's economic relationship with China: 5, 45, 48; policy changes, 50; Taiwanese businesspersons (taishang), 46–49; Taiwanese fear, 106
Taiwan's elections: 2012 general election, 48–49, 56–57; 2014 local election, 194, 198–199; 2016 general election, 195, 198–199
Taiwan Solidarity Union, 105, 109, 179, 195, 200–201
Taiwan's post-Sunflower activism, 183–186; comparison with Hong Kong, 191–193
Taiwan's pro-government protests, 137, 165, 208

Taiwan's youth, 5–6, 19–20, 176, 191; economic grievances, 75–77; expansion of higher education, 16; postmaterialism, 78; public perception, 77–78; "Seventh Graders," 74–79; "tribe of strawberries," 74; student movement clubs, 80–81
Tang, Henry Ying-yen, 125
Ta-pa-ni Incident (Taiwan), 24
Tapu land expropriation (Taiwan), 66–67, 88
Tarrow, Sidney, 10–13, 96–97, 146, 153–154, 194, 216–217
Tear gas, use of, by Hong Kong police, 2, 127–128. *See also* Threat
Ten Years, 28
Thinking Taiwan Foundation, 83. *See also* Tsai Ing-wen
Third force (Taiwan), 195, 199–200. *See also* Taiwan's post-Sunflower activism
30-second Incident (Taiwan), 102, 105–106, 116. *See also* Threat
Threat, 13, 19–20, 106–107, 116, 128–129, 140, 145, 180; definition, 95–97; moral shock, 140
Tiananmen Massacre (China), 5, 14–16, 37–38, 52, 57, 64, 74, 133
Tianxia (civilization state), 17, 220
Tien, James Pei-chun, 126
Tilly, Charles, 11–12, 73, 96–97, 153–154, 216–219
Ting Hsin International Group, 56
Tong, Ronny Ka-wah, 126–127
Transnational social movement network, 5, 19, 70, 74, 91, 120, 204; Taiwan–Hong Kong nexus, 91–93, 203, 207
Trans-Pacific Partnership, 202
Trees Party (Taiwan), 194
Tsai, Eng-Meng, 56
Tsai, Ing-wen, 83, 109, 184, 198, 201, 205, 208, 215; debate with Ma Ying-jeou over the ECFA, 56–57, 99; and the 2016 election, 180, 195
Tsang, Donald Yam-kuen, 49, 229
Tsang, Kin-chiu, 161, 173
Tuan, Yi-kang, 105
Tung, Chee-hwa, 44, 49
Turner, Ralph, 146

Umbrella Movement: attacks from localists, 142, 144, 182; bullet shield group, 173; Causeway Bay occupation, 129–132, 136, 155, 173, 176; decision making, 122–124, 130, 138–139; dialogue with officials, 132–135; expatriates, 160; five-party platform, 132, 141, 143; handicraft making, 158; image of civility, 159–160; imprisonment, 178, 208; infographics, 157; injunctions, 137; international support, 2–3, 201–202; leader characteristics, 131; leadership, 7, 132, 140–144, 152, 175; LGBT, 170; Lion Rock banner, 161; logistic support, 139, 154–156; main stage in Admiralty, 131–132; master of ceremonies, 131–132; militants, 135–136; Mong Kok occupation, 129–130, 132–134, 136–138, 143, 155, 165, 171–173; November 30 siege, 136, 160–161, 171; on-site survey of participants, 5; origin of the name, 2, 155; prosecution, 178; security brigade, 120, 139, 164; singing "Happy Birthday," 15, 165; South Asians, 160; support in poll, 136–137, 179; Tsim Sha Tsui occupation, 130; "Umbrella Revolution," 133; Umbrella study corner, 159–160
Umbrella soldiers, 196, 200, 206, 215. *See also* Hong Kong's post-Umbrella activism
Undergrad, 84–85, 178, 198
United Democrats of Hong Kong, 37. *See also* Hong Kong Democratic Party
United States: responses to Sunflower Movement, 202–203; responses to Umbrella Movement, 3, 202
University of Democracy to Come (Hong Kong), 139
University of Hong Kong personnel controversy, 187–188. *See also* Hong Kong's post-Umbrella activism
University Student Rights Investigation and Evaluation Team (Taiwan), 82

Victoria Harbor Preservation Movement (Hong Kong), 92

Walder, Andrew, 217
Wang, Jin-pyng, 104, 106, 115, 134
Want Want Holdings Limited, 56, 58–59. *See also* Anti–Media Monopoly Movement
Watchout (Taiwan), 157, 186–187. *See also* Taiwan's post-Sunflower activism
White terror (Taiwan), 27
Wild Lily Movement (Taiwan), 15, 36, 80–81, 84

Index

Wild Strawberry Movement (Taiwan), 57–59, 74, 79–82, 91
Wild Strawberry's Song, 79
Wings of Radical Politics, 144, 194. *See also* Taiwan's post-Sunflower activism
Wong, Joshua Chi-fung, 55, 92–93, 123–125, 131, 176–178, 197–199, 202, 207–208; in Anti–National Education Movement, 86, 88; entry denied at Bangkok, 204; imprisonment, 206; speech on September 26, 2
Wong, Raymond Yuk-man, 126–127, 142, 197
World Trade Organization, 6–7, 44, 92, 127
Wu-she Incident (Taiwan), 24

Xi, Jinping, 17, 202, 221; meeting with Ma Ying-jeou, 205
Xu, Jiatun, 43

Yau, Wai-ching, 197, 206
Yesh Atid (Israel), 193
Yeung, Alvin Ngok-kiu, 190
Yiu, Edward Chung-yim, 206
Young Girls' Heart (Hong Kong), 182
Young Plan (Hong Kong), 26, 28
Youngspiration, 196–197, 200. *See also* Hong Kong's post-Umbrella activism
Youth against Oppression in Taiwan, 186. *See also* Taiwan's post-Sunflower activism
Youth Occupy Politics, 186. *See also* Taiwan's post-Sunflower activism
Youth Synergy Taiwan Foundation, 83

Zen, Joseph Ze-kiun, 128, 140
Zhang, Zhijun, 204

Ming-sho Ho is a Professor of Sociology at National Taiwan University. He is the author of *Working Class Formation in Taiwan: Fractured Solidarity in State-Owned Enterprises, 1945–2012.*